DISCARD

IDEAS
HAVE A HISTORY

Perspectives on the Western Search for Truth

Frederika Oosterhoff

University Press of America,® Inc.
Lanham · New York · Oxford

Copyright © 2001 by
University Press of America,® Inc.
4720 Boston Way
Lanham, Maryland 20706

12 Hid's Copse Rd.
Cumnor Hill, Oxford OX2 9JJ

Library of Congress Cataloging-in-Publication Data

Oosterhoff, F. G.
Ideas have a history : perspectives on the Western search
for truth / Frederika Oosterhoff.
p.   cm
Includes bibliographical references and index.
1. Faith and reason—History. I. Title.
BR50 .O56 2001   261.5—dc21   2001027484 CIP

ISBN 0-7618-2031-0 (pbk. : alk. paper)

⊖™ The paper used in this publication meets the minimum
requirements of American National Standard for Information
Sciences—Permanence of Paper for Printed Library Materials,
ANSI Z39.48—1984

"All Scepticism originates from the impression that our certainty depends upon the result of our scientific research." Abraham Kuyper, *Principles of Sacred Theology*, p. 125.

"We must now recognize belief once more as the source of all knowledge.... No intelligence, however critical or original, can operate outside ...a fiduciary framework." Michael Polanyi, *Personal Knowledge*, p. 266.

Contents

Preface

This book is the product of several years of teaching, and I gladly use the opportunity to thank my students for cooperating with me in attempting to understand the past of our civilization and to learn from it.

I am also deeply grateful to the relatives, friends, and colleagues who encouraged me in writing the book and/or who helped me in completing it. As to the latter category, a very special word of thanks goes to Dr. William Helder of Hamilton and to Dr. Jitse van der Meer and Dr. Wytse van Dijk, the last two of Redeemer College in Ancaster, for reading all or part of the manuscript in various stages of readiness, pointing out errors, and making suggestions for improvements.

The Board and Principal of Covenant Teachers College in Hamilton contributed to the work by allowing me to try out the book's conclusions on their students, which turned out to be quite a learning experience not just for these students but also for me. I hope I have made a good use of their comments and insights in preparing the book's final version.

Finally, I express my sincere thanks to Kirsten Sloots for her editorial assistance, to Tim Nijenhuis for helping me with the technicalities of formatting the manuscript, and to Diana Lavery and Beverly Baum at University Press of America for their help and prompt attention to my questions.

Introduction

Knowing our times

This book is about our civilization's mental journey. It speaks of ideas that have moved western men and women in the past and that continue to move them today. One could therefore call it an intellectual history, or a history of ideas, but then in a limited sense. My purpose in writing it was not to provide a systematic account of our intellectual past, but rather to draw attention to those ideas that have a close connection with the dominant belief systems of today.

In the majority of cases description has been combined with interpretation. This means that I trace the origin and development of selected ideas and attempt to explain them with reference to the historical period wherein they arose. The book's goal, however, is constantly kept in mind, and that goal is to help us to understand our own times. Specifically, it is to find answers to questions that are common among Christians today. One of these is how we must explain the decline of Christian faith and the skepticism and moral relativism in a civilization that was shaped and nourished by Christianity. A second question, related to the first, is how we can detect the philosophical underpinnings of today's mentality, and so find the intellectual means to evaluate and challenge it. A good deal of attention will, in this connection, be given to the function of epistemologies or theories of knowledge.

An answer to the first of our questions requires a historical survey. The second one can be answered without historical references. Those who look for an answer to the question can benefit, however, from an approach that pays attention to the role of ideas in history. For in spite of what philosophical materialists proclaim, ideas play a part in moving the world, and ideas have a history. If we want to understand today's belief systems, it helps to trace the ideas that inform them to their roots. Doing so enables us to see how and why they arose, how they operated in the past, and what their consequences have been.

Science and religion

Because religion, philosophy, and science are especially important in the formation of these belief systems, the focus will be on ideas derived from them. In the chapters on Greece and the Middle Ages, philosophy and religion will be our main concern, but when dealing with the modern period we will concentrate on the role of science. In connection with that topic attention will be given to the relationship between science and religion, to the question of science's role in the turn to secularism, and to the manner in which it has influenced the modern theory of knowledge.

On the first of these issues there has been a good deal of controversy. In the positivistic nineteenth century a school arose which described the relationship between science and the Christian religion as antagonistic. Opposed to Christianity and greatly impressed with the successes of the scientific pursuit, its members portrayed science as the instrument of enlightenment while representing the church and the theologians, especially the Roman Catholic ones, as forces of superstition and darkness. This view did not, however, remain unchallenged. There were also historians who stressed the positive relationship between science and the Christian faith. A leader among them was the Anglo-American philosopher Alfred North Whitehead who, writing in the 1920s, explained the rise of modern science with reference to medieval Christianity. For a society to turn to science and to persevere in the scientific pursuit, he argued, it must be convinced that science is indeed possible. Belief in the possibility of science, in turn, requires faith in a rational God, and such a faith modern Europe inherited from the theology of the Middle Ages. Its presence explained why Europe, unlike other civilizations, developed the mentality necessary for a truly scientific culture.[1]

Twentieth-century historians have increasingly followed Whitehead's lead. They have provided support for his view that Christianity played a vital role in the rise of western science and also shown that for centuries, and well into the modern period, there was a great deal of co-operation between science and theology. Indeed, until the late eighteenth century no real boundary line existed between them. Early-modern scientists concerned themselves not just with specifically scientific issues, but also with metaphysical and theological ones, and in their theorizing they made use of the work of theologians. Many a theologian, in turn, supported the work of scientists and used scientific conclusions in support of the Christian faith.

Harmony did not, however, rule at all times. The relationship between science and religion, as historian John Hedley Brooke has pointed out, is a complex one and does not allow for simple generalizations.[2] There was conflict as well as agreement. The best-known example of conflict in the early period is of course that of Galileo, who got into trouble with the Roman Catholic Church on the issue of Copernicanism. Although less vehement in their opposition than Rome, Luther and Calvin also criticized Copernicus' theory, but they did so without treating it as a theological heresy. In fact, in his commentary on Psalm 136 Calvin stated that the Holy Spirit "had no intention to teach astronomy." Nor did Calvin believe that a Bible passage such as Joshua 10:12 (where Joshua told not the earth but the sun to stand still) proved the heliocentric theory to be unbiblical. In Joshua 10 it was simply a matter of the Bible accommodating itself to the worldview of the time.[3] Calvin's followers also were of two minds on the Copernican issue, with some of them rejecting the new model and others defending it. A similar situation prevailed among Lutherans and Roman Catholics.

In conclusion, then, the early-modern centuries do not support the scenario of constant and relentless warfare between science and religion that the nineteenth-century positivist school painted. There were, as later chapters will show, various instances of harmony and of very close co-operation. Some of that harmony survives even today: Christians are among those who defend the scientific enterprise by insisting, against postmodern skeptics, that truth exists and can be found. But it is also true that conflicts did occur, already in the early-modern period, and increasingly so since the rise of Darwinism in the nineteenth century.

Science and the decline of Christianity

The second question, that of science's role in the decline of

Christianity, also does not admit of a simple answer. The idea that science was the enemy of religion was inspired mainly by the conflict on Darwin's evolutionary theory. There is little doubt that Darwinism became a stumbling block for Christians and contributed both directly and indirectly to the process of secularization, but about the role that science in general played in this process it is less easy to generalize. On the one hand, early scientists were convinced that their work made manifest God's glory and majesty and served to prove the truth of Christianity. Many theologians, as we noted, agreed with this view and made use of scientific conclusions in their apologetic work. Religious considerations influenced even the choice of modernism's mechanistic cosmology, which, according to many an early-modern scientist and theologian, safeguarded better than any competing theory the confession of God's transcendence and absolute sovereignty.[4]

The mechanistic or clockwork model could also, however, support the view of a universe that operated in an automatic fashion. Already in the seventeenth century, and increasingly so in the eighteenth, mechanism served to bolster the claims first of deists, who professed divine creation but denied divine providence, and then of atheists as well. The move toward deism was also encouraged by the habit of apologists to stress God's general revelation, that is, his work in creation, more than his special revelation, the written Word. Meanwhile the great successes of science gave rise to the opinion that the scientific approach to truth could perhaps compete with the religious one. Among the early scientists there were some who, impressed with the power of mathematics as a scientific tool, held that mathematical truths were eternal and existed independently of God.[5] This belief was soon followed by the idea that mathematics and science as sources of truth could not only compete with revelation but replace it. Science's explanatory powers, and later the realization of its tremendous technological potential, made this a popular creed.

All this is not to suggest that the scientific pursuit in itself was hostile to religion. More often than not, anti-religious implications of scientific theories were drawn not by scientists but by philosophers and other non-scientists, who used science to promote their own political or social or ideological agendas. And even if it is true that science played a role, whether directly or indirectly, in the decline of religion, it was not by any means the only secularizing force. The process was advanced by other factors, such as the break-up of Christian unity, a variety of political, socio-economic, and technological developments, and the growing acquaintance with and appreciation for non-western civilizations and religions. In addition there were the changes in the media of communication (for example, the invention of printing with movable type in the fifteenth century, and of electronic means of communication in the twentieth), which, while contributing to the spread of the Gospel, had at the same time a secularizing effect.[6] Yet another contributing factor, as sociologist Peter Berger and others have observed, was the rise of pluralism. Itself an instance of the declining role of Christianity in society, pluralism also furthered it. It did so, for example, by forcing the evacuation of religion from the public sphere and by so contributing to the privatization of religious faith.[7]

Not in the last place, there was the creed of the all-sufficiency of the so-called scientific method. According to this creed only that which can be observed and measured and logically demonstrated deserves to be called true knowledge; all the rest is mere subjective opinion. This brings us to the third topic we raised in connection with western science, namely the nature and function of the modern epistemology.

Theory of knowledge

Before we turn to the modern version, something must be said about the concept of epistemology in general. The term epistemology or theory of knowledge refers to the system of thought that for any given society answers the questions as to what can be known, how and why it can be known, and how certain human knowledge is. As will become apparent in following chapters, these theories have an impact on people's beliefs even if the people themselves are not aware of the nature of the ruling theory, and perhaps do not even know that such things as theories of knowledge exist. Often they operate as assumptions in human thought – the type of assumptions which, in the words of philosopher Alfred North Whitehead, "appear so obvious that people do not know what they are assuming because no other way of putting things has ever occurred to them."[8]

It should also become evident, however, that if Christians indeed want to understand their times they cannot be satisfied with this situation but must do what they can to become aware of the ruling epistemology and its nature. They must be conscious especially of its religious implications.

For epistemologies are not religiously neutral – although that has often been assumed, even among Christians – but reflect a society's beliefs about God and man and the universe, and therefore also about the nature and ultimate source of truth.

Although in this book other theories of knowledge will be noted, we will give special attention to the modern one, which ruled the West for three hundred years or more. That theory was based on the belief in full scientific objectivity. Modern thinkers used it to judge the validity of all truth claims, including religious ones. It also served them as a basis for their belief in unlimited progress, a belief that long survived but at last collapsed, together with the scientist ideal, amid the disasters of the twentieth century.

Later chapters will show that there is a direct connection between the scientist belief and the process of secularization, and between that same scientist belief and the postmodern denial of all truth, religious as well as secular. They will also show the groundlessness of the modern epistemology with its claim that, whereas the personal element intrudes in other fields of research, full objectivity can be reached in science. A variety of examples given throughout this book will make clear that this claim cannot be substantiated: that the presence of the subjective element is not only unavoidable and pervasive, but indeed essential in science, just as it is in other fields of knowledge. Belief in the so-called objective ideal, in short, is a false belief, and can be shown to be so. Extra-scientific factors, including the scientist's own insights, presuppositions, and idiosyncrasies, as well as the expectations and beliefs of his culture, intrude at practically every stage of his work.

The scientist epistemology is false not only because it denies the subjective element in knowing, but also because it relegates whatever cannot pass the grid of the so-called scientific method to the realm of personal opinion rather than knowledge proper. Adherents of scientism ignore the fact that a great many truths cannot be established in a scientific manner and that all human knowing, including the scientific kind, involves unproven and unprovable presuppositions. Among these presuppositions is the belief that truth exists and that the human mind can discover it, that the world exists independently from us, that creation is orderly and uniform, and that regularities and laws can be discovered in nature. None of these assumptions can be demonstrated; they must be accepted on trust and indeed are so accepted. All knowledge, critics of the scientist philosophy have reminded us, takes place within a framework of trust. If we insisted on absolute certainty for all we believe and do, the pursuit of knowledge, and indeed life itself, would be impossible.

Foundationalism

Similar objections apply with respect to a closely related aspect of the modern epistemology, namely the theory of classical foundationalism.[9] This theory states that some of our beliefs are held on the basis of other beliefs, while others are immediate or basic, in the sense that they stand by themselves. The immediately held beliefs include propositions that are self-evident or evident to the senses (such as the proposition that I and other people exist, or that two plus two equal four). These beliefs are held to be rational without the need for further evidence. Other beliefs, however, can be considered rational only if they are based on and supported by such basic ones. The latter, serving as foundation for the former, provide the evidence that these former ones are indeed true. In this manner, classical foundationalists held, a body of knowledge could be constructed that was indubitably certain, built, as it was, on unshakable foundations.

Among the beliefs which, according to classical foundationalism, were not immediate or basic and could therefore not be accepted without further proof, were religious ones. Here we have the origin of the so-called evidentialist challenge to religious faith: the claim that it is irrational to accept Christianity as true unless proper evidence can be marshalled in its support. It explains the popularity in the modern period of natural theology with its attempts to provide logical and experimental arguments to prove the truth of Christianity.

Classical foundationalism, which remained strong throughout the modern period, collapsed around the same time as the objective ideal of scientism. The causes also were similar. The belief that human reason can establish any permanent truths was severely challenged by the rise of non-Euclidean mathematics and quantum physics.[10] People realized, moreover, that the foundationalist theory itself lacked foundations, and it also became increasingly clear that what is held to be self-evident at one time may well be, and in fact often is, considered questionable at a later date. Here as elsewhere the subjective element intrudes. Critics of the modern epistemology reasoned further that if no proposition is to be considered rational unless it is self-evident or evident to the senses or unless it is based on such immediately held beliefs, then many of the assumptions on which we operate in daily life become irrational – including such notions as that there are other people when we do not see any. Christians among these critics pointed out that if, on the other hand, that notion is indeed properly basic and rationally held, then so is belief in God. The claim that religious faith requires evidentialist support can then not be maintained, which means that it is unnecessary for a Christian to depend on so-called theistic arguments. As Calvin already observed, if faith indeed had to rely on such arguments, it would never be secure.

If the causes of foundationalism's demise were similar to those of the collapse of the objective ideal, so were the consequences. Some postmodern thinkers have concluded that the bankruptcy of foundationalism means that no true knowledge at all can be had; others argue that it means that one can no longer distinguish between what is rational and what is irrational, so that "everything goes." The implication is that the individual decides what is appropriate or true for him or her at any given moment. Such conclusions, however, are obviously illogical. To show that indubitable and exhaustive knowledge cannot be had here below is not at all to prove that the achievement of reliable knowledge is impossible. Experience tells us that such knowledge can indeed be had, in science as in other fields.

The reaction of skepticism and relativism is, fortunately, not the only one in our days. There are late-modern and postmodern thinkers who, while rejecting the extravagant claims of the modern epistemology, insist that universally valid truth can be found, and who are establishing the outlines of a theory of knowledge which acknowledges that fact while at the same time attempting to eliminate the defects of the modern theory. The choice, in other words, is not between the modern belief in scientific infallibility and the postmodern reaction of all-out skepticism and relativism. There is a better way. The last four chapters of this book will speak of that way.

Scope

As to the book's scope: the first four chapters are devoted to ancient Greece and the Middle Ages. The rest, and that is by far the larger part, is concerned with modern and postmodern times, that is, with the past four hundred years or so. The modern period began in the seventeenth and eighteenth centuries with the scientific revolution and the so-called Age of Reason (the Enlightenment).[11] These two centuries saw the development of modern science, the spread of rationalistic and naturalistic philosophies, and the invention of the modern theory of knowledge. Tracing the variety of ideas that gave birth to that theory, noting their consequences, and judging their validity, is a major concern of the later chapters. So is the analysis of the alternative theory of knowledge that is being proposed by a number of late-modern and postmodern thinkers.

The prior excursion into the civilizations of Greece and the Middle Ages is justified by the fact that ideas have roots, which can go deep. It is in ancient Greece that we must look for the origins of much of western philosophy, western science, and western theories of knowledge. An acquaintance with Greek history is of interest for yet another reason. Classical Greek culture forms the secular foundation of western civilization. This is probably why the history of Greece often seems to provide a model of the history of Europe, and why the study of the ancient Greek past contributes in so many ways to an understanding of the present.

Medieval history also is relevant to our theme. The Middle Ages form the first phase of our own civilization. The period began with the fall of Rome and the Christianizing of a largely barbarian western Europe. An offspring of the Roman empire and an heir to Greco-Roman culture, medieval society forms the link between the classical period and the modern age. Its thinkers worked hard to preserve classical learning while at the same time attempting to integrate it with Christianity. And so the Middle Ages transmitted to the modern West not only the teachings of both Christianity and the classical world, but also their own peculiar interpretation and synthesis of these messages. It was with this medieval heritage that western scholars would be occupied in the centuries that followed. The modern and postmodern periods cannot be understood apart from their medieval predecessor.

******

In a volume like the present one, which is of modest size but tries to deal with more than two thousand years of intellectual history, it is not possible to provide a great deal of background information. I am assuming that the reader has some knowledge of the history of western culture and some familiarity with the scientific and philosophical concepts discussed in this book. To provide some help to non-specialists, however, I have provided a chronology or time line and indicated in the Index where definitions of certain terms and concepts can be found. Endnotes and bibliography should be of help to those who want to read up on the history of western thought and/or wish to pursue in greater depth any of the topics this book deals with.

NOTES

[1] Alfred North Whitehead, *Science and the Modern World* (New York: New American Library, Mentor Books, 1964 [Macmillan, 1925]), p. 19.

[2] John Hedley Brooke, *Science and Religion: Some Historical Perspectives* (Cambridge: Cambridge University Press, 1991).

[3] *Ibid.*, pp. 96f.

[4] See chapter 6 below.

[5] See below, p. 226.

[6] On this issue see Walter J. Ong, *The Presence of the Word: Some Prolegomena for Cultural and Religious History* (Minneapolis: University of Minnesota Press, 1986 [1967]), pp. 287-95.

[7] Peter L. Berger *et al.*, *The Homeless Mind: Modernization and Consciousness* (New York: Random House, 1973), pp. 79-82.

[8] Whitehead, *Science and the Modern World,* p. 50.

[9] On this issue see Alvin Plantinga and Nicholas Wolterstorff, eds., *Faith and Rationality: Reason and Belief in God* (Notre Dame: University of Notre Dame Press, 1983), especially the Introduction and the articles by Plantinga and Wolterstorff; and Nicholas Wolterstorff, *Reason Within the Bounds of Religion* (Grand Rapids: Eerdmans, 1976).

[10] On these topics see ch. 17 below.

[11] The choice of the seventeenth century as the beginning of the modern age can be defended but remains somewhat arbitrary. It is also justifiable to move it back to about 1500, as many historians do, or even to move it forward to the French Revolution.

I.   Early Greek Thinkers

The search for wisdom

The Jews, the Apostle Paul writes in the first chapter of his first letter to the Corinthians, demanded miraculous signs, and the Greeks sought wisdom. The context makes it clear that Paul refers to human wisdom, the "wisdom of the world," as he calls it in the same chapter.

When the letter to the Corinthians was written, the Greek search for wisdom had been going on for several centuries. Historians locate the first Greek philosophers in the early sixth century before Christ. These thinkers are usually referred to as the Pre-Socratics. The name was chosen not only because the schools they founded date from the period preceding the death of Socrates in 399 B.C., but also because their approach was quite different from that of the great Athenian philosopher. This explains why we meet Pre-Socratics who were contemporaries of Socrates.

The Greek philosophical tradition underwent many changes during the six centuries preceding the Christian era, and it boasted several different schools. The philosophers Paul referred to had other concerns than the Pre-Socratics, and these, in turn, had interests that differed from those of Socrates. The business of the Pre-Socratics was largely (although not exclusively) with the physical world, the focus of natural science; that of Socrates was with man and his society. Many of the Hellenistic philosophers (such as the Stoics and Epicureans Paul may have had in mind) similarly concerned themselves primarily with man, although other philosophical traditions also found adherents in the Hellenistic period. What the Pre-Socratics, Socrates, and the philosophers of Paul's days had in common was that in their search for wisdom they relied not on revelation or religious traditions, but on human reason.

The birth of the philosophical tradition in ancient Greece was of great historical importance. It signified the division between the Greek (and western) view of God and man and nature, and its oriental counterpart. The Greek tradition was to stamp western thought and can be recognized in the rationalistic bent of our civilization and its scientific achievements. Even the cult of irrationalism, which more and more characterizes our own age, cannot be understood without reference to the Greek tradition: it is a revolt against it. The tradition has influenced western religion as well, although some of the strongest attacks upon rationalism have also come from Christianity. In any event, to understand our civilization we have to understand its Greek foundations.

We will begin our survey with the Pre-Socratics, and then move on to the Sophists. The next chapter will be devoted to the great Athenian philosophers Socrates, Plato, and Aristotle.

The birth of natural philosophy

A major concern of the Pre-Socratics was to find the basic stuff out of which the universe was made and which served as its unifying principle. A few also tried to account for motion in the physical world, hoping thereby to solve the problem of the relationship between permanence and change. Some, moreover, speculated about the origins of the cosmos, and some occupied themselves with such subjects as astronomy and geometry. These various concerns show that there were similarities with modern science.

It is true that the context of Pre-Socratic science was altogether different from that of the modern version, and also that the early thinkers were theorists who did not attempt to test their theories by observation and experiment. They therefore cannot be called scientists in the modern sense of the word. Yet they anticipated ideas of modern science in a variety of ways, and for that reason are generally assigned a place not only in histories of philosophy but also in histories of science.

Basic to their approach was that they separated speculation about the universe from religious traditions. This did not necessarily make them atheists. Practically all the Pre-Socratics believed in the existence of the gods, and many of them still assumed the divinity of nature. But they were searching for natural, rational explanations of physical phenomena, and that was a revolutionary development. Before the rise of the Pre-

Socratics, Greeks had been satisfied to explain these phenomena with reference to the Olympic gods, who personified nature and natural forces and directed them. The genealogy of these gods was described in the seventh century B.C. by the poet Hesiod, and myths about them were preserved in the works of ancient bards, foremost among whom was the eighth-century epic poet Homer. Homer's gods were made in the image of man. They were moved by similar desires and afflicted with similar foibles and often engaged in blatantly immoral activity. The gods were immortal, however, and far more powerful than men, ruling both man and nature.

In breaking with the tradition of explaining natural phenomena with reference to religion and myth, the Pre-Socratics moved from a largely magical view of nature to a largely analytical one. Natural cause-and-effect relationships became important, and naturalism – the view that nothing exists except the physical world – was adopted by the Pre-Socratics, at least for methodological purposes. Natural phenomena, in other words, were to be understood with reference to nature alone (even though the material world was not necessarily devoid of gods). Although their efforts to understand and explain the universe led to theories that may seem primitive from our modern vantage point, there were, as we will see, also striking anticipations of modern ones. But whatever the validity of the outcomes, the work was inspired by assumptions similar to those underlying modern science.

These included the belief in the intelligibility of the universe and in its inherent order, in the ability of man to take his distance from nature in order to theorize about it, and in the ability of human reason to understand and explain nature. Also, the importance of mathematics was recognized by at least some of the early Greek thinkers. And, again like modern scientists, these thinkers attempted, as we saw, to reduce the universe to a single principle or set of principles. Throughout Greek history there was a strong desire for simplicity, order, and an underlying unity in a world of seemingly endless diversity. Here is the origin of the philosophical debate on the One and the Many, and on the related question regarding the relationship between being and becoming (or permanence and change) and between universals and particulars. These issues, which passed from the Pre-Socratics to the Greek Sophists and the Athenian philosophers, would engage the attention of philosophers and scientists also in later ages. We will meet them again in subsequent chapters.

Naturalism and its effects

There are similarities not only in the underlying assumptions of ancient and modern science and in the questions that were asked, but also in the effect which in both periods science had upon society.

In the history of European civilization the rise of modern science coincided with and helped bring about the transition from the Middle Ages to the modern era. The Middle Ages are often referred to, and on the whole rightly so, as an age of faith. The modern era has been an age of ever-increasing religious skepticism, and the popular view of science has played a role in that development. Impressed by science's track record, people began to consider the scientific approach to reality and knowledge as the only valid one. And so scientific theories began to be reflected in the general climates of opinion of the modern period; materialism and naturalism came to dominate them, and the so-called scientific method was used to elucidate all manner of issues, divine as well as human. Sense experience and logic became the only ways of knowing and the only criteria of truth.

To state this is not to imply that the rise of science was the only development signalling the arrival of the modern period, nor that science (or rather, the materialistic worldview which the success of science encouraged) initiated the modern secularizing trend. That trend preceded the rise of science and, in a sense, contributed to it. But the reverse was also true. In later chapters we will come back to this point. For now the question is: was the rise of scientific speculation in ancient Greece accompanied or followed by similar developments? Do we find an early instance here of the conflicts between tradition and modernity and between faith and reason that we can notice in the history of modern civilization?

That question has to be answered in the affirmative. Of course, there are important differences between the situation in ancient Greece and the Christian West, differences that make the drawing of parallels a risky business. Nevertheless, when comparing the background and influence of scientific speculation in the two periods, one cannot but note similarities. They apply to the scientists' religious attitudes. We have seen that the naturalism of the Pre-Socratics did not necessarily make them skeptics. Most of them were convinced that the gods existed and played a role in the world of nature. In their case naturalism simply meant that scientific questions could not be answered with reference to the Olympic gods, and that they should not be answered with reference to any other supernatural power.

They were, therefore, naturalists *qua* scientists. That is, they tried to explain physical phenomena without reference to the supernatural, but also without rejecting its existence. That applied to many western scientists as well, certainly in the early-modern period. Practically all these people made it clear that they pursued science in order to show God's might and glory as displayed in creation.

That with such beginnings science could nevertheless nourish the skepticism, naturalism, and materialism of modern thought tells us something important about the human predicament. It shows the limitations which, because man is finite and his reason imperfect, characterize his thought, including his analytical thought. As the philosopher William Barrett described it: "The more specialized a vision the sharper its focus; but also the more nearly total the blind spot toward all things that lie on the periphery of this focus."[1]

Science's analytical visions are restricted by their very nature. An important contributing factor is the role of the imagination in human knowing. This is evident, for example, in the use of metaphor, which allows us to envision the unknown by looking at the known. Such usage implies restriction: we see only what the metaphor allows us to see. The existence of these inevitable limitations does not make scientific conclusions invalid, but it does mean that science cannot account for or explain all that exists. The theories of the Pre-Socratics, like those of their successors of the modern age, were subject to these limitations. This fact was often ignored also in their time, and the absolutizing of scientific conclusions that we encounter in the modern period played a role in classical Greece as well.

The influence of the Pre-Socratics upon the general climate of opinion was not as potent and widespread as would be the case with modern science. One reason was that their speculations did not result in applied science and technology and were therefore of little practical value; another that the period of their activity was comparatively brief. Even so, the influence was noticeable. It can be seen most clearly in the ideas of an intellectual elite consisting of philosophers and other opinion-makers such as the Sophists. To give an idea of the way in which the Pre-Socratics influenced the Greek climate of opinion (and also to indicate their contributions to modern science), we will describe some of their ideas.[2]

Pre-Socratic theories

The first of the Pre-Socratics was Thales of Miletus in Ionia, who lived around 600 B.C. and foretold the eclipse of the sun which occurred in 585 B.C. (Apparently he was able to do so not because he knew the real causes of solar eclipses, but because of his acquaintance with ancient Babylonian records.) Searching for the universe's basic principle or unifying element, Thales, like most of the early Pre-Socratics, chose a material one, namely water. That choice was perhaps influenced, as Aristotle suggested later, by the fact that much of the natural world originates in water and is also nourished by it. Another influence may have been the element's flexibility. Water can assume various forms: it can be liquid, solid (in the form of ice), and vapour.

One of Thales' Ionian successors opted for air as the unifying principle, and another Pre-Socratic, Empedocles of Agrigentum in Sicily, proposed four basic elements: water, air, earth, and fire. These four elements accounted for all phenomena by combining, separating, and recombining. The Pythagoreans, a school in southern Italy which concentrated on mathematics, proposed number as the basic principle of nature, thereby anticipating the modern doctrine that mathematics holds the key to the secrets of the universe.

The type of theorizing engaged in by these Pre-Socratics was revolutionary because of its naturalism, but was perhaps not otherwise too disturbing to the Greek mind. It was different with the theory of Heraclitus of Ephesus (about 500 B.C.), who proclaimed that not permanence but change is the essence of things. He did believe in a unifying principle or law, which he called the *logos*, but even the *logos* (which he seems to have identified with fire as the world's basic material element) was in constant motion. Heraclitus coined the well-known maxim that we can't step into the same river twice, because the river and its contents are in everlasting flux and subject to constant change. The same applies to everything else that exists. The problem with his theory was that it seemed to make the pursuit of knowledge all but impossible. If the object we study changes under our hands, how can we ever know and understand it? A century and a half later, Plato, and then Aristotle, were to struggle with this problem and propose solutions to it.

So did Heraclitus' younger contemporary Parmenides. His answer to Heraclitus was an opposite theory: according to him nothing changes. Being is eternal, and eternally the same. What we perceive as becoming, as change, is simply appearance, not reality. It is not the senses that tell us what is real, but reason. And that there is no becoming can indeed be demonstrated, according to Parmenides. He argued as follows: for something to become, it must arise either out of being or non-being. If it is to arise out of being, it does not *become* because it already *is*. If it is to arise out of non-being, on the other hand, it is nothing, since for something to come out of it, non-being must already be something, which is of course a contradiction. Becoming and change are therefore logically impossible. Logic proves that the world remains forever the same; and logic decides the issue.[3]

Parmenides' view was opposed to common sense, observation, and experience, but it has had staying power. The theory is of interest because of the distinction it drew between appearance and reality, and between empiricism (reliance on sense impressions) and rationalism. His conviction that only reason can be trusted, rather than the senses, makes Parmenides one of the first rationalists. And he had a point: it is true that sense experience can be deceptive. Don't we, for example, "see" the sun rising and setting, even though science tells us that the sun is stationary relative to the earth, and that it is the earth that moves? The question is, of course, whether logic provides a safer guide. Parmenides believed it did. So did Plato, who admired Parmenides and would make use of his ideas in developing his own philosophy.

One more natural philosopher requiring our attention is Democritus of Abdera in Thrace. He flourished around 420 B.C. and was therefore a contemporary of Socrates and the Sophists. Inspired by the teachings of Leucippus of Miletus, Democritus suggested that water, air, and so on – the so-called "first principles" of his predecessors – were not ultimate themselves but consisted of still more basic elements. These elements, which were infinite in number, constituted all that exists in the universe. They were uncreated, invisible, indivisible, and indestructible, and whirled around in an infinite void. Democritus called these particles atoms, which means uncuttables (because they could not be subdivided).

With this theory Democritus accounted not only for the basic substance of the universe, but also for its origin and for the phenomenon of change. His theory of origins was that the larger atoms had come together to form the earth and the heavenly bodies; finer ones formed water, air, and fire. Since the number of atoms and the space wherein they moved was infinite, there was an infinitude of universes, some similar to our own, others different. Also, some were being born, others had reached maturity, and still others were dying; for all things, except the eternally existing atoms and void, have a beginning and an end.

The atomists explained the origins of earthbound beings, including humans, in similar terms. Like some other Pre-Socratics, they subscribed to a theory of evolution. It stated that life had developed out of a primeval slime. Like the earth and the heavenly bodies, and like animals and plants, man came into being as a result of a particular combination of atoms, and he ceased to exist when these atoms dispersed. The soul was extinguished together with the body.

The atomic theory could have accommodated a non-material agency. Another Pre-Socratic, Anaxagoras, seems to have tried to introduce such an agency when, in a somewhat different theory, he proposed that the particles constituting the original chaos had been brought together by a cosmic Mind or *Nous*. Such was not Democritus' view. While not denying the existence of the gods, he did not allow them any significant function, and he specifically withheld from them the power of creation and providence. As to the operations of the universe, he appears to have believed in a naturalistic, mechanistic necessity.

The atomic theory was not only mechanistic but also materialistic. In a sense that had already been true of the theories of earlier philosophers, who had chosen a material element as the world's unifying principle. In their case, however, matter was still divine; no real distinction had yet been made between what we now call matter and spirit. Ancient Greek "materialism" therefore was quite different from the modern kind. It was also different from that of Democritus. For him the only things that had real existence were not the gods but atoms and the void.

Like the theories of some of his predecessors, those of Democritus could be made use of for non-scientific purposes. He himself did so. Aware of the unreliability of sense perceptions and of the subjective element in observation, he concluded that the relativity which characterizes our knowledge of the external world must affect also our moral reasoning, and indeed our knowledge of reality as a whole. Truth was relative; ultimately it was the individual who decided what was good or evil, true or false. The criterion the individual used, Democritus taught, was whether or not a certain belief or action was conducive to his own feeling of well-being. Because he was convinced that moderation contributes to personal happiness, Democritus did not advocate a crude hedonism; yet such an attitude was no longer irrational once the hedonistic basis of ethics was accepted.

Similar conclusions were drawn by Democritus' follower Epicurus (341-271 B.C.), the founder of Epicureanism, a dominant philosophy in the Hellenistic period.[4] Epicurus shared Democritus' religious views and held that although the gods existed, they did not really matter, since they had nothing to do with humanity. He also taught, again like Democritus, that the main source of human anxiety was fear of the gods and of death and divine judgment, and that the atomic theory should be used to deliver people of those fears. Human existence was accounted for by the chance combination of atoms, and human death by their chance dispersion. There was no after-life and no final judgment: death was the absolute end. Well-known is his slogan: "When I am, death is not; when death is, I am not." Since there would be no reckoning afterwards, one was free to enjoy life.

Reactions to scientific naturalism

Although Pre-Socratics were active throughout the fifth century B.C., interest in natural philosophy declined in the course of that century. One reason for the decline may well have been the skepticism and subjective relativism of a theorist like Democritus, and his message that all that exists can be explained in terms of atoms and the void. Although under attack from many sides, religion was still important, and in any event, people then as now wanted to know about the purpose of the universe and of human life. Democritus did not answer this type of question, and neither did any of the other natural philosophers. Nor did these thinkers manage to contribute a unified, generally accepted view of the universe. Every school had its own theories, which often conflicted with those of the next one. The entire endeavour seemed to lead to little more than disagreements, and even to stalemates, such as the one between Heraclitus, who insisted that all was change, and Parmenides, who seemed to have proved the opposite.

In the end, Pre-Socratic philosophy was too theoretical, too remote from human concerns, to satisfy the Greeks of the classical period. In the course of the turbulent fifth century B.C. there is evidence of a kind of existential revolt against the theories of the natural philosophers. It signified a growing concern with the question about the nature and destiny of man. These concerns are reflected in the Delphic imperative "Know thyself!" and in Socrates' creed that "An unexamined life is not worth living." They are also evident in the fact that the fifth century became the century of the great classical tragedians, and that it witnessed, with the work of Herodotus, Thucydides, and others, the flourishing of Greek historiography.

The kind of objection that arose against the Pre-Socratics' naturalism – and that has a modern ring to it – is well described in the *Phaedo*, Plato's dialogue that recounts the last day of Socrates. Condemned to death by the Athenians and waiting for the cup with the deadly hemlock to arrive, Socrates sought to comfort his grieving friends, Plato tells us, by arguing that death is not to be feared, because there are good reasons to believe that the soul is immortal, and that in a future existence the righteous will reap great rewards.

In the course of the discussion he recalled that as a youth he had been very much interested in the speculations of the natural philosophers, because they supposedly explained the causes and meaning of things. He had been especially happy with the statement of Anaxagoras that not matter but Mind ruled the world. That implied, Socrates had believed, that all was ordered for the best; that the universe had a purpose, and that the end was rational and good. But as it happened, Anaxagoras had grievously disappointed him. It seems that he had been something of a Greek deist, believing that Mind set everything in motion but then left the universe to run on its own. In any event, when it came to the explanation of mundane matters, Socrates said, Anaxagoras had recourse to the same material factors as the others. He did not deal with questions of plan and purpose; all he was concerned with was the "how" of happenings, not the "why."

In his particular case, Socrates said, the natural philosophers (Anaxagoras included) would be of no help at all. They would explain the fact that he did not run away from his trial and execution with reference to the properties of bones, tendons, muscles, and other material elements, all the while ignoring the fact that it was Socrates himself who had chosen to undergo the trial and to submit to death, in obedience to Athens' laws. They confused causes with conditions, and refused to allow for the existence of Mind.[5] So Socrates had turned away from the natural philosophers and embarked upon his search for a wisdom that would be useful for man.

The Sophists

That search involved a lifelong battle against the teachings of the Sophists, a group of itinerant teachers and philosophers who applied the naturalism of the Pre-Socratics to intellectual, moral, and social matters. Their name is derived from *sophia*, the Greek word for wisdom, and the Sophists said that wisdom was indeed what they were after. Historically they have had a bad press. They may well have deserved it, although it is true that we know about them primarily (although not exclusively) through Plato, who cordially disagreed with their teachings and probably made a point of painting them in the darkest possible colours. It may well be that not all their theories were without merit or socially destructive, but it is hard to judge, because the Sophists' writings (like most of those of the Pre-Socratics) have disappeared.[6] Only fragments and summaries survive.

The Sophists flourished in the second half of the fifth century B.C. The century had opened with the victory of Greece in the Persian wars. As a result of that victory, Athens had become the undisputed naval power which dominated the Aegean area commercially and politically. Ultimately the city's predominance and heavy-handedness led to the suicidal Peloponnesian wars, in which Sparta defeated and humiliated Athens, but by mid-century that nemesis still lay in the future. The larger part of the fifth century was for Athens a period of confidence and expansiveness. It witnessed the Athenian Golden Age, the period of the city's greatest cultural achievements, which made it not only "the school of Greece" but also the school of its successor civilizations, including our own.

The fifth century was also a period of rapid social and intellectual change. International trade and commerce, together with Athens' imperial concerns, opened up a new world for Athenians and acquainted them with religions, laws, and customs quite different from their own. This led, as is common in such cases, to a questioning of inherited customs and traditions and so reinforced the skepticism inherent in Pre-Socratic teachings. Religion did not escape the type of critical questioning people increasingly engaged in. Although many temples were built during the Golden Age, traditional religious truths were more and more being relativized, as were traditional moral values. It was in furthering these developments that the Sophist movement played a prominent role. Its members hailed from various areas in Greece, but several converged upon Athens, where they enjoyed the patronage of the Athenian leader Pericles and of other leading citizens.

According to Plato these Sophists (whose teachings, as Plato describes them, bear an uncanny resemblance to those of postmodern days) were skeptics and subjective relativists. They said that objective, universally-valid norms did not exist, or, if they did, that humans could not know of any. Indeed, there was preciously little that people could know. Since Heraclitus proclaimed his theory of incessant flux nothing was certain, not what previous generations had believed about the gods, nor the conclusions reached by the Pre-Socratics, nor anything else. The teachings of skeptics like Democritus had similar implications.

Indeed, although they relativized the theories of the Pre-Socratics, the Sophists had learned much from these thinkers. They echoed their ideas and followed their principle of explaining reality without reference to the gods. Traditional laws and norms and customs, the Sophists said, were not of divine but of human origin. This was obvious and could be ascertained by anyone who took the trouble to look around and compare the laws and standards of foreign states with each other and with those of Athens. There were so many differences that these systems could not possibly be explained with reference to Zeus or any other universal lawgiver.

Since laws and customs were neither divinely-given nor "natural" (that is, part of an unchanging natural order) but simply man-made, they could not be proved to be binding on society and on the individual. For why should we be told, the Sophists asked themselves and their audience, to obey laws that were established by people as fallible as ourselves and who lived in times so different from our own? After all – and again reference could be made to Heraclitus – reality was nothing but flux. All one could ever really know about the physical world was the impressions that he received via the senses, each one disappearing sooner or later. It followed that only those things could be considered true which the individual himself experienced as true at any moment. And what applied to the physical world applied to ethics. Moral standards also were in constant flux. What was good today was not necessarily good tomorrow, and what was right for one person was not necessarily right for his neighbour. This being so, each individual had to decide on his own, and every moment anew, what he for himself would consider to be true or good.

Among the people who spread these doctrines was Protagoras, one of the founders of the movement and probably the most highly regarded among the Sophists. In religious matters he posed as an agnostic, explaining that he could not possibly tell whether or not the gods existed, or, if they did, what they were like: human life was too short to reach certainty on so obscure a subject. His maxim was that "Man is the measure of all things, of things that are that they are, of things that are not that they are not." In the absence of absolute norms it was man – ultimately the individual – who set his own norms and standards. Protagoras' maxim, and the teachings of his followers, implied a thoroughgoing epistemological and moral uncertainty. Although Protagoras himself refused to admit it, the danger of moral chaos became evident when other Sophists, not as moderate as the master, said that "Might is right" and that "Justice is the interest of the stronger."

Sophist ideas spread rapidly in fifth-century Athens. The Sophists tended to make a living as teachers, and the more famous among them were very popular. They taught a well-rounded liberal arts curriculum combined with subjects that were primarily of a practical nature. Sophist teaching, in other words, was both humanistic and career-oriented. The latter orientation was to be expected. If truth cannot be found, if it probably does not even exist, one may as well concentrate on what is useful and settle for the comforts of the material.

There was a market for the Sophist curriculum. A direct democracy and an expanding city-state and empire with far-flung political and economic interests, Athens offered great career opportunities to the brightest of her sons, and the Sophists were ready to prepare these young men for their tasks wherever they might be found, in Athens or abroad. Among their concerns was the teaching of skills and devices that would guarantee success in politics and diplomacy. As we read in the *Protagoras,* the Sophists' teaching focused on debating techniques ("the art of making clever speakers") so that the student could become "a real power in the city, both as speaker and man of action."[7] And since norms were relative, students did not have to be concerned with old-fashioned values like honesty, justice, or mercy. They could concentrate on learning the tricks that would enable them, as Socrates' accusers put it, to make "the worse into the stronger argument."[8] Relativism was rife, and the Sophist ethics that "justice was the right of the stronger" was widely practised. Athens' weaker neighbours experienced it.

It was these relativistic and ultimately nihilistic Sophist principles that Socrates encountered. Like his disciple Plato, he considered them so destructive of society and the individual that he would spend a lifetime attempting to refute them. He went about his task by reasserting the reality of the One in the moral realm, thereby proving the existence of moral norms which are valid for all people, regardless of time and place and circumstances.

NOTES

[1] William Barrett, *Irrational Man: A Study in Existential Philosophy* (Garden City, New York: Doubleday, Anchor Books, 1962 [1958]), p. 5.

[2] A good resource on the life and work of the Pre-Socratics is Kathleen Freeman, *The Pre-Socratic Philosophers: A Companion to Diels,* Fragmente der Vorsokratiker, 2nd ed. (Cambridge, Mass.: Harvard University Press, 1959). See also Drew A. Hyland, *The Origins of Philosophy: Its Rise in Myth and the Pre-Socratics. A Collection of Early Writings Selected, Edited, and with Explanatory*

Essays (New York: Putnam, Capricorn Books, 1973).

3. See for this explanation Frederick Copleston, *A History of Philosophy, I, Greece & Rome,* Part I (Garden City, New York: Doubleday, Image Books, 1962 [Westminster, Maryland: Newman Press, 1946]), pp. 65, 67. See also W. K. C. Guthrie, *The Greek Philosophers: From Thales to Aristotle* (New York: Harper and Row, Harper Torchbooks, The Academic Library, 1960 [1950]), pp. 46-49.

4. The poem *De rerum natura* by the Roman Epicurean poet Lucretius also shows the abiding attraction of Democritus' atomic and evolutionistic theories. This poem would, in turn, influence early modern scientists in their acceptance of atomism.

5 Plato, *Phaedo*, 96-99.

6 See G. B. Kerferd, *The Sophistic Movement* (Cambridge: Cambridge University Press, 1984 [1981]) for a somewhat more favourable view of the Sophists than the traditional one.

7. Plato, *Protagoras*, 312D, 319A.

8. Plato, *Apology*, 19b.

II. The Athenian Philosophers

Socrates

Before we proceed with the account of Socrates' life and teachings, a note on the sources is in order. Socrates himself did not leave any written works, and most of what we know about him comes to us via Plato, Socrates' disciple.[1] Because Plato enlarged on his master's teachings but continued to use Socrates as his mouthpiece, it is not always clear whether the ideas in the Platonic dialogues are his own or those of Socrates. In the following account it has been assumed that in the earlier dialogues the Socratic element is the stronger, and that in the later works the Platonic one is predominant.

Although he was a life-long opponent of the Sophists, Socrates' contemporaries often identified him with them. That happened also at his trial in 399 B.C. The trial took place a few years after the Athenian defeat by Sparta in the Peloponnesian War, at a time when Athenian democracy, which the Spartans had suspended, had been restored. The Athenian people, led by conservatives, looked for a scapegoat, someone who could be blamed for the disastrous defeat and the increasing social and moral anarchy. Recognizing the socially destructive nature of the principles taught by the Sophists, they picked the man they believed to be the most influential member of that group, and that man was Socrates.

The mistake was understandable. Socrates was popular among young Athenians, and he spent much of his time arguing with them. Also, like the Sophists, he was a skeptic, at least as far as belief in the Olympic gods was concerned, and at this particular time that was a crime. The

Olympic religion was still the religion of the community. As often happens in times of national crisis, religious devotion had increased, and people were quick to explain the humiliating outcome of the war as divine punishment for the apostasy of Athens' intellectual leaders. This explains the charge against Socrates: he was accused of having corrupted the youth of Athens and of having introduced foreign gods.

It was not just the contents of Socrates' teachings that led to his death. His approach also had been an irritant. In his search for the moral absolutes that the Sophists had denied - that is, in his search for norms and standards that are the same for all times and all people - he employed what has become known as the Socratic method. His search was for definitions of concepts of morality and truth. Acting as a hornet or gadfly (his own description), he would enter into discussions with people and force them, by constant questioning and by constant testing of the opinions they expressed, to refine their concepts. In the process they were forced to admit that they did not know what they had thought they knew. That was annoying for the victims, and Socrates knew that he was making enemies. At his trial he told his accusers that he could not help it. He had not chosen the task himself; heaven had laid it upon him.

Why did Socrates not simply proclaim what he believed to be the objective, unchanging standards of right and truth? The reason was that traditional values had been under attack for too long. Socrates himself may have regarded these values highly, but he knew that they could no longer be imposed from outside. The individual had to establish for himself the validity of the norms he followed. And he could do that without falling into the abyss of subjective relativism, Socrates believed, if he knew how to use his reason. In his case reasoning was not, as it was for the Sophists, simply a matter of rhetoric and debating techniques. For Socrates human reason was grounded in the Reason that, he believed, ruled the cosmos. It was because of this relationship that it could enable man to find the One behind the Many and so discover standards and truths of abiding validity.

The Socratic method was the means to that end. Its goal was to move toward a single definition of a concept (such as truth, justice, piety, temperance, and so on) that was impervious to counter-arguments. If this could be done, it would show that there were norms which transcended the opinions of individual men and women. The stress was on the individual's personal search. Generally, the Socratic dialogues did not lead to a conclusion. They were not intended to. Socrates insisted that he himself knew nothing, and that his task was not to dictate answers, but simply to act as a midwife (another of his self-descriptions), helping others give birth to truth. Instead of indoctrinating them, he wanted people to find the truth for themselves. That is, he wanted to help bring to birth a truth that he believed was already present in people's minds, even though they themselves were not aware of it; hence his insistence that he acted as a midwife. Instead of teaching the essence of virtue, he taught a method by means of which people could arrive at it on their own. At the very least, they would learn to examine their opinions and so strip away errors. The Socratic method was primarily a method of clear and critical thinking.

Obviously, then, Socrates was not a traditionalist, that is, someone who preaches that one must follow certain norms and believe in certain truths simply because tradition or authority (including religious authority) affirms them. In this sense he was in agreement with the Sophists and their Pre-Socratic mentors. He opposed their subjectivism and relativism, but like them he believed that simply to legislate morality was no longer possible in the times wherein they lived. Tradition and religion might well have the right answers, but in an age of skepticism it took personal conviction rather than outside authority to affirm them.

Convinced of the effectiveness of his approach, Socrates kept insisting that moral reform would follow intellectual enlightenment. He was able to say this because of the conviction, basic to all his philosophy, that no one does evil willingly, that evil is the result of ignorance, and that those who know the good are willing and able to do it. Morality was its own reward. Against the prevailing opinion Socrates insisted that virtue and happiness were intimately connected, and that the same applied to vice and unhappiness. The moral law was a law of life.

Socrates' legacy

What has been the effect of Socrates' teachings? They no doubt served to check the subjective relativism taught by Protagoras and the other Sophists, at least among some of his hearers. His influence has not been restricted to his contemporaries either. Socrates has been a source of inspiration for centuries. Christians were among those who admired the man and his teachings. The second-century apologist Justin Martyr, for example, believed that Socrates was "a Christian before Christ," the Renaissance scholar Erasmus called him a saint, and not a few Christians in the early and medieval church admired him as an outstanding pagan philosopher to whom Christians would do well to listen.

The unbounded admiration of Socrates has been waning in late-modern times. This is in the nature of the case. Socrates was a humanist with a strong belief in man's essential goodness and rationality. For him it was not the unconscious drives that ruled the intellect; the opposite was true. The mind was in control, and the mind was good and willed the good. This explains why he kept insisting that no one does evil willingly, and that those who know the good will do it. Such an optimistic view of human morality does not agree with the beliefs of our post-Freudian, postmodern world.

It is not in agreement with biblical teachings either. Although Socrates can indeed serve as an inspiration, his message cannot be accepted uncritically. He was not really "a Christian before Christ," and neither is he an infallible guide. Some of the weaknesses underlying his philosophy - its humanism and rationalism - have already been mentioned, but our critique has to go further. It has to include his implicit denial of human finitude. It is true, Socrates rejected the idea that human reason is on a par with divine wisdom. If there were Greek thinkers who were guilty of such hubris, Socrates was not among them. His one claim to wisdom was, as he explained to his contemporaries, the fact that he was aware of his utter ignorance. And yet in his system the human being in the end takes the place of God as the source of laws and standards. Man is responsible to himself alone and becomes his own standard. Ultimately, therefore, Socrates too makes man the measure of all things, and thereby puts a greater burden on mortals and their society than they can well bear.

That the burden was indeed too heavy becomes clear from the subsequent history of ancient Greece. It also becomes clear from the history of modern Europe. For the Christian West followed Socrates in his belief in human reason as the source of morality and truth, and it did so with less justification than Socrates. All that Socrates and his fellows could do, as the Apostle Paul was to express it in his speech on the Athenian Areopagus more than four centuries after Socrates' death, was to take notice of God's providence so that, inspired thereby, they might "perhaps reach out for him and find him" (Acts 17). But until Paul preached the gospel to them, the Greeks did not know God. Nor did they know that he who had established the moral law had also provided for the way in which it was to be known and obeyed. The western world knew the way and rejected it.

Plato

Did Socrates consciously "reach out" for God, or at least for the supernatural? This question is a difficult one to answer. On the one hand, there is Socrates' perpetual skepticism and the fact that in the search for objective standards he did not have recourse to the supernatural. In his system the acquisition of moral knowledge was the result of thinking, and of thinking only.

On the other hand, there are dialogues like the *Phaedo* which portray him as someone who believed in the existence of an afterlife. In the *Phaedo* the Platonic element is already becoming strong, however, and the discussion on immortality may be more Platonic than Socratic. In the earlier *Apology,* which deals with his trial, Socrates comes across as what has been called "a hopeful agnostic." The thing that does seem reasonably clear is that he searched for a purpose and, in connection therewith, for a Mind that had ordered reality and had done so for the good. Plato tells us, as we have seen, that this search led him to Anaxagoras in the vain hope of finding an alternative to the materialism and determinism of the Pre-Socratics.

The search for a benevolent supernatural principle or being would be continued by Plato, who was Socrates' disciple as well as his biographer and was moulded by him. He was also affected by the ideas of the Pre-Socratics, more so than his teacher had been. Heraclitus and Parmenides especially influenced him. Heraclitus was the man who said that the essence of reality is flux and change. This theory seemed to be exemplified by the times in which Plato lived and which he found utterly disturbing. Political and social instability was as characteristic of the fourth century B.C. as it had been of the late fifth. The century had opened, moreover, with the execution of his teacher Socrates, a perversion of justice that upset and angered Plato. This experience no doubt played a role in the development of his philosophy. In any event, convinced that truth can never be found in the contemplation of the chaotic visible world, Plato began his lifelong search for a transcendental realm where changelessness ruled.

While Heraclitus saw nothing in the visible world but flux, he believed that underlying the chaos was a rational principle or reason (the *logos*), which governed the cosmos. This theory, too, served Plato as a motivation. So did the ideas of Parmenides, who had said that only our reason can be trusted, not our sense experiences, and that the change and decay we see all around us are only appearance. True reality is eternal and unchanging and can be known by reason only. It was in accordance with these teachings that Plato came to speak of two worlds: the visible world - that is, the world of our senses, the world of becoming - and the invisible or intelligible world, the realm of being, of universals, of the One. The former was the shadow and temporal image of the latter. Those who searched diligently for the invisible realm would find deliverance from the world of flux and change.

Plato's search led him to his theory of Forms or Ideas. It was especially through this theory that he enlarged upon the teachings of Socrates and attempted to meet the latter's demand for purpose and meaning. His Forms could be compared to the definitions of Socrates, in the sense that they represented the unchanging essences of things. Unlike Socrates' definitions, however, they were not just mental concepts but real entities, which existed apart from the sensible objects. Also, they referred not only to moral norms but to all of reality. In addition to the Forms of justice, piety, temperance and the other concepts that Socrates had been concerned with, there were Forms for physical things and beings. Each object, like each concept, was represented by (or participated in) its own Form, of which it was an image. To give an example: humanity was the Form, individual men and women were the shadowy, imperfect images of that ideal. For Plato, essence came before existence; the general or universal before the particular.

By replacing Socrates' definitions with these Forms and by separating them from the sensible world and placing them in the intelligible one, Plato kept them safe from flux and decay. Concepts and definitions might sooner or later come under attack and undergo change; words could be said to be mere conventions (as the Sophists in fact had taught) rather than having a direct and necessary connection with the things they denoted; but the Platonic Forms, existing as they did in the supersensible world, were beyond human interference. The theory of the Forms served additional purposes. Plato used it, for example, as a theory of knowledge, stating that man could know the eternal essences of things because his soul, being spiritual, was related to the Forms. According to the theory of recollection, which Plato introduced in the *Meno* dialogue, the human soul had known the Forms in a previous existence. Life in the flesh had all but erased that knowledge, but it could be brought back to a person's memory in a number of ways. One of them was the Socratic method of questioning. The questioner here served indeed, in Socrates' words, as a midwife.

Plato's theology

As the foregoing suggests, the theory of the Forms could function also as a theology, and even as a soteriology, a doctrine of salvation. It could do this because knowledge of the Forms redeemed man from the aimlessness and purposelessness of the present world, and also because the theory implied the separate existence of the soul and its relationship with the eternal. It was this relationship that enabled Plato to posit the pre-existence and immortality of the soul.

Not in the last place, the theory of the Forms provided for the existence of the cosmic Mind for which Socrates had been searching. It located that Mind in the intelligible realm, and showed how it could be known. In Plato's system the philosopher's goal was firstly the contemplation of the individual Forms, but ultimately these served as stepping-stones to the knowledge of the highest Form, which was the Form of the Good. It was that Form that functioned as Socrates' cosmic Mind. The Form of the Good ordered the cosmos, directed it toward a benevolent end, and served as the source and nurturer of all that existed. It can therefore be defined as the supreme Platonic God.

Plato was influenced not only by Heraclitus and Parmenides, but also by the Pre-Socratic Pythagoreans, members of a school of mathematics that was at the same time a religious brotherhood. From them he learned about the importance of mathematics for philosophy, and he was inspired by their religious teachings as well. The two were connected: for the Pythagoreans mathematics was a sacred subject. Their brotherhood, which dates from the sixth century B.C., appears to have been influenced by a number of ancient mystery religions, including that of the Orphics (named after the legendary singer and poet Orpheus). The Pythagoreans, it appears, taught the immortality of the soul, the transmigration of souls, the reality of a world beyond the visible one, and the effect of man's present actions upon his fate in a future life. With its stress on the soul, their religion was unlike the Olympic one, which granted the soul only a shadowy existence after death. Pythagoreans considered the soul to form the essence of man, believing that it had its origin in the heavens but had fallen to earth, where it became imprisoned in the body. Salvation meant the soul's release from the body and its eventual return to the intelligible realm.

These ideas, then, are reflected in Plato's dialogues. Often he tried to prove them by logic, but at times, when the language of logic could not express the ineffable, he had recourse to myth. This was the case, for example, in the *Phaedo*, when he tried to prove the immortality of the soul and the reality of a future life, and in the *Republic*, in connection with his attempt to show that virtue will be rewarded and vice punished in the world to come.[2]

Plato's myths and mysticism have endeared him to mystics, Christian and non-Christian ones alike. The religious elements in his philosophy made him popular among Christian philosophers and theologians, beginning with some of the early church fathers. Often they became acquainted with his ideas not only via Plato's own works, but also via Neoplatonism, a system of thought that mixed Platonic ideas with those of other religious and philosophical traditions and often stressed mysticism even more than Plato had done. Neoplatonism continued to be popular in the Middle Ages. Together with Platonism proper it served as an inspiration in the Renaissance and, directly or indirectly, the early modern period.

The measure of Plato's influence was not only his mysticism, but also his belief in human reason and his conviction that reason was the means of leading man to knowledge of the Absolute. That belief would be reinforced by the philosophy of Aristotle, Plato's most brilliant student and the last of the great Athenian triad that begins with Socrates.

Aristotle

In the early sixteenth century the Italian Renaissance artist Raphael produced a painting entitled "The School of Athens." In the centre of this painting, surrounded by ancient philosophers and scientists, stand Plato and Aristotle. Plato points upward, to the realm of Ideas, and Aristotle points downward, to the physical world. Raphael's painting suggests that the ideal philosophy is one which synthesizes the ideas of Plato and Aristotle. Attempts to bring about such a synthesis had often been made, both in the ancient world and in the Middle Ages. Often an eclectic approach was followed, with people choosing what appealed to them in the two systems and ignoring or adapting what seemed less congenial.

A student of Plato for many years, Aristotle was strongly influenced by him, but he also turned against a number of Plato's central constructs, such as his theory of transcendental Forms. Aristotle did not share Plato's extreme otherworldliness. As Raphael's painting suggests, his concern was less with the heavens than with mankind's habitat, the earth.

Although he rejected Plato's Forms, Aristotle did not believe that the visible object was the ultimately real. For the Platonic Forms he instituted concepts, the so-called universals, which corresponded to the essences of objects. To come to know these universals was, for Aristotle as for Plato, the proper goal of philosophy and science. But unlike Plato's, Aristotle's universals did not have a separate existence. They could be apprehended by the mind, but only via the individual object, the particular. The universal or general was to be recognized in the particular and abstracted from it. To return to our example: humanity was a universal, a concept derived from observation of the particulars, that is, of individual men and women, and it was knowable only through them. There was no separate and independent entity up in the heavens called "humanity."

This change had a number of important implications. Firstly, with his theory of universals and particulars Aristotle returned to the individual the significance that Socrates had also given it but that Plato had denied. (For Plato, as we saw, the Form or Idea was more "real" than the concrete particular.) Secondly, he redefined the ancient problem regarding the relationship between universals and particulars and between being and becoming; a point to which we return later in this chapter. And thirdly, Aristotle's revision of Plato's theory meant, as Raphael's painting suggests, that for Aristotle and his followers knowledge cannot be had by simply focusing on the transcendental. Although his goal is the contemplation of eternal truth, the philosopher must find it by first of all turning to the physical world. And knowledge of the physical world depended, for Aristotle as for future empiricists, on sense perception.

Turning to the natural world (and to the world of humanity) was indeed what Aristotle did, and what he made his students do. A man of universal interests and encyclopedic knowledge, he observed, collected, and classified a very large body of data and left writings on practically every subject under the sun, ranging from physics, astronomy, and biology to metaphysics, ethics, rhetoric, politics, and poetics. In the process he had to invent much of the terminology and many of the intellectual tools he needed. One of his greatest achievements in that regard was the creation of a system of logic, which would guide thinkers for centuries to come.

Aristotle's theology

For all his concern with the world here below, Aristotle was not a materialist. He remained a disciple of Plato and Socrates. Although an empiricist, he believed that ultimate truths are deductive and therefore intellectual ones. They alone are necessarily true. And he agreed with his mentors in their insistence that knowledge of the "wherefore and why," of the purpose or *telos* of things, was of far greater relevance than knowledge of the "how."

Important in this connection was the analysis of causation which he gave in Book II of his *Physics,* and his explanation of the way in which we must use that concept to understand phenomena. He distinguished four causes, and illustrated them with reference to the work of an artist or artisan, such as a sculptor. The first cause, the *material* one, was the raw material the sculptor used; then came the *formal* cause, namely the form that would be given to or impressed upon the material; the *efficient* cause was the sculptor; and the *final* cause was the purpose for which the statue was made. Although he was too much the scientist to ignore material and formal and efficient causes, ultimately Aristotle was the man of the final cause. In the words of classical historian F. M. Cornford, Aristotle's thought, like that of Plato and Socrates, was governed by the idea that "the true cause or explanation of things is to be sought, not in the beginning, but in the end." [3]

Aristotle also admitted the existence of the supernatural, but here again there were important differences with Plato. For one thing, Aristotle did not need a Creator, because his cosmos was uncreated and eternal. He did need a supernatural being, however, to account for motion in the universe. Aristotle helped build the model of the cosmos that, with certain adaptations, would rule for some two thousand years. In this model the earth was the stationary centre around which all the heavenly bodies revolved. Beyond sun, moon, and planets were the fixed stars, and beyond them were the heavens, the abode of God. He was the cause of all motion, not only in the heavens but ultimately also on earth. Aristotle referred to him as the Unmoved Mover.

This Unmoved Mover moved the world not by force, but by attraction. He could do that because he was absolutely perfect, and as such the object of the world's desire. This meant that each thing on earth moved because, consciously or unconsciously, it strove to reach the degree of perfection of which it was capable, and thereby come closer to God. It was therefore also possible to say that everything on earth was moved by love. It was, however, no more than a disembodied and intellectualized love. The Unmoved Mover could never be the protector, provider, and redeemer of man and nature, nor could he be the object of mankind's loyalty and worship.

The God of Aristotelianism was a philosophical construct, the result of logical necessity. Cornford observes that the argument used to demonstrate his existence "strikes a chill to the religious consciousness." [4] The same could be said of his nature. The Unmoved Mover was wrapped up in himself. He desired nothing and, being conscious of nothing but himself, had nothing to do with the world. His activity was restricted to eternally contemplating himself as the height of perfection. There was little left of Plato's God with his moral demands, his concern for human happiness, his provision of rewards and punishments in a future life. The philosophy of Aristotle did not provide for the immortality of the individual soul. The part of man that did survive, but only in an impersonal mode, was the intellect. As the seat of thought, it was divine and shared, in some abstract fashion, in the eternal Mind.

In Aristotle's theology we find the culmination of the Greek tradition of rationalism that began with the Pre-Socratics. For in his rationality Aristotle's God was like man. Since it was the possession of reason that distinguished man from other living beings, Aristotle argued, reason must be considered man's essence. It followed that one's happiness consisted in the use of one's rational faculty. This intellectual type of happiness was what Aristotle himself pursued as the highest good, and it was also what he assigned to the First Mover of his cosmos. In that sense he created his God in his own image. The heart and the emotions played no role in the contemplation of the eternal.

Aristotle and Plato

While Aristotle discarded some of the insights that Christians have found most congenial in Plato, he also improved on the ideas of his teacher. Among the more important changes were, as we already noted, his restoration of the importance of the concrete individual and, in connection therewith, his rejection of Plato's extreme otherworldliness. Plato had exalted the eternal world of the Forms over the temporal world of the senses, reason over sense experience, and the soul over the body. The divisions were drawn so sharply that dualisms resulted. The world of matter and of sense experience was only a shadow of the intelligible or real world and greatly inferior to it, and the body was the prison of the soul. Salvation consisted, for Plato as for his Pythagorean mentors, in the soul's release from the body and in the escape from the temporal world into the intelligible one.

For Aristotle, on the other hand, the sensory world was eminently real, and therefore a worthy object of study. His belief in the reality of the visible world implied not only a renunciation of the otherworldly tendencies in Plato's thought. It also inspired him to a more fruitful solution of the problem left by Parmenides and Heraclitus regarding the relationship between changelessness and change, or being and becoming, than Plato had achieved. Distinguishing between *potentiality* and *actuality*, Aristotle showed that development and becoming are real, and that they are not, as Plato believed, to be deplored. Change and growth are essential in the objects' striving for maturity and lead to the degree of perfection of which their natures are capable. By moving from potentiality to actuality, the seed, for example, develops into the plant, the bud into the flower, the embryo into the child, the child into the adult.

Another important concept he used in this connection was that of *Form* and *matter*. Matter was the raw material, which Form arranged into an essence, a final product. Form was the permanent element, which survived throughout the untold generations of the perishable individual. It was also capable of evolving and so become the matter for a higher Form. Development was continuous: the child, for example, was the Form of the embryo but the matter of the adult. This meant that Aristotle, although starting from different premises, followed Plato in replacing the Pre-Socratic idea of material causation with the concept of Form as ultimate cause, and therefore also as the true reality and the abiding essence of things. It was by affirming this abiding essence that, like Plato and Socrates, he responded to the subjective relativism of the Sophists, and also to their skepticism: if the One indeed underlies the Many, then knowledge is possible. Meanwhile Aristotle did make clear that growth, and therefore change, was inevitable and, for organic beings, a natural and desirable thing.

In order to reach their essence, these objects had to be able to produce their own kind, as in fact they did. An acorn developed not into a maple but into an oak. Similarly, a scorpion's egg hatched a scorpion, not a hummingbird. Aristotle believed that that capacity was inherent in nature, rather than being imposed, as Plato had taught, from outside. Organic beings possessed an immanent vitalistic principle, the vegetative soul, which programmed the reproductive process.

In this manner Aristotle brought down "the Platonic Form of the species... from its heaven of unchanging reality, and plunged [it] in the flow of time and sensible existence."[5] As we will notice later, early-modern scientists and philosophers rejected Aristotle's organic theory, believing that it gave too much power to nature and could be used in support of pantheism. Inspired by the Pre-Socratic Democritus and his Hellenistic followers, they preferred the atomic model of the universe with its mechanistic implications. More recently, however, appreciation has grown again for Aristotle's view, since it provides a better model for the biological sciences than does the mechanical one.

But while the capacity for development was immanent in nature, there was for Aristotle a higher teleology as well. Ultimately the object's potential was actualized through the attraction of the First Mover. This constituted the relationship between the Unmoved Mover and nature.

Aristotle's influence on Christian theology

Aristotle did not fully eliminate the sharp dualisms inherent in Plato's philosophy. The one between the supernatural and the natural world, between God and man, remained. Aristotle's theology, with its removed and impersonal God, would in fact strengthen that dichotomy. As we will see in later chapters, Aristotle's view of God would be reflected in Christian theology in the Middle Ages and in later centuries.

But his work had positive effects in the history of Christian doctrine as well. Plato's idealism - that is, his belief that no certain knowledge can be had by attending to the world of the senses, because the latter is no more than a shadow or symbol of true reality - had a negative effect on biblical studies. It encouraged the tendency among theologians to concentrate on the search for a "hidden" meaning of Scripture at the expense of the literal sense, and so contributed to the excessive allegorizing of the biblical message that so marred the theology and preaching of the early church and the church of the Middle Ages.

It was Aristotle's empiricism - his belief that what we know comes first of all from the senses - that would serve as a correction to this habit. In the Middle Ages it would encourage the philosopher Thomas Aquinas to promote the primacy of the literal interpretation of the Bible.[6] Aristotelian ideas also played a role in Thomas' rejection of a sharp duality between body and soul, another Platonic element in early Christian and medieval theology.[7] Whereas for Plato the soul was separate from the body, which served as a temporary prison, for Aristotle it was the Form of the body and therefore inseparable from it. The two formed a unity. As a Christian, Aquinas did of course believe the soul to be immortal; it survived when the body died. But he also believed that without the body it was incomplete; hence full restoration would not come about until the body was resurrected and reunited with the soul.[8]

The perennial philosophy

There are other distinctions between Aristotle and Plato. Ultimately, however, the differences between the two are probably less important than the similarities. Both men were disciples of Socrates and upheld the philosophy that he had taught and exemplified. We have seen that this philosophy was humanistic, intellectualistic, and dualistic. These characteristics were inherited by western philosophy and explain the stubborn western beliefs that unaided human reason can establish eternally valid truths, and that the philosopher and scientist are not participants in the world, but mere observers. The modern cult of intellectualism and of a dualistic, objectivistic scientism, against which postmodernism has rightly begun to rebel, had its origins in the Greek intellectual tradition.

But we have noted that the perennial philosophy contains insights of lasting value as well. The Athenian philosophers opposed materialism, skepticism, and subjective relativism; they insisted that there is a universally binding moral law which man must attempt to find; they taught that the individual is responsible for his actions, and that the moral life is a matter not simply of isolated acts, but of character and habit. Not in the last place, they showed that mankind does well to attend to universal issues: to that which abides.

It was this philosophical tradition that Aristotle bequeathed to the Middle Ages. Medieval thinkers inherited it as part of, and together with, his work on logic, biology, physics, ethics, and a multitude of other disciplines. They eagerly and gratefully used his contributions to logic and to the knowledge of man and nature, and were both attracted and repelled by his rationalism. They greatly worried about the elements in his system that contradicted the Christian Scriptures. Aristotle's work was so rich, so promising, and (on the whole) so convincing that medieval philosophers looked for ways of incorporating it into Christian philosophy and theology. The attempt to reconcile Aristotle (and often also Plato) with Christianity would occupy the energy of several of the period's greatest thinkers.

NOTES

1. Plato's account can be supplemented with information from other contemporary and near-contemporary sources, such as Aristophanes, Xenophon, and Aristotle.

2 Plato, *Phaedo*, 105ff., *Republic*, 614ff.

3. F. M. Cornford, *Before and After Socrates* (Cambridge: Cambridge University Press, 1965 [1932]), p. 90.

4. *Ibid.*, p. 100.

5 *Ibid.*, p. 99.

[6.] Norman L. Geisler, *Thomas Aquinas: An Evangelical Appraisal* (Grand Rapids: Baker, 1991), pp. 52f. This is not to say that Aquinas and his disciples abandoned the allegorical approach altogether. It remained popular throughout the Middle Ages and into the Renaissance.

[7.] F. C. Copleston, *A History of Medieval Philosophy* (New York: Harper and Row, Torchbook Library, 1972), p. 188.

[8.] For a critique of the scholastic conception of the soul as determined by the Greek "form-matter" concept, see Herman Dooyeweerd, *Roots of Western Culture: Pagan, Secular, and Christian Options,* trans. John Kraay, eds. Mark Vander Vennen and Bernard Zylstra (Toronto: Wedge Publishing, 1979), pp. 32f.

III. Reason and Revelation in the Middle Ages

Augustine on ancient learning

When they turned to the study of ancient philosophy, medieval scholars continued a tradition established by the early church. The Christian church was born in the advanced Hellenistic culture of Greece and Rome, and many Christian converts had been steeped in classical learning. Since this was pagan learning, they had to decide whether its pursuit was appropriate for believers. Was all contact with ancient wisdom to be avoided, or could classical learning be used to advance the faith?

Scholars in the early Christian centuries spent much time debating the issue. They reached no unanimous conclusion. Some, believing that there were no points of contact " between Jerusalem and Athens," warned that Greek learning should be left alone. The African church father Tertullian, who died around 220, is the best-known spokesman for this opinion. Others argued that if properly adapted and carefully used, ancient learning could benefit the church and should be pursued. How else would the church be able to reach the surrounding culture? Moreover, just as Israel of old had been told to despoil the Egyptians, so the church was to despoil the pagans. The second opinion gained dominance. In the western church its validity was demonstrated, for example, by the church father Jerome (c.342-420), who used his knowledge of languages to translate the Bible from Hebrew and Greek into Latin, and by the work of Jerome's contemporary Augustine, bishop of Hippo (354-430).

It was especially Augustine who convinced the church that it could and should make use of ancient learning. He did not do so, however, without subjecting the Greek rationalistic view of human knowing to a thoroughgoing critique. In the process he developed the outline of an alternate theory of knowledge, one which has inspired later thinkers, down to our own days. We will meet him again when dealing with late-modern and postmodern critics of the modern scientist tradition.

His critique of Greek rationalism

Although he challenged the premisses of classical rationalism, Augustine did not despise human reason. On the contrary, he valued it highly, believing that it was God's gift to mankind, the means whereby he had made man superior to the animal and capable of serving God. "We could not even believe," he wrote, "unless we possessed rational souls." [1] The Greek view of the excellence of human reason therefore contained an important element of truth. The great flaw in the classical approach was that it denied the existence of any authority beyond reason. Rejecting that humanistic belief, Augustine affirmed the fact of human dependence. The individual was a created being, a person who depended in all things, including his reasoning, on God. Augustine was convinced that only in God's light do we see light. This did not mean that faith came in the place of knowledge, but rather that it was the necessary condition of understanding, and also the only means of reaching cognitive certainty.

Augustine went on to expose the failure of rationalism to examine its own presuppositions. Rationalists believed that reliance on autonomous reason yielded objectively valid truth, but that religious faith, and knowledge based on religious faith, provided no more than subjective opinion. Augustine responded by showing that all knowledge depends on faith. The rationalists' trust in reason was itself impossible without it, for reason's pretension that it could reach objective truth had never been proven and indeed could not be proven; it was simply believed. The choice facing all human beings therefore, Augustine concluded, was not between scientific objectivity and superstition, but between two kinds of religious belief – one admitting man's dependence on God, the other Promethean.

Faith preceded reason, and true knowledge was possible only if reason submitted to divine revelation. This conviction explains Augustine's maxim that unless we believe we shall not understand. In the

Augustinian tradition the Christian scholar does not try to understand so that he may believe, but believes so that he may understand. Reason has a positive function in his life and work, including his philosophical work, but it is trustworthy only when it is subordinated to faith in revelation. But again, while insisting that ultimate authority rests with revelation, Augustine does not see faith as a substitute for reason, but rather as "the condition that makes genuine rational activity possible. Christian faith provides the foundation, the blueprint, and the materials, without which no sound philosophical structures can be built." [2]

With this conviction Augustine began his lifelong task of studying, teaching, and writing. The result was "one of the most comprehensive and enduring attempts to understand the Christian faith which has ever been made. Augustine developed a specifically Christian ethic as an alternative to the veiled Stoicism of the Pelagians. He elaborated the first Christian philosophy of history.... He worked out a theory of the Church and a theology of grace which remained in equilibrium with each other through the Middle Ages.... He built Neo-Platonism into the structure of Christian thought and became the true founder of Christian philosophy."[3]

Although the Augustinian tradition remained alive for centuries to come, its influence was especially strong in the Middle Ages. It was in that same period, however, that part of Augustine's work – including his warnings against an uncritical adoption of pagan-classical ideas – began to be ignored. This process started during the High Middle Ages, after the rediscovery of Aristotle's works. Before turning to that topic we will briefly describe the status of philosophy in the preceding centuries.

The Early Middle Ages

The Early Middle Ages comprise the four or five centuries immediately following the dissolution of the Western Roman Empire in the late fifth century.

This period was far from reaching the intellectual level of either the early Christian centuries which preceded it, or of the High Middle Ages which followed it, but it was not without intellectual activity. The Bible, Augustine, and other Christian writers were studied, attempts were made to preserve and copy ancient manuscripts, and in some cases attention was given even to ancient philosophy. The emphasis was on Platonism, and especially on Neoplatonist versions of that philosophy (for little of Plato's own work was known), rather than on Aristotle. The popularity of Platonic philosophies derived in part from the fact that they could be of service to Christian theology. The Platonic theory of the Forms, for example, could serve as an illustration of biblical truths such as the existence of God, the immortality of the soul, and the nature of morality and justice. It was possible, in short, to use Platonism both for an explanation of the faith and for its defence.

The possibility of adapting it to Christian theology was not the only reason for Platonism's appeal. The example of Augustine, who had come to Christianity via Neoplatonism, played a role as well. Furthermore, Platonism's view of reality – its stress on the universal rather than the particular, and its otherworldliness – agreed with the period's general view of life. The early medieval centuries were times of little individualism, of political chaos and steep cultural decline, and of a widespread conviction that the end of the world was near. Platonic and Neoplatonic philosophies with their stress on the transcendent fitted such times better than Aristotle's.

During these centuries, moreover, Aristotle shared Plato's fate in that not much of his work was known, at least not as a separate philosophical tradition. Some Aristotelian elements were present in Neoplatonism, there were commentaries on a number of his writings, and a few of these writings were available in translation, including part of his work on logic. Much of this was due to the efforts of Boethius, a sixth-century Roman philosopher, whose writings included translations of and commentaries on some of Aristotle's work on logic. These writings would arouse far less interest, however, during the early medieval centuries than during the High Middle Ages.

Early scholasticism

The period of the High Middle Ages lasted from about 1000 to about 1300. By the year 1000 the foreign invasions, which had plagued Europe for centuries, had ended. The political and social situation became more stable, agriculture improved, and the revival of trade and re-urbanization followed. Meanwhile the Cluniac monastic movement, which had begun in the early tenth century, contributed to a reform of religion and a revival of learning and of the arts. Monastic schools began to flourish, as did, somewhat later, the cathedral or episcopal schools. In the late twelfth and early thirteenth centuries universities were established in Italy, France, and England, and in the course of the Middle Ages the institution would spread to various other parts of Europe. The cultural awakening was further evident in the revival of architecture, the renewed interest in classical language and letters, and the flourishing of vernacular literature.

It was in the expansion of literary culture rather than in increased philosophical study that the renaissance was first of all evident. Dialectic increasingly gained ground, however, and would be taught at the schools from the middle of the eleventh century onward. Medieval dialectic was based on Aristotelian logic, and its popularity signified a reviving interest in Aristotle. That interest did not imply the eclipse of Platonism, which continued to have many followers throughout the Middle Ages. Nor was there any immediate danger that the theological use of logic and disputation would weaken the faith. Although medieval thinkers were keenly interested in intellectual matters, their age was first and foremost one of faith and only then of reason. In the second medieval period as in the first, thinkers looked for means to make the faith intelligible, and like Platonism, Aristotelianism was used for that purpose. Yet it is true that the spread of the latter philosophy signified an increasing concern with matters of this world, and also that it would be accompanied by the rise of religious skepticism. In the end this would lead to the great medieval conflict between faith and reason. But in the eleventh century that development lay still in the future.

The revival of interest in Aristotle in the eleventh century was not the result of an influx of newly found manuscripts. It was only in the later twelfth and the thirteenth centuries that the great rediscovery of ancient texts would take place and Aristotelian sources began to reach the West in any volume. The eleventh-century scholars had little more than fragments of Aristotle's work and the commentaries on that work by later thinkers such as Boethius, much of which had been around for centuries. Their use of Aristotle was restricted mainly to parts of his work on logic. To that discipline, which had largely been ignored during the early medieval period, they turned with a passion.

Logic as a branch of knowledge can be defined as the science of correct reasoning. Socrates and Plato had been concerned with it, but it was Aristotle who had systematized it and provided sets of rules that must be followed in the reasoning process. Like that of his predecessors, Aristotle's logic insisted upon a proper definition of terms, and upon careful, analytical thinking. It also helped people impose order on the perplexing variety of facts they encountered: to arrange, categorize, and classify.

As a method of reasoning, logic was deductive, which means that it moved from the general to the particular. Its practitioners often made use of Aristotle's favourite type of argument, the syllogism. Syllogistic reasoning is a type of reasoning wherein one draws a conclusion or inference from two premisses. The school book example of a syllogism is: *All men are mortal* (a general truth, used here as the major premiss), *Socrates is a man* (the minor premiss, again a known truth, but now applying to a particular case), *therefore Socrates is mortal* (the conclusion, or the answer to the question that was asked). As this example shows, the conclusion is a necessary one. This applies to all valid syllogistic reasoning. If the premisses are true and the proper logical method is used, then the conclusion has to follow. It is this aspect of deductive reasoning that explains its appeal to medieval thinkers, whose search was not for probabilities, but for the establishment of indubitable truths.

In the eleventh century, then, thinkers turned increasingly to Aristotle's logic. Now that times were improving and learning was reviving, people were hungry for new knowledge and eager to make use of the intellectual tool that Aristotle provided them with. That tool enabled them to develop the dialectical manner of reasoning, which was the typically medieval approach to learning. It began with a question (for example: Whether God can be known in this life by natural reason), followed it up by arguments for and against, and, after these had been discussed at length, formulated a conclusion. Applied to theology and philosophy, the dialectic formed the basis of what became known as medieval scholasticism, an approach wherein faith guided rational inquiry and was, in turn, supported by that inquiry. Scholasticism, in short, was "knowledge within a dogmatic framework," so that "ultimately, faith and reason had to harmonize. When they no longer did so, scholasticism disintegrated."[4]

One of the greatest early scholastics was Anselm (c. 1033-1109), the Italian-born abbot of the monastery of Bec in Normandy, who was later appointed archbishop of Canterbury. An Augustinian, Anselm established the primacy of faith over reason. He used the dialectic as a means to illuminate the truths of revelation. Following his mentor in confessing that unless we believe, we shall not understand, he originally entitled one of his books *Fides quaerens intellectum*, faith seeking understanding, and coined the well-known maxim *Credo ut intelligam*, I believe so that I may understand. "As a basis," historian David Knowles writes, "he presupposes an unshakable faith in the revealed doctrines .... His dialectic, therefore, is directed neither towards establishing revealed truth nor towards criticizing it; his primary aim is to penetrate with dialectic the truth held by faith."[5]

Another well-known early scholastic was the itinerant scholar and dialectician Peter Abelard (1079-1142). Abelard's fame rests in part on his ill-fated love affair with Heloise, the niece of a Parisian canon, in part on his sometimes violent disputes with Bernard of Clairvaux and other Augustinians, but in large part also on the genuine contributions he made to scholastic learning. He dominated the intellectual scene during the first four decades of the twelfth century, involving himself in such matters as the debate on universals, theological disputations, and the development of scholastic methodology. An influential methodological text was his book *Sic et Non,* which contained a collection of apparently contradictory theological and philosophical statements. The book's purpose was to help readers harmonize what seemed to be discordant opinions in authoritative writings.

The rediscovery of Aristotle's works
The dividing line between early and later scholasticism falls in the second half of the twelfth century, which saw the beginning of the great influx of Aristotelian and other ancient writings into Christian Europe. The first manuscripts came from Muslim Spain. They had been translated into Arabic and were often supplied with Muslim or Jewish commentaries. Before long additional works arrived, in the original Greek, from Constantinople. Translating all these works into Latin became an important industry, and the schools, as well as the newly established universities, experienced an Aristotelian renaissance of major proportions. Soon western Christendom was in possession not only of the entire corpus of Aristotle's logic, but also of most of his other works. Scholars got busy studying and assimilating them.

How did the church react? Augustinians considered the replacement of Plato by Aristotle an impoverishment to theology. It was becoming increasingly clear that when applied to theology, Aristotle's rationalistic method constituted a danger to the faith, and so did some of the conclusions he had drawn. The church was uneasy about the issue, and on occasion it restricted or forbade the teaching of certain works of Aristotle, but it was unable to stop the trend. And so arose the inevitable conflict between revelation and reason.

Or was it inevitable? To understand the situation it helps to look at what would happen several centuries later, when Darwin's theory of evolution was introduced. The reason why Christians often found it hard to cope with that type of scientific theory was their belief in the full objectivity of the scientific method. That method being what it was, scientific conclusions, it was felt, must be true. The same kind of awe with which the modern age regarded the scientific method was in the Middle Ages reserved for Aristotle's system of logic. Indeed, his entire corpus was seen as a superhuman achievement. Overwhelmed by Aristotle's wisdom and encyclopedic knowledge, some medieval thinkers believed that the man must have known Moses, or perhaps received his wisdom via King Solomon. It was quite normal for scholars to refer to Aristotle simply as "the Philosopher."

Difficulties arose almost at once. While some of Aristotle's work could be reconciled with revelation, there were also conclusions which contradicted the faith. Among them were Aristotle's ambiguous attitude with respect to the immortality of the individual soul, his belief in the eternity of matter (which implied a denial of the biblical doctrine of creation in time and out of nothing), and his rejection of a personal God, divine providence, and rewards and punishments in a future life. In the eyes of Aristotle's medieval admirers none of these views and conclusions could be shrugged off as pagan nonsense. Aristotle had arrived at them by the application of what was believed to be his infallible logical method, and the Christian scholars who followed his reasoning had to admit it: the conclusions were logically necessary. No one who used his method could gainsay them.

Medieval scholars reacted to the problem posed by the intrusion of Aristotelianism in a number of ways. Some believed that the works of Aristotle which contradicted Scripture should be ignored, and if necessary forbidden, and that his logic should not be applied to matters of the faith. Others, perhaps a majority, tried to hold on to both the Christian faith and to Aristotle. They were convinced that the Bible contained divine and absolute truth, but, try as they might, they could not disprove Aristotle's conclusions that went against the faith. These people attempted to live with Aristotle by proclaiming his conclusions to be logically necessary, even if they were not true from a biblical standpoint. Perhaps one could compare them to modern Christians who refuse to deny the Bible but also try to live, however uncomfortably, with conclusions of a naturalistic science that contradict biblical teachings.

And finally, there were people who rejected the Bible in favour of Aristotle. Atheism, of course, was forbidden to medieval clerics (and medieval scholars were practically always clerics). In most cases these men therefore continued to make at least a superficial show of orthodoxy, but their opinions spread. The fact that many of them were university teachers did not help. For the first time in medieval history skepticism and unbelief were becoming intellectually respectable.

Thomas Aquinas and the medieval synthesis

Theology and philosophy faced a crisis, and something had to be done to resolve it. The man who rose to the challenge was Thomas Aquinas (1225-74). A member of the Italian nobility, Thomas had, against the wishes of his family, joined the newly established Dominican Order. He studied and lectured at a number of schools, including the University of Paris. The German Dominican Albert the Great was one of his teachers and prepared him for what would become Thomas' great mission: the fight against unbelief by harmonizing revelation and reason and, as part of the process, the creation of a Christian philosophy.[6]

Thomas was not the first to attempt the harmonization of faith and reason. Earlier Muslim and Jewish scholars had already tried it. Best known among the former was Averroes, a man who had written commentaries on Aristotle that were widely read also in Christian Europe. He had upheld Aristotle even when the latter went against the faith, and those who took a similar position in Christian Europe were called Latin Averroists. In the end Averroes' synthesis had failed to gain the endorsement of his culture. After years of acclaim as Islam's foremost scholar, he aroused the ire of orthodox leaders and died in exile.

That Thomas succeeded where Averroes failed is perhaps a result of the fact that he did his work under the supervision of his Order and, in a sense, at the church's behest. An important task of the Dominican Order, and also of the Franciscan, was to fight the heresies that began to flourish in the burgeoning cities of the High Middle Ages and were making inroads in the universities. One way of defending the faith (a way that appealed especially to the Dominicans) was to show its rationality. The fact that Thomas did his work on behalf of his Order and of the church did not mean that he ran no risk of theological disapproval. It did mean, however, that he was able to pursue his work under church protection, an advantage that Averroes had lacked.

A closely related reason for Thomas' success was that he managed to avoid a drastic break with official religious teachings. Thomas refused to admit to Aristotle's infallibility. Biblical truth came first, and when Aristotle contradicted the Bible, Aristotle was in error. Still a third factor may have been his legendary serenity in the face of opposition, and his unshakable self-confidence. Whatever the complex of causes, Thomas was able to produce the synthesis for which his times had been waiting. It was given in a number of works, of which the *Summa Contra Gentiles*, a work of apologetics, and the *Summa Theologiae*, his famous compendium of theology, are the most important.

Like many of his contemporaries, Thomas had a high respect for Aristotle, and also for Averroes. He referred to them as "the Philosopher" and "the Commentator" respectively. They were not, however, the only philosophical sources he used. Thomas referred to commentators other than Averroes; he relied on Augustine and other Christian philosophers, and he made much use of Plato and Neoplatonism as well.

In developing his philosophy, Thomas followed his Greek mentors in assigning an important function to the intellect, also in matters of religion. While affirming the essential unity of all knowledge, he at the same time separated theology and philosophy, stating that each had its own domain. Whatever truth could be known by natural reason belonged to the sphere of philosophy; whatever could not be so known belonged to that of faith. Thomas was able to assign even many matters of revelation to the domain of philosophy, which meant that they could be proved by reason.

One of these was the existence of God. Following Aristotle, Averroes, and the Jewish Aristotelian Maimonides, Thomas defended the doctrine of God's existence with reference to arguments that the universe must have a first mover, a first cause, and so on. Having done this, he was able to find proofs for additional biblical truths, including some of those that Aristotle had denied or questioned. Among them were the doctrines of God's omniscience and providence and of the immortality of the soul. These truths, Thomas said, were not necessarily articles of the faith, at least not for everybody. The uneducated might have to take them on the evidence of divine revelation, but for all those who could establish them by reason they merely served as introductions or preambles to the faith. Essentially, they were matters of common sense.

There were, however, also truths that reason could not establish. These were the *mysteries* of the faith: the Trinity, the Incarnation, Christ's sacrifice on the cross, the Resurrection, and the Last Judgment, as well as original sin, and the creation of the world in time. These truths were known to the believer through divine revelation and church teachings only and therefore belonged to the realm of faith proper. In that realm the will had primacy, not the intellect, which meant that belief in these truths was first of all a matter of moral rather than intellectual affirmation.

But if these mysteries of the faith could not be established by reason, neither were they contrary to reason. Once they had been received by faith, one could apply one's thinking processes to them and show that they were highly probable. Reason therefore could be used to uphold them in the face of attacks by heretics and skeptics. If ever reason contradicted the faith, Thomas said, it was not revelation that was in error, but reason. It had been applied wrongly.

Reason and revelation, then, supported each other, pointing as they did to the same truths. This suggested that at bottom they were one, even though revelation was dominant, and this was a conclusion most people in the Middle Ages would in fact have expected. In the words of historian Steven Ozment: "Ultimately reason and revelation, philosophy and theology, nature and grace, the state and the church, secular life and religious life were neither strangers nor antagonists, but close relations. Reality is one; truth is one – no conviction was more medieval than that. This was the belief behind the Thomist maxim that grace does not destroy nature, but perfects it...."[7]

Thomas and his age

Thomas, it would appear, achieved what his age needed. Reason and philosophy had been rescued and faith was unassailable. Every Christian doctrine could either be demonstrated by reason or, if it spoke of the "mysteries," could be shown to be rationally defensible. Skepticism and atheism once again would cease to be intellectually respectable, heresy could be countered, and the Christian character of European civilization was assured.

As to the last point, it is instructive to have a look at the relationship between Thomism and the society wherein it arose. The Thomist synthesis came at a time when medieval culture was at its height, and the synthesis of faith and reason was representative of that culture. It was in accord, one could say, with the period's worldview, with the spirit of the age.

Thomism, as we saw, confirmed the typically medieval belief in the unity of all reality and truth. At the same time it upheld the dominant position enjoyed by the church. Indeed, by asserting that grace perfects nature, it provided a philosophical justification for that position.[8] In addition, Thomism reinforced the optimism that by this time had largely replaced the Augustinian teachings concerning man's total depravity and his utter dependence on divine grace and illumination. Although revelation and grace – both prevenient and co-operative grace – were indispensable, man was able to reach up to God at least partly by his own intellectual and moral powers. Thomist theology supported that belief. Anselm's maxim "I believe in order that I may understand" was in danger of being turned into its opposite.

The synthesis was typical of the age also in its comprehensiveness and orderliness. All knowledge, both of things visible and invisible, things human and divine, was accounted for, and every aspect of that learning was put into its proper compartment. It is not surprising that more than one historian has compared Aquinas' *Summae* to two of the other great cultural achievements of the period: the Gothic cathedral and the greatest epic poem of the Middle Ages, Dante's *Divine Comedy*. They too formed compendiums of all knowledge – theological, ethical, natural, and historical; they showed the same symmetry, orderliness, and explicitness as the *Summae;* and, most clearly so in the case of Dante, they manifested the Thomist belief in the cooperation between man's natural powers and divine grace.[9]

The reception of Thomism

The fact that his system was in accord with the spirit of the times did not safeguard Thomas from being censured. Already during his lifetime his philosophy was questioned. Among the earliest critics were members of his own Dominican Order. Shortly after his death, however, the Order adopted his philosophy, and in 1323 the church canonized Thomas. Ultimately Rome would follow the lead of the Dominicans and accept the substance of Thomas' teaching as church doctrine. But not everybody followed Rome in its approval of Thomism. As we will see in the next chapter, the century following Thomas' death saw a sustained assault upon his synthesis, one that would greatly weaken the prestige of scholasticism in general. It would also become a symptom of the decline of medieval civilization.

Though attacked, Thomism survived the Middle Ages, and the consensus which late-medieval scholastics attempted to reach is still being sought today. The continuing debate on Thomism is a testimony to the enduring relevance of the questions Thomas dealt with and the issues he raised. Among these issues is the use of natural theology. This discipline, which is as old as Plato and Aristotle, refers to the use of human reason apart from revelation as a means to know God. In the Christian tradition, which bases itself on such texts as Romans 1:20 (where we read that "God's invisible qualities – his eternal power and divine nature – have been clearly seen, being understood from what has been made"[10]), the objects of natural religion are similar to those of the Platonic tradition. They include proof of God's existence and of those of his attributes that can be known through his works, of the human soul, and of the immortality of the soul.

Natural theology was for Thomas a means to defend Christian doctrine by providing rational proofs of the truth of revelation and so to confound atheists and skeptics. Many Christian apologists have through the centuries followed his example, but others have questioned both the utility and the legitimacy of Thomas' approach. The questioning began in the Middle Ages. Among those who subjected natural theology to a sustained critique were the medieval scholastics John Duns Scotus and William of Ockham. Their critique was revived by the Protestant reformers and – to restrict ourselves to these few examples – by the Enlightenment philosophers David Hume and Immanuel Kant, by the nineteenth-century Christian existentialist Søren Kierkegaard, and by twentieth-century dialectical theologians like Karl Barth and Emil Brunner.

On what grounds have Christians criticized natural theology? One incontrovertible argument is that even if nature can be said to point to an intelligent designer, it does not reveal God as he has made himself known in Christ. And this, as Martin Luther was to remind believers, is the only way in which God allows himself to be known. Thomas, of course, knew this and had no intention of denying it. As recent authors have argued, Protestant critics have at times underestimated the sincerity of Aquinas' efforts to uphold the priority of revelation.[11] Nevertheless, the importance assigned to rational proofs did tend to push God's self-revelation in Christ into the background.

There are other reasons to be cautious with the approach followed by Thomas. It implies that knowledge of God by faith is inferior to knowledge based on reason. Whereas intellectuals can, in the Thomist system, arrive at the so-called preambles of Christian doctrine by reason, the uneducated have to accept them by faith. But this is a false distinction. Revelation was given because the human mind, no matter how brilliant, is by definition incapable of reaching up to God. The finite cannot comprehend the Infinite. The approach will lead in practice to the creation of two distinct Gods, one of whom is the object of faith, the other the outcome of human reasoning. An explanation of divine matters in natural terms also brings with it the risk of the rejection of Christian doctrine as soon as an increase in scientific knowledge undermines the arguments' credibility.

Yet another problem with natural theology is that faith is not simply a matter of logical necessity, but also of the will. As the Lord told the Jews, certainty that his teachings were indeed true would come only by obedience, that is, by their choosing to do God's will (John 7:17).

Religious understanding does not precede faith but follows it. Reliance on arguments and proofs suggests, moreover, that faith is rational only if it can be logically demonstrated. But logical demonstration cannot be a sufficient ground for religious certainty, for reason is not neutral, nor are its pronouncements definitive. As the history of natural theology shows, counter-arguments can always be found, so that certainty forever eludes those who rely on logical proofs. Reliance on arguments and proofs suggests, moreover, that human reason is a better means of knowing God than revelation and the work of the Holy Spirit. It ignores the fact that man and his reason are finite.

Philosophical objections can be added to the religious ones. If God's existence is believed to be necessary because all things must have a cause, the question inevitably arises how God is to be exempted from the law of cause and effect. Must he not be caused as well? And if so, by whom or what? Furthermore, as Scotus and Ockham already remarked, to derive God's existence and attributes from nature is to risk subjecting him to the determinism that rules the natural realm. The approach may lead to a concept of God similar to that of the Aristotelian deity. Ceasing to be the personal God of the Scriptures – the Creator and Redeemer of man and nature – he becomes little more than an impersonal First Mover, a mere logical postulate. That this risk is not an imaginary one is shown by the conclusions of the theologians and philosophers who, in the early modern period, turned to natural theology to prove the existence of God and ended up by encouraging the movement toward deism.

Does this mean that no use can be made of the insights of natural theology for apologetic purposes? There are people who think so. Kierkegaard and Barth and Brunner were among them. Because they hold that faith alone leads to knowledge of divine matters and that reason and historical evidence can be disregarded, the attitude of these believers is referred to as fideism. But opposition to natural theology does not necessarily lead to an extreme fideist attitude. John Calvin, certainly no friend of natural theology, nevertheless believed that, if properly used, arguments in support of the credibility of Scripture can be "useful aids." Calvin did not speak of rational arguments in the manner of Thomas Aquinas, however, but of the *testimony* creation gives to God's wisdom and glory. And he made it clear that these "aids" could not, by themselves, lead to faith in revelation. ". . .The only true faith," he wrote, "is that which the Spirit of God seals in our hearts." And ". . .unless this certainty, higher and stronger than any human judgment, be present, it will be vain to fortify the authority of Scripture by arguments, to establish it by common agreement of the church, or to confirm it with other helps. For unless this foundation is laid, its authority will always remain in doubt."[12]

Nevertheless, Calvin agreed that creation gives witness to God. Scripture itself teaches this. It does so, for example, in Psalm 19 and Romans 1, but also in other places, such as the final chapters of the book of Job. In brief, the choice for Christians is not between a rationalistic natural theology and an extreme fideism. Historian George Marsden is among those who have argued this point. Observing that arguments in support of Christianity are, especially since Darwin, not logically compelling unless one already believes in a benevolent Creator, he adds that they nevertheless "may have great psychological and even intellectual force, particularly for those who are wavering in their resolution to deny the presence of God and his Word." [13] A modern apologist makes a similar point when distinguishing between knowing and showing.[14] We know Christianity to be true by the witness of the Spirit; we show it to be true by pointing to the witness of creation and providence. Christianity is indeed a reasonable faith. Although not founded on argument and evidence, it does make use of them. On this point Aquinas was right.

NOTES

[1.] Charles Norris Cochrane, *Christianity and Classical Culture: A Study of Thought and Action from Augustus to Augustine* (New York: Oxford University Press, A Galaxy Book, 1964 [1940]), p. 401. Much of what follows in this section is based on Cochrane's study.

[2.] David C. Lindberg, "Science and the Early Church," in *God and Nature: Historical Essays on the Encounter between Christianity and Science*, eds. David C. Lindberg and Ronald L. Numbers (Berkeley: University of California Press, 1986), p. 28.

[3] E. Harris Harbison, *The Christian Scholar in the Age of the Reformation* (New York: Scribner's, The Scribner Library, 1956), pp. 17f.

[4.] Gordon Leff, *Medieval Thought: St. Augustine to Ockham* (Harmondsworth: Penguin Books, 1965 [1958]), p. 92.

[5.] David Knowles, *The Evolution of Medieval Thought* (London: Longmans, Green and Co., 1963 [1962]), pp. 100f.

6. On the rediscovery of Aristotle, the problems it caused, and the Thomist solution, see Etienne Gilson, *Reason and Revelation in the Middle Ages* (New York: Scribner's, Scribner Library Books, 1938); *idem, The Spirit of Thomism* (New York: P. S. Kenedy and Sons, 1964); and the relevant chapters in Copleston, *A History of Medieval Philosophy;* in Knowles, *op. cit.;* and in Leff, *op. cit.;* as well as Steven Ozment, *The Age of Reform 1250-1550: An Intellectual and Religious History of Late Medieval and Reformation Europe* (New Haven: Yale University Press, 1980).

7. Ozment, *The Age of Reform,* pp. 11f.

8. *Ibid.,* p. 20.

9. The similarities between scholasticism and the Gothic Cathedral have been well described by Erwin Panofsky, *Gothic Architecture and Scholasticism* (Cleveland: World, Meridian Books, 1968 [1951]). The builders of the cathedrals, Panofsky shows, were in constant contact with scholastic advisers. A good description of the parallels between Thomism and Dante's epic is given by Dorothy L. Sayers, "The Divine Poet and the Angelic Doctor," in her *Further Papers on Dante* (Westport, Connecticut: Greenwood Publishers, 1957), pp. 38-52 and *passim.* For an account of the differences between the philosophies of Dante and Thomas, see Etienne Gilson, *Dante and Philosophy* (New York: Harper and Row, Harper Torchbooks, The Academic Library, 1963 [Sheed and Ward, 1949]), pp. 153f. and *passim.*

10. Unless otherwise indicated, biblical quotations in this work are taken from the New International Version.

11. Works by evangelical authors that attempt a revision of anti-Thomist Protestant views include Norman L. Geisler, *Thomas Aquinas: An Evangelical Appraisal,* and Arvin Vos, *Aquinas, Calvin, and Contemporary Protestant Thought: A Critique of Protestant Views on the Thought of Thomas Aquinas* (Washington/Grand Rapids: Christian College Consortium/Eerdmans, 1985).

12. John Calvin, *Institutes of the Christian Religion,* ed. John T. McNeill, trans. Ford Lewis Battles (Philadelphia: Westminster Press, 1967 [1960]), I, vii, 5; viii, 1.

13. George Marsden, "The Collapse of American Evangelical Academia," in *Faith and Rationality,* eds. Plantinga and Wolterstorff, pp. 254f.

14. William Lane Craig, *Reasonable Faith: Christian Truth and Apologetics,* rev. ed. (Wheaton, Illinois: Crossway, 1994 [1984]), p. 48.

IV. Late-Medieval Culture

The assault upon his system began during Thomas' lifetime but increased in seriousness in 1277, three years after his death. In that year Pope John XXI, concerned about rumours that errors were being taught at the University of Paris, ordered the bishop of Paris, Etienne Tempier, to make inquiries. Tempier responded by publishing a condemnation of 219 theses. Many of these were derived from Aristotelian and Averroist teachings, but some of Thomas' propositions were included as well, although he was not mentioned by name. Later that year the archbishop of Canterbury, a Dominican, followed the example of Paris and censured a number of Thomist teachings at Oxford.

A major problem, as Thomas' critics saw it, was the determinism implied in Aristotelian philosophy and theology. The term determinism refers to the doctrine that all that happens on earth happens necessarily, and divine determinism means that God himself is bound by the laws of cause and effect and the conclusions of logic. That Aristotle's philosophy indeed runs the risk of making God the captive of whatever definition is used of him was made clear by several of the 219 theses Tempier condemned. Among them were statements implying that it was logically impossible for God to have created, to have created in time and out of nothing, to have made more than one world, and to have created a void.[1] This determinism was found especially in the teachings of Aristotle and Averroes. Thomas tried to safeguard God's freedom, yet he did not fully escape entanglement in the determinism of his Greek and Arab mentors, not in his theology and not in his cosmology either.[2]

Leaders of the late-medieval attack upon Thomism were the two Franciscan philosophers we already met, John Duns Scotus and William of Ockham.[3] Both objected to Thomas' determinism, complaining that he had compromised God's absolute power and freedom, and both criticized his belief that God's existence and many of his attributes could be established by logic. As to the latter objection, Scotus was willing to admit that the existence of an infinite being that was all-knowing and perfect, could be demonstrated. In the case of most other Christian doctrines, however, logic could do no more than show their probability. Revelation was the only valid source of religious knowledge, and faith, rather than reason, the way to achieve that knowledge. And faith should be manifested in love. The will (and therefore the heart) had primacy over the intellect. Loving God, Scotus said, was of far greater worth than understanding him.

William of Ockham completed the work that Scotus had begun. Like the latter, he was a voluntarist, which means that he stressed the primacy of the will: of man's will over his reason, and of God's absolute freedom over the logical necessity of Aristotle's philosophy. Ockham went further than Scotus in rejecting the possibility of establishing the truth of Christian doctrine by logical argument. He said that one might be able to prove that there must be a first cause, but added that this was not the same as demonstrating the existence of the Christian God. The theistic arguments did not even prove the existence of *one* first cause. It was quite possible, Ockham argued, to posit a plurality of first causes, just as it was quite possible to posit a plurality of worlds.[4] Here, then, was the beginning of the long war against natural theology to which we already referred in the previous chapter.

Neither Scotus nor Ockham despised reason. They considered it an important tool, but one whose usage was limited to its own sphere. If they objected to natural theology they did so not simply to safeguard reason, but also to defend God's sovereignty and to ensure the primacy of faith in matters of religion. Reason of course continued to have a place in their theology, but its function was far less exalted under voluntarism than under Thomism. Another important implication of voluntarist theology was the vindication of God's mercy in his dealing with mankind. Voluntarist teachings implied that "the present order, the means offered for salvation, and even human reason, were such not by necessity but out of God's loving kindness."[5] Rationalist influences had obscured that truth. It was for this reason that Luther would later speak of reason as "the devil's whore." Luther was no irrationalist, but he distinguished between reason as a power that stands above revelation and judges it, and reason that submits to it, and he allowed only the latter.

The rise of nominalism

In its rejection of the Thomist synthesis, the voluntarism of Scotus and Ockham was joined by late-medieval nominalism. Nominalist philosophy was the opposite of what in the Middle Ages was called realism. Medieval realists harked back to the teachings of Plato and Aristotle on the matter of universals, which we discussed in the second chapter of this book. The followers of Plato believed that universals such as genera and species, as well as beauty, goodness, justice, humanity, and so on, were real entities, which existed apart from the particulars that manifested them. (This explains the term realism, which is derived from the Latin word *res,* meaning thing.) Plato had located these universals, which he called Forms or Ideas, in the transcendental world. Medieval Platonists, following Augustine, placed them in the mind of God. Because in Plato's view the universals alone were truly real, they, and not the visible world, were for him and his medieval followers the proper object of study. The particulars were mere shadows.

Nominalists reversed this doctrine and insisted that true reality belongs only to the concrete particular. Nominalism therefore not only rejected Plato's doctrine but also went beyond Aristotle's ideas on universals. Aristotle had taught that universals do not exist apart from the particulars, but that they are authentic metaphysical entities and constitute the final object of knowledge. The nominalists rejected this view and stated that universals were only sounds or names (*nomina –* hence the term nominalism). Because they had no real existence, one could not, in a deductive fashion, derive truths from them. Nominalists turned their attention instead to the concrete particular, making use of universals or concepts only to impose some kind of order on the multiplicity of phenomena.

Although there had been nominalists in the eleventh and twelfth centuries, nominalism did not become a potent force until the fourteenth century. Most of the earlier scholastics were realists, either in the Platonic or the more moderate Aristotelian tradition. Thomas Aquinas, who also dealt with the issue, adopted the Aristotelian position that the universal can be known only in and through the concrete particular. This was in agreement with his empirical philosophy, according to which nothing is known by the intellect which has not first been in the senses. But if for Thomas physical nature revealed the universal, so the universal, in turn, illuminated the particular. Both sense experience and reason were necessary for the attainment of knowledge; the two complemented each other. Instead of opposition, there was harmony.

Nominalism as the *via moderna*

The unity of all knowledge which Aquinas had sought in attempting to harmonize faith and reason, then, he also sought in his solution to the problem of universals. Because belief in the essential unity of knowledge and truth was typical of the Middle Ages, the approach of Aquinas and his fellow realists became known as the "ancient way," the *via antiqua*. It was Ockham and the fourteenth-century nominalists who challenged this belief in unity and so introduced the *via moderna*.

Although Ockham may not have adhered to every aspect of the nominalist philosophy,[6] there were important similarities between his voluntarist position and the position of the nominalists. Specifically, he agreed with them in their concern with the particular and with their belief that reason's proper theatre of operation was the physical world. The simultaneous emergence of these voluntarist and nominalist views shows that an important change was underway from the classical and medieval view of reality to the modern one. For Plato and Aristotle and for their realist followers, including Thomas Aquinas, true knowledge meant knowledge of the universal, the unchangeable, the realm of being. Nominalism, on the other hand, was concerned with the particular and the world of change and becoming.

Nominalism, together with voluntarism, would affect the scientific pursuit, but that was only one of its consequences. A person's view of the relationship between universals and particulars has implications for his general worldview. A society that believes in the reality of the universal will have criteria of truth, goodness, and beauty, and so on, that are permanently and universally valid. Realists are assured that, in spite of the flux and fragmentation all around them, life has an inherent unity and possesses meaning. A serious danger in a radical and single-minded realism, however, is that the approach can be used to support collective and tyrannical political and philosophical systems. This threat was among the reasons for the existentialist revolt against realism in late-modern times.

Nominalism, on the other hand, acknowledges the individual and the particular. This is one of its positive characteristics. The disadvantage of a nominalist approach, if relentlessly pursued, is that in the end it will destroy meaning and bring about fragmentation, relativism, and political and moral anarchy. It was this danger, which became evident under the Greek Sophists, that inspired Socrates' attempts to demonstrate the existence and accessibility of universal standards, and Plato's and Aristotle's theories of unchanging Forms. The Sophist experiment had shown that if the reality of the universal is denied, criteria of truth and morality shift from the eternal and unchangeable to the temporal and particular, that is, to the judgment of the individual human being. An attitude of subjective relativism is the inevitable result.

Modern and postmodern times have once again demonstrated the negative consequences of a consistent nominalism. In the Middle Ages, however, these effects were not immediately apparent, at least not to their fullest extent. As long as it was believed that religious truths and moral standards are not a matter of personal choice but are objectively valid since they have been given in revelation (and most medieval nominalists still believed this), the relativistic implications of nominalism were kept within bounds. With the increasing trend toward secularism these safeguards would disappear, and the idea of the subjective nature of religious beliefs and moral criteria would come to dominate the modern worldview.[7] Obviously the need – today as much as it was in the past – is for an approach that does justice to both the universal and the particular.

Religious uncertainty

If the Thomist system was in accord with the spirit of the High Middle Ages, the voluntarist and nominalist attacks upon Thomism attested to the decline of medieval culture. They not only symbolized that decline but also contributed to it, and they did so first of all by creating a new uncertainty in the realm of religion. If faith was not supported by reason, then it stood largely on its own. The rational tools with which to fight heresy, skepticism, and agnosticism, as well as personal doubt, were lost.

Religious uncertainty was intensified by the extreme voluntarism of the Ockhamist tradition. In his reaction against determinism, Ockham followed the bishop of Paris in stressing the absolute power and sovereignty of God. Theologians had traditionally distinguished between God's absolute power, that is, his omnipotence pure and simple (the *potentia absoluta*), and his ordained or covenanted power (the *potentia ordinata*). The latter referred to his will as revealed in Scripture. The church had always upheld both doctrines and refused to give primacy to God's absolute over his ordained power. It admitted that God could suspend natural laws and indeed frequently did so. Miracles were a case in point. But it also taught that God's ordained will was irreversible in the sense that the believer could rest in it. By exalting God's absolute power over his ordained will, Ockham challenged that belief and put in doubt, at least by implication, the trustworthiness of divine revelation.

Or rather, his followers did so. Ockham himself attempted to guard against a conclusion of divine arbitrariness by stressing God's covenant faithfulness, which, he insisted, makes it possible for us to believe that our knowledge of God and his works, if not infallible, is nevertheless reliable. "If God has freely chosen the established order, he *has* so chosen," he wrote, "and while he can dispense with or act apart from the laws he has decreed, he has nonetheless bound himself by his promise and will remain faithful to the covenant that of his kindness and mercy, he has instituted with man."[8]

Not all his followers, however, held to this position. For some Ockhamists God did become an arbitrary power, absolutely free to declare good evil and evil good. What he had promised in his Word would not necessarily come to pass, for God was free to reverse himself. It was therefore impossible to know God's will for one's life. No mortal could really be sure as to what would please and what displease him. The burden this placed on the believer was made the heavier by the Pelagianism of the Ockhamist school, a position Ockham had defended with reference to God's sovereignty and man's freedom.[9]

The full effect of Ockhamism in the later Middle Ages may never be known. We do know that it caught on quickly and penetrated several universities, and we also know that Luther was among those who were influenced by it. Luther's Ockhamist background helps explain the intensity of his search for a God who could be trusted, as well as his hatred of scholastic speculation.

Mysticism and the Modern Devotion

There were other reactions to the weakening of the medieval synthesis. The endless conflicts among philosophers caused many of the educated to lose interest in scholasticism altogether. In the absence of a rational undergirding of the faith, and desperate for certainty in an uncertain age, some people looked for support for their beliefs in the "inner experience" of either an evangelical or a more eclectic (and sometimes semi-pagan) mysticism.

Others, ignoring Thomas, Scotus, Ockham, as well as the official church, turned to revelation alone, trusting the Bible to be self-authenticating and faith its own justification. The return to the Bible would culminate in the Protestant Reformation of the early sixteenth century. It was evident in such late-medieval reform movements as those of John Wycliffe in England and John Huss in Bohemia.

Another movement that was inspired by a distrust of philosophy and by religious discontent but that did not break openly with Rome was the so-called Modern Devotion, which arose in the Northern Netherlands and spread to much of north-western Europe. This movement stressed piety and practical Christianity. Rejecting theological speculation, it at times downplayed the value of learning for the life of faith. The devotional *Imitation of Christ*, which comes from this group and has been attributed to Thomas a Kempis, contains statements like the following:

> Of what use is it to discourse learnedly on the Trinity, if you lack humility and therefore displease the Trinity?... If you knew the whole Bible by heart, and all the teachings of the philosophers, how would this help you without the grace and love of God? 'Vanity of vanities, and all is vanity,' except to love God and serve Him alone.... A humble countryman who serves God is more pleasing to Him than a conceited intellectual who knows the course of the stars, but neglects his own soul.[10]

Not all members of the Modern Devotion spurned learning. The movement promoted education and worked for the establishment of schools. This was one of the means by which it would play a role in the emergence of the Christian humanism of the Northern Renaissance: Erasmus and Agricola were among those who attended its schools. The movement also helped prepare the way for the Reformation, and it did so not only by raising the people's level of literacy. Its members also made it their task to copy (and later to print) the Bible and to study its original languages. One of them, the learned John Wessel Gansfort, taught Hebrew and Greek. Although there were theological differences between Gansfort and Luther,[11] the former anticipated several of Luther's attacks upon church policies and teachings. Luther himself noted this, and in Protestant Germany Gansfort became known as "a reformer before the Reformation."

The revival of science

The attack on Aristotelianism and Thomism affected not only philosophy and religion, it also influenced the study of science. It is true that the revival of science, which became most clearly evident in the fourteenth century, did not await classical scholasticism's decline. The translation of Greek and Arabic scientific works, including those of Aristotle, had stimulated an already reviving interest in science as early as the thirteenth century. It was accompanied by the demand for an empirical approach. The Franciscan bishop of Lincoln, Robert Grosseteste (c. 1175-1253), for example, who studied astronomy and optics, objected to an uncritical reliance on authorities and advocated observation and experimentation.

Roger Bacon, another thirteenth-century Franciscan, joined Grossteste in stressing the need for observation. Bacon also seems to have been among the medieval thinkers who believed that science could be used for the improvement of man's life here on earth. He has, at any rate, been credited with making a list of technological marvels which science could make available – prototypes of the automobile, the submarine, and the airplane being among them. Bacon's ideas were considered so outlandish, we are told, that his contemporaries began to suspect him of practising black magic, and his Order found it necessary to reprimand him. The General of the Franciscan Order, Bonaventura, warned that "The tree of science cheats many of the tree of life, or exposes them to the severest pains of purgatory."[12]

In emphasizing the need for observation, these early natural philosophers departed from the rationalistic approach to science. Rationalism had been the method of choice for most Greek philosophers. It was based on the assumption that the universe was rational, and that whatever happened in nature was logically necessary. Man, who partook of the same reason (or *logos*) as that which ruled the world, could understand nature by logical thought. Observation was not necessary for there was no contingency or unpredictability in nature: whatever happened, happened necessarily. A prime example of a Greek rationalist was Plato. We have seen that Aristotle objected to Plato's rationalism and proclaimed the empirical creed that all knowledge begins with the senses. He did not, however, always follow this own maxim. His mechanics and cosmology, for example, were based as much on deductive reasoning as on observation. This rationalistic tendency explains the "necessity" of his conclusions and the determinism inherent in his philosophy.

Early Christian philosophy had turned against the rationalist tradition. It adopted what historians of science have called the ancient-creationist view, which was based on Hellenistic, Jewish, and Christian teachings.[13] Rejecting the widespread belief in pantheism, according to which nature is divine, and in panentheism, which makes creation a part of the divine, Christians taught that nature was separate from God, and also that, as the creation of a rational God, it operated in a regular, law-like, orderly manner, in accordance with the covenant God had established in the beginning. It possessed a degree of autonomy. That autonomy was not absolute. Nature had not emerged but was created, and the laws that governed it had been imposed by the Creator. These divinely instituted laws made rational investigation of nature possible but could not themselves be discovered by speculation or rational deduction. In short, although the cosmos was orderly, its order was contingent. It did not have to be the way it was; God could have ordered it differently. One "could not just think up a rational blueprint and then say that because it is rational nature has to be that way."[14] Observation remained necessary. It was this tradition to which the thirteenth-century natural philosophers returned.

The interest in science, which continued in the fourteenth century, received an important impulse from Bishop Tempier's condemnations of Aristotelianism in 1277. These condemnations helped scientific development not so much by encouraging an empirical approach to science; much of fourteenth-century natural philosophy was of a speculative nature.[15] Tempier's document served as a stimulus because, in the words of historian of science R. Hooykaas, in the condemnations "not only the *theology* of necessity was at stake, but also the *natural science* of necessity."[16] Scientists and philosophers were now encouraged to go beyond Aristotle in their speculations about the cosmos, and this new freedom made possible scientific hypotheses and theories that were strikingly modern. Some of these hypotheses proposed changes in the authorized model of the cosmos. That model was still the Aristotelian-Ptolemaic one and featured a universe consisting of one solar system with a central, stationary earth around which the sun and the other heavenly bodies revolved in perfect circular motion. The heavenly bodies were embedded in separate concentric spheres, each of which was moved by both the outer sphere of the *primum mobile* and by its own intermediate mover – in the medieval system an intelligence or angel.

The new approach to science, on the other hand, encouraged the revival (by Jean Buridan, rector of the University of Paris, who died c.1358) of the ancient impetus theory. With the help of this theory the movement of the heavenly bodies could be explained without reference to intermediate movers, which made for a greatly simplified model of the cosmos. Ockham stressed the importance of simplicity in scientific thinking throughout, declaring that "it is vain to do with more assumptions what can be done with fewer." Although not invented by Ockham himself, this principle became known as "Ockham's razor."

A number of medieval natural philosophers anticipated other modern theories. Several worked on the impetus idea, and some suggested the daily rotation of the earth on its axis, the possible infinitude of the universe, and the possible multiplicity of solar systems. Frequently this was done with explicit reference to the condemnations of 1277. Buridan's student Nicholas of Oresme, for example, who developed the theory of a rotating earth, referred to the condemnations and argued the inability of Aristotelian logic to establish that the earth *must* stand still or that the heavens *must* have a circular motion.[17] Apparently his motivation was more religious than scientific. His primary goal was to demonstrate not that the earth moved, but that reason could not prove the opposite. And if reason and experience could not decide on this issue, he argued, they certainly could not judge matters of faith.[18] Nor was Oresme the only voluntarist among natural philosophers. Fourteenth-century thought experiments were often inspired by the confession of God's absolute power.

These natural philosophers, then, anticipated theories that would be revived during the scientific revolution of the late sixteenth and seventeenth centuries. In their own period they still formed a minority, however, and their ideas did not lead to a drastic change in the fields of astronomy and related disciplines. One reason why they were not implemented was the fact that there was no framework capable of accommodating the new ideas. That framework was not established until the seventeenth century, with the acceptance of mechanism. Aristotle's laws of motion and the Aristotelian-Ptolemaic model of the universe would survive until the time of Copernicus and beyond.

The Waning of the Middle Ages

Historians disagree as to the dividing line between Middle Ages and Renaissance. Some believe that the fourteenth and fifteenth centuries form the closing phase of the Middle Ages; that it was a period of decline, rather than renewal. Others insist that these centuries already witnessed a rebirth of culture and so belong to the Renaissance. Both sides are right. During these two centuries there was a slow decline in medieval institutions, customs, and beliefs – indeed, in medieval culture as a whole – while with the advantage of hindsight we can see that at the same time new forms were arising.

We have already noted some of these non-medieval forms in the late-medieval period: the search for faith apart from rational proof, the renewed interest in natural science, and the arrival of Renaissance humanism. There was also the spread of nominalism, which symbolized, among other things, the emerging respect for the individual over against the typically medieval concern with the collective. The turn against collectivism can also be recognized in the increased use of vernacular languages instead of Latin and in the rise of the nation state and capitalism during the late Middle Ages and the Renaissance.

Contemporaries did not have our advantage of hindsight, however. And the impression is that especially in north-western Europe (in Italy the Renaissance came earlier) people often experienced the time in which they lived more as a period of decay and death than of rebirth. They had reasons for it, and these concerned not only the divorce of faith and reason. Their period also suffered physical dislocations. In the Late Middle Ages western Europe experienced a lengthy period of economic depression. Trade declined, arable land returned to waste, and there was a steep decrease in population.

This decline in population was not the result of economic dislocations only. The problem was aggravated by what appears to have been a prolonged cycle of bad weather, which led to famines, and by epidemics such as the Black Death. That disease visited Europe for the first time in the late 1340s and would return at regular intervals, well into the seventeenth century. The first visitation lasted three years and it has been estimated that it killed between one-third and one-fourth of the population. The demographic problem was also worsened by a prolonged period of violence. The fourteenth and fifteenth centuries witnessed a variety of civil and international wars (including the Hussite Wars and the Hundred Years' War between England and France), as well as feudal disorders, peasant revolts, and urban uprisings.

The boundaries of Christendom itself were not even inviolate. An Islam offensive, this time led by the Ottoman Turks, was launched against south-eastern Europe. Constantinople fell in 1453, a disaster that was followed by the Turkish conquest of much of the rest of the Balkans. Later Hungary was overrun as well, and even Austria was threatened. Advances in Spain against the Muslim Moors, which had characterized the High Middle Ages, were halted until well into the fifteenth century, and Mongols were advancing in eastern Europe. Clearly, Europe was no longer on the offensive, as it had been at the time of the crusades.

The feelings of uncertainty that these developments aroused were compounded by the steep decline in the power and prestige of church and papacy. The fourteenth and early fifteenth centuries were the period of the so-called Babylonian Captivity, when for some seventy years the popes were the virtual captives of the kings of France, and of the Great Western Schism, when two and later three men fought for the papal throne. Believers throughout Christendom were convinced that the political and other disasters they experienced were God's punishment on the sins of the church and its members. Doomsday feelings were widespread. There was a renewed search for the gospel and for personal piety, but the period also witnessed a rise in heresy, witchcraft, Satanism, and other manifestations of the occult. The Inquisition worked overtime, and groups of penitents (the so-called flagellants) moved around the country, scourging each other as a sign of repentance and crying out for God's mercy.

A bridge to the modern era

Clearly, the fourteenth and fifteenth centuries witnessed the decline of much that the Middle Ages had stood for, and there are good reasons for calling that period, as Johan Huizinga did, the autumnal or waning phase of medieval culture.[19] The signs of renewal, however, were there. They were present in practically every aspect of late-medieval life and thought: in religion, philosophy, and general learning, in science and technology, in political and economic organization, and also, toward the end of the fifteenth century, in the beginnings of trans-oceanic exploration.

It was this confused and confusing situation that provided the background for the scientific revolution. It also provided a bridge. The accomplishments of the fourteenth-century scientific renaissance were not forgotten: when science revived in the late sixteenth and seventeenth centuries, it was able to build on these medieval achievements.[20] Another important motivation for scientific research was the desire to prevent a recurrence of the natural and social disasters of the late-medieval centuries. Promoters of modern science rejected medieval scholasticism, which had been notoriously unable to deal with these disasters. Looking for more "useful" knowledge, they turned not only to the fourteenth-century natural philosophers, but also to the thirteenth-century Roger Bacon's dreams about the potential benefits of science and technology. Interestingly, it was Roger's seventeenth-century namesake, Sir Francis Bacon, who became the great champion of progress through science. In that capacity he became the herald of the new age.

NOTES

[1] For the bishop of Paris's theses in English translation, see Arthur Hyman and James J. Walsh, eds., *Philosophy in the Middle Ages: The Christian, Islamic, and Jewish Traditions* (Indianapolis: Hackett Publishing Company, 1974), pp. 540-49.

[2] Examples of deterministic implications in Thomist cosmology can be found in Arthur O. Lovejoy, *The Great Chain of Being: A Study of the History of an Idea* (New York: Harper and Row, Harper Torchbooks, The Academy Library, 1965 [1960]; [Cambridge, Mass.: Harvard University Press, 1936]), pp. 73-81.

[3] On Scotus and Ockham, see the relevant chapters in Copleston, *A History of Medieval Philosophy*; in Knowles, *The Evolution of Medieval Thought*; and in Leff, *Medieval Thought: St. Augustine to Ockham*. See also Harry Klocker, *William of Ockham and the Divine Freedom* (Milwaukee, Wisconsin: Marquette University Press, 1992); Gordon Leff, *The Dissolution of the Medieval Outlook: An Essay on Intellectual and Spiritual Change in the Fourteenth Century* (New York: New York University Press, 1976); and Ozment, *The Age of Reform 1250-1550*, pp. 33-42, 55-63. On the nominalist tradition in general, see Heiko Augustinus Oberman, *The Harvest of Medieval Theology: Gabriel Biel and Late Medieval Nominalism* (Cambridge, Mass.: Harvard University Press, 1963).

[4] Leff, *Medieval Thought*, p. 287.

[5] Justo L. Gonzalez, *A History of Christian Thought*, II (Nashville: Abingdon Press, 1983 [1971]), p. 318.

[6] Leff, *Dissolution*, p. 12; see also the Introduction to the same author's *William of Ockham: The Metamorphosis of Scholastic Discourse* (Manchester: Manchester University Press, 1975).

[7] On nominalism and its impact on modernism, see Richard M. Weaver, *Ideas Have Consequences* (Chicago: University of Chicago Press, 1948); Danie F. M. Strauss, "Rationalism, Irrationalism and the Absolutized Horizon of Knowledge as Ideals of Knowledge in Philosophy and Science," in *Facets of Faith and Science*, II, ed. Jitse M. van der Meer (Lanham: The Pascal Centre for Advanced Studies in Faith and Science/University Press of America, 1996), pp. 99-121; as well as the articles by Rousas John Rushdoony and Arthur F. Holmes in *Jerusalem and Athens: Critical Discussions on the Theology and Apologetics of Cornelius Van Til*, ed. E. R. Geehan (N.p.: Presbyterian and Reformed Publishing Comp., 1971), pp. 339-48 and 428-44 respectively.

[8] Quoted by Margaret J. Osler, *Divine Will and the Mechanical Philosophy: Gassendi and Descartes on Contingency and Necessity in the Created World* (Cambridge: Cambridge University Press, 1994), p. 34. See also Oberman, *The*

Harvest of Medieval Theology, pp. 37, 39, and *passim*.

9. Ozment, *The Age of Reform*, pp. 40-42, 233f.

10. Thomas a Kempis, *The Imitation of Christ*, trans. Leo Sherley-Price (Harmondsworth: Penguin Books, 1965 [1952]), pp. 27f.

11. Gerhard Ritter, "Romantic and Revolutionary Elements in German Theology on the Eve of the Reformation," in *The Reformation in Medieval Perspective*, ed. Steven Ozment (Chicago: Quadrangle Books, 1971), pp. 35f.

12. Stephen F. Mason, *A History of the Sciences* (New York: Macmillan, Collier Books, 1973 [1962]), p. 115.

13 See Christopher Kaiser, *Creation and the History of Science* (London/Grand Rapids: Marshall Pickering/Eerdmans, 1991), pp. 1-34 and *passim*.

14 Diogenes Allen, *Christian Belief in a Postmodern World: The Full Wealth of Conviction* (Louisville, Kentucky: Westminster/John Knox Press, 1989), p. 25.

15. This in spite of the fact that both voluntarism (with its stress on nature's contingency) and nominalism (with its interest in the particular) would seem to demand an empirical approach to the study of nature. Empirical science, however, did not really become important until the early-modern age. See on this point David C. Lindberg, *The Beginnings of Western Science: The European Scientific Tradition in Philosophical, Religious, and Institutional Context, 600 B.C. to A.D. 1450* (Chicago and London: University of Chicago Press, 1992), pp. 243f.

16 R. Hooykaas, *Religion and the Rise of Modern Science* (Edinburgh: Scottish Academic Press, 1984 [1972]), p. 32; italics added. On the effects the condemnations of 1277 had upon the development of science, see *ibid.*, pp. 31-35, as well as Kaiser, *Creation and the History of Science*, pp. 76-94, and Edward Grant, "Science and Theology in the Middle Ages," in *God and Nature*, eds. Lindberg and Numbers, pp. 49-75 (see especially pp. 54-59).

17. Hooykaas, *Religion and the Rise of Modern Science*, p. 33.

18. Brooke, *Science and Religion*, p. 62.

19. J. Huizinga, *The Waning of the Middle Ages*, trans. F. Hopman (Harmondsworth: Penguin Books, 1965 [1924]). The Dutch original, entitled *Herfsttij der Middeleeuwen* was first published in 1919.

20. See Lindberg, *The Beginnings of Western Science*, especially pp. 363-68.

V.   The Scientific Revolution

One of the insights to be gained from our survey so far is that what we have chosen as the main elements constituting worldviews and epistemologies in western society – namely religion, philosophy, and science – have not always been present in equal doses. In the ancient world the dominant element was philosophy. In the Middle Ages religion was the leader, followed by philosophy as a close second. Science played a minor role in that period, and its cultural influence was limited.

The reversal came in the modern period, which established science as the dominant cultural force. It did so not only for Europe, but increasingly also for the rest of the world. For it was science and technology that enabled the West to rule the world, first militarily and economically, then also intellectually. They account for the world's westernization and explain the present-day phenomenon of the global village.

The curious thing in this development is that Europe was a latecomer on the scene. Science flourished in ancient China, India, the Mediterranean region of Greece and Rome, and later in the Muslim world, well before Europe entered upon the global stage. And when it did enter upon that stage, these older civilizations would for centuries – during the later Middle Ages and into the early modern period – serve as mentors of European scholars. Yet none of these civilizations developed a scientific, technological, and industrialized society. Only Europe did.

The question why this happened will have our attention in the present chapter. Its aim is to illustrate the thesis that in their scientific work scientists are influenced by extra-scientific factors, and that these include the belief systems and the perceived needs of their culture.

The influence of Christianity

An important element in the rise of modern science, most modern historians agree, is the Christian religion. Christianity provided for a view of the cosmos that was in a number of important ways the opposite of the classical and other pagan ones. For one thing, as we saw in the previous chapter, it taught that nature was orderly, but that its order was contingent or non-necessary, so that an empirical approach to science was needed. This was opposed to the Platonic view – and to some extent also to the Aristotelian one – that truth about the universe could be had by speculation alone.

In the second place, Christianity taught that creation was good and matter not to be despised; a belief that was the opposite of the Platonic tradition, which held matter in contempt and therefore discouraged the study of nature. That tradition was strong in Greece and in several oriental cultures, and it threatened to infiltrate Christianity via such dualistic religions as Gnosticism and Manicheism. The church steadfastly fought these influences. It upheld the biblical message that God had created the universe and proclaimed it good, and that Christ had redeemed matter and, by his incarnation, sanctified it. The Christian religion was also opposed to pantheism, another belief that was widespread in the Hellenistic world. The scientific implications of pantheism were similar to those of classical dualism in that it, too, discouraged the investigation of nature.

The Greek and oriental traditions were tenacious, and the struggle waged by the early Christian scholars was a lengthy one. Nor did it lead to a complete victory. Platonic ideas, such as the dichotomy between body and soul, influenced medieval and even post-medieval theology. They were also present in monasticism, with its tendency to escape from the world and to exalt the soul at the expense of the body. This type of dualism, however, did not result in a turning away from creation. Western Christianity never followed the oriental practice of scorning nature and despising matter. In fact, monks and nuns were in the front ranks of early-medieval farmers, craftsmen, and inventors.

An important factor here was, as Christopher Kaiser has shown,[1] the tradition of Christian compassion and selfless service, and the conviction that the forces of nature should be harnessed in order to alleviate suffering, improve the conditions of life, and help the poor. That tradition encouraged first of all the healing ministry of the early church and the Middle Ages. Public and monastic hospitals were established and much effort was devoted to the study of medicine. The tradition also encouraged the development of technology and the mechanical arts, including the art of agriculture and cattle breeding.

The work in these areas had important social and economic consequences. Already in the early-medieval centuries agricultural improvements increased the supply and variety of foodstuffs, and once the invasions ended, these advances allowed for rapid population growth, the revival of trade, and the re-emergence of towns. The application of mechanical power similarly increased production. It also decreased human drudgery and made possible the elimination of slavery. Neither Greece nor Rome nor any other ancient civilization had accomplished this. In the words of historian Lynn White, Jr.: "The chief glory of the Middle Ages was not...its cathedrals, its epics, its vast structures of scholastic philosophy, or even its superb music; ...it was the building for the first time in history of a complex civilization which was upheld not on the sinews of sweating slaves and coolies but primarily by non-human power."[2] Because of the effectiveness of these efforts, and also because they were inspired by the conviction that power was to be used for the benefit of others rather than for personal aggrandizement, they resulted in a positive assessment of technology and, later, of science.

The Christian religion encouraged scientific pursuits also because of its message that God is a trustworthy God and that he himself (and not a subordinate deity such as Plato's demiurge or the evil deity of Gnosticism) had created nature and man, endowing the latter with the ability to understand creation. Because of this, man could indeed fulfil the cultural mandate. Often the doctrine of man's being created in God's image was used as an additional argument. It was combined with the so-called *logos*-doctrine, inherited from Neoplatonism, according to which man participates in the divine rationality and so is enabled to "think God's thoughts after him." But whatever their background beliefs, Christians generally held that nature could be known. And because creation was God's handiwork, its study was seen as a means of glorifying God. By revealing the order and grandeur of nature, scientists revealed something of the majesty of its Creator.

Medieval and Renaissance roots

Christian teachings and the traditions of the early church were important factors in preparing Europe for the scientific revolution, but they were not the only ones. The Middle Ages also played a role. They transmitted to the modern age the belief in a rational, orderly cosmos as well as the scholastic tradition of careful logical reasoning. Early modern scientists benefited, moreover, from the work of medieval scholars who transmitted the natural philosophy of the Greeks, and from the achievements of the fourteenth-century scientists. They could also make use of the technological advances of the medieval centuries, a point to which we return in the next section.

Hardly less important for the rise of modern science was the revival of ancient learning and ancient traditions during the so-called Renaissance. A period of some 200 to 300 years in length, the Renaissance was wedged between the Middle Ages and the modern age. As is common in transitional periods, it reacted negatively to the culture of the centuries immediately preceding it. It was the people of the Renaissance who gave the Middle Ages its name. In choosing it they expressed their evaluation of the medieval past: it was no more than an in-between period, a time of superstition and cultural decline that had unfortunately ended the much higher civilizations of Greece and Rome.

The classical past stood, in their opinion, for the height of human achievement and therefore served the Renaissance as its supreme inspiration. This explains the name Renaissance, which contemporaries invented. The implication was that their times had broken with the preceding period and witnessed a rebirth of classical civilization. Renaissance interest in the classics affected the scientific revolution in a number of ways. It led to the rediscovery of ancient works on mathematics and of a variety of scientific theories that would inspire modern scientists. As will be shown in the discussion of the Copernican revolution, it also helped bring about the revolt against the medieval model of the universe, while at the same time providing ideas for its replacement.

The taming of nature

Yet another contribution of the Renaissance to the rise of modern science was the development of technology. In their concern with technology, Renaissance craftsmen and engineers continued a late-medieval tradition. Although important technological inventions had taken place in Western Europe even during the so-called Dark Ages and throughout the Middle Ages, it was not until the later Middle Ages and the Renaissance that people became truly obsessed with what one historian has called the urge to "tame nature."[3]

That urge is understandable in view of the problems society faced in these centuries. The threats posed by the late-medieval famines and epidemics stimulated a search for means to help man escape the cruelties of nature and, in a positive sense, to use nature's energies for human wellbeing. Not nearly all the contrivances that were produced in these centuries could be put to use, but the output of usable tools and instruments was impressive. The Late Middle Ages and Renaissance witnessed, among other things, the introduction of the pendulum, mechanical clocks, scales, printing with movable type, gunpowder, and a variety of navigational devices, including the magnetic compass.

The obsession with mechanical devices, and the scrutiny of nature to which it gave rise, continued into the early modern period and formed, historian John Hale writes, "an essential prelude to the science of the Newtonian century that followed...."[4] So far head and hand had tended to operate separately, as they had done in ancient Greece. The vision of medieval and Renaissance artisans and engineers contributed to the modern tradition of combining the two. Many of the artist-engineers, moreover, made a point of studying ancient works on mathematics, architecture, optics, physics, and engineering, and of disseminating the classical knowledge they found.[5] The result of these various endeavours would be rapid scientific advances. Like his medieval namesake Roger Bacon, the early-modern philosopher, statesman, and advocate of experimental science Sir Francis Bacon (1561-1626) believed that eventually science would contribute to the further development of technology.

Science and magic

Technology was not the only means of controlling nature. There was also the occult, and it, too, played a role in the advancement of science.

The relation between belief in occult forces and the development of science was long ignored by historians of science, and even today most textbooks pay little or no attention to it. But as twentieth-century historians of Renaissance science have shown, the relationship was a close one. Many an early-modern scientist who became famous for his contributions in astronomy, physics, or chemistry was seriously involved in the pursuit of astrology and alchemy as well. Indeed, until at least the time of Francis Bacon, "advanced scientific thought moved on parallel, often overlapping paths" with natural magic.[6] The astronomer Johannes Kepler was a firm believer in astrology, as was his colleague Tycho Brahe, who was interested in alchemy as well. Both men transgressed the church law which forbade the casting of horoscopes. Galileo also dabbled in astrology. And as his unpublished manuscripts show, even Sir Isaac Newton was a believer in the occult, attaching as much importance to his studies in alchemy as to his work in science proper.

This concern with the occult – among scholars and among the population at large – was not a new development. As noted in the previous chapter, the later Middle Ages already had experienced an interest in esoteric knowledge, a phenomenon that must in part be explained by the doomsday and millenarian expectations which prevailed during much of the period. These expectations did not disappear with the arrival of the early-modern age. In the sixteenth and seventeenth centuries also there was a widespread belief that the world was running down and that a collapse of civilization, and perhaps even of the cosmos as a whole, was imminent. Among the factors that now contributed to the belief were the break-up of Christian unity, religious and dynastic wars, and profound political, social, and economic changes. Expecting catastrophic developments, many people followed the medieval occultists in turning for solace and help to ancient magic.

Interest in magic was whetted by the rediscovery in the Italian Renaissance of ancient writings on the occult. These included Neoplatonic works as well as a number of manuscripts known as the Hermetic corpus. The latter consisted of a medley of ancient philosophy, Platonic and Stoic theology, and works on astrology, alchemy, and other forms of natural magic. The Hermetic writings dated from the first to third century of the Christian era. During the Renaissance, however, they were believed to be the work of a mythical Egyptian priest by the name of Hermes Trismegistus (Hermes the Thrice-Greatest) who was purported to be either pre-Mosaic or a contemporary of Moses. In a period when it was believed that the greater the antiquity of a tradition the greater was its wisdom, the assumed age of the Hermetic corpus ensured it an enthusiastic reception. Together with Neoplatonic writings, it served as a major inspiration for those who in the early-modern centuries turned to esoteric knowledge.

These centuries witnessed various manifestations of the occult, ranging from witchcraft and Satanism to natural magic such as alchemy and astrology. It was the last two that exerted a direct influence on the development of science. Alchemy's goal was to find the elixir (or the philosopher's stone) for changing base metals into gold and to discover other means of control over nature. Although its practitioners at times tried to enlist help from occult forces, alchemy had affinities with experimental science and aided its development. Most alchemists engaged in a serious study of nature, and their work contributed to such arts and sciences as metallurgy, dye-making, pharmacology, chemistry, and, in some cases, mathematics. It also contributed to a growing interest in magnetism and electricity.[7] Alchemy was associated, however, with mysticism and magical forces, and as time progressed these concerns would gradually transform it into an all-embracing philosophy. Once that happened, "alchemical transformation was frequently linked to the spiritual transformation of the alchemical experimenter, and it was believed by some that the elixir not only transformed base metals into gold but also conferred immortality."[8]

Astrology, arguably the most popular occult practice of the Middle Ages and the early modern centuries, also aimed at control. It originated in the ancient belief that stars and planets influence both nature and human destiny. Although its association with pagan idolatry and its implied determinism and fatalism made the practice of astrology a contentious issue in the Christian Middle Ages, it was never fully suppressed. Usually a distinction was made between what was called vulgar astrology, such as the casting of horoscopes and the prediction of propitious times for certain actions, and the study of the physical influences which the heavens were believed to exert upon man and nature. The former practices were frequently forbidden, while the latter were allowed. Like alchemy, astrology had an experimental basis and contributed to the development of astronomy.

Sir Francis Bacon

Although the occult was popular among scholars and the populace at large, not everyone believed in its efficiency or in its benevolent nature. Skepticism about the power of magic was expressed throughout the early-modern period. It was also becoming clear that in an age when apocalyptic and millenarian expectations were widespread, messages that the stars foretold social unrest such as peasant wars and sectarian uprisings could be self-fulfilling prophecies. The same could be true even of predictions of famines, since they might lead merchants to hang on to supplies in order to raise prices and profits.[9] The pantheistic implications of some Neoplatonic and Hermetic teachings were another cause of serious concern in a Christian society. Not in the last place, there was the fear that the preoccupation with magic would lead to a conception of man as the manipulator of nature for the sake of personal power. This threat inspired the English playwright Christopher Marlowe (1564-93) to write

The Tragicall History of Dr. Faustus – the story of a practitioner of black magic whose desire for forbidden knowledge caused him to sell his soul to Satan and so to bring about his own destruction.

The threat of Faustianism played a role in Sir Francis Bacon's attitude toward magic. Bacon was a man of his times and aware of the attractions of the occult. He himself accepted some aspects of alchemy and astrology, believing, for example, that by means of the latter one "could be forearmed against the Antichrist... and forewarned of the exact time of his coming."[10] Bacon was also influenced by the current millenarian expectations, and it is probably no coincidence that he spoke of his system as "the great instauration," a term used by millenarians to describe the restoration of peace and righteousness that would descend when the present age had run its course.[11] Bacon in fact believed that, by applying itself to the study of nature, mankind could regain the dominion over nature that it had lost by the fall into sin. In his opinion as in that of the magicians, knowledge implied power over nature.

But unlike the magicians, Bacon increasingly referred not to the power of the occult but to that of scientific knowledge. Although he was indeed influenced by the magical tradition, he in the end rejected it, and he did so largely on moral grounds. Knowing that humanity's original sin was inspired by the desire for forbidden knowledge so that man might be "like God," he feared any approach that sought to transcend man's creaturely limitations. The pursuit of learning was legitimate only if it was done in humility and aimed not at self-aggrandizement but sought, in accordance with the ancient Christian tradition, the glory of God and the well-being of humanity. The magus ideal, on the other hand, was inspired by pride and self-centredness and its pursuit, he believed, constituted a second fall into sin.[12]

And so Bacon became an example of scientific rectitude, a man who spent much of his life fighting the influence of Renaissance occultism. Because that heritage was more and more becoming an embarrassment in any case, concerted attempts would be made in the seventeenth century to forswear and repress it. But it did not disappear without leaving a trace. Current research suggests "that the major contribution of Hermeticism to the Baconian sciences and perhaps to the Scientific Revolution was the Faustian figure of the magus, concerned to manipulate and control nature...."[13]

The revolution in astronomy

Astronomy and physics were not the only disciplines to attract the attention of early-modern scientists. Advances were made in other fields as well. A well-known example is Andreas Vesalius' study on human anatomy, which was published in the same year as Copernicus' work on astronomy. But although important work was done in a variety of scientific fields, the development of a new astronomical model of the universe was central to the scientific revolution. It was also the process wherein the two other factors we mentioned as contributing to the rise of modern science – the switch in general worldview and the interest in ancient traditions – became especially noticeable.

The search for the new model began in the late Renaissance. It was in that period, in the year 1543, that the Polish astronomer Nicolaus Copernicus started the process by publishing his book *On the Revolutions of the Heavenly Spheres*, wherein he argued for the replacement of the old earth-centred model with one wherein the sun was the focus. It meant that, instead of the sun revolving around a stationary earth, the earth would revolve around a stationary sun. In the rest of this chapter we will concern ourselves with the causes and implications of the Copernican vision.

Copernicus was not the first to propose a new model of the universe. The ancient Pythagoreans already believed that the earth moved, and the Hellenistic astronomer Aristarchus of Samos, who lived in the third century B.C., anticipated Copernicus by proposing a solar system with an earth that rotated daily on its axis and revolved annually around the sun. Aristarchus had been unable, however, to convince his peers. Theories of a stationary sun and a moving earth went against common sense and raised serious scientific and philosophical problems. And so the ancient model continued to rule supreme, both in the Hellenistic world and during the Middle Ages. We have seen that medieval scientists who considered changes to the old model (such as the rotation of the earth on its axis) also failed to make a dent in the traditional model. Copernicus' theory, on the other hand, even though it was not immediately accepted, had staying power and was eventually vindicated.

Why did Copernicus succeed where his predecessors failed? The answer is threefold. In the first place, there was an increasing impatience with the inadequacies of the old model. It is true that it was still a serviceable tool. A lot of observation and mathematics had gone into it, and it allowed for quite accurate predictions. Nevertheless, it contained discrepancies, and the many adjustments that had been necessary to account for all the observed phenomena had made it cumbersome.

In the second place, the modern period's mathematical knowledge was superior to that of the Hellenistic and medieval worlds, and so was its array of technological aids. As a result modern scientists, unlike their predecessors, were able to provide the mathematical and empirical evidence and tools that the new model required. A well-known example of a helpful empirical tool was the telescope, developed in Holland, which in the early seventeenth century allowed Galileo to demonstrate the greater probability of the new model over the old.

And in the third place, there was the role played by the change in worldview and by the renewed interest in the classical past. Unlike the Hellenistic and medieval mentalities, that of the Renaissance would stimulate the search for a new model and encourage its acceptance, and it would do so at a time when the rediscovery of ancient traditions provided new concepts for that model.

It is here, incidentally, that we meet with one of the complexities in the development of the modern world. Living in a period that saw a revival of interest in classical antiquity, Renaissance and early modern scientists in developing their theories were inspired and aided by a variety of ancient traditions. But as it happened, the success of their work would lead to a weakening of the very traditions that had so generously nourished it. The inaccuracies of Aristotle's physics and mechanics, the inadequacy of the old astronomical model, and the shortcomings in the works of other ancient thinkers became increasingly apparent, a development that contributed to the slow erosion of belief in the superior wisdom of the classical past. It therefore also contributed to the decline of the Renaissance itself, to the replacement of regressive and cyclical views of history with a progressive one, and so, ultimately, to the victory of the typically modern belief in progress.

The old model

The interaction between the Renaissance mentality and the scientific developments of the time can best be illustrated by means of a description of the old model. That model had been centuries in the making, from the time of the Pre-Socratics to the late-Hellenistic age. Aristotle had provided much of the framework, but later scientists continued working on the model's astronomy. Their work was synthesized by the Hellenistic astronomer Ptolemy, who lived in the second century of the Christian era, and the model is usually called the Ptolemaic one. The Ptolemaic system was more than an astronomical model. It entailed a cosmology, and in that capacity guided people in ordering their view of man, nature, and the spiritual world. This cosmology served first the Greek and Hellenistic worlds and then, after men like Roger Bacon, Albert the Great, Thomas Aquinas, and the poet Dante had tried to Christianize it, the later Middle Ages.

The Middle Ages liked the model, which looked as if it had been expressly designed for integration with the medieval worldview. The stationary earth was at the centre and therefore also at the lowest point of the system (with the exception of hell, which, situated in the very bowels of the earth, was lower still). For medieval man the location of the earth underlined the biblical message not just of humanity's central position in creation, but also of its fallenness.

The low estate of man's habitat (in comparison with the heavenly bodies) was illustrated also in other ways. The earth was made up of four elements (earth, water, air, and fire) which symbolized changeableness, corruption and decay. The heavenly bodies, which were composed of a luminous "fifth element," the so-called quintessence, were immutable. And just as change implied decay, so changelessness symbolized perfection and permanence. The manner in which the heavenly bodies moved gave further testimony of their flawlessness. Unlike earthly motion, heavenly motion was circular, which meant that no change in location occurred. Circularity ensured immutability and therefore perfection. The difference between the earth and the heavens was radical.

The fact that the heavenly bodies were perfect did not mean that they were perfectly equal. Equality was not a virtue in the Middle Ages. Gradations in rank existed in church, civil government, and society, and they also permeated the universe. There was a straight ascending line from hell and earth to the lowest of the heavenly bodies, and from there to the highest heavens, the abode of God.

The heavenly bodies did not move freely but were embedded in concentric spheres. The lowest of these contained the moon; beyond it were the spheres of Mercury and Venus, then came the sphere of the sun, followed by those of Mars, Jupiter, and Saturn. In most versions the eighth sphere contained the so-called fixed stars; the ninth was called the *primum mobile* or first mover, because it moved the lower ones; and the tenth sphere was the Empyrean Heaven, where the angels were located. God, who was enthroned beyond the created heavens, was the ultimate source of all heavenly motion. The *primum mobile* was moved by love of God, as were the other spheres. Intermediaries, however, were also present. The spheres had as movers their own set of intelligences or angels, and here also the proper hierarchical order was observed. The highest angels took care of the highest spheres, lower angels of the lower ones. The *primum mobile* itself was moved by the Seraphim, the pre-eminent order in the angelic hierarchy.

The medieval model was finite, and this was yet another characteristic to appeal to the Middle Ages. Medieval astronomers did not believe that the cosmos was small and cozy; they knew that the distances between planets and stars were unimaginably large. Even so, their universe was limited. There was only one solar system, not the billions which the new model would accommodate. And where the new model would posit limitless space, the old one saw space as bounded, first by the spheres of the fixed stars and the *primum mobile*, then by the Empyrean Heaven itself.

The people of the Middle Ages, as one historian put it, still lived in a walled universe, just as they still lived in walled towns,[14] and in both cases the walls gave a sense of security. Indeed, God himself surrounded the universe. He also controlled and governed it, day by day. Miracles were still possible, and angels were everywhere. So was a multitude of lesser spiritual beings, both good and evil. The medieval universe left little room for a naturalistic materialism.

Objections to the medieval model

The correspondences between the medieval belief systems on the one hand and the medieval model on the other explain why people in the Middle Ages felt at home in their universe, and why astronomers were willing to put up with the model's inadequacies. They also suggest why, with the decline of medieval civilization and the coming of the Renaissance, the old model was liable to come under attack.

A variety of Renaissance characteristics would cause difficulties for the Ptolemaic model. For one thing, the period tended to be more humanistic and more secular than the Middle Ages, and therefore less enamoured of a universe that in so many ways mirrored the medieval-Christian view of man and his world. The Renaissance was also critical of authority, particularly of the authority of the medieval church, medieval religion, and the medieval intellectual tradition, all of which had been closely allied to the old cosmology.

Another trait that ran counter to the old model was the Renaissance's expansiveness. A static and limited universe had suited medieval society, which, on the whole, had been inward-looking. It did not suit a period like the Renaissance, which more and more directed its attention outward. As art historians have remarked, Renaissance artists conquered space by inventing linear perspective at a time when Columbus and other explorers conquered space by crossing the world's oceans. The same desire to move beyond ancient boundaries contributed to the dislike of the spatial limitations which the old model had imposed on nature. The belief in a boundless universe, containing a plurality of solar systems, grew during the Renaissance.

Not in the last place, the Renaissance disliked the old model's hierarchical set-up. With their increased self-confidence, Renaissance humanists could not be happy with a model that located man's habitat right at the bottom of the system. Humanity deserved better, and so did the earth. The desire to promote the earth and portray it as a "noble star" – made of the same stuff as the heavenly bodies and sailing with them around the sun – was present well before Copernicus published his theory.

The role of the classics

Yet another element in the scientific revolution, as we noted earlier, was the classical revival. Of special importance was the discovery of Platonic, Neoplatonic, and Hermetic manuscripts.

Renaissance interest in Platonism affected science in a number of ways. For one thing, it stimulated the study of mathematics and convinced astronomers that that discipline provided the key to the knowledge of the cosmos. Modern scientists learned from Plato (and via him from the Pythagoreans) that proportion and orderliness characterized the universe, and that both could be expressed in mathematical formulas. One reason why Copernicus questioned the old model was its complexity and his belief that a sun-centred model would be much simpler mathematically than the earth-centred one. Simplicity was what counted. The Creator was too good a mathematician, Copernicus reasoned, to prefer a complex and arbitrary system to a simple, precise, and fully rational one.

Copernicus himself left too much of the old system intact to achieve the desired simplicity, but that did not detain his followers. The belief that the operations of the universe could be expressed in precise mathematical terms, and that in this respect the Copernican model was potentially superior to the Ptolemaic one, motivated later Copernicans such as Kepler and Galileo.

Copernicanism attracted scientists not only because of its potential for a better explanation of the heavenly motions. Many of them also liked the system because of the dominant position it gave to the sun, and here again Platonism was influential. In the *Republic*, Plato had referred to the sun as symbol and image of the highest of all the Forms. It was the earthly God, the ruler of the cosmos. Common sense confirmed this high estimation of the sun. After all, it was the source of life and light in the earthly realm, and it was only natural for it to occupy the central position in the universe. Copernicus himself appears to have drawn that conclusion,[15] and so did several of his followers, the astronomer Johannes Kepler being an outstanding example.

The Platonic tradition served as a source of ideas for other features of the new model. It was in proposing these features that earlier thinkers, including non-scientists, played a role. Some of them, although living before Copernicus, came closer to outlining the new model than he did. Copernicus would do little more than switch the location and status of the earth and the sun, and, by implication, destroy the Aristotelian distinction between terrestial and heavenly regions. Practically everything else was left intact, including the spheres, the walled-in appearance of the universe, and the idea that there was only one solar system. There were earlier thinkers, however, who explicitly stated that the earth and the heavens were made of the same stuff and therefore equal. Similarly, there were pre-Copernicans – both in the late Middle Ages and in the Renaissance – who considered the possibility of a rotating earth and suggested that the universe might well be infinite and contain a large number of solar systems.[16]

This type of speculation had been impossible under the rule of Aristotle, but was, since the spread of voluntarism, possible from the point of view of God's sovereign freedom and omnipotence. As historian Arthur O. Lovejoy has shown, some of the ideas themselves – especially those concerning the infinity of the universe and the plurality of solar systems – were inspired by the idea of plenitude, which was a Neoplatonic concept.[17] The idea of plenitude was derived from Plato's God, whose nature was a dual one. On the one hand he was self-sufficient and kept his distance from the world of becoming and change. On the other hand he was very much involved in that world because he was the source of all that was. He had given rise to the cosmos and all that it contained because he was good, and for Plato goodness in this context did not mean compassion, but lack of envy, and hence the desire to give existence to all that could possibly exist.

That "all" had to be taken in the most literal sense. Perfect goodness meant a total lack of envy, and that implied the creation of an infinite universe, containing an infinitude of "worlds" and populated by an infinitude of beings. This conclusion, which seemed to follow from the premisses, was indeed drawn by Renaissance thinkers and disseminated well before modern scientists had begun to work on the new model. By the early sixteenth century, that is, before Copernicus published his work, "the theories of the plurality of solar systems and of inhabited planets, of the infinity of the number of the stars and the infinite extent of the universe in space, were already common topics of discussion."[18] In the course of the seventeenth century scientists would develop a model that contained these features.

NOTES

[1.] Kaiser, *Creation and the History of Science,* pp. 34-52. For a similar account see the same author's *Creational Theology and the History of Physical Science: The Creationist Tradition from Basil to Bohr* (Leiden/New York/Köln: Brill, 1997), pp. 60-83. For the influence of Christianity on the rise of science see also the detailed account in Nancy R. Pearcey and Charles B. Thaxton, *The Soul of Science: Christian Faith and Natural Philosophy* (Wheaton, Ill.: Crossway, 1994), ch. 1.

[2.] Lynn White, Jr., *Dynamo and Virgin Reconsidered* (Cambridge, Mass.: Massachusetts Institute of Technology, 1968), pp. 70f. See also Mason, *A History of the Sciences,* ch. 10.

[3.] John Hale, *The Civilization of Europe in the Renaissance* (New York: Macmillan, 1993), ch. 10.

[4.] *Ibid.,* p. 564.

[5.] Thomas S. Kuhn, *The Essential Tension: Selected Studies in Scientific Tradition and Change* (Chicago: University of Chicago Press, 1977), pp. 55f.

[6.] Hale, *The Civilization of Europe in the Renaissance,* p. 582. On what follows in this section and the next see also Kuhn, *The Essential Tension,* ch. 3; Marie Boas, *The Scientific Renaissance 1450-1630* (New York: Harper and Row, Harper Torchbooks, The Science Library, 1962), ch. 6; Charles Webster, *From Paracelsus to Newton: Magic and the Making of Modern Science* (Cambridge: Cambridge University Press, 1984 [1982]); Robert S. Westman and J. E. McGuire, *Hermeticism and the Scientific Revolution* (Los Angeles: William Andrews Clark Memorial Library, University of California, 1977); and Frances A. Yates, *Giordano Bruno and the Hermetic Tradition* (London: Routledge and Kegan Paul, 1964) and subsequent essays. Yates was among those who did pioneering work on the role of the Renaissance magus in the scientific revolution.

The trailblazing study on the relationship between magic and science in general is Lynn Thorndike's monumental work *A History of Magic and Experimental Science*, 8 vols. (New York: Columbia University Press, 1923-58).

[7.] Kuhn, *The Essential Tension*, p. 54; Lindberg, *The Beginnings of Western Science*, p. 290. In fact, the practice of alchemy was generally considered a scientific one well into the early modern-period. As Stephen Toulmin has shown, alchemy originated in Aristotle's organic view of nature, according to which the ingredients of matter are not stable but in process of development toward their most "noble" form. Alchemists attempted to accelerate this "natural" process by artificial means. It was not until the eighteenth and nineteenth centuries, with the work of the chemists Lavoisier and Dalton, that a different theory of matter was adopted and alchemy became a pseudo-science. Stephen Toulmin, *Foresight and Understanding: An Inquiry into the Aims of Science* (New York: Harper and Row, Harper Torchbooks, The Science Library, 1963 [1961]), ch. 4.

[8.] Lindberg, *The Beginnings of Western Science*, p. 290.

[9.] Hale, *The Civilization of Europe in the Renaissance*, p. 568.

[10.] Brooke, *Science and Religion*, p. 59.

[11.] Webster, *From Paracelsus to Newton*, p. 30.

[12.] Frances A. Yates, *Ideas and Ideals in the North European Renaissance, Collected Essays*, III (London: Routledge and Kegan Paul, 1984), p. 62.

[13.] Kuhn, *The Essential Tension*, p. 54.

[14.] Lovejoy, *The Great Chain of Being*, p. 101.

[15.] "In the centre of everything," Copernicus wrote, "rules the sun; for who in this most beautiful temple could place this luminary at another or better place whence it can light up the whole at once? ... In this arrangement we thus find an admirable harmony of the world, and a constant harmonious connection between the motion and the size of the orbits as could not be found otherwise." Quoted by Mason, *A History of the Sciences*, p. 133.

[16.] Lovejoy, *The Great Chain of Being*, pp. 111-116.

[17.] On this concept and its effect on late-medieval and Renaissance thought, see *ibid.*, especially chapters 2-4.

[18.] *Ibid.*, p. 115; see also p. 344, n28.

VI. A Clockwork Universe

The revolution in astronomy began in 1543, when Copernicus published his theory of a heliocentric universe. It took his followers close to a century and a half to work out the implications of Copernicanism. That work was not completed until 1687, with the publication of Newton's *Mathematical Principles of Natural Philosophy*. The cause of the delay was not simply that a great deal of evidence had yet to be collected in support of Copernicus' theory. No less daunting a task was the putting together of a model of the universe, one that explained the variety of data and combined them into a framework.

The establishment of such a framework was the work of Newton and his colleagues. As a replacement of the old system, its function was to accommodate the new astronomy and at the same time to serve as a cosmology. This meant that it had to satisfy not only scientific but also extra-scientific requirements – specifically theological and socio-political ones. The manner in which these factors contributed to the final product is the topic of the present chapter, which will concentrate on the reasons for and the consequences of the close alliance that was forged between science and theology. But before we turn to that issue, something must be said about the search for evidence on behalf of the new astronomy.

After Copernicus

From the start, Copernicus had inspired scholars to complete the work he had begun, and already in the sixteenth century information had been forthcoming that supported the new theory, or at least cast serious doubts on the adequacy of the old one. In 1572, for example, a supernova had been observed, and five years later a comet appeared whose orbit, astronomers showed, lay beyond the moon. Both phenomena disproved the old idea that the heavens were perfect and unchanging, and they threw serious doubt on the existence of the crystalline spheres as well.

The efforts on behalf of the new model continued in the seventeenth century. In 1609 Galileo pointed his telescope at the skies and found additional evidence against Ptolemy's model. He noted that neither the sun nor the moon were the perfect, luminous bodies that the old system assumed them to be. The sun showed spots, and the moon's surface was disfigured by craters and other irregularities. Galileo also discovered that the planet Venus had phases, which suggested that it revolved around the sun, and that Jupiter had four moons circling around the mother planet, which proved that heavenly bodies could revolve freely in space and yet stay in orbit. If the moons of Jupiter could do it, then so could the earth – although Galileo could not explain how it happened. He further noted that the Milky Way consisted of an enormous number of stars, an observation which suggested that the universe was much larger than had previously been thought. Those who were so inclined could interpret it as an argument for the infinity of the universe and the multiplicity of solar systems.

In the year that Galileo introduced the telescope, his colleague Johannes Kepler published the first two of his three laws of planetary motion. These laws established that the orbits of the heavenly bodies were not circular, as Aristotle and Ptolemy and their followers had believed, but elliptical. They also provided the mathematical formula by which the orbits of the planets could be calculated. Kepler's findings showed that heavenly motion was of a mechanical nature and so reinforced the notion, which late-medieval scientists had already entertained, that the solar system operated as a clockwork, in an automatic fashion.

These and various other discoveries showed the inadequacy of the Ptolemaic model and were used in support of the Copernican one. But many quandaries remained, some of them of a scientific, some of a philosophical nature. A prominent one within the former category concerned the mechanics of heavenly motion. Among the questions that urgently demanded an answer was how, in the absence of the Ptolemaic spheres, the earth and the other planets could stay in their orbits when moving around the sun, and also how they were able to move in the first place. Furthermore, if the earth was indeed in motion, it had to be explained why human beings and other terrestial objects were not flung off into space but constantly "fell" back toward the earth, and why people did not even notice that their planet was in motion.

Partial answers to these questions had been given by Galileo, Kepler, René Descartes, Christian Huygens, Robert Hooke, and other scientists. Their observations and speculations had resulted, among other things, in the development of the theory of inertia (a further development of the medieval work on the impetus theory), which dispensed with the need for the continuous application of force to keep an object in motion. While this still implied the necessity of a first mover to account for heavenly motion, it provided yet another argument against the need for spheres and their attendant intelligences. To explain why freely revolving planets stay in their orbits around the sun and why terrestial objects fall toward the earth rather than being flung off into space, notions of gravity were developed, and it was also suggested that the two phenomena in question, that of the sun's and the earth's gravitational attraction, could perhaps be explained with reference to the same theory.

Newton's synthesis

It was these various theories that Newton inherited, adapted, and synthesized into his laws of universal gravity and inertial motion. By doing this he answered the questions that previous scientists had left unanswered and made possible the framework the age had been waiting for. Completing the demolition of the old distinction between the earth and the heavens, Newton showed that the same laws apply to heavenly and earthly motion, and that the same gravitational force which keeps the earth, the other planets, and the moon in their orbits accounts for the fact that terrestial objects fall toward the earth. That force, which operated between all particles of matter in the universe, he described in a simple mathematical formula. Newton, in short, confirmed Kepler's notion of the universe as a beautifully designed clockwork that, once God had set it going, operated in obedience to mathematical laws which God had instituted.

The clockwork or machine metaphor facilitated the acceptance of the Copernican-Newtonian universe among the people at large – at least among those who had no special interest in Neoplatonism and related traditions. For it was not only the scientific evidence supplied by Newton and his predecessors that convinced people of the new model's correctness. Few could follow the difficult mathematical reasoning in any case. But there was considerable interest in the idea of a clockwork universe, and indeed of mechanical explanations of all sorts of phenomena. The obsession with mechanical contrivances that had characterized the later Middle Ages and the Renaissance remained strong in the early-modern period. The model that was now being established satisfied the desire for a mechanical approach to problems, and so helped introduce the mechanistic worldview that would characterize western civilization for the next two hundred years or more. In what follows we will have a closer look at the extra-scientific reasons for its acceptance.

How does God relate to nature?

The mechanistic model was inspired by the discovery of yet another Greek tradition, that of the Pre-Socratic atomists, whom we met in the first chapter of this book. As was noted there, the ancient atomists speculated that nature was composed of infinite numbers of particles, which moved in an infinite void and formed all things by their chance combinations and recombinations. Although materialistic and associated with atheism, the atomic theory had appeal for modern scientists. It fitted the ideas of the great extent of outer space, the free movement of planets, the very large number of stars, and the parity of the earth and the heavenly bodies, and it allowed for a mathematical approach to physical science. Furthermore, it could be adapted to Christianity. All that was needed was to assume that the atoms were not eternal, as the Pre-Socratic atomists had thought, but created entities, and that their movements were governed by laws imposed by God.

To the scientific reasons for the choice of the new model, non-scientific ones were added. Unlike the architects of the Ptolemaic astronomy, Copernicans believed that their model was not simply a descriptive one, but that it was physically true. That belief was shared by their culture, and it intensified the need for scientists to attend to the system's philosophical and religious implications, so that it could serve as an acceptable cosmology. The religious implications especially were important. As recent historians of science have shown, and as became clear also in the previous chapter, religion and science were still closely connected in the early-modern centuries.

An overriding concern in the time of Newton was to find a scientific model that gave an appropriate answer to the question of the relationship between God and nature. For two millennia people had lived by the answer that the old model had provided. Now that with its astronomy and mechanics the Ptolemaic cosmology had been destroyed as well, the question had to be answered anew. Modern historians have shown that the task of doing so constituted one of the most urgent problems that scientists and their advisers faced in the seventeenth century.[1]

In attempting to resolve it, they were able to choose from three models, namely Neoplatonism, Aristotelianism, and a mechanistic concept based on the atomic theory. Neoplatonism and Aristotelianism allowed for divine immanence in nature. This was considered both an asset and a liability. It was an asset in that it could serve as a defence against the threat of a materialistic explanation of nature, a threat that was already evident, for example, in the philosophy of a mechanist like Thomas Hobbes. But as was becoming increasingly clear, an approach stressing divine immanence contained dangers of no less serious a nature. The Neoplatonism of the time proclaimed the indwelling of God in nature, his being present there as a sort of world soul. This could and indeed did lead to pantheism and similar heresies. A well-known illustration of its dangers was provided by the case of Giordano Bruno, an Italian philosopher. An ardent advocate of a sun-centred universe, Bruno had mixed his scientific messages with pantheistic ones, which he derived from Neoplatonism and Hermeticism. Because no such opinions were allowed in the Italy of the Counter-Reformation, Bruno was, in the year 1600, burned as a heretic.

His extremism was no isolated phenomenon. Neoplatonic and Hermetic traditions fuelled a virulent type of sectarianism which plagued England and other European countries at various times during the seventeenth century.[2] Although increasingly suppressed in this period, occultism survived, and it did so especially among members of the lower classes. Indeed, magic often functioned as "the science of the non-numerate, the potential power of the unprivileged."[3] Some of the sectarians were inspired by socialist and even communist ideas, and a number of them used occult religious mysticism to prove that all individuals, rich and poor, male and female, could attain to spiritual enlightenment, and that therefore all people were equal. This type of teaching implied a questioning of the legitimacy of social, political, and ecclesiastical hierarchies. There were, in short, good reasons for scientists to turn their back on Neoplatonism and to opt for a view of nature that excluded any suggestion of divine immanence.

That decision implied the rejection not only of the Neoplatonic view of nature, but also of the Aristotelian one. Aristotle had explained natural processes with reference to a vitalistic principle within nature itself. It was the Form (or the vegetative soul) in organic beings that guided their development and ensured, for example, that an acorn developed into an oak, and a fertilized human ovum into a human being. Thomas Aquinas had adopted this model. In his philosophy Aristotle's vital principles became powers which God had instilled in nature. Growth and order in nature were for Thomas, and for Christian Aristotelianism in general, the result of a process wherein God co-operated with these powers. The scientific establishment rejected that view. Convinced of the need to counter the threats inherent in immanentism, it vetoed not only theories that allowed for a divine presence in nature, but even those that gave a measure of independence to nature itself, however small.

This left mechanism based on the atomic theory. Although it was realized that it could encourage materialism and atheism, scientists and their advisers felt that it nevertheless was the best choice, both from a scientific and a theological point of view. Its greatest theological asset was that it allowed for the explanation of celestial motion and of all other natural processes with reference to a wholly transcendent God who operated nature by means of laws which he himself had established. This construction provided additional religious warrant for the mechanistic model. It not only countered pagan heresies but also did justice to God's sovereignty and freedom.

Science and theology

The choice of mechanism, then, was influenced by various extra-scientific considerations, including theological ones. Historians have shown that in shaping their model scientists drew on two theological traditions, namely those of medieval voluntarism and of the Protestant Reformation.[4]

The voluntarist tradition gained force in the later Middle Ages, the period following Thomas Aquinas' attempted synthesis of Christian doctrine and Aristotelian philosophy. As was described in chapter four of this book, Thomas' synthesis was attacked for a number of reasons, one of which was that it threatened to compromise the freedom and sovereignty of God. Reacting against the deterministic tendencies of Aristotelianism and Thomism, the philosophers Duns Scotus and William of Ockham and their followers made it their task to stress God's absolute freedom and his radical sovereignty.

These voluntarist ideas were still alive in the seventeenth century and had affinities with   Reformation teachings. This is not to say that the Reformers were voluntarists in the late-medieval sense of the term. In fact, they criticized the tradition, opposing, among other things, the Ockhamist dichotomy between God's absolute and ordained power.

Where Ockhamists had held that at any time God's absolute power could arbitrarily override his ordained will, so that not even the Scriptures could be relied upon, the Reformers, in accordance with the principle of *sola scriptura,* confessed the utter trustworthiness of the divine Word. And although Reformation theology did agree with voluntarism in its belief in God's transcendence and absolute sovereignty, the differences with Ockhamism were again great. For the Reformers the belief in God's sovereignty implied that salvation is wholly God's work and therefore received by faith only, whereas Ockhamist voluntarism led to the Pelagian belief that it is achieved by human effort.[5]

In matters of theology, then, the similarities between Ockhamism and Reformation theology were often more apparent than real. Yet their confession of God's transcendence and his sovereign freedom set voluntarists and Reformers apart from the classical cosmologists. Luther and Calvin confessed that the natural realm, rather than being autonomous, depends upon a transcendent God who upholds both nature and the world of men. Mechanists therefore could support their scientific framework with arguments derived from Protestant theology. In turn, many a Protestant theologian subscribed, for religious and socio-political reasons, to scientific mechanism.

Mechanism had the added advantage that it could serve as a foundation for natural theology. Since it still required a first cause and supernatural designer, it could serve as proof of God's existence, and such proofs were much in demand in the early modern period. The rise of materialism and skepticism in the seventeenth century became a matter of concern for all Christian thinkers. Following Thomas Aquinas, many scientists and philosophers turned to natural theology and devised theistic arguments, pointing to nature as proof for the existence of a divine lawgiver and designer and so providing what they believed was a secure foundation for the Christian faith.

Mechanism and divine providence

Their justification of the mechanistic model shows that seventeenth-century scientists were not at all ready to break with Christianity. It is true that religion was not the only factor to explain mechanism's appeal. The theory also served important scientific functions. But there is no reason to believe that the mechanists were hypocritical in justifying their theory with reference to religion. The evidence makes it abundantly clear that they believed their model of the universe was the best one possible to vindicate religious orthodoxy, take the wind out of the sails of pantheists and related heretics, and serve as a defence against skepticism.

Yet all was not well on a religious front where people chose to rely on a fallible scientific model as a means of support for the faith. It soon became clear that a harmonization of belief in God's sovereignty with a belief in mechanism caused theological difficulties. By stressing God's transcendence one might indeed guarantee his freedom, but that freedom disappears when the universe must also be seen as a machine. For a machine, once it has been started, runs automatically and in a predetermined manner. The mechanistic universe may have been designed and set in motion by God, but once in operation it does not really allow for divine intervention. General providence can still be professed, but acts of special providence are no longer likely.

This, of course, went squarely against the teachings of the Reformation. Gary B. Deason has expressed the difference between mechanism and the theology of Luther and Calvin. "For the Reformers," he writes, "the radical sovereignty of God filled not only intellectual needs but spiritual and pastoral ones as well. Medieval theories of salvation had so stressed the active participation of human beings in their salvation that many believers worried whether they had done enough to be saved.... Luther saw the radical sovereignty of God as offering the only reliable assurance of salvation. Accepting on faith that God alone saves, the Protestant was freed from doing good works and penance as preconditions of salvation...."[6] In short, Luther's rediscovery of the gospel of free grace had everything to do with theology and nothing with science and cosmology.

Similarly, when the Reformers taught God's transcendence and his sovereign control of nature, the intention was not to explain the work of a type of cosmic Clockmaker or Engineer, who had set the universe in motion and ensured that the laws of nature would henceforth function as they should. The intention was to assure the believer that he could put his trust in the personal God of the Scriptures, a God who was both transcendent and present. God's special providence applied to creation as a whole and to every part of it, including each individual human being, including even each sparrow. The difference with the mechanistic concept was again profound. To quote Deason once more: "Nothing could contrast more sharply with the mechanists' view of God and the world. For [the mechanists], although God was sovereign over a world that He created and, in principle, could suspend or change natural laws to accomplish a special purpose, in practice He did not tamper with the laws of nature.... In the mechanical worldview, God [had become] a cosmic legislator.... The sovereign Redeemer of Luther and Calvin became the sovereign Ruler of the world machine."[7]

An awareness of this danger led in some circles to attempts to formulate a modified mechanism, one that left room for God's intervention. This was attempted by Sir Isaac Newton himself, who, as recent historians have shown, has wrongly been depicted as a mechanist of the Cartesian stripe.[8] A student of the seventeenth-century Cambridge Platonists, Newton feared the materialistic implications of the prevailing mechanistic theories, and a major reason why he paid a great deal of attention to the study of alchemy, and also to biblical prophecy, was to counteract this threat. His work in alchemy was to provide evidence of God's presence and activity throughout the realm of nature, and his biblical and historical studies were intended to prove God's providential action in the moral realm.

Nor were these the only means to prove God's active governance of the world. The same purpose was served with Newton's belief that God periodically had to adjust the orbits of the planets, and with his theory of gravity. According to Newton, gravity was not inherent in matter as a type of "divine energy," and neither was it a mechanical principle. It depended on God's immediate action. In their own fight against deism and atheism, Christian apologists would make use of this explanation. Gravity, for them, became the equivalent of grace: just as grace activated the believer, so gravity activated matter.[9] But to leave these openings for divine intervention was no more than a stop-gap measure. The arguments' credibility would be undermined when further discoveries provided mechanical solutions to the remaining problems.

There were other dangers to religion in the promotion of natural theology. The attempts to prove God's existence with reference to his works, rather than his Word, threatened the integrity of biblical Christianity and would in the end lead to the replacement of the God of Scripture with a pagan type of deity. Again, some scientists and theologians were aware of this danger and refused to replace reliance on revelation with reliance on observation and reason.[10] But not nearly everybody did so. Among natural theologians even the religiously orthodox tended to see God primarily as Creator, rather than as Creator and Redeemer. Richard Westfall has noted this, for example, in the case of the chemist Robert Boyle, one of the leading mechanists. Boyle, he states, never considered natural religion as a substitute for Christianity, stressed the priority of the Scriptures over natural religion, and acknowledged God the Redeemer. Nevertheless, he worshipped God the

Creator and Governor, and made few references in his writings to Christ.[11]

In the course of the century the Trinitarian faith would increasingly come under attack. Newton himself was an anti-Trinitarian, as was the philosopher John Locke, and for many of their contemporaries Christianity turned into a non-biblical theism. This development paved the way first for deism, and then for the spread of religious skepticism and atheism.

The moral of the story

The story we have told in this chapter illustrates the risks of attempting to safeguard religious truths with reference to a scientific model. It also shows the difficulty of avoiding such attempts, for the influence of a scientific cosmology upon our view of reality is powerful. In the words of historian Jacques Roger, "...Few can resist the intellectual trends of their age, and, in any case, it is much easier to identify the error of the past than to see the misunderstanding of the present."[12]

This does not mean, of course, that past errors have nothing to teach later generations, for they do have a message. Christians who supported the mechanistic model on religious grounds and, in turn, attempted to defend the faith with reference to that model, did so with the best of intentions, but the religious consequences were negative. The alliance between cosmology and theology secularized the gospel and it did not really succeed in harmonizing religion and science. For the God of the mechanists was not simply an absentee God; essentially he was no more than a God of the gaps. He was needed to account for those aspects of nature that scientists could not yet explain on naturalistic grounds (or that they did not as yet want to explain in that manner). Ultimately, however, such naturalistic explanations would be forthcoming, and the reference to God as an explanatory hypothesis would no longer be necessary. Christianity then lost credibility, and the modern universe became a closed, materialistic, and wholly deterministic one. Instead of guaranteeing the truth of nature's dependence on God, mechanism ended by establishing nature's autonomy.

The secularization of the model began in the seventeenth century. The process greatly accelerated in the eighteenth, the so-called Age of Reason. Before turning to that period, we must look at the contributions which seventeenth-century philosophy made to the new worldview. We will focus on the work of the French rationalist René Descartes and of the English empiricist John Locke.

NOTES

[1.] Jacques Roger in "The Mechanistic Conception of Life," in *God and Nature*, eds. Lindberg and Numbers, pp. 277-95, see esp. p. 279; Gary B. Deason, "Reformation Theology and the Mechanistic Conception of Nature," in the same volume, pp. 167-91. For what follows see these authors, as well as Hooykaas, *Religion and the Rise of Modern Science*, pp. 1-26; Osler, *Divine Will and the Mechanical Philosophy*, pp. 1-35; and Kaiser, *Creation and the History of Science*, pp. 150-186 and *passim*.

[2.] On the issue of sectarianism see Christopher Hill, *The World Turned Upside Down: Radical Ideas During the English Revolution* (Harmondsworth: Penguin Books, 1982 [1972]); David Kubrin, "Newton's Inside Out!: Magic, Class Struggle, and the Rise of Mechanism in the West," in *The Analytic Spirit: Essays in the History of Science; In Honor of Henry Guerlac*, ed. Harry Woolf (Ithaca and London: Cornell University Press, 1981), pp. 96-121. Instances of sectarian and social unrest on the continent are given in Carolyn Merchant, *The Death of Nature: Women, Ecology, and the Scientific Revolution* (San Francisco: Harper and Row, 1982 [1980]).

[3.] Hale, *The Civilization of Europe in the Renaissance*, p. 580.

[4.] See Deason, "Reformation Theology," esp. pp. 169f.

[5.] See above, p. 52.

[6] Deason, "Reformation Theology," p. 186.

[7.] *Ibid.*, p. 187.

[8] See on this point B. J. T. Dobbs, *The Janus Face of Genius: The Role of Alchemy in Newton's Thought* (Cambridge: Cambridge University Press, 1991), and Kaiser, *Creational Theology*, ch. 4. Webster (*From Paracelsus to Newton*, pp. 88-100 and *passim*) shows that Newton's fear was shared by other scientists, and that it caused a number of them, and even the Royal Society itself, to go slowly in supporting the rising attack on persecutions for witchcraft. They saw belief in demons, and in spirits in general, as a defence against a materialistic atheism.

[9.] Deason, "Reformation Theology," p. 185.

[10.] Richard S. Westfall, *Science and Religion in Seventeenth-Century England* (New Haven: Yale University Press, 1964 [1958]), pp. 140f, ch. 6. For the spread of natural theology and its implications, see the same work, ch. 5 and *passim*.

[11.] *Ibid.*, pp. 124f.

[12.] Roger, "The Mechanistic Conception of Life," p. 293.

VII. Descartes' Quest for Certainty

The problem of skepticism

The seventeenth century was a period of great trust in human reason, a trust that seemed to be fully justified by the accomplishments of science. Paradoxically, it was also a time of uncertainty, doubt, and skepticism. It was the problem of skepticism that occupied much of the attention of the period's philosophers, rationalists and empiricists alike.

Early-modern skepticism had many causes. The break-up of medieval Christianity and the accompanying religious uncertainties contributed to it, as did the religious wars, which lasted into the seventeenth century. The voyages of discovery also played a part. A growing awareness of the existence of different cultures and religions led to a questioning of the uniqueness, and even the superiority, of one's own civilization and religion. What had happened in Greece in the fifth century B.C. repeated itself in early-modern Europe.

The assault upon what had long been considered absolutes derived further strength from the disappointing performance of the ancients. The seventeenth century had not yet adopted the idea of progress. Especially during the first half of the century, many still believed in the superiority of the "ancients" over the "moderns" and continued to look for inspiration and wisdom to the classical past. Nevertheless, the trust in the ancients' infallibility was under attack. New technologies, new scientific theories, as well as the discovery of lands unknown to the Greeks and Romans, caused many an early-modern thinker to wonder whether the ancients were really as safe a guide as had been thought. The result was not yet a general feeling of triumphalism, although that feeling was not absent. But it also led to a sense of abandonment, of being adrift in an uncharted sea.

The revolution in astronomy had similar effects. The Ptolemaic universe had been limited and walled in, and had consisted of only one solar system. The Newtonian universe was boundless and probably infinite, and contained untold numbers of solar systems. Although many were happy with the new model, the sense of satisfaction was not universal. Well-known is the complaint of the philosopher and mathematician Blaise Pascal that the "eternal silence of those infinite spaces" frightened him. Questions were also raised about the implications for Christianity if, as was widely assumed, there were more inhabited planets, perhaps an infinite number of them. How did this fit in with revelation? And what did a plurality of inhabited planets and the boundlessness of space imply about man's status in the universe?

The old model had, it is true, located him at the lowest point of the cosmos, but that lowest point was also the centre. There had been a definite place for humanity and its planet. That place was gone. Infinitude meant that there was neither circumference nor centre, and that, as the poet John Donne expressed it, both the sun and the earth were lost. The same applied to heaven, the abode of God. An infinite universe was by definition a closed one, in the sense that there could be no spatial heaven above or beyond it. The cosmos appeared to have been bereft of God. In fact, it was being despiritualized altogether. A clockwork universe did not need angels to keep the planets in their courses, and a materialistic universe could not accommodate ghosts and spirits. And so the modern period witnessed, to borrow sociologist Max Weber's expression, the world's "disenchantment."

In a period when so many certainties were already under attack, the classical past provided Europeans with a philosophical justification of skepticism. Among the ancient manuscripts that Renaissance humanists had brought to light was a compendium of the teachings of the Pyrrhonists, a Hellenistic school of skeptics who taught that neither the senses, nor reason, nor anything else could lead to indubitable knowledge. In the uncertain climate of the sixteenth and seventeenth centuries these teachings were taken seriously and they spread rapidly, threatening both the Christian faith and scientific progress.

I think, therefore I am

It was in this situation that René Descartes (1596-1650) began his career. A mathematician and one of the chief architects of the clockwork universe, Descartes developed his philosophy in large part in response to the rising tide of skepticism. Like others among his contemporaries, he was looking for a new method of inquiry, one that would replace the outdated system of the medieval scholastics. The new method was to guarantee the advancement of science by establishing a sure and certain foundation for knowledge, one that would prove the skeptics wrong. And it was not to be concerned with the progress of science only. Descartes would also use it to combat the cultural uncertainties of his time, and, not in the last place, to fight the evils of philosophical materialism and atheism. His method would demonstrate the independence of the human mind and the existence of God.

Descartes outlined his methodology in a number of writings, among which the *Discourse on Method* of 1637 and the *Meditations* of 1641 are the best known. In his search for certainty he followed the skeptics' own approach. That is, he began by doubting away everything he had ever learned, read, or experienced. To doubt what he had been taught and read was not difficult. As often as not, authorities disagreed with each other, and one might therefore as well begin, Descartes reasoned, by considering them all to have been wrong. But sense experience, he knew, was deceptive as well. We see, for example, stars like pinpoints, but know that in reality they are of a very large size. We also see the sun rise and move and set, even though modern science tells us that it is stationary relative to the earth. And we can be grievously deceived even by our body: people who have had a leg amputated continue to have sensations "in" the missing limb.

In view of the unreliability of sense experience, Descartes decided to doubt the reality of the entire world of the senses, including his own body. Visible nature could, for all he knew, be nothing but a dream. But having doubted everything away, he concluded that one thing could not be doubted, namely the mind that did the doubting. And so Descartes came to the first and founding principle of his method. It was the famous *cogito ergo sum:* I think, therefore I am. The implication was, Descartes said, that man's essence was his being a "thinking thing," rather than a unity of mind and body. And it was human reason, properly employed, that constituted the road to certainty.

Having demonstrated the existence of the human mind, Descartes established the general rule that "all things which we clearly and distinctly conceive are true." Such truths were innate, which meant that they were not the fruit of experience. Human beings were born with them; ultimately they were implanted by God. This applied to the *cogito* principle, which was to be accepted as an axiom, a clear and distinct idea. It was, he insisted, of the nature of an unshakable conviction, an intuitive, self-evident truth, similar to such mathematical verities as that two plus two equal four. Its truth was so firm and assured, Descartes said, "that all the most extravagant suppositions of the skeptics were unable to shake it" (*Discourse*, Part IV). And from this indubitable principle, by careful logical reasoning, he deduced further truths.

Descartes had the mind of a mathematician, and his method was deductive-mathematical. Just as in mathematics one reasons from clear and distinct ideas to further truths, so it was to be done in other matters, including science, philosophy, and theology. He could say this because in his view all knowledge and all the sciences were ultimately one, reflecting, as they did, one reality. This being so, he believed that one method could be applied to all types of knowledge, and for Descartes the mathematical method was superior to all others. As long as one began with first principles or self-evident ideas as foundational truths and applied careful logical reasoning, one would reach demonstrative, universally valid truth. And again, the foundation stone, the first principle in the search for all further truths, was the *cogito* argument.

I think, therefore God is

Having laid the foundation of his theory of knowledge, Descartes proceeded with his theistic proofs. They were necessary as the ultimate safeguard of his method. For the possibility had to be considered, he believed, that an evil demon deceived man, so that what appeared self-evident might in fact be false.[1] The only means of removing that threat was to prove the existence of a benevolent God who would guarantee the trustworthiness of the conclusions drawn by human reason. Descartes realized, of course, that men will make mistakes because of impatience and careless reasoning, but he wanted assurances that those who followed the proper method and did not deal with matters beyond human judgment could reach certain, objectively valid truth. This implied – a point that was equally important – that they would also be able to recognize untruth.

To prove the existence of God, then, was Descartes' next task. He used a number of proofs, the most important of which was a version of the ontological argument which the medieval scholastic Anselm had made famous, and which Descartes combined with a causal one. To put it briefly, he reasoned (in the ontological argument) that he had the idea of an absolutely perfect being, one whose perfection implied its necessary existence. Obviously, the idea of such a being could not be the product of the senses, for no such being had ever been encountered, and neither could it be conceived by the unaided human imagination. It must therefore be innate, implanted by God, and hence beyond all doubt. From this clear and distinct idea further truths were deduced about God's attributes.[2]

Descartes probably did not introduce the proofs of God's existence simply for philosophical reasons. He considered himself a faithful Roman Catholic, who wanted to provide rational confirmation of revealed doctrine in order to persuade doubters, skeptics, and atheists of the truth of Christianity. At least, this is what he wrote in his letter to the Faculty of Theology of Paris, with which he prefaced his *Meditations*, and there seems to be no reason to question his sincerity. Nevertheless, the God of Cartesianism was little more than the guarantor of Descartes' method and epistemology, certifying the validity and trustworthiness of the *cogito* principle. He provided the proofs which reason could not provide on its own, and he solved the problems which, if he could not be proven to exist, would remain without a definitive solution.

Descartes and his times

Descartes' epistemology constituted a decisive break with that of the Middle Ages. Whereas the preceding epoch had recognized the positive and indeed essential role of community, tradition, and authority in the pursuit of knowledge, Descartes rejected these sources. In his theory it was the solitary and fully autonomous thinker, armed with what was considered an infallible method, who became the arbiter of all truth claims. That theory would be widely followed throughout the modern period. Indeed, Descartes became the philosopher and epistemologist *par excellence* of modernism. He is therefore also one of the main targets of attack in the postmodern age.

To explain the nature of Descartes' influence, it is good to begin by looking once more at the times in which he lived. The seventeenth century has been called "The Century of Genius," and rightly so. It was a period of brilliant achievements in many areas: in science and philosophy, in literature and the arts, in economics and in overseas exploration. But it was at the same time a deeply troubled age. We already noted the danger posed by the spread of skepticism. When in dealing with that threat Descartes showed the need for a rigorously logical, mathematical approach to science, he did much to set the scientific enterprise on a firm footing and so helped ensure its brilliant achievements both in his own age and in subsequent centuries.

Intellectual skepticism was only one of the problems Descartes and his contemporaries had to cope with. The period also experienced socio-political and economic dislocations. Politically, the European situation remained, at least until the middle of the century and in many areas well beyond that, unstable. Much of Germany was devastated by the disastrous Thirty Years War (1618-48), in which at one time or another most European states participated. France struggled with religious divisions. England suffered first the upheavals of a civil war and then the unrest caused by a number of constitutional revolutions. In addition to the array of political problems, there were severe economic depressions which affected most of western Europe. Poverty and unemployment joined with all the other factors – with wars and political upheavals, with often severe religious persecution, and with the general feeling that the times were out of joint – to exacerbate the radical sectarianism and the accompanying social unrest to which we referred in the two previous chapters.[3]

In short, the period desperately needed certainty and stability, and Descartes' epistemology promised to fulfil these needs. Believing in the power of human reason and the uniformity of human nature, Descartes taught that all thinkers, as long as they built on the proper foundation and followed the proper method, could and indeed would reach the same conclusions. This would serve not only as an antidote to skepticism. The approach would also advance the quest for religious peace, and that, in turn, would help ensure political and social stability. If everybody dealt with theological matters according to the Cartesian method, then everybody would draw the same theological conclusions. Religious divisions and rivalries, which were such an important cause of war and civil unrest, could so be eliminated.

Order would also be enhanced by the new cosmology, to the establishment of which Descartes devoted much effort. As we noted in the previous chapter, one reason for the choice of the mechanistic model of the universe was to fight the Neoplatonic type of pantheism that had been feeding the flames of sectarian unrest. The new model had additional socio-political functions. It was used, for example, as a symbol of what was held to be the "natural" kind of government. In the turbulent seventeenth century the natural system was, for many politicians, royal absolutism. These people reasoned that just as the sun, in splendid isolation, ruled the solar system, so the king, and he alone, was to rule the terrestial estate. It is revealing that the most famous of the century's absolute rulers, Louis XIV of France, chose to be known as *le roi soleil,* "the sun king." Other rulers, from England in the West to Russia in the East, tried to follow Louis' example of royal absolutism. Ecclesiastical hierarchies also liked to refer to the cosmic model as the example society had to follow. This happened, for example, in England, where sectarian egalitarianism threatened the ecclesiastical as well as the political order.

Dualism and the progress of science

Descartes' promise to solve the intellectual and socio-political problems of his times is one reason for the popularity of his philosophy. Another is that the dualistic method he promoted contributed to the success of the scientific enterprise. Because of the important role his dualism has played and continues to play in our culture, we will give some attention to its nature and implications.

Cartesian dualism sets the mind over against the physical world. For Descartes this was a means to counter the threat, which he and his contemporaries justly recognized as a real one, of a materialistic worldview. Wanting to establish the primacy and independence of the mind, he drew a distinction between the intellect and whatever else makes up the human being. The mind ruled. It was the only source of knowledge. The senses, the imagination, and the emotions were unreliable and of little use to the philosopher and scientist. Man's essence was that he was a thinking being, rather than a being that felt, believed, and imagined.

In addition to the mind there was matter, which comprised the natural world: inorganic nature, plants, animals, as well as the human body. The mind was fully separate from that world. It alone was truly alive; physical reality for Descartes was nothing but matter in motion. This applied even to organic nature. The human body and all other living beings were essentially machines which, like the cosmos itself, functioned mechanically, in obedience to natural laws. Descartes in fact believed that animals had no consciousness and were unable to feel pain. They might give the impression they did and even cry out, but that was little more than a mechanical reaction. There was no true apprehension and therefore no real bodily and emotional suffering.

Descartes further adopted the distinction between what later would be called primary and secondary qualities. Primary qualities were the aspects of nature that were capable of being weighed, numbered, and measured, and that therefore lent themselves to investigation in the empirico-mathematical manner. Secondary qualities, which included sensations like smell, colour, and taste, were not quantifiable. They were held to have only subjective existence. Without measurable qualities such as extension and motion they were incapable of being the object of scientific study and therefore of no value to natural scientists.

Descartes' approach was not the most appropriate one for the life and human sciences, and the attempt to follow it in these areas would be among the causes of the Romantic and postmodern reactions against a mechanistic science. But it did benefit the study of physical nature, the material world of matter and motion, and in the early-modern period this was science's main concern. Early-modern science meant, with only a few exceptions, physics and astronomy, two disciplines concerned with phenomena which could be investigated in a largely impersonal manner, the approach that the dualistic view of the world encouraged.[4]

Cartesian rationalism

Descartes was a rationalist. While not denying the importance of observation and of an empirical verification of scientific theories, he disagreed with the empiricists that all knowledge ultimately depends on sense experience. Convinced that the human mind possesses innate dispositions and ideas, he believed that we can reach truth apart from observation.

Descartes' denial of the all-sufficiency of empiricism was to the point. A single-minded reliance on the senses leads to the positivist belief that whatever cannot be observed does not deserve the label of knowledge and truth. This means the negation of religious truth and it also places in doubt the validity of historical knowledge and the existence of universal moral norms, and indeed of all things whose truth cannot be established in an empirical manner. Positivistic empiricism denies the reality of what is invisible, is by definition materialistic, and therefore necessarily hostile to Christianity.

A positive aspect of rationalism is that, unlike empiricism, it does extend the field of the knowable to that which cannot be seen and touched. It also allows for the existence of a universal, overarching truth to which the human mind has access. In that sense the rationalism which Descartes promoted has affinities with a Christian view of knowledge. There are, however, also important differences. The most important one is Descartes' denial that faith in God as the source of all truth was to play a role in science. Indeed, he removed religious faith from scientific thinking, convinced that it would interfere with the acquisition of truly objective knowledge. Here we come to the central weakness of Descartes' epistemology. Having with his theistic arguments attempted to provide his theory with a metaphysical basis, he in practice removed that basis. As a result, and in spite of the important contributions he made to the success of early-modern science, he was unable to solve the problem that had inspired his philosophy in the first place, namely that of the rising tide of philosophical and religious skepticism.

Cartesianism and skepticism

Some of his contemporaries were aware of this failure. Already in Descartes' own days objections were raised, for example, to his natural theology. A well-known case is that of Blaise Pascal, who rejected "the God of the philosophers," confessed his faith in "the God of Abraham, Isaac, and Jacob," and warned against making deductive reason the road to all truth. Not logic but faith led to knowledge of the personal God of the Scriptures. "The heart has its reasons," Pascal wrote, "of which reason knows nothing." Without faith there can be no religious certainty.

The validity of Descartes' *cogito* principle came under attack as well, as did his theory of innate ideas in general. The weakness of the *cogito* principle was that it had to carry more weight than it is capable of carrying, since it cannot be shown to be a necessary truth. According to his empiricist opponents, the theory Descartes built on it was also contrary to experience. Among those who raised that objection was Descartes' contemporary Pierre Gassendi, a leading empiricist. Gassendi pointed out that people may consider their ideas to be clear, distinct, and indubitable, and may be willing even to die for them, when in fact these ideas are false. In case of opposing beliefs, who was to decide which one was correct and which one not? Gassendi had similar objections to Descartes' ontological proof of God's existence. If God had indeed impressed the idea of himself upon man's mind, he argued, then all people capable of logical thought would believe in the same God as Descartes, which was evidently not the case.[5]

In defence of Descartes it can be argued that the human mind, even if it does not possess innate ideas of God, at least has dispositions that guide it toward an acknowledgement of the supernatural. The Bible teaches this, for example in Romans 1. John Calvin, who was certainly no rationalist, even spoke of a "sense of divinity" and of a "seed of religion" that had been implanted in the human mind. But Calvin also taught that neither reason nor natural revelation can lead to a saving knowledge of God. That knowledge is contained in Scripture alone, and its certainty can be had in no other way than by the witness of the Spirit.[6]

Instead of acknowledging man's need for divine revelation and the testimony of the Spirit in the human heart, Descartes tried to build religious certainty on the fallible foundation of human reasoning. Gassendi was right in attacking that position.

The skeptical implications of Cartesianism in both the religious and the philosophical sense were exacerbated by Descartes' guiding principle that tradition and authority are suspect and that doubt is the beginning of all wisdom. To criticize this approach is not to imply that his critical methodology lacked positive elements. There were good reasons to stress the need for objectivity and a critical attitude in the pursuit of knowledge. Far too long thinkers had considered Aristotle, Ptolemy, and other ancient authorities to be the end of all wisdom. Unless that attitude changed and thinkers began to rely on their own insights and observations, few advances in knowledge could be made. The problem with Descartes' method was its propagation of *universal* doubt. Scientific and other intellectual pursuits require a critical attitude but (as the early Christians already knew, and as twentieth-century critics of Cartesianism have once again shown) they also require faith and reliance on authority.

It was in the religious area and in the related field of Christian ethics that Descartes' epistemology has had some of the most disastrous effects. It is true that he tried to prevent religious uncertainty by insisting that he did not apply the method of systematic doubt to revelation. Religious truths were a matter of authority and were to be received by faith. But as a commentator remarks, skepticism in one field easily spreads to another. Once systematic doubt was used as a method to achieve philosophical certainty, "the truths of faith could not be permanently insulated from the quest for compelling demonstrations.... What an earlier age had readily accepted as truths above reason...might well appear contrary to reason in an age of systematic doubt."[7]

And so they did appear to a subsequent age. The deity of Cartesianism succumbed to the attacks of Enlightenment skeptics. Gassendi's objection to Descartes' ontological argument was shared by many, and the belief that a mechanistic universe is capable of managing without a supernatural engineer and designer would, in time, demolish causal proofs of God's existence as well. Meanwhile Descartes' rejection of tradition and authority and his advocacy of universal doubt could be and indeed were applied in the fight against revealed religion. What remained, after Descartes' natural theology had been rejected, were the Cartesian habit of disqualifying the claims to truth of whatever surpasses human understanding and the belief that the only way to reach knowledge is to begin with systematic doubt. Instead of containing the tide, Descartes' method opened the floodgates to religious skepticism.

Religion was not the only victim. Descartes' dualism – that is, the gap he created between the mind and the outside world – left open the question how the mind could truly know that world. Any guarantee that mental representations of external objects corresponded to these objects themselves was lacking, which meant that the world could be altogether different from the picture held by the mind. This uncertainty about external reality Descartes bequeathed to his philosophical successors, rationalists as well as empiricists.

And finally, he placed in jeopardy the human mind, whose independent status he had tried so hard to safeguard. The fact that the scientific method was successful in its own area ensured that it would be applied, as Descartes had intended, to other disciplines, including the humanities and social sciences. This implied a naturalistic and mechanistic approach to human studies. In practice it meant that the human mind, like the human body and the rest of nature, was reduced to a machine, capable of being understood and manipulated by recourse to "scientific laws" that were modelled on those of the physical sciences. The mind came to be viewed as part of the world of nature, and consciousness, intellect, thought, and sensations as products of physical and chemical processes.

Instead of being separate from and exalted above nature, as Descartes had intended it to be, the mind was swallowed up by nature. In this sense Cartesianism anticipated the conclusions of Darwinism.

NOTES

[1] According to Amos Funkenstein, *Theology and the Scientific Imagination from the Middle Ages to the Seventeenth Century* (Princeton, N. J.: Princeton University Press, 1986), pp. 122f., among the sources of this idea is Descartes' radical voluntarism. (On this tradition, see ch. 4 above.)

[2] For Descartes' proofs of God's existence, see his *Discourse on Method*, IV, and *Meditations*, III and V.

[3] A good account of the relationship between Descartes' philosophy and the times in which he lived is given in Stephen Toulmin, *Cosmopolis: The Hidden Agenda of Modernity* (Chicago: University of Chicago Press, 1992 [1990]); and in the same author's *The Return to Cosmology: Postmodern Science and the Theology of Nature* (Berkeley: University of California Press, 1982), Part Three.

4. Toulmin, *Return to Cosmology*, pp. 240, 247.

5. *The Philosophical Works of Descartes*, trans. Elizabeth S. Haldane and G.R.T. Ross (Cambridge: Cambridge University Press, 1967 [1911]), II, 152, 174.

6. John Calvin, *Institutes of the Christian Religion*, I, iii; iv,1; vii,5; viii, 1.

7 Richard S. Westfall, "The Rise of Science and the Decline of Orthodox Christianity: A Study of Kepler, Descartes, and Newton," in *God and Nature*, eds. Lindberg and Numbers, p. 226. Westfall deals here with the objections which the Jesuit Fr. Bourdin, a contemporary of Descartes, raised against the latter's method of systematic doubt.

VIII. John Locke on Human Understanding

Descartes was the founder of modern philosophy and his work defined many of the problems that would occupy his successors. Among these was the Englishman John Locke (1632-1704). For Locke as for Descartes, skepticism was an important philosophical issue. He spent much time wrestling with the problem, and in the process of doing so developed theories of knowledge and of the mind that proved as influential and lasting as Descartes'. In this chapter we give attention to Locke's theory of knowledge. His ideas on psychology and political theory – additional areas in which he helped set the stage for modern developments – will be dealt with in the next chapter.

Although there are rationalistic elements in his philosophy, Locke was, like practically all thinkers from the British isles, an empiricist. This means that he rejected Descartes' theory of innate ideas and subscribed to Aristotle's doctrine that "nothing is in the understanding that was not first in the senses." All knowledge depended on experience: on external experience (the evidence of the senses) and internal experience (the mind's reflection on that evidence). The mind by itself was not a source of knowledge. Deprived of innate ideas of any kind, it was at birth nothing but a blank sheet, a *tabula rasa*, waiting to be filled with the knowledge that only the sense impressions and the mind's reflection on those impressions would provide.

Locke worked on his theories of knowledge and of the mind for close to two decades. In 1690 he published the conclusions he had reached in his *Essay Concerning Human Understanding*. In this work he made clear his opposition to rationalists, objecting to both their method and to what he implied was their intellectual pride and ambition. In distinction to such speculative thinkers he revealed himself as the common-sense Englishman who would stay away from matters too deep and wonderful for human understanding. Doubt and skepticism arise, he explained, when we try to go beyond the capacities of our mind. Humility is required: we have to accept the limitations placed on our understanding and not demand knowledge where only probability has been given. If we insist on reaching indubitable knowledge, we will necessarily be disabused and may well end up as someone "who would not use his legs but sit still and perish, because he had not wings to fly." That is, we run the risk of disclaiming *all* knowledge, simply because *some* things cannot be understood.[1]

Locke's philosophy was to be a practical one, with limited, but definite goals. His famous analogy of the sailor's line expressed his intentions well. "It is of great use to the sailor," he wrote, "to know the length of his line, though he cannot with it fathom all the depths of the ocean. It is well he knows that it is long enough to reach the bottom at such places as are necessary to direct his voyage, and caution him against running upon shoals that may ruin him. Our business here is not to know all things, but those which concern our conduct. If we can find out those measures whereby a rational creature ... may and ought to govern his opinions and actions, ... we need not to be troubled that some other things escape our knowledge."[2]

Abstract theorizing, in other words, was out. The proper objects of mankind's study were man and nature, not supernature. It was a restricted but also a necessary and even a promising, pursuit, and Locke warned his readers that the limitations of their minds should not keep them from their tasks. "It will be no excuse to an idle and untoward servant," he wrote, "who would not attend his business by candlelight, to plead that he had not broad sunshine. The Candle that is set up in us shines bright enough for all our purposes."[3] Those purposes included, besides the study of nature, the pursuit of the good and virtuous life. Indeed, Locke insisted that knowledge was not to be a person's main aim: the health of the body and the destination of the soul were more important, and morality was man's proper business.

The appeal of Locke's philosophy

Locke's philosophical modesty did nothing to diminish his popularity. His influence was very great, both in England and on the continent. Even in France it surpassed that of France's native son, René Descartes. Descartes, it is true, was never fully eclipsed. There was a grandeur to Cartesianism that continued to appeal to moderns, and especially to Frenchmen. Descartes still philosophized in the grand metaphysical manner. Unlike Locke's sailor, he believed that man was capable of understanding the mysteries of the cosmos; that his intellect could scale the heavens and plumb the oceanic depths. In principle, nothing was hidden from his understanding. In that sense he can be compared to the great Greek philosophers and to medieval scholastics like Thomas Aquinas. Of course, Descartes was a man of his times. He neither denied nor scorned the practical benefits of science and showed an interest in technology. Understanding, however, received more emphasis than utilitarian outcomes.

The British empiricist school to which Locke belonged stressed these utilitarian outcomes. It had done so from the start. Francis Bacon, the theorist of early British empiricism, had had little good to say of the rationalist type of theory that the mind could achieve worthwhile knowledge simply by attending to its own cogitations. That amounted to building systems which might appear impressive but had little substance and even less utility. If man wanted to achieve knowledge of the outside world, Bacon said, he would have to rely on evidence from that world, that is, on sense experience. Knowledge acquired in that manner would have practical value.

Bacon showed his pragmatic bent in the aphorism that knowledge (and he meant scientific knowledge) is power, in that it provides man with the means to control nature. As we saw in previous chapters, the relation between science and magic was still close in the seventeenth century, and for Bacon science had much the same function that the occult had for Renaissance magicians: it had to serve mankind's well-being. According to Bacon the twin goals of science were the glory of God and "the relief of man's estate" (that is, the improvement of humanity's temporal life); and the second aim was no less important than the first.

The eighteenth century sympathized with the empiricists' goals. It wanted a practical approach to knowledge. Philosophy and science had to concentrate on a method that gave tangible results, and the fact that Locke promised these results goes a long way in explaining his great popularity. His psychology and political theory, as we will see in the next chapter, provided what appeared to be infallible blueprints for the overhaul and improvement of society. His general theory of knowledge with its focus on realizable goals promised to have equally great potential in the study of nature.

That potential was obvious for all who had eyes to see, for Locke's method had been vindicated by the mathematical empiricism of Newton and his fellow-scientists. The message Locke's empiricism brought to the eighteenth century was that trying to comprehend the infinite is a vain endeavour, but that by concentrating on the finite, mankind will be able to push back, little by little but inexorably, the limits of both its understanding and its power. There was no need to reach the depths of the oceans, and neither was it necessary to climb up to the heavens. Following the approach outlined by Locke, science would ensure that the equivalent of a heavenly city could be built on planet earth.

Empiricism and skepticism

Empiricism was popular because it worked, not because it solved the problem we have been concerned with, that of doubt. In his *Essay* Locke dealt with that issue, but rather than solving it, his theory of knowledge, like that of Descartes, strengthened the tendencies toward skepticism.

Locke was a realist in the sense that he believed in the reality and independent existence of the external world. He also believed in the ability of the mind to have knowledge of that world, but he warned his readers that such knowledge was limited. This was so, first of all, because we can be aware of only a small part of the objects around us. Moreover, our observations are frequently inaccurate and our sense perceptions relative: colours may change depending on the light, and water that is felt as cold by one hand may seem warm to the other.[4] Locke knew that the distortions we experience are a result of the way we observe and are not part of the objects themselves. Objects are not mind-dependent. But the fact remains that the deceptiveness of our senses makes it difficult for us to have true knowledge of these objects.

The problem was compounded by the fact that, for Locke as for Descartes, whatever contact the mind had with the outside world was indirect. The senses, in Locke's theory, produced "ideas" and impressed these upon the mind. The mind interpreted them, but because it was not able to bypass the senses and look "beyond" them, it had no way of knowing whether the ideas were true representations of outside objects. For all the mind knew, the world could be quite different from the picture the senses conveyed.

Locke provided further openings for skepticism by stating that we have sensory knowledge only of actually present objects. He did not believe that memory was unimportant in any theory of knowledge, but he did insist that, since we can't be absolutely sure that what we perceive today will exist tomorrow, we can only speak of belief or opinion here, not of knowledge proper.[5] A few chapters earlier he had already declared that "we cannot with certainty affirm: that all men sleep by intervals; that no man can be nourished by wood or stones; that all men will be poisoned by hemlock...." In some of these matters, he explained, we must appeal to trial, and in others we must be content with probability rather than achieving certainty.[6] Clearly, the realm of the empirically knowable was severely reduced. Steps were set on the road to the explicit skepticism which one of Locke's empiricist successors, the Scot David Hume, would proclaim in the next century.

Hume was a natural skeptic. Locke was not. It is true that he refused to believe in the possibility of achieving indubitable knowledge in all areas, and that he was not nearly as afraid of uncertainty as Descartes had been. But while admitting that uncertainty was inevitable – and its acknowledgement salutary – he also wanted to set limits to it. He was particularly careful to safeguard the scientific enterprise. Realizing the skeptical implications of his theory of knowledge, Locke went to considerable lengths to ensure that the mind could know the objects science concerned itself with. He followed Galileo and Descartes in distinguishing between an object's primary qualities (weight, shape, motion, and number) and its secondary ones (such as colour, taste, scent, and sound). Our ideas of secondary qualities, he said, were not resemblances of objects, but mere sensations, and therefore perceiver-dependent. Primary qualities, however, existed objectively in things and so did reveal the outside world.[7] Science, therefore, was able to go on with its work. In science, if nowhere else, objective knowledge could be found. In most other areas mankind had to make do with belief or opinion.

Locke tried hard to substantiate his conclusion about the certainty of scientific knowledge. It did not necessarily follow from his premises, however, and would come under attack by critical successors. He would have done better, one cannot help thinking, to dispense with his representative theory of knowledge and return to the ancient-creationist doctrine, which states that the world is real because God created it, and that we can have reliable (even if not exhaustive) knowledge of the world because God made man capable of understanding the world's structures.

Locke could also have adopted a less restrictive definition of empirical knowledge. On this point the contemporary philosopher Leibniz, a rationalist, criticized Locke the empiricist. In his *New Essays on Human Understanding*, Leibniz wrote that the terms "knowledge" and "certainty" can be extended beyond actual sensations. He added: "...It would certainly be insane to doubt in earnest that there are men in the world when we do not see any. To 'doubt in earnest' is to doubt in a practical way...." On this definition of certainty, Leibniz said, evidence from history can be adequate. We can be sure, for example, that Alexander the Great, Julius Caesar, and Constantine once lived, for we have trustworthy testimony about them. And the same thing applies, Leibniz added, to all matters that one cannot doubt without madness.[8] The fact that we do not have demonstrative proofs in such cases does not mean that we cannot have moral certainty of their truth.

Locke's tightrope

Locke probably realized this. The problem is that he was walking a tightrope. He wanted to ensure the progress of science and to defeat a Pyrrhonist type of skepticism, but he also wanted to convey his belief that human understanding is limited. His call for intellectual humility was not simply a justifiable reaction to the grandiose claims of rationalism; it was also inspired by the times in which he lived. Indeed, Locke's ideas cannot be understood unless attention is paid to the character of those times. As has been noted before, the seventeenth century had been, especially for England, an age of uncertainty and turmoil. The country had experienced a civil war, which had culminated in the execution of an anointed king and led to a short-lived republican experiment. It had also been the scene of fierce religious persecution and a disturbing multiplication of extreme religious sects, including such well-known groups as Levellers, Diggers, Fifth Monarchy Men, Ranters, and Seekers. Moreover, in 1688, just before the publication of the *Essay*, Parliament had deposed yet another anointed king, the Stuart James II, a Roman Catholic and a friend of Louis XIV of France. This event, the so-called Glorious Revolution, culminated in Parliament's replacement of James with his daughter Mary and her Dutch-Calvinist husband William III, Louis' sworn enemy.

Locke approved of Parliament's action but was anxious to prevent a repetition of the turmoil that had preceded it. Convinced that the problem was ultimately the result of faulty belief systems, he made it the goal of his *Essay* to determine the manner in which people acquire their beliefs. This was not meant to be a mere theoretical exercise. Locke was a utilitarian, interested in social reform. Ways and means had to be found to ensure that people rejected socially destructive beliefs and accepted socially beneficial ones.

He considered religious fanaticism, which had manifested itself in persecution and caused war, revolution, and sectarian unrest, one of society's greatest enemies. This conviction helps explain his insistence that few of our beliefs are absolutely certain. In the majority of cases we have probabilities only, and that, Locke kept repeating, is all we really need, in religious and in most other matters. Such probable knowledge, which he called belief or opinion rather than knowledge proper, gave varying degrees of assurance, depending on the reliability of the source. Locke established strict criteria to determine degrees of reliability,[9] for he wanted the fight against skepticism to continue. But he also insisted on the right to speak of religious and other non-scientific knowledge as mere belief or opinion, and that desire was in large part inspired by the perceived need to battle dogmatism. To deny the label of knowledge to religious belief would weaken the case of sectarian enthusiasts, who were convinced that what they stood for was indubitable truth. It would also discredit the policy of religious uniformitarianism. If religious belief was only belief, rather than certain knowledge, a policy of religious toleration was the only logical one.

Revelation and reason

If Descartes' philosophy had left room not just for philosophical doubt but also for religious skepticism, so did that of Locke. Decisive was his pronouncement that whereas science yields true knowledge, religion yields only opinion.

It is true that, more so than Descartes, Locke made a point of stating his faith in divine revelation. He did this both in his *Essay* and in a number of subsequent works, of which the *Reasonableness of Christianity* (1695) became the best known. His attitude toward revelation was ambivalent, however, and his religious argumentation inconsistent. On the one hand he admitted that man could not know God without the help of revelation. Human reason, finite and feeble, was unable to comprehend the infinite God. Furthermore, although the message of Scripture surpassed human reason, this was no argument against its truth. On the contrary: faith, Locke wrote, "as perfectly excludes all wavering as our knowledge itself; and we may as well doubt of our own being, as we can whether any revelation from God be true."[10] Faith in revelation was the more certain because of the high ethical norms the Bible taught, and because its truth was attested by miracles and by the testimony of reliable witnesses. In short, faith in revelation was built on a proper foundation and capable of meeting evidential challenges. If the stringent canons of probability which he himself had established were applied to the biblical sources one could be fully assured, Locke said, that the Bible was divine revelation.

In the end, however, he could not leave well enough alone. Having personally experienced the social unrest caused by radical religious sects, he was mortally afraid of what he and his contemporaries called religious "enthusiasm." He therefore made a point of stating that revelation could not be contrary to reason. Faith in revelation leaves no room for doubt, he wrote, but he immediately added, "Only we must be sure that it be a divine revelation ...."[11] And that was a matter for reason to decide. In another place, also when speaking of revelation, he delivered what has been called the motto of the *Essay*: "Reason must be our last judge and guide in everything."[12] It is true that this maxim must not be divorced from its context. In coining it, Locke opposed both "the manipulatory use of the Bible by authoritarian Anglican bishops and the deceptive and often manipulatory claims of 'enthusiasts' to know God's will privately."[13] The statement nevertheless implied that it was up to the individual to decide whether or not a certain part of revelation was to be accepted as reasonable. But as Locke well knew, reason was an untrustworthy yardstick; after all, as he kept reminding his readers, it is feeble and often fails us.

Reason nevertheless had to ensure that whatever appeared unreasonable in the Christian religion was eliminated. Christianity could survive only if it was rational, and for Locke this implied, for example, that the Trinity and the divinity of Christ had to be denied. Although he wanted to come across as an orthodox Christian, Locke relativized the importance of doctrine and so became a spiritual ancestor of the English deists. Locke himself was not a deist. He reserved a place for revelation in his interpretation of the Christian faith and in his search for moral norms and he accepted the possibility of miracles. At the same time he regarded matters of doctrine of secondary importance and tended to reduce religion to ethics.

Locke's proofs and method

Meanwhile Locke's empirical supports for the faith – the moral excellence of Christianity, the reliability of biblical witnesses, and the accounts of miracles – proved to be less substantial than he had believed. Books on travels in non-European lands, containing highly embellished accounts of non-Christian civilizations like those of China and Persia, threw doubt on the moral superiority of Christianity, and in the eighteenth century David Hume, following the example of various deists, would do his utmost to show the "unreasonableness" of believing in the biblical witnesses and the biblical accounts of miracles.

Indeed, Locke's entire natural theology came under attack. Like most other philosophers of his period he developed theistic proofs. Although rejecting Descartes' idea that we have an innate idea of God, he nevertheless believed that the evidence we have of God's existence is equal to mathematical certainty.[14] His proofs were a mixture of empirical arguments and intuitive ones. He argued, for example, that since we exist, and since nothing cannot produce anything, there must be an eternal being, one who has the power of cognition (since he is the cause of cognitive beings such as man). This type of argument had been used before, but by Locke's time the persuasiveness of theistic proofs was beginning to be questioned, and in the course of the next century philosophers like Hume and Kant would deny these proofs all validity.

It was not just through the contents of his work that Locke contributed to the rise of both religious and intellectual skepticism. The fact that he made science the only road to true knowledge had a similar effect; for science, and especially empirical science, does not admit any certainty to the knowledge of things that are beyond observation. Nor does it allow for the concept of final truth in its own realm. Science advances by the discovery of new and always changing knowledge. This necessarily tentative nature of scientific conclusions was applied also to non-scientific knowledge, encouraging the belief that all truth is impermanent.[15]

For these reasons Locke's empiricism was no more successful in the battle against Pyrrhonism than Cartesian rationalism had been. This is not to say that his stress on the limitations of reason was not to the point. It was. But by declaring the scientific method to be the only reliable guide to truth, Locke effectively eliminated the possibility of reaching both religious and philosophical certainty. The psychological effect of his approach was "to nurture a skeptical frame of mind, which took little on trust, which was on the whole quite nominalistic, and which demanded facts or sensible evidence for the objects of investigation."[16] That frame of mind has typified the modern age from the eighteenth century onward.

NOTES

1. John Locke, *An Essay Concerning Human Understanding*, ed. Alexander Campbell Fraser (New York: Dover, 1959 [1894]), I, Introduction, 4-6.

2. *Ibid.*, Introduction, 6. Spelling and punctuation in quotations from the *Essay* have been modernized.

3. *Ibid.*, Introduction, 5.

4. *Ibid.*, II, viii, 19-21.

5. *Ibid.*, IV, xi, 9, 11.

6. *Ibid.*, IV, vi, 15.

7. *Ibid.*, II, viii, 15ff.

8. G. W. Leibniz, *New Essays on Human Understanding*, trans. and eds. Peter Remnant and Jonathan Bennett (Cambridge: Cambridge University Press, 1982 [1981]), pp. 444f.

9. Locke spoke in this connection of two "grounds of probability." The first one was conformity with what we ourselves have already observed or experienced; the other depended on the testimony of others. In the case of the latter attention had to be given to the following factors: the number of witnesses, their integrity and skill, the design of the author (when the testimony came from a book), the consistency of the parts and the circumstances of the relation, and contrary testimony. The degree of assent to be given to propositions and beliefs depended on the weight of evidence awarded them according to these criteria. *Essay*, IV, xv, 4, 5. See also James Tully, *An Approach to Political Philosophy: Locke in Contexts* (Cambridge: Cambridge University Press, 1993), pp. 193-96.

10. Locke, *Essay*, IV, xvi, 14.

11. *Ibid.*, IV, xvi, 14; xviii, 10.

12. *Ibid.*, IV, xix, 14.

13. Anthony C. Thiselton, *Interpreting God and the Postmodern Self: On Meaning, Manipulation and Promise* (Grand Rapids: Eerdmans, 1995), p. 4.

14. Locke, *Essay*, IV, x, 1. See the same chapter for Locke's arguments for the existence of God.

15. For the skeptical implications of Locke's theory (and of empiricism in general), see Franklin L. Baumer, *Religion and the Rise of Scepticism* (New York: Harcourt, Brace, 1960), pp. 93-5.

16. *Ibid.*, pp. 94.

IX.   The French Enlightenment

The eighteenth century Enlightenment was not limited to any one country. Its ideas spread as far as Russia in the East and England's American colonies in the West. But Western Europe was its place of origin and France became its centre. It was also the country where the socially destructive implications of its teachings first revealed themselves: the French Revolution, including its radical phase, was inspired by Enlightenment principles. Because of its central position, we will, in this brief survey of the Enlightenment, focus on France.

The leaders of the French movement were the so-called Enlightenment philosophers. Among them were playwrights, poets, journalists, scientists, and members of still other professions. Very few were philosophers proper, and to distinguish these Enlightenment thinkers from the professional brand of philosophers, the French term *philosophe* is generally used for them. What united these men was the desire to bring about cultural enlightenment and political reform.

Much of the work aiming at cultural enlightenment was done via the *Encyclopédie*, a multi-volume work edited by Denis Diderot, to which several of the *philosophes* contributed. Much was also done by means of essays, histories, political treatises, and literary works. Aimed at the non-specialist and usually well written and witty, these works found a large reading public, especially among the members of the well-educated French middle class. The message was that, thanks to the new reliance on human reason and the advancement of science, a new age was beckoning, one whose perfections would surpass anything the world had witnessed before.

The message's utopianism, which surpassed that of the English empiricists, shows that the modern belief in progress was taking hold. Progress, it is true, was not yet believed to be automatic, nor was the belief in perfectibility universal. More than one *philosophe* clung to the idea that the historical process was perhaps cyclical after all, or even that the modern age was one of decadence and decline.[1] Nevertheless, the belief in the possibility of progress dominated, as did the conviction that every effort was to be expended to make it a reality. Among the prerequisites for its achievement was the extension of the rule of reason, specifically the establishment of a rational political and social environment. And that, the *philosophes* taught, required the defeat of the forces of tradition, superstition, and intolerance. Their goal was to bring about that defeat.

Concretely, they demanded the reform of an absolute and increasingly ineffective monarchy, the end of the privileged status of the nobility and clergy, and the political and social emancipation of the middle class, to which most of the reformers themselves belonged. England served them as an example. The Glorious Revolution had enhanced that country's political stability. The threat of royal absolutism had been ended for good and all, and the power of parliament had been increased at the king's expense. England had seen improvements in the religious situation as well. The Church of England continued to be the state church, but in 1690 the government of William III had passed an act which gave freedom of worship to practically all Protestant dissenters. Politically and socially England fared well under the new rules, and the French *philosophes* demanded the same types of political and religious reforms for their country.

Locke's psychology in Enlightenment France

It was not only the English political system that inspired the French reformers; they made use of English ideas as well. The *philosophes* preferred the English empiricists to the continental rationalists and spent much of their time popularizing the ideas of men like Bacon, Newton, and Locke. They gave special attention to those of Locke. His work on human understanding and the human mind was popular, and for good reasons. A basic element of his theory was that the mind at birth was a blank sheet or *tabula rasa*, which meant that it was altogether without innate ideas, and that all knowledge was a result of sense impressions alone. That idea had important implications. It could be interpreted as a denial of the biblical doctrine of original sin, and therefore as an affirmation of the belief in mankind's essential goodness. It also suggested that human beings were free from the burden of heredity, a conclusion that bolstered the Enlightenment belief in the equality of all men. Moreover, by implying that the world is new for every person entering it,[2] it encouraged the idea that what previous generations have built can be destroyed with impunity and replaced by something altogether different. Tradition and history could be ignored. The French revolutionaries would act upon this belief and symbolize it by their introduction of a new calendar which designated the year of the establishment of the revolutionary order as year one.

And not in the last place, the concept of *tabula rasa* provided opportunities for influencing people's mental, emotional, and moral development; and that, in turn, held promises for the unlimited amelioration of man and society. If the individual was nothing but the product of his environment, then all that was needed to bring about the golden age was to change that environment. This, of course, was theory. To assume that it could be translated into practice required a belief in unrelieved human determinism, and there were not many Enlightenment thinkers who were willing to go that far. Nevertheless, Locke's psychology did make people aware of the need to concentrate on transforming the environment. To achieve this was a task that the *philosophes* had set for the natural scientists and for themselves. The scientists were to improve the physical environment, which included the battle against disease, famine, and other cruelties of nature; the social reformers would concern themselves with the remaking of society.

The appeal of Locke's political theory

Locke's political theory captured the imagination of the French reformers as much as did his psychology. He had presented his political ideas in the *Two Treatises of Government*. Like his work on human understanding, these treatises were published in 1690, although much of their content had been written earlier. The publication took place shortly after the Glorious Revolution, and one of its aims was to legitimate that revolution and the rule of William III.

Locke was not the only one in his age to present a political theory. The seventeenth century with its political and social instability had inspired a number of theorists. But whereas many of them had been believers in absolute rule as the means to guarantee law and order, Locke proposed the opposite solution. He did so because of a growing conviction that the old system did not work. It played havoc with people's rights and led to religious intolerance, social unrest, and civil war. The time had come, Locke believed, to rethink the old questions about the origin and limitations of political power and about the mechanisms for the prevention of abuse.

In dealing with the origins of political power, Locke, like some of his predecessors, made use of the ancient myth of the social contract. According to this myth, government had originally been established by means of a contract between the people and their rulers. Before such a contract was drawn up, people lived in what was called the "state of nature," a primitive kind of existence that was evaluated differently by different authors. Thomas Hobbes, an earlier English theorist and the author of the famous political treatise *Leviathan* (1651), had lived through the turbulent period of England's civil war and concluded that strong government was the only guarantee of law and order. He had therefore portrayed the state of nature in altogether negative terms. According to him, existence in that state had been so precarious (primitive life, in his famous phrase, having been "solitary, poor, nasty, brutish, and short") that in return for security people had been willing to surrender all their rights to the civil authority. Hobbes' government was truly a Leviathan. Absolute in might, it was man's "mortal God," the only power on earth that could ensure peace and must therefore be unconditionally obeyed.

Locke's description of the state of nature was far less negative than Hobbes', but in his case also people ultimately began to feel the need for a civil authority, one that could enforce laws, protect the people's freedoms and property rights, and defend them against foreign aggression. The government the people subsequently established was a limited one. They transferred their political powers to the ruler, but only conditionally. The citizens were and remained free, equal, and self-governing, and the government's power was derived from them. Therefore, if the ruling authority broke the people's trust and without their consent alienated their property rights (a term that for Locke included their civil and religious freedoms), the people were allowed to resist, if necessary by force of arms, to protect their rights. The American revolutionaries of 1776, taught by Locke, did exactly that.

Locke disagreed with earlier theories that the right of resistance always belonged to the "lesser magistrates," such as parliament or the nobility, and never to the people as such. He rejected that solution because the lesser magistrates often were hand-in-glove with the ruler.

For that reason the right of resistance had to be an individual right (as well as a collective one). Locke agreed with the English Dissenters in their resistance to the uniformitarian religious policies of king and parliament. In 1685, while in exile in the Netherlands, he published *A Letter Concerning Toleration*. It was directed against the religious policies of both the English government and the French king, who in that same year had revoked the Edict of Nantes and intensified the persecution of the Huguenots.[3]

It is not surprising that Locke's theory with its doctrines of toleration, natural rights, popular sovereignty, and the right of rebellion appealed to the French reformers. In order to remake the human environment, political changes were essential; after all, most of the problems society faced could be traced to abuses in the political system. It is true that the *philosophes* were far from being revolutionaries. They were not interested in a violent political upheaval, and they were also little inclined to declare the sovereignty of the common people. What they wanted was the liberalization of society, not its overthrow, and they believed that their aim could be achieved in a non-violent manner.

But they did demand political influence for their own class, and to accomplish that goal they were anxious to promote Locke's political doctrines. These, as it turned out, were more prone to a truly revolutionary interpretation in France than they had been in England. In the 1760s the philosopher Jean-Jacques Rousseau would make use of them in working out a far more radical political theory than Locke's, one that would do much, a few decades hence, to inspire the French revolutionaries. We will turn to Rousseau's theory later in this chapter.

The attack on Christianity

The radicalization of English ideas was a common feature of the French Enlightenment. It happened also in the religious area. This can best be illustrated by the case of Voltaire, who was the most influential of the *philosophes* and also one of the most persistent in the attack on Christianity.

Voltaire (1694-1778), was a man of letters, who until the end of his long life used his pen to attack religious "superstitions," as well as ecclesiastical, political, and social abuses. He had a clever wit, and his attacks were often ruthless. They earned him a number of imprisonments and led to a period of exile in England (1726-29). His exile provided Voltaire with the opportunity to study at first hand the work of Newton and Locke, as well as that of the English deists, all of which he would promote in France. He also became an admirer of the English political system and was among those who made a practice of contrasting English liberties with the absolutism and intolerance of France's political and ecclesiastical establishments.

Voltaire was a deist, not an atheist, at least not openly so. He felt that belief in personal immortality, for example, was necessary to ensure law and order and declared that it would be unwise to admit to atheistic ideas in front of one's servants. No longer restrained by fear of punishment in a future life, they might rebel and even turn criminal. In short, religion had too important a social function to be abolished altogether. But he was outspoken in his hatred of Christianity. This was true of many of the French Enlightenment writers, and the country's ecclesiastical situation was among the causes of this attitude. Whereas England since the Glorious Revolution had greatly extended freedom of worship, the French church (which was very closely allied with the government) clung to its monopoly position. During the reign of Louis XIV the suppression of Protestantism had been taken up with renewed zeal. In an age of secularization this caused resentment, and Voltaire's battle cry against the church (*Ecrasez l'infâme!* – Crush the infamous thing!) was echoed by large numbers of Frenchmen.

The efforts of Voltaire and his colleagues on behalf of religious freedom had positive effects. They served to diminish the frequency and severity of the religious persecutions and would ultimately be crowned with the proclamation of full religious freedom. It is necessary to stress the positive aspects of the *philosophes'* work, for as a modern author remarks, Christians have too often seen the modern concern with human rights simply as apostasy,[4] a replacing of the worship of God with the worship of man. The abolition of the Christian religion was indeed the goal of the French Enlightenment, but the fact remains that many of the humanitarian reforms the *philosophes* helped bring about were overdue, and also that they were often in accordance with biblical principles of justice. By exposing the injustices of religious intolerance and by agitating on behalf of political reform, civic freedoms, and social and judicial equality, the Enlightenment brought real enlightenment to France, and also to much of the rest of Europe.

The problems the French Enlightenment brought in its wake, then, were not inherent in the reformers' desire for justice. They were a result, rather, of the radicalism of their approach. This radicalism was an effect of their rationalistic ideology, which was influenced by Locke's psychology. The idea of *tabula rasa* suggested that social amelioration can be achieved by simply following a method and encouraged the idea that political and other innovations can be introduced into a society quite apart from its cultural and historical background. Enlightenment thinkers relied on abstract reason. They ignored customs and traditions and, in general, the lessons of what they considered to have been an irrational past.

Postmodern enemies of the Enlightenment have criticized the Enlightenment's habit of decontextualizing whatever it touched and have shown the destructiveness of that approach. They are not the first to do so. What they are saying had already been said by the philosopher Edmund Burke, an English conservative and a contemporary of both the *philosophes* and the French revolutionaries. As he made clear in his *Reflections on the Revolution in France* (1790) and other writings, Burke approved of the Glorious Revolution of 1688 and the American War of Independence of 1776, arguing that both were justified because they built on age-old British traditions. As a result they were constructive, capable of providing for a system of "ordered freedom." But he rejected the French Revolution, and well before the Reign of Terror began, Burke predicted that, because it ignored historical developments and depended on untested principles, the revolution would result in chaos and bloodshed.

Rousseau on politics

The writings of Jean-Jacques Rousseau (1712-1778) have, no less than those of Voltaire, moulded modern thought. As a political thinker Rousseau was a follower of Locke, but his political theory is not as easy to classify as that of the Englishman. A seminal thinker, Rousseau was also a somewhat incoherent and contradictory one whose ideas have been interpreted in different ways. His authority has been invoked by liberals and authoritarians alike, and he has been called the father of both full-fledged democracy and modern totalitarianism.

Although he played an important role in the arrival of democracy, Rousseau did not himself advocate a democratic form of government.[5] He doubted that it was practical, except perhaps for a very small state such as Geneva, the place of his birth, and he was not sure that even there it could work. But if no democrat, Rousseau was a believer in egalitarian politics. His efforts on behalf of egalitarianism were influenced by his experience and personality. Rousseau's mother had died shortly after his birth, and when Jean-Jacques was still a lad, his father, a watchmaker, had abandoned him. His background, as well as his lack of formal education, contributed to the inferiority complex that afflicted him all his life. He also had a suspicious nature, quarrelled with several of the *philosophes*, and suffered from persecution complexes. On the whole Rousseau felt that the world treated him badly, and his efforts to reform society were influenced by his own need for acceptance.

Rousseau's attitude toward society was ambivalent. On the one hand, he saw it as the source of all evil. A Romantic at heart, he exalted the primitive "state of nature" when, he believed, humanity had been self-sufficient, innocent, and free. That happy state had ended with the coming of civilization and the establishment of organized society, events that for Rousseau were equivalent to the Christian doctrine of the Fall. They were responsible for the introduction of inequality, exploitation, alienation, and every other social evil. Yet, catastrophic as the coming of civilized society had been, Rousseau did not advocate a return to primitivism. Society was here to stay, and if properly organized it was capable, he believed, of erasing the evils that had plagued mankind since the beginning of civilization. Having been the cause of humanity's misery, society could become the means of human redemption.

This would only be possible, however, if it became a true community. Rousseau accepted much of Locke's political theory and agreed with the new human-rights philosophies. But he also feared them, realizing the individualistic implications of the new theories.[6] Society had always been a battlefield among competing interests and goals. Now that the new philosophies made people independent of religious authority and free to pursue their own selfish interests, things could only become worse. Instead of an atomized society where man was a wolf to man, Rousseau wanted a close-knit community where love and compassion reigned. It was to the blueprint of such a community that he devoted his major political writing, *The Social Contract* of 1762.

Social contract and general will

In this work Rousseau followed Locke in making use of the social contract idea, but he introduced an important change. In Rousseau's version the contract was not between the people and its rulers. The rulers were only servants, whom the people appointed and whom they could dismiss at will. The contract concerned the people alone, and it involved the surrender of each individual with all his rights to the community. That community, the state, became a public person with a will of its own. It was the true sovereign, although the people who created it partook of the sovereignty. As participants in the sovereign authority they were citizens; as beings owing obedience to the laws of the state they were subjects.

Under this type of contract the dangers of exploitation and inequality would be reduced, Rousseau believed, because each individual gave his entire self to the community, so that the conditions under which the citizens lived were the same for everyone. No one therefore had any interest in making life burdensome for others. And while it was true that in society people must obey laws which in the state of nature were non-existent, these laws were made with their consent. Obedience to one's own laws did not mean servitude but lifted one to a higher level of liberty than existed before.

Still another safeguard against exploitation, and easily the most important one in Rousseau's opinion, was that in his system each individual agreed to surrender not only his rights but also his will to the community, promising to subject himself to "the supreme direction of the general will." In spite of the importance he assigned to the general will, Rousseau did not really make clear what he meant by it. He neither explained the concept itself nor its relation to the individual will of the citizens, except to say that whereas the individual will could err, the general will always looked "to the public good."[7]

Although undefined and ambiguous, the idea of a general will has had staying power and has served many a future leader well, particularly men of a totalitarian bent. They either presented themselves as the incarnation of the general will or they acted as the people's representatives, qualified to interpret the general will on the people's behalf.

Rousseau did not choose the concept to pave the way for tyrants. He championed freedom and introduced the idea of the general will simply as a means to ensure society's well-being. Its function was to overcome passions like greed and selfishness that threatened the proper operation of state and society. Nevertheless, in situations where the state's interests cannot be reconciled with the freedoms of the citizens, Rousseau was willing to sacrifice the latter.

This was evident in his discussion of the people's involvement in the legislative process. Rousseau defined political sovereignty as inalienable and indivisible, and these characteristics implied for him the rejection of a representative system. He did not like majority rule: the will of the community should be one, not simply in theory but also in practice, and this united will should be expressed in the law-making assemblies. The problem was, however, that whereas the general will could be trusted, individuals could make the wrong choices. If that happened, Rousseau said, it would be necessary to go by majority decision and presume that it expressed the general will. Dissenters would simply have to conform their will to that of the majority. After all, one was to be ruled by laws to which one agreed, not by laws that one opposed. This was a major criterion of freedom. Therefore, Rousseau said, "Whoever refuses to obey the general will shall be constrained to do so by the entire body politic, which is only another way of saying that his fellows shall force him to be free."[8]

By equating compulsion with freedom Rousseau gives an example of the double-speak he at times engaged in and at the same time shows the totalitarian potential of his theory. These totalitarian implications are also evident in his attitude toward organizations that could become too influential within the state. The issue arose in the course of his thoughts on legislation. He continued to be concerned with the problem of ensuring that the nation's laws were in conformity with the general will. The difficulty was that if the individual could err, so could the majority. Rousseau believed that, if they followed their own inclinations, most people would come to the right decision. Their innate goodness and wisdom would see to that. Problems could arise, however, in the case of divided loyalties. For that reason it was best to discourage "partial societies" within the state, that is, organizations with their own collective wills, which might compete with the will of the state and draw people away from their civic duties. The most dangerous of such "partial societies" was the Christian church, whose evil effects upon the people Rousseau described at length.[9]

A civic religion

Although he wanted to see the powers of the church eliminated, Rousseau did not want his state to be a secular one. There was to be a religion. It had to be radically different from Christianity, however, even from a Christianity that made no claims to temporal power. No form of the Christian religion would do because Christianity was by definition otherworldly, so that for its adherents a single-minded service of the state was out of the question. What Rousseau's state needed was a religion that exalted the community as humanity's highest good and created a citizenry which truly cherished its political duty and freely risked all for the sake of the earthly fatherland.

The religion Rousseau proposed was indeed a civic one. Its creed would express sentiments "without which no man can be either a good citizen or a loyal subject." It would assert the existence of God, the reality of a future life, the happiness of the just, the punishment of the wicked, the sanctity of the social contract and the nation's laws, and the inadmissibility of intolerance. If in addition to his adherence to this civic creed an individual wanted to cling to another faith, the state could allow that, as long as its dogmas were not at variance with the obligations of the citizen.

Rousseau wanted the new religion to be taken seriously. While admitting that the state could not oblige anyone to believe the civic creed, he nevertheless gave it the right to banish those who refused to do so. Furthermore, the death penalty was to be reserved for the apostate, that is, for those who had publicly committed themselves to the creed's tenets and then acted as if they did not believe them. There was a limit to religious tolerance in Rousseau's state.[10]

These are the final, contradictory conclusions of *The Social Contract*. They are contradictory in the sense that Rousseau was sincere in his desire to guarantee the individual's well-being. He had started with the rights and freedoms of the individual and with the need to protect them; yet he ended with an all-powerful state capable of destroying these freedoms. Although inspired by Locke, he left Locke's implicit liberalism behind and ended with what amounted to an apology for totalitarianism.

The reasons for the differences between the systems of Locke and Rousseau include differences in personality and in social and political backgrounds. No less important than these, however, was the progress of secularization. Locke had still been able to refer to divine law as a moral guide. In Rousseau's society recourse to such a law was no longer fashionable. In his educational theory Rousseau would allow man's feelings and conscience to serve as his moral guide, and in *The Social Contract* he assigned the task of moral taskmaster to the community. The state became responsible not only for mankind's behaviour, but also for its moral renewal. That is too difficult an assignment for any state. As Rousseau was forced to admit, the attempt necessarily implied religious intolerance, thought control, and physical force.

The moral function Rousseau gave to the state followed from the fact that in his system it had truly become the "mortal God." Rather than seeing the state as a necessary evil, Rousseau assigned to it a fullness of redemptive powers. This explains why the individual had to surrender himself unconditionally to the community, retaining none of the rights that Locke had believed to be inalienable. It also explains why Rousseau could call civic apostasy "the greatest of all crimes" and make it punishable by death. His conclusions followed from the premisses. No one among his radical followers, from the French revolutionary leaders onward, has been able to avoid them.

NOTES

[1] On the pessimistic currents in Enlightenment thought, see Henry Vyverberg, *Historical Pessimism in the French Enlightenment* (Cambridge, Mass.: Harvard University Press, 1958).

[2] Peter Laslett in his Introduction to John Locke, *Two Treatises of Government* (Cambridge: University Press, 1960), p. 83.

[3] On Locke's attitude toward religious toleration, see Tully, *An Approach to Political Philosophy: Locke in Contexts*, pp. 47-62.

[4] Wolfhart Pannenberg, "How to Think About Secularism," *First Things*, No. 64 (June/July 1996), p. 28.

[5] Rousseau, *The Social Contract*, III, iv.

[6] See Allan Bloom's Introduction to his translation of Rousseau's *Emile, or On Education* (New York: Basic Books, 1979), pp. 5f.

[7] Rousseau, *The Social Contract*, II, iii.

[8] *Ibid.*, I, vii.

[9] *Ibid.*, IV, viii.

[10] For Rousseau's description of the civic religion, see *ibid.*

X.   The Limitations of Reason: Hume and Kant

The Enlightenment, a commentator wrote, was abandoned, not refuted. And indeed, although as a cultural period it went the way of all flesh, many of its ideas have survived and influenced later ages, including our own.

Among these ideas is the Enlightenment's contradictory view of human reason. On the one hand, the period exalted the powers of reason highly, proclaiming it capable of solving any problem humanity faced. On the other hand, it retained an earlier and far more skeptical view of reason's competence. These two views were often aired simultaneously. The Enlightenment never managed to resolve the contradiction, and neither have its heirs. It is still with us and helps explain the schizophrenic character of postmodern times.

The belief in reason's unlimited powers was strongest when the Enlightenment was still young. It was in its later phase, after the middle of the eighteenth century, that more and more attention was being paid to those who suggested limits to the power of human reason. Among the thinkers who set the trend in France were Voltaire, whose skepticism increased with age, and Jean-Jacques Rousseau, who had from the beginning downplayed reason, exalting the emotions over the intellect. By doing so he helped inspire the Romantic movement, which would spread across western Europe in the second half of the eighteenth century.

Other contributors to the weakening of the Enlightenment belief in human reason were two non-French philosophers, David Hume (1711-1776) and Immanuel Kant (1724-1804). They will have our attention in the present chapter. Hume was a Scot, born into a Presbyterian family; Kant a German of Scottish descent, who came from a Pietist background. Hume was the outspoken skeptic; Kant the man who tried to rescue what could be rescued of rational and religious certainties after Hume's onslaught. It is with Hume's ideas, therefore, that this chapter must begin.

David Hume

Hume was an empiricist, a member of the school of John Locke. We have seen in a previous chapter that Locke had hoped to eliminate the threat of skepticism but in the end failed to do so. Rather than weakening the tendency toward skepticism, his theory of knowledge in fact strengthened it.

Locke was not a doubter by choice and he was far from drawing out all the skeptical implications of the prevailing theory of knowledge. That work was reserved for Hume. A philosophical Pyrrhonist, Hume was, in the words of his biographer Antony Flew, also "a complete unbeliever, the first major thinker of the modern period to be through and through secular, this-worldly, and man-centered." That he did not openly refer to himself as an atheist was, according to Flew, a result of his prudence and of the fact that he was too much the principled skeptic to proclaim with any finality on the existence or non-existence of God. The most he was prepared to affirm "was the bare existence of a Deity, about the essential nature of which nothing whatever can be known; and which could, surely, not be identified as an entity separate and distinct from the Universe itself."[1]

Hume's skepticism has often been seen as altogether negative; as destructive of religious as well as scientific certainties. As the following pages should make clear, that verdict is largely correct. Hume was an enemy of religion and intent on destroying its credibility, and although he wanted to protect the trustworthiness of scientific beliefs, his attack on the rational basis of the scientific epistemology placed them in jeopardy as well. As recent commentators have shown, however, there nevertheless are limits to the destructiveness of Hume's skepticism.[2] He distinguished between beliefs that are based on rational arguments and beliefs that have their foundation in human nature, and while rejecting the former, he generally maintained the necessity, and even the inevitability, of the latter.

Hume's work must perhaps be explained, at least in part, by his realization that the Cartesian response to the crisis of Pyrrhonian skepticism had failed.[3] A major aim of his philosophy was to show that most of our certainties are not rational but psychological ones; that they cannot be logically demonstrated or empirically proven but have their basis in habit, the imagination, and human nature in general. And so, although a religious skeptic himself, Hume could nevertheless write that contemplation of the apparent design in nature forces one to adopt "the idea of some intelligent cause or author," and add that the human propensity to believe in such an intelligent power "may be considered as a kind of mark or stamp, which the divine workman has set upon his work...."[4]

But this type of conclusion was not supported by the bulk of Hume's work, and in any event, he made it clear that any belief in an intelligent cause was based in human nature and had no foundation in reason. Although it could be called "reasonable" in a psychological sense, it was unreasonable in a rational one. (In Hume's system a belief could be reasonable without being true. The important thing was whether or not the belief had positive practical consequences.[5])

Hume on causation

Hume had published his first work on philosophy by 1740, when he was in his late twenties. Entitled *A Treatise of Human Nature*, it failed to make a stir. Rewriting it, he produced two new volumes, an *Inquiry Concerning Human Understanding* (the so-called First Inquiry, with which we will be concerned in this chapter) and an *Inquiry Concerning the Principles of Morals*. These later publications found more readers than the first one, both at home and on the continent. Other works followed, including some on religion, as well as a history of England.

In his philosophical work Hume dealt with the question whether the human mind can have true knowledge of the outside world. That question was at least as old as Cartesianism. Anxious to safeguard the freedom of the mind, Descartes had established an airtight division between the mind and the world of matter, thereby leaving open the question how in that situation the mind can come to know the material world. The ancient-creationist doctrine having for all practical purposes been discarded, there was no guarantee that man's scientific knowledge was in accordance with outside reality. Rationalists, who relied more heavily on innate ideas and deductive reasoning than on observation, could perhaps ignore the urgency of the problem. This was not possible for empiricists, for whom all knowledge comes via the senses. If they kept to Descartes' dualism, which generally speaking they did, any guarantee that their scientific theories adequately described the external world was lacking. This was the conclusion which Locke had been forced to draw, and which Hume accepted as well.

Hume adhered to the central creed of British empiricism that we cannot know anything apart from sense experience. One consequence of this theory was that pivotal scientific assumptions were in jeopardy. Hume used the principle of causal relationships as an example, showing that we can never be sure of the validity of this principle because it can neither be observed nor rationally demonstrated. We experience regularities in life; we notice that generally speaking event B follows event A, and we assume that this sequence will always be there. Grounds for that assumption are lacking, however, because we have no proof of the principle of uniformity, according to which the future will be like the past.[6] We do, of course, live our daily lives *as if* the world were one of cause and effect, and *as if* such notions as the principle of uniformity were true. If we didn't, life would become impossible. Similarly, science, if it is to proceed, must assume the validity of these notions, but it has no evidence that this assumption is warranted. The idea that it is warranted is a result of habit, not of empirical or demonstrative proof.

Hume went on to show that the certainty of causation is not the only belief we have to abandon if we follow empiricist premises. The entire world can be called into question, for all our mind has before it is images, and neither inductive nor deductive arguments can demonstrate the continued existence of natural objects once they are absent from the senses.[7] Empiricism therefore can well lead to solipsism: the belief that only the self exists, or at least that the self can be certain of nothing but its own experiences. Locke had refused to draw the solipsist conclusion, but Hume showed that on empiricist premises it was not at all an illogical one. He again agreed that such a skeptical attitude is ridiculous and cannot possibly be maintained in day-to-day life. Nature is too strong for principle, and that is all for the good. The skeptical life can't be lived. But the fact remained that not reason or logic, but only "the strong power of natural instinct" could free one from excessive doubt. Hume rejected Descartes' solution that a benevolent God guarantees the trustworthiness of our senses. If that were the case, he argued, our senses would be infallible, because a benevolent God would not deceive. And in any case, once the external world had been called into question, it would be difficult to find arguments by which to prove the existence of God or any of his attributes.[8]

Hume on religion

If it was difficult to derive absolutely certain conclusions from scientific work, it was altogether impossible to derive them from metaphysics and theology, including natural theology. Hume drove home that point in the well-known concluding paragraph of his *Inquiry*, where he exclaimed: "When we run over libraries, ...what havoc must we make? If we take in our hand any volume - of divinity or school metaphysics, for instance - let us ask, *Does it contain any abstract reasoning concerning quantity or number?* No. *Does it contain any experimental reasoning concerning matter of fact and existence?* No. Commit it then to the flames, for it can contain nothing but sophistry and illusion."

As this paragraph makes clear, the attack on religious certainty was part of Hume's project. In the *Inquiry* he turned to the topic more than once. Especially important are the Sections "Of Miracles" and "Of a Particular Providence and of a Future State" (Sections X and XI respectively). He also wrote a number of separate works on religion. They include brief essays, as well as *The Natural History of Religion* of 1757, and the *Dialogues Concerning Natural Religion,* which was published in 1779, a few years after his death.

Hume's goal was not to prove the *impossibility* of miracles or of the existence of God. His intention was rather to show that these doctrines could not be proven, in the sense that they could not be shown to be more probable than their opposites.[9] If he succeeded in doing so, it would become clear that natural theologians who tried to defend religion with reference to the canons of probable reasoning were engaged in a hopeless quest. Religion would become a matter of simple faith, not of evidence, and the supports of the faith in which Locke and many other latitudinarians had put their trust – such as miracles, prophecy, and the reliability of biblical witnesses, as well as various arguments of design – would be declared invalid.

Much of Section XI of the *Inquiry* was devoted to an analysis of the traditional arguments for the existence of God. Hume's view on causation already implied the questioning of theistic proofs that were based on the idea of God as first cause, designer, and so on, but he added that there were additional difficulties with these proofs. If I argue from effect to cause, he said, I have to keep in mind that all I can infer about the cause is what I see in the effect. Therefore, I may be justified in thinking that the universe points to a Creator as its cause, but I cannot infer from this belief the existence of any divine attributes that are not evident in the effect. I certainly can't infer from it such doctrines as divine providence, human immortality, and a future life.

Furthermore, as he would argue in the *Dialogues*, the idea of an ultimate cause does not necessarily lead to the conclusion that only one deity exists. Just as houses usually have more than one builder, and towns and commonwealths more than one founder, so the universe may have more than one supernatural cause.[10] In short, God's existence can't be proven, which means that natural theology has become impossible. Religion is a matter of faith, not of rational proofs or empirical evidence.

On miracles

The Section in the *Inquiry* on theistic arguments was preceded by the one on miracles. For Locke miracles and prophecy had constituted proof of the truth of revelation, but in the skeptical atmosphere of the eighteenth century the historicity of miracles was bound to come under attack. In fact, already in Locke's own days deists and others were questioning the rationality of the belief in miracles. Hume followed the example, deriving many of his arguments from his predecessors' works.[11]

He divided the section on miracles into two parts. In the first one he stated that evidence for the truth of the Christian religion is less persuasive than the evidence for the truth of our sense impressions. This is so because the authority of Scripture is based on testimony, a testimony that has been passed from one group to another and in the process must have lost part of whatever accuracy it originally may have possessed. Hume applied the same principle to the evidence for miracles. "A wise man," he said, "...proportions his belief to the evidence," and testimony in support of miracles needed even more scrutiny than did most other accounts. Among the reasons why this was so was that a miracle violated the laws of nature, which had been established by "a firm and unalterable experience."[12] Ignoring the fact that on his own showing the existence of these laws could not be demonstrated, he declared that they constituted a direct argument against the probability of any of the biblical miracles.

As C. S. Lewis has argued in his book on miracles, Hume performed something like a conjuring trick here. To ask whether nature is absolutely uniform *and* to ask whether miracles occur is really asking the same question phrased differently. If nature is absolutely uniform, miracles are impossible. Therefore, if the first part of the question is answered in the affirmative, the second must be answered in the negative, and that is what Hume did.[13] His real assignment as a philosopher would have been to *prove* the absolute uniformity of nature, but that task was, by its very nature, beyond him. Indeed, the central message of his work was that it could not be done. Hume's reply was also insufficient because it was of an *a priori*, that is a non-empirical, nature, whereas an empiricist ought to come with empirical evidence. He realized this and added that his conclusion about the impossibility of miracles would be overturned if "superior opposite proof" could be found.

That was the question to which he turned next. He answered it in the negative. One argument was the untrustworthiness of the witnesses on whose reports the accounts were based. The very fact that these people reported miracles implied, for Hume, that they lacked the good sense necessary to distinguish fact from fiction and fraud. Furthermore, reports of miracles were found mainly among backward nations, which constituted another reason to take them with a grain of salt. Finally, Hume questioned the historicity of miracles with the argument, which he failed to substantiate, that every account of them had been opposed "by an infinite number of witnesses," and that all religions came with accounts of miracles, so that they could have little value as testimony to the truth of any specific one. *Ergo*, miracles provided no proof for the truth of Christianity. Faith alone could bring that conviction, and such a faith, Hume concluded sarcastically, was itself a miracle.[14]

Although similar arguments had been voiced before, it was Hume's work that came to epitomize the Enlightenment attack upon religion. Reference is still being made to it, by supporters and opponents alike. There is no space in this chapter for an adequate summary of the replies that Hume's work has evoked from critics. For such a summary the reader is referred to studies specifically devoted to the topic.[15] Here only a few points can be made. The first one is that Hume, like practically every Enlightenment thinker, ignored the fact that one's preconceptions can blind one to the available evidence. Convinced *a priori* that the belief in miracles and prophecies was irrational, Hume selected the evidence in accordance with that conviction.

He also limited himself, as more than one critic has remarked, to the analysis of verbal testimony and failed to deal with the implications of the central Christian miracle, that of Christ's resurrection. Had he seriously considered that miracle, he could hardly have avoided taking into account the evidence of drastically changed lives - among the apostles and other disciples and among later believers - as well as that of the establishment of the Christian Church. Nor could he have avoided mentioning the hundreds of witnesses who were said to have been alive when the account was written. Ignoring such evidence, Hume proceeded to suggest the unreasonableness of belief in the resurrection by providing a mock-account of a reappearance by Queen Elizabeth after she had been dead and in the grave for some time.[16]

Yet another weakness was Hume's failure to make a serious use of what has been called the coherence theory of truth. It is based on the tendency of looking for organic connections among beliefs; connections that, if they can be found, enhance the plausibility of the object of faith. Such connections exist between New Testament accounts (for example, that of Christ's incarnation, his passion, and the miracle of his resurrection) on the one hand and the Old Testament ceremonial laws, Old Testament prophecies, and indeed the Bible's entire redemptive-historical account, on the other. Hume ignored this, and by doing so violated his own rule that one must proportion one's belief to the evidence.

In view of the approach he followed, his contradictions were inevitable. Hume is to be commended for exploding the exorbitant claims of reason and for showing that many so-called verities are accepted simply on trust. But he collapsed into incoherence by attempting to prove, by means of the rationalistic arguments whose validity he had earlier denied, the irrationality of religious faith.

Immanuel Kant

Kant summed up and concluded early-modern and Enlightenment philosophy. His aim was to break the deadlock between rationalism and empiricism and in the process counter the skepticism of Hume's philosophy. He began his career as a rationalist but changed directions after he read Hume, who, he said, had roused him from his dogmatic slumbers.

Kant rejected Hume's skeptical conclusions but realized that they followed logically from the premises on which the prevailing theory of knowledge was based. He therefore saw it as his task to submit these premises to a critical analysis. The central question he had to answer concerned again the nature and function of human reason. Were its powers, as the empiricists said, restricted to simply explaining our experiences? Or were the rationalists right in believing that reason had the power to decide, apart from experience, on such matters as the validity of natural laws, including the law of causality? Also, what was the relationship between reason and religious faith? Was it indeed true that reason could prove the existence of God, or was Hume right in denying the validity of natural theology and theistic proofs? Kant tackled these and related questions in a number of writings, which during the final decades of the eighteenth century followed each other in quick succession. Among them were the *Critique of Pure Reason* of 1781, with a revised edition following in 1787, the *Foundations of the Metaphysics of Morals* of 1785, and *The Critique of Practical Reason* of 1788, three works that will have our special attention.

His first concern was with the question of reason's competence in the realm of scientific knowledge. Having studied science early in his career, Kant was acquainted with Newtonian physics and convinced that real, objective knowledge of the world is possible by the methods applied by Newton and his colleagues. Indeed, for Kant Newtonian physics, together with the Euclidean geometry that had served the physicists as their tool, established universal and permanent truths. Because of Hume's questionings, he had to provide proofs for these convictions. The problem was especially difficult because Kant believed that all knowledge begins with sense experience, but as both Locke and Hume had made clear, empiricism (if it takes no account of God the Creator) inevitably leads to skepticism. Kant dealt with this problem in his first *Critique*. Herein he tried to resolve the Lockean and Humean conundrum while at the same time attempting to reconcile the differences between rationalism and empiricism. His solution was to give a far more active role to the human mind than the empiricists had done, while nevertheless maintaining that the content of knowledge comes from sense experience alone.

The mind, Kant taught, was not simply a blank sheet which passively receives the images conveyed by the senses. It possessed structures of its own. They consisted of the forms of time and space, and of the so-called categories of thought.[17] The mind employed these forms and categories to organize and interpret sense data, and in doing so applied to them the various "natural laws," including the law of causation. These laws were *a priori*, that is, they were not derived from observation but belonged to the structure of the mind. Yet they were applicable to the outside world. This meant that it was not nature that established natural laws, but that the mind established them and imposed them upon nature.[18]

His 'Copernican revolution'

By thus giving greater powers to reason than the empiricists had allowed, Kant reclaimed the validity of scientific knowledge. He compared his theory to Copernicus' one in astronomy, and the comparison was apt. Instead of nature being central, that place was given to the human mind. The mind, it is true, did not operate apart from the senses. It needed them for the content of its knowledge. But the mind shaped the world the senses brought to it. A consequence of the theory was therefore that the mind, whose existence Humean skepticism had all but called into question, was again given a place of eminence.

Even so, a price was exacted. Where the old rationalism had proclaimed near-universal powers for human reason, Kant's epistemology denied it that scope. According to Kant we cannot know objects as they are in themselves; we can know only what our mind makes of the sense impressions coming to it from without. This means that our knowledge is limited to appearances, to what Kant called phenomena. The thing-in-itself, which he called the noumenon, cannot be known. This applied to material objects and, no less strongly, to the world beyond the senses.

Kant's solution was therefore not a real guarantee against skepticism. Uncertainty was increased by the fact that he followed the empiricists in placing a screen between the mind and the world, thereby throwing doubt on the possibility that we can truly know phenomena. Indeed, as critics have argued, by allowing the human mind to determine the shape of reality, Kant rescued science by sacrificing the physical world. His solution also implied the danger of an all-out subjective relativism. Kant denied the reality of that danger by saying that the categories of thought are the same for all people, so that everybody sees nature in the same way. But he was unable to prove this, and his theory can be used in support of the postmodern belief that truth is relative to the beholder.

Kant's epistemology certainly contributed to the habit of relegating *religious* truths to the subjective realm. This was a result of the dualisms he established between the noumenal and the phenomenal worlds and between the ways in which we can know these two worlds. It is through these dualisms, no less than through his "Copernican revolution," that Kant has profoundly influenced later philosophy and theology. For a proper understanding of these effects some knowledge of his religious views is necessary.

Kant on religion

After he had rescued Newtonian science, Kant turned to the metaphysical beliefs that a naturalistic empiricism called into question: the belief in the existence of God, in the reality of the soul and of a future life, and in human freedom. The last of these issues was not the least important one for Kant, who spent much effort attempting to prove that man, although organically part of a mechanistic and deterministic nature, is nevertheless a free moral agent and therefore fully responsible for his actions.

Kant's theory of knowledge made it impossible for him to accept the traditional proofs for the existence of God and the human soul. The mind was equipped to deal only with what the senses experienced, and God and the soul cannot be observed. Nor can they be rationally conceived, since they belong to the noumenal world to which the mind has no access. Theoretical reason therefore was in no position to establish the truth of God's existence, and all attempts to prove that it was able to do so, Kant showed, led to contradictions. Although this conclusion cost him the support of some Christians, he himself did not consider it an attack upon religion. He argued that, if theoretical reason could not prove the truth of religion, neither could it demonstrate its untruth. It simply was not qualified to deal with supersensory matters.[19] Kant did believe that reason and science should *assume* the existence of a superhuman being, but added that this could be no more than a hypothesis, necessary to account for the world's order and intelligibility.[20]

Natural theology, then, was once again declared an illusion. But unlike Hume, Kant did not leave it at that. By showing that theoretical reason could not prove the existence of God, Kant had made room, he said, for faith,[21] and faith in Kant's system was more powerful than in that of Hume. It was capable, among other things, of establishing the reality of the noumenal world. Kant was not referring, however, to faith in the doctrines of biblical Christianity. He had exchanged the Pietist religion of his youth for deism. As a deist he rejected divine revelation and demanded a thoroughly "rational" religion, and when referring to faith he seems to have considered it primarily as a mental function, common to all men. Kant further believed that religion's primary function was to serve as basis for morality. This belief in the ethical function of religion was typical of the Enlightenment as a whole, but it was especially strong in Kant, who came from a devout Pietist family and whose entire life bore witness to the strength of the moral convictions he had formed in his youth. In the end, he did not simply value religion as a basis for morality, he virtually equated the two.

Looking for a means to establish the validity of belief in God, in a future life, and in human freedom, Kant turned to what he called the moral law. He devoted his *Critique of Practical Reason* to this project. (In Kant's system the pure reason was concerned with theoretical knowledge; the practical reason with the will and morality.) This second

Critique was based on an earlier work, the *Foundations of the Metaphysics of Morals* of 1785. Herein Kant had stated that human beings have a strong, innate sense of moral obligation. He called this sense of duty "the categorical imperative." It was an imperative because it was indeed an obligation; and it was categorical because it was unconditional and a good in itself, rather than being a means to an end. Furthermore, it was a dictate not of an external lawgiver, but of man's own reason. Having come of age (a point Kant insisted upon throughout), man was autonomous, capable of functioning as his own moral legislator. He was also capable of following the moral laws his reason had set, and to do so for their own sake, apart from any promise of reward or threat of punishment. And finally, Kant stated that the moral law was based on universal reason and was therefore the same for all people. It required every rational being to act in such a way that he would want the principles upon which his own actions were based to become universal law.

It was this moral law, then, the law of the practical reason, which, Kant insisted, assured the human being of religious truths that were beyond the boundaries of the theoretical reason. These truths, all of them postulates of the categorical imperative, were the following three. Firstly, the moral law led to the affirmation of human freedom. Although as an organic being man was subject to the cause-and-effect determinism that governed nature, as a moral being he was free and therefore morally responsible. The "I ought" implied an "I can." Secondly, it led to a belief in a future life. To be perfectly virtuous meant to be in perfect harmony with the universal moral law, and this goal could not be reached in the individual's earthly life but required an "infinitely enduring existence." And thirdly, the categorical imperative showed that there must be a God. For although virtue was its own reward, it nevertheless should lead to happiness. This combination of virtue and happiness, which Kant called the *summum bonum* or highest good, was rarely experienced in this mortal life, and therefore God was necessary to guarantee it in a future life. [22]

Kant had to convince his culture of the validity of his views on the relation between the Christian religion and his own moral theory. He therefore devoted his last major work, *Religion Within the Limits of Reason Alone*, which was published in 1793, to a comparison between his religious philosophy and Christian doctrine. It implied a drastic reinterpretation of Scripture, and the outcome was little more than the old deism in a new dress. On Kant's showing, people could earn God's approval by following the moral law. Christ served as the great example, not as the Redeemer of a human race lost in sin, for no redeemer was necessary. Man could save himself by obeying the law he set for himself. As in the world of the senses, so it was in religion: the human being was at the centre of things.

Conclusion

More so than Hume, Kant tried to be constructive. His aim was not only to save science, but also to place religious faith on a firm basis, and in the process to rescue morality from the naturalistic interpretations that were being marketed in his days. He intended to slay the dragons of materialism, skepticism, atheism, and moral hedonism and in doing so provide an alternative to the dominant mechanistic view of man. Although he was part of nature and to that extent determined, man was morally free and therefore responsible for his actions. And to be truly moral, these actions had to reflect a level of disinterestedness that make Kant's theory far more attractive than other man-made ethical theories of his period.

This is no doubt one of the reasons why his philosophy, although rejected by orthodox theologians, appealed to many liberal ones. It is true that his "proofs" for the existence of God, of the soul, and of a future life are weak. As Herman Bavinck wrote,[23] if the entire world, physical nature, and the human being itself in its organic aspect belong to the realm of neutral reason, and if all these areas fall not under the rule of God but of a mechanistic determinism, then it seems hardly logical to make an exception for the moral life, proclaim that it belongs to the realm of freedom, and use this proclamation as an argument for the existence of God and the immortality of the soul. If God is not needed for the origin and existence of the world of nature and if even the moral order finds its origin in the human being, it is hardly logical to "prove" God's existence by the need to compensate virtue and ensure man's future happiness.

The fact that Kant's arguments were based more on wishful thinking than on logical reasoning was widely ignored. His ideas about religion and morality were convincing in an age when belief in humanity's innate goodness continued to be strong. The appeal of his system was further heightened by the fact that he separated religion from the sphere of theoretical reason and made it independent of divine revelation. Grounded in man's moral sense alone, faith became subjective, and was therefore impervious to rationalist attacks. It had nothing to fear, for example, from the historical-critical approach to biblical scholarship that was already beginning in Kant's own days and that would dominate the theological scene in the nineteenth century and beyond. In its struggle against skepticism and unbelief, liberal theology was happy to follow Kant in choosing a non-rational faculty as the foundation of religious faith. Some would adopt Kant's own choice of that faculty, namely man's innate moral sense. Others would locate religious certainty in the emotions, which had been Rousseau's approach and would be widely followed in the Romantic period.

Religion would be saved by denying it an objective basis. This at least was the assumption. As it turned out, religious subjectivity was not as unassailable a defence against skepticism as Kant and his liberal followers had thought. In a scientific age subjective convictions have little standing; objective truth is what counts. What Kant in the end accomplished was, in the words of one critic, "to show that whatever can be known belongs to the sphere of the sciences, and that metaphysics is not only not science but also meaningless. At best it can have only 'emotive' significance. And this is what Kant's theory of practical faith really amounts to, when it is given its cash-value."[24]

This verdict takes us back to the Kantian dualisms. In Kant's system the theoretical reason knew only the phenomenal world, the world that it met via the senses. The knowledge of that world was restricted to appearances. This did not make it unreliable, however. Far from it: the accomplishments of Newton and his colleagues proved that the scientific approach yielded knowledge that was objectively certain. Over against this phenomenal realm – the realm of science and cause-and-effect relationships – stood the noumenal one. Here objective certainty was lacking. Neither nature nor theoretical reason could point to God, and the Bible as objective record of divine revelation had been declared largely spurious. In a culture where the critical reason and what was held to be an objective scientific method were widely believed to be the only means to provide reliable knowledge, the relegation of religion to the subjective realm implied its dismissal as a universally valid way to truth.

And what applied to religion applied to the noumenal world in general, including the realm of morality. Kant's dualisms gave support, for example, to the fact-value distinction that plays such an important role in modern and postmodern days. The distinction refers to the division between what I know and what I believe. What I *know* are "facts," which belong to the "objective" realm, that is, to the world of science where they can be tested. My *beliefs* are concerned with religion, morality, aesthetics, and similar matters. The objects of these beliefs are only "values" and belong to the subjective realm. Facts are objectively and universally valid; the validity of values is a matter of private opinion. Not an external, objective law, but the individual decides which values are to be considered true or false. As was taught by the Sophists of old, what is true for me is not necessarily true for my neighbour, and what I consider good today I may well consider wrong tomorrow.

The bankruptcy of Kant's moral theory has not led to a repudiation of the view that man can settle moral issues without reference to the laws established by God. This continues to be an article of the secular creed. Yet there have been important changes since Kant. Divinely revealed norms are still denied, but so is Kant's belief in human freedom. Today a deterministic conception holds sway again, and it is a more fatalistic determinism than the old mechanistic one that Kant fought against. It is the evolutionistic belief that man is part not of a benevolent and essentially moral nature, as the early mechanists assumed, but of an amoral one, and that he has been pre-programmed to follow the dictates of that nature.

NOTES

[1.] David Hume, *Writings on Religion*, ed. Antony Flew (La Salle, Ill.: Open Court, 1992), Editor's Introduction, p. vii.

[2.] See several of the contributions in *Hume: A Re-evaluation*, eds. Donald W. Livingston and James T. King (New York: Fordham University Press, 1976).

[3.] Donald W. Livingston, "Introduction," *ibid.*, p. 7.

[4.] Hume, *The Natural History of Religion*, in David Hume, *Writings on Religion*, pp. 180, 181.

[5.] Páll S. Árdal, "Some Implications of the Virtue of Reasonableness in Hume's *Treatise*," in *Hume: A Re-evaluation*, eds. Livingston and King , pp. 103-5.

[6.] Hume, *An Inquiry Concerning Human Understanding*, in David Hume, *On Human Nature and the Understanding*, ed. Antony Flew (New York: Collier-Macmillan, Collier Books, 1965 [1962]), IV, ii; V, i, and *passim*.

[7.] Árdal, "Some Implications," in *Hume: A Re-evaluation*, eds. Livingston and King, pp. 101f.

8. Hume, *Inquiry*, XII, i-iii.

9. Jeffrey Stout, *The Flight from Authority: Religion, Morality, and the Quest for Autonomy* (Notre Dame, Indiana: University of Notre Dame Press, 1981), ch. 6.

10. Hume, *Inquiry*, XI; *Dialogues Concerning Natural Religion*, V, in *Writings in Religion*.

11. Colin Brown, *Miracles and the Critical Mind* (Grand Rapids: Eerdmans, 1984), p. 79.

12. Hume, *Inquiry*, X, i.

13 C. S. Lewis, *Miracles* (New York: Macmillan, 1947), p. 124.

14. Hume, *Inquiry*, X, ii.

15. See the fine study by Colin Brown, quoted previously; for additional titles see its bibliography.

16. Hume, *Inquiry*, X, ii.

17. Kant distinguished twelve such categories, which he placed into four classes, namely 1. Quantity (unity, plurality, totality), 2. Quality (reality, negation, limitation), 3. Relation (inherence and subsistence, causality and dependence, community), 4. Modality (possibility-impossibility, existence-non-existence, necessity-contingency). Immanuel Kant, *Immanuel Kant's Critique of Pure Reason*, trans. Norman Kemp Smith (London/New York: Macmillan/St. Martin's Press, 1968 [1929]), p. 113 (A80, B 106).

18 *Ibid.*, pp. 65-119 (B31–B116).

19 *Ibid.*, p. 602 (A753, B 781).

20. *Ibid.*, pp. 565-9 (A695-A702; B723-730).

21. *Ibid.*, p. 29 (Bxxx), p. 597 (A745, B773).

22. Kant, *Critique of Practical Reason*, trans. and ed. Lewis White Beck (Indianapolis: Bobbs-Merrill, A Liberal Arts Book, 1956), pp. 114-36.

23. H. Bavinck, *Christelijke Wereldbeschouwing*, 3rd ed. (Kampen: Kok, 1929 [1904]), p. 82.

24 Copleston, *A History of Philosophy*, VI (Westminster, Maryland: Newman Press, 1960), p. 433.

XI. The Rise of Darwinism

One of the most spectacular events in the nineteenth-century world of ideas was the triumph of evolutionism. The novelty was not merely that evolution was proposed as an explanation of the origin of species, or even of the world as a whole. What set the nineteenth century apart from its predecessors in the matter of evolutionism was that now, for the first time, the theory gained widespread adherence, and also that people began to see all of life in developmental terms.

For evolution as a simple theory of origins was not new. Some of the early Greek philosophers had already suggested it, and for a while the tradition had been kept alive by the ancient Epicureans. It resurfaced during the Renaissance and in the seventeenth century and, increasingly so, in the eighteenth. But neither in the ancient world nor in the early-modern period was it universally accepted, and no evolutionistic *worldview* arose until the nineteenth century. Although modern history had made preparations for it, it was only in the age of Darwin that the old world of changeless being would truly be replaced by a dynamic, ever-changing world of becoming. Darwin's theory of evolution was a catalyst of this change.

It was also one of its effects, for the reason why evolutionism triumphed in the nineteenth century was not simply that more data became available in support of evolutionary theories. It is true that that factor played a role. Geologists and biologists had been busy collecting evidence, and evolutionary theories had been proposed well before the publication, in 1859, of Darwin's *Origin of Species*. But neither Darwin's theory nor those of his contemporaries sprang from these data alone. Belief in a developing world had been growing before the amassing of facts and apart from it. As had been the case with Copernicanism, the search for evidence was as much a result of a widespread demand for the new model as a cause.

This meant, among other things, that incontestable proof for Darwin's ideas was not essential. His hypothesis, as is quite generally admitted, was accepted in the absence of conclusive evidence. A far more important factor was its explanatory power. When Darwin published the *Origin,* rival theories were still being proposed. Darwin's prevailed in large part because it came with a simple mechanism to account for the evolutionary process, a mechanism that appealed to many not only on scientific but also on philosophical grounds. That mechanism was natural selection. For Darwin it was the means by which the most favoured individuals survive in the struggle for existence so that they are able to reproduce, while the less favoured ones are eliminated. In that manner, he proposed, new species are able to develop.[1]

The mechanism of natural selection was philosophically attractive because it operated in a purely mechanistic manner, and Darwin, like many of his contemporaries, wanted nature to proceed autonomously. The philosophy underlying Darwinian evolutionism was a mechanistic naturalism, and therefore based on belief not in design, but in necessity or chance. This was a major reason why large numbers of people were willing to accept Darwin's theory and why they clung to it, even though the fossil evidence failed to support it and various other problems remained.

It is not the aim of this chapter to provide a critique of Darwin's theory. That has been done by others, Christians as well as non-Christians.[2] Our concern is not so much with biological or geological developmentalism as such as with the genesis and nature of evolutionism as a philosophical and worldview system. The present chapter deals with the question why and how the belief in evolutionism arose at this particular time; the next one will consider some of the implications of an evolutionist worldview.

The idea of progress

An important condition for the acceptance of evolutionism was a new view of history, one based on the belief that progress is the law of life. This view, which implied the perfectibility of man and nature, matured in the eighteenth and early nineteenth centuries.

It was a revolutionary development, one that set the modern period apart from preceding ages. Most earlier cultures had seen the movement of history either as regressive, with the Golden Age in the past, or as cyclical. According to the latter view, worlds and societies arose, prospered, and declined, making room for others that went through the same cycle. There was nothing new under the sun; whatever had been would be again. Ancient evolutionists had subscribed to this cyclical view. According to them also worlds evolved to a certain level and then decayed, to give rise to new ones that would repeat the process, and so on, *ad infinitum*. Unlike the modern one, these early evolutionary theories were not associated with a belief in continuous progress.

Regressive and cyclical theories of history were not confined to the ancient world. Pushed into the background during much of the Christian Middle Ages (although the regressive view was not uncommon during that period), they were back in force at the time of the Renaissance. Some Renaissance thinkers held the regressive view; others adopted the cyclical one, believing that all they could expect for their age was a return to the heights of classical antiquity. To surpass it was out of the question. These beliefs explain the period's tendency of looking to the classical past for guidance. But well-established as the old view of history was in the Renaissance, it was in the course of this same period that people began to doubt the traditional wisdom and wonder if modern man was not surpassing the ancients in at least some areas. Among the reasons for the doubts, as we noted in an earlier chapter, were modern technological and scientific achievements, as well as the discovery of lands that had been unknown to the Greeks and Romans.

The doubts led to the battle between the "ancients" and the "moderns," that is, between those who affirmed the superiority of the ancients over the moderns and those who held the opposite view. Members of the latter group included Sir Francis Bacon, who believed that science could make possible the restoration of man's dominion over nature that he had lost because of the Fall, so that in the future the world's felicity would surpass that of ancient times. Although not everybody among the "moderns" was quite so confident, all agreed that modern man was capable of surpassing the ancients at least in science and technology. Whether he could also compete with them on the moral level remained, for the time being, a question. It did not remain so for long. Among those who answered it in the affirmative were the followers of Locke. The *tabula rasa* concept implied the possibility of moral progress. Education and legislation could do for the taming of mankind what science and technology promised to do for the taming of nature.

The optimism to which these beliefs gave rise was strengthened by other factors, such as the increasing prosperity and relative peace that the eighteenth century enjoyed. The result of all these developments was that before the middle of that century the battle had been largely decided in favour of the "moderns." Although there were prominent Enlightenment thinkers who continued to cling to a more pessimistic view of history, the progressive one prevailed. At first this did not imply belief in inevitable progress, but before the end of the century that shift was being made as well. A well-known example is that of the Marquis de Condorcet. A supporter of the French Revolution, Condorcet had run afoul of the more radical revolutionaries, fled, was captured, and died in his cell, possibly by suicide. Shortly before his death he wrote his *Outlines of an Historical View of the Progress of the Human Mind,* wherein he expressed his unshaken belief in continuous progress.

While for Condorcet progress was guaranteed, he still believed that education and legislation would advance it. For the Scotsman Adam Smith, the theorist of laissez-faire capitalism, progress could be automatic. In 1776 Smith published his famous work *On the Wealth of Nations.* Herein he pleaded for unrestricted economic freedom, arguing that it would benefit society as a whole. Individuals were motivated by self-love and greed, and that was all for the good. People's self-interest, together with the law of supply and demand, would guarantee a self-regulating economic system wherein production and wealth increased to their greatest possible extent. As in the physical universe, so it was in the economic one of Adam Smith: there were natural laws that must not be interfered with, and there was an "invisible hand" which guided all for the ultimate good of all, even if some of the weak were eliminated in the process. As long as the system was left alone, over-all progress was ensured.

Adam Smith was not alone in holding such views. When he published his work, commerce was thriving in England, and the industrial revolution was just beginning. Merchants, industrialists, and many members of the middle class as a whole found his theory congenial. So did imperialists. The idea of progress, combined with the laissez-faire principle with its exaltation of freedom and competition, was well established when Darwin provided what was believed to be its scientific basis.

Romanticism and the historical temper

Belief in progress was important for the rise of evolutionism. But although it may have been a necessary condition, it was not a sufficient one. It could co-exist with a belief in special creation, in the fixity of species, and in the permanence of human nature and human institutions. During much of the eighteenth century it did so co-exist. The Newtonian system itself was a static one and encouraged belief in universality and immutability. The mechanistic metaphor did not allow for evolutionism either: a machine operates in a uniform manner. No change is involved.

Another necessary ingredient in an evolutionary worldview is a sense of historical continuity and development, and that, too, was lacking in early-modern society. It is true that the Enlightenment was not an unhistorical period. Much historical research was done in the eighteenth century and many histories were written. Attempts were even made to bring about a revolution in the writing of history. Voltaire, for example, rebelled against the tendency to make history a chronicle of nothing but political and military events, and his *Essay on the Manners and Customs of Nations* constituted a watershed in the history of historiography.

But although innovative, Enlightenment historians (with the exception of some German ones) pursued goals that were quite different from those of their colleagues in a truly historical century such as the nineteenth. Unlike the latter, Voltaire and his fellow historians were not interested in historical development as such. Their concern was with the present, which for them constituted the height of human achievement. The past was important only in so far as it made clear the unique character of the age of reason or anticipated its ideals. Consequently epochs like the ancient world and the Renaissance were admired; periods like the Christian Middle Ages were despised precisely because they were Christian. The past was studied to illustrate the reality of progress and the superiority of the age of reason. To borrow the words of the Enlightenment historian and statesman Lord Bolingbroke, history was nothing more than "philosophy [and he meant Enlightenment 'philosophy'] teaching by example."

An evolutionistic worldview required not simply a progressive view of history, but a truly developmental one. It demanded the belief that history is continuous, that consecutive epochs are organically related, that development is the law of life, and that the simple passage of time guarantees growth and leads to real change, to transformation. And those ideas were still absent in the Enlightenment. They had to await the triumph of Romanticism in the late eighteenth and early nineteenth centuries.

Romanticism was a complex movement, which cannot be adequately defined in a brief statement. It was similar to the Enlightenment in its concern for freedom and its belief in progress, but was opposed to many other ideas of the preceding epoch. Romantics exalted feeling, the emotions, and the unrestricted imagination, rather than reason. They rejected the universalism and cosmopolitanism of the Enlightenment and stressed instead racial and historical differences among peoples. They preferred, at least in theory, nature to civilization, and they substituted a love of movement, diversity, and the unexpected for their predecessors' delight in stability and predictability. They were among the first to realize the negative implications of science and technology, disliked the mechanistic view of the universe, and urged a return to nature, which for them was an organism, a living and growing one. They also urged a return to the supernatural, which, for many, was closely related to the natural. Neoplatonism and pantheism experienced a revival in the Romantic period.

With their organic view of nature the Romantics strengthened the tendency toward developmentalism. They did this also by their attitude toward the human past. Unlike Enlightenment historians, those of the Romantic era (and of the nineteenth century as a whole) had a sense of historical continuity. Regarding the remote past as the childhood of the race and nation, they were vitally interested in that past and avidly studied primitive and medieval history. The differences between periods might be great, but there was an organic connection between earlier and later ages, so that the present could not be understood apart from the past.

The struggle for survival

Although the Romantic view of history created an atmosphere wherein evolutionism could and indeed did thrive, it did not influence Darwin directly. Romantics tended toward Neoplatonism, whereas Darwin was a mechanist, unwilling to allow vitalistic or supernatural ideas to taint his theory. Also uncongenial for Darwin was the benevolent character which many Romantics (although not all of them) assigned to nature. Darwin saw nature as morally neutral. He was more in tune with the views of men like Adam Smith and Jeremy Bentham (founder of the Utilitarian School of political economy), who believed that progress depended on competition and struggle.

Not all political economists of the period agreed with Adam Smith and his school that a laissez-faire policy would bring automatic progress. A notable exception was Thomas Malthus. In his *Essay on the Principle of Population* of 1798, Malthus, a clergyman by profession, wrote that people multiplied much faster than the food supply. As a result there was, instead of the promise of progress, a continual threat of starvation for the masses of mankind. Measures of relief through social legislation were not the answer, since they did not lead to an increase in the supply of food. Moreover, they increased apathy, dissipation, and idleness among the poor and raised the financial burden for the rest of the population.

Although Malthus believed that certain government policies, such as the encouragement of agriculture, could alleviate the problem of poverty to some extent, generally speaking he put the onus on the poor themselves. Unless they could be persuaded to limit the number of their offspring, the inadequate food supply could only lead to ever-increasing misery and vice. The misery included hard labour, insufficient food, high infant mortality, famines, and epidemics; the vice, war, immorality, abortion, and infanticide. Malthus' theory, at least in its original form, explains why his type of economics was referred to as "the dismal science."[3]

Among the people who took to heart Malthus' ideas of scarcity and of a perpetual struggle for existence were Charles Darwin, Karl Marx, and Herbert Spencer. All three, however, drew different conclusions from them than Malthus had done. It had been Malthus' intention to refute the ideas of men like Condorcet about automatic progress, and also to prove wrong those who blamed the suffering of the poor on the imperfections of social institutions. The horrors of the French Revolution, especially in its later stages, had shown what the Enlightenment type of criticism of society could lead to. Malthus wanted to demonstrate that a change in the lifestyles of individuals was more likely to reduce the problem of poverty than a revolutionary change in institutions.[4]

Darwin – to begin with him – ignored Malthus' main thesis. His attention focused on the parallels between the struggle for existence in human society and in nature. But rather than seeing this struggle as an argument against perfectibility, Darwin concluded that it constituted a road to progress. While reading Malthus' essay it had suddenly struck him, he wrote, that as a result of the incessant struggle for survival "favourable variations would tend to be preserved, and unfavourable ones to be destroyed. The result of this would be the formation of new species."[5] This insight provided him with the mechanism he needed: descent with modification by means of natural selection. Darwin was especially pleased with his discovery of Malthus because he wanted a principle that operated without interference either by man or by supernatural agency; one that was "self-explanatory, self-sufficient, and self-regulating."[6] That principle Malthus' study suggested to him.

The same mechanical principle appealed to Karl Marx. Marx also agreed with Malthus about the increasing pauperization of the masses and the inevitability of the struggle for existence. But in his view the struggle was not among individuals but among classes, and the victory would not be for the strong, as Malthus implied, but for the weak. The impoverished workers would rise against their capitalist oppressors, overthrow them, and so bring about the socialist paradise. For Marx as for Darwin, scarcity and the struggle for survival led to progress.

Herbert Spencer, finally, took Malthus' theory much as Darwin had done, and the system he built on it would become almost as influential as Darwinism proper. An evolutionist before the appearance of Darwin's *Origin of Species*, Spencer developed a philosophical system that tried to explain not only the geological and biological world, but all of reality in evolutionary terms. Organic nature and the physical universe, as well as institutions and moral systems, had evolved over time. His attempts (and those of his followers) to apply evolutionary principles to economic and social policy became even better known than his general philosophy, and his system is generally referred to as Social Darwinism.

Spencer equated free economic competition with Darwin's struggle for existence. By ensuring the elimination of the unfit and the survival of the fittest, both economic competition and natural selection were necessary for progress. The struggle for economic survival was therefore good and should not be interfered with. Like the Enlightenment philosopher Adam Smith, Social Darwinists believed in a laissez-faire policy in social and economic affairs.

The spread of evolutionism

The second half of the nineteenth century was a period of rapid industrial and technological advances, of increasing international competition for land, markets, resources, and investment opportunities, and of ruthless capitalism. In view of the character of the age, it is not surprising that economic and socio-political considerations as expressed in Social Darwinism were reflected in both the general worldview and in the scientific model that was in part derived from it.

They were not the only factors, however, in the triumph of Darwinism, nor were they present everywhere to the same extent as in

Adam Smith's and Herbert Spencer's England. The motivations for accepting evolutionism varied from country to country. In England the belief in unrestricted competition helped pave the way for it, and the same would happen in the United States. The latter country would also, more so than most other nations, embrace Social Darwinism. In France anti-religious sentiments and belief in political and social progress were among the factors that helped make the idea of evolutionism (although not at first the Darwinian theory) congenial. In Germany the philosophy of Idealists such as Hegel, together with Romantic-pantheistic ideas, had a similar effect.[7]

Racism also played a role in the triumph of evolutionism, as did the intensified militarism and the race for colonies of the late nineteenth century. In these cases it was a matter of proving that one's own race or country or empire was fitter than the rest, and therefore justified in subjecting other peoples and nations. Not in the last place, there were, then as now, militant atheists who supported naturalistic evolutionism as much for religious as for scientific or social reasons.

The problem of evil

As the foregoing shows, evolutionism had many causes and served a variety of functions. One of its functions, which has not yet had our attention, was that for many it provided an answer to the problem of evil. The attempt to find a solution to that problem played an especially important role in the rise and adoption of radical or pan-evolutionism.

A perpetual human concern, the problem of evil had become particularly urgent in the early-modern period. Christianity had explained the existence of evil with the doctrine of the Fall, but with the rise of natural theology and deism that explanation was increasingly being questioned. Although belief in God continued for a while, he was seen as Creator only, not as Redeemer, for mankind was not in need of redemption. The question the early-modern centuries wrestled with, was: if man is by nature innocent, and if God is, as the philosophers describe him, omnipotent and wholly good, then whence comes evil? Does it not appear that God is either unwilling or unable to prevent it?

Various answers were given. Some thinkers resorted to a kind of Manichean dualism, according to which the world is the theatre of a permanent conflict between good and evil forces. There were also those who, with Rousseau, placed the burden of guilt on neither God nor man but on society and its institutions. And still others constructed theodicies, philosophical attempts to justify the ways of God with man. Among these was a system based on the ancient concept of the Great Chain of Being. It was this theodicy that, in an indirect way, contributed to the rise and acceptance of evolutionism.

The Great Chain of Being

The Great Chain was of Neoplatonic origin. One of the ideas used in its construction was that of plenitude. The idea implied, as we saw in chapter 5, that God, being good and therefore without envy, had created an infinite universe, which contained an infinitude of phenomena. All possible varieties of all possible beings and things were present. A related idea in the concept of the Great Chain was that of continuity, which referred to the fact that the differences between one species and the next are gradual, often barely perceptible. This reinforced the idea, implicit in the idea of plenitude, that every possible intermediate form must be present on the Chain. There could be no missing link.

The countless numbers of beings that constituted the Great Chain were arranged in a hierarchical order. At the top of the Chain was the highest created being or, in some versions, God himself. Then came the rest of the spiritual world, and then humanity. Man, being partly spiritual and partly corporeal, was at the centre. Following him were the phenomena of the material world: the various species of animals in descending order of complexity, the plants, and finally, at the bottom, inorganic nature. This Chain was eternally perfect and complete. There were no missing links, and no change had ever occurred or would occur. Each being had its own form and place, and both were fixed.

The most influential promoter of the Great Chain in the early-modern period was the German philosopher Gottfried Wilhelm Leibniz (1646-1716). Leibniz taught that God, when confronted with the need to create one world out of an infinitude of possible worlds, had created the best of the series, so that the present world was the best of all possible ones. This was for Leibniz the logical deduction from the fact that God was wholly good. It was also the only way, for Leibniz and for many of his contemporaries, to prove that creation was not a chance affair. There was a good and sufficient reason for all that was, including the imperfections that marred the world and human life. It was this belief that served Leibniz as his theodicy. A universe which was as full as possible and which accommodated every conceivable phenomenon could not contain good things only, but had to contain imperfect ones as well. The presence of evil was a logical necessity.[8]

Leibniz's system provided the basis for what is often called

Enlightenment optimism. That term does not refer to hopefulness, but to the belief that evil was the necessary shadow side of good, and that the present world, if not as good as one could wish, was nevertheless the best of all possible worlds. Although hardly a cheerful philosophy, it had its attractions. It justified, for example, the maintenance of the social and political status quo (improvements in a world that was the best of all possible ones were by definition out of the question), and it provided assurances of the world's intrinsic rationality. And in any event, evil was not without fruit. Somehow the world's imperfections served a purpose and led to a greater good. One of Leibniz's popularizers, the English poet Alexander Pope, even implied that evil was only an illusion. Man might think that it existed, but that was a misapprehension, a result of the fact that he was finite and could not oversee the whole.

> All Nature [Pope explained] is but Art, unknown to thee;
> All Chance, Direction, which thou canst not see;
> All Discord, Harmony not understood;
> All partial Evil, universal Good:
> And, spite of Pride, in erring Reason's spite,
> One truth is clear, 'Whatever *is*, is *right*.'
> (*Essay on Man*, I, 289-94)

It was a soothing philosophy for those who could be satisfied with logical conclusions. Not everybody could. Early in the eighteenth century the Anglo-Irish writer Jonathan Swift had already satirized the superficiality of the rationalism of his age. The well-known author and lexicographer Dr. Samuel Johnson was among those who consistently refused to accept the idea of the Great Chain. He criticized Pope and others who used it to justify human and social imperfections.[9] After the middle of the eighteenth century these men were joined by Voltaire, the prince of the Enlightenment *philosophes*. Voltaire's indignation at Enlightenment optimism was aroused by the manifestation of natural evil in the disastrous Lisbon earthquake of 1755, and by that of human evil in the Seven Years' War, which broke out the year after the earthquake.

From Being to Becoming

The exposure of the essential hopelessness of Enlightenment optimism, combined with a persistent belief in progress, led to a widespread questioning of the concept of the Great Chain of Being and to a demand for change. The manner in which that demand was met was striking. It led not to the rejection of the Chain, or even of the ideas of plenitude and perfection implied in it, but to its temporalizing. From a Chain of Being, symbolic of a static, non-evolutionary world, it became a Chain of Becoming, symbolic of a dynamic and evolutionary one.[10]

The idea of a dynamic Chain was inspired by the criticisms of men like Swift, Dr. Johnson, and Voltaire, and by scientific considerations. An important scientific reason was the growing realization that the fullness of plenitude could not be present at any one moment. For all possibilities to be realized, an extended time-scale would be required, one that involved the past and the future as well as the present. That conclusion was supported by the findings of empirical scientists, who drew attention to gaps in observable nature and the fossil record and to the disappearance of species. Evidence of this kind strengthened the belief that the cosmos was not, as the original concept taught, eternally complete. It suggested, rather, that it was in a process of constant change.

Even Leibniz himself, in contradiction to much of the rest of his philosophy, had considered the necessity of a dynamic world.[11] Before the middle of the eighteenth century poets and other authors had taken over the idea of developmentalism, and in the 1750s the philosopher Kant used the new dynamic version of the idea of plenitude to develop a theory of stellar evolution. Others followed the turn to developmentalism, increasingly so as the century advanced.

Although not all eighteenth-century developmentalists defined evolutionism in the same terms as their successors in the next century, many of the later ideas were already present. There were suggestions, for example, of the transformation of species, of pan-evolutionism, and of continuing cosmic progress. It is true that there were also theories suggesting development within species only (micro-evolution), and evolutionism was even combined with the ideas of degeneration and cyclical development. (Kant's stellar evolutionism, for example, was cyclical.) In the midst of all this speculation about developmentalism the belief in the unchangeableness of the cosmos and the fixity of species survived as well. Nevertheless, the process of temporalizing the Chain of Being had begun and would accelerate in the next century, making Darwinism possible.

Becoming and the problem of evil

The temporalizing of the Chain and the acceptance of evolutionism would solve for many the problem of evil. It is true that they did not do so for every one. There were those who objected to evolutionism not only because it clashed with revelation but also because, in their view, it exacerbated the problem of evil. The great stumbling block was Darwinist theory, since it described the process of evolution as ruthlessly competitive and implied that even man was the product of an amoral nature.[12]

Darwin was aware of the moral difficulties implied in his theory and tried to minimize them. Early in the *Origin,* at the end of the chapter on the struggle for existence, he wrote: "When we reflect on this struggle, we may console ourselves with the full belief, that the war of nature is not incessant, that no fear is felt, that death is generally prompt, and that the vigorous, the healthy, and the happy survive and multiply."[13] Furthermore, the outcome made everything worthwhile. "...As natural selection works solely by and for the good of each being," he told his readers, "all corporeal and mental endowments will tend to progress towards perfection."[14] And he concluded the book with the well-known words: "Thus, from the war of nature, from famine and death, the most exalted object which we are capable of conceiving, namely, the production of the higher animals, directly follows. There is grandeur in this view of life...that, whilst this planet has gone cycling on according to the fixed law of gravity, from so simple a beginning endless forms most beautiful and most wonderful have been, and are being, evolved."[15]

Many of his contemporary followers drew a similarly optimistic conclusion. The negative implications of evolutionism, although recognized in Darwin's time, would not constitute a major problem until the end of the century, when they would contribute to the wave of *fin de siècle* pessimism. In Darwin's days the positive view dominated. The idea of progress survived and flourished, with the belief in evolution providing a satisfactory solution to the problem of evil.

And indeed, a dynamic model gave a far more credible base for optimism than the old static one had done. The transformation of the Chain helped bring that message home. The idea of perfection, for example, which in the old Chain had become an irritant, now became an asset. For in the temporalized Chain – and this was the great innovation – this perfection was seen not as actual, but only as potential. That which existed was still in a process of striving *toward* the final goal of perfection. This was true of every link in the Chain: of the physical universe, of the world of plants and animals, of man, of the spiritual hierarchy, and even of God. Evolving together, neither man nor God was responsible for the evil that existed, nor were they as yet capable of fully eradicating it. As Leibniz had said, imperfections were inevitable. But the explanation of the advocates of developmentalism was far superior to that of Leibniz and the Enlightenment optimists: evil was now seen as temporary, as something that would gradually diminish and in the end be overcome.

Pan-evolutionism was a revolutionary concept. For those who wanted proof that evil would disappear it was also a most satisfactory one, since it made allowance for the reality of present evil without sacrificing the idea of future improvement. Rather, it made progress inevitable. It is therefore no wonder that scientists were anxious to find empirical evidence for evolutionary theories, nor is it surprising that their contemporaries greeted these theories with enthusiasm. In the nineteenth century the acceptance of evolutionism, both as a theory of origins and as an explanation of the world's operation and destiny, was an all but foregone conclusion.

NOTES

[1] Darwin stated that natural selection, although the main evolutionary mechanism, was not the exclusive one. Darwin, *On the Origin of Species: A Facsimile of the First Edition* (Cambridge, Mass.: Harvard University Press, 1966 [1964]), p. 6. (Among the other mechanisms were use and disuse, the effect of climate and environment, and sexual selection.)

[2] See, for example, Gertrude Himmelfarb, *Darwin and the Darwinian Revolution* (New York: Norton, Norton Library, 1968 [1959]); Marjorie Grene, "The Faith of Darwinism" in her *The Knower and the Known* (London: Faber and Faber, 1966), pp. 185-201; as well as more recent critical assessments such as Phillip E. Johnson, *Darwin on Trial* (Downers Grove, Ill.: InterVarsity, 1993 [1991]); and Michael J. Behe, *Darwin's Black Box: The Biochemical Challenge to Evolution* (New York: The Free Press, 1996).

[3] In later editions Malthus modified his theory. He suggested, for example, that improvements in the lot of the poor could be made by means of legislation and education and by cultivating a spirit of pride and independence. Generally, however, people ignored these modifications and defined Malthusianism according to the arguments of the first edition. See Gertrude Himmelfarb's introduction to her edition of Malthus' essay: Thomas Robert Malthus, *On Population*, ed. Gertrude Himmelfarb (New York: Random House, The Modern Library, 1960).

[4] *Ibid.*, pp. xivff.

[5] Darwin, *The Life and Letters of Charles Darwin, Including an Autobiographical Chapter,* ed. Francis Darwin (New York: D. Appleton and Company, 1896), I, p. 68.

[6] Himmelfarb, *Darwin and the Darwinian Revolution,* p. 165.

[7] *Ibid.,* pp. 303ff.; Mason, *A History of the Sciences,* p. 412.

[8] Lovejoy, *The Great Chain of Being,* chs. 5, 7.

[9] Basil Willey, *The Eighteenth-Century Background* (Harmondsworth: Penguin Books., 1965 [1962] [Chatto and Windus, 1940]), pp. 52-9.

[10] On the temporalizing of the Chain, see Lovejoy, ch. 9.

[11] *Ibid.,* pp. 255-62.

[12] Darwin did not proclaim human evolution until 1871, when he published *The Descent of Man.* That human evolution was implied was clear to most readers of the *Origin,* however. Darwin himself suggested it in the earlier work when he wrote that in the future, as a result of his theory, light would also be thrown "on the origin of man and his history." *Origin,* p. 488.

[13] *Ibid.,* p. 79.

[14] *Ibid.,* p. 489.

[15] *Ibid.,* p. 490.

XII. Radical Evolutionism

Radical evolutionism – that is, the application of an evolutionary theory to all of life – was not a primary concern of Darwin himself. He was first and foremost a scientist, rather than a philosopher. By the time he reached middle age his interest in religion had become limited as well. Darwin had begun as a believer in divine creation, but later turned to agnosticism: the conviction that nothing can be known about the supernatural. To think otherwise, he argued, was to deceive oneself.

This was a logical deduction from his belief in human evolution. Since the human mind had evolved from the mind of the lower animals, one could not help entertaining, he wrote to a friend, a "horrid doubt" as to the trustworthiness of metaphysical ideas. "Would any one," he asked, "trust in the convictions of a monkey's mind, if there are any convictions in such a mind?"[1] The only intellectually honest attitude was one of agnosticism.

But although Darwin tried to avoid drawing out the metaphysical implications of his theory, he did not always succeed, nor could the strategy satisfy in the long run. Since Darwinism claimed to explain not only man's organic but also his mental development, it had implications for theology, ethics, epistemology, and anthropology, for political and social theories – indeed, for practically every area of human knowledge and belief systems. Darwin himself admitted this, and a number of his contemporaries, less hesitant than Darwin, speculated freely on the wider implications of developmentalism. Ideas on universal evolutionism had been around before the appearance of the *Origin of Species*. The number of its adherents would increase after the rise of Darwinism.

In this chapter we will first deal with what is probably the best-known of these speculative theories, namely that of the Englishman Herbert Spencer, the founder of Social Darwinism. We will then turn to the arguments of Darwin's friend and supporter Thomas Huxley, who spelled out the negative implications of an evolutionary approach in the field of ethics. In dealing with the ideas of these two men some attention will also be given to Darwin's own views on the topic of radical evolutionism.

Evolution and morality: Herbert Spencer

Herbert Spencer (1820-1903) was an avowed evolutionist. Already in the 1850s, before the publication of Darwin's *Origin of Species*, he had concluded that theories of evolution should be applied not only to biology and geology, but to every other phenomenon under the sun. The conviction inspired his ten-volume *Synthetic Philosophy*, which dealt with such topics as biological evolutionism, the evolution of mind and consciousness, of society and government, and of morality. In Spencer's system everything developed from primitive beginnings to complex systems. Everything would also, in the end, suffer decay and dissolution. Unlike Darwin, Spencer held to a cyclical philosophy of history and at times admitted to a feeling of pessimism. He tended, however, to push the world's and humanity's ultimate fate into the distant future, and on the whole his philosophy was an optimistic one. Evolution meant progress.

As the title of the work suggests, Spencer tried to synthesize the knowledge of his day. But his ultimate concern was with morality, and the two volumes on ethics constituted both the conclusion and the summit of his synthetic work. It was Spencer's aim to put together a "science of ethics." He wanted to develop a system of morality that was fully supported by the findings of natural science, and that could replace the traditional moral code, which was based on religion. He believed it to be a matter of some urgency. As he wrote in the preface to the first volume of his *Principles of Ethics*, "Now that moral injunctions are losing the authority given by their supposed sacred origin, the secularization of morals is becoming imperative. Few things can happen more disastrous than the decay and death of a regulative system no longer fit, before another and better regulative system has grown up to replace it."[2]

In drawing up this "better regulative system," Spencer was inspired by Malthus, Darwin, and some of the earlier evolutionists. Darwinism especially was important. It served to strengthen Spencer's belief that in the final analysis human behaviour was to be judged by the criterion whether or not it contributed to evolutionary progress. This principle Spencer applied in his social theory as well. Competition in society and in economics was necessary for progress in that it allowed for the elimination of the unfit. Already in 1851 he had written: "The poverty of the incapable, the distresses that come upon the imprudent, the starvation of the idle, and those shoulderings aside of the weak by the strong, which leave so many 'in shallows and in miseries,' are the decrees of a large, far-seeing benevolence."[3] Here we are at the core of Spencer's theory of Social Darwinism.

Callous as he may seem, Spencer was not as radical a Social Darwinist as some of his followers. He increasingly worried, for example, about the colonial rivalry and the militarism that plagued Europe in the later nineteenth century and that their advocates justified with reference to the creed of Social Darwinism. He also objected to British aggression in South Africa (the Boer Wars), an attitude that earned him much scorn from English nationalists and imperialists. Furthermore, he believed (as did Darwin) that the social struggle for survival was temporary. It belonged to the period when mankind was still close to its animal ancestry. Some day, when human development had reached its proper level, competition and struggle would be replaced by co-operation and peace and mutual sympathy. But until perfection had been reached, the natural process would have to continue functioning as moral guide.[4]

Spencer's conviction that morality was to be based on evolutionary biology found much support, in his own days as in ours, but it also aroused strong opposition. Some of that opposition came from Darwin's inner circle. The attitude of Darwin himself was ambivalent. Although critical of Spencer's speculative approach, Darwin more than once expressed agreement with the conclusions of the Social Darwinists.[5] He believed that in order for mankind to keep evolving to a higher level, the struggle between civilized and "lower" races and between more and less civilized societies had to continue. But at the same time he worried about the consequences of this struggle, for he could not help feeling that civilized nations and peoples had obligations to those lower in the scale. Darwin never quite succeeded in resolving the conflict between his admiration for the "higher morality" of Christianity and his belief that competitive struggle was essential if humanity was to reach the perfection of which it was capable.[6]

Thomas Huxley on evolutionary ethics

Among those who rejected Spencer's evolutionary ethics were some of Darwin's closest associates. They included Alfred Russell Wallace, co-inventor with Darwin of the theory of natural selection, the geologist Charles Lyell, and Darwin's long-time friend Thomas Huxley, whose unwavering and vociferous support of Darwinism earned him the nickname "Darwin's bulldog."

Huxley was the most outspoken of the three. He had begun as an evolutionary ethicist, in agreement with Spencer. Unlike Wallace and Lyell, he continued to accept Darwin's view of the role which natural selection had played in human evolution, but he came to oppose the type of ethical theories that Spencer, and to a lesser extent Darwin himself, based on it. A summary of his critique follows. It serves to show the nature and implications of an evolutionary ethics. It also demonstrates that it is difficult to avoid such an ethics if one holds to an evolutionistic worldview. Refusing to abandon Darwinism, Huxley was unable to provide a solution to the problems that Darwin's evolutionism raised in the ethical realm.

Huxley's best-known diatribe against evolutionary ethics is to be found in the Romanes lectures, which he delivered in 1893, two years before his death, under the title "Evolution and Ethics." As is clear from the Prolegomena to these lectures, Huxley was concerned not only about the ruthlessness implied in Spencer's Social Darwinism, but also about theories like those of Darwin's cousin Francis Galton, one of the early eugenicists. The idea of speeding up the evolution of humanity through selective breeding was catching on. Although careful not to promote an outright eugenicism, Darwin himself, in the *Descent of Man*, implied that the idea was not without merit. He wrote that civilized nations, by such policies as the building of asylums and hospitals and the institution of poor-laws, did their utmost to prolong the life of the weak, as a result of which these people managed to "propagate their kind." "No one," he commented, "who has attended to the breeding of domestic animals will doubt that this must be highly injurious to the race of man."[7]

But he was also quick to explain that "the aid which we feel impelled to give to the helpless is mainly an incidental result of the instinct of sympathy, which was originally acquired as part of the social instincts...." And he added, "Nor could we check our sympathy, even at the urging of hard reason, without deterioration in the noblest part of our nature." Even so, although his admiration for the "higher morality" remained strong, Darwin did suggest that it would be good if the weaker members of society refrained from marrying, and he proceeded to summarize at some length the arguments of eugenicists on the issue of natural selection as it affected civilized nations.[8]

More so than Darwin, Huxley recognized the connection between negative eugenics - measures to prevent procreation by the "weak members" of society - and the actual elimination of the unfit. He spoke of the disastrous consequences a policy of eugenics would have on the bonds that keep society together. And who, he asked, could possibly possess the wisdom to decide, "with the least chance of success, those who should be kept, as certain to be serviceable members of the polity, and those who should be chloroformed, as equally sure to be stupid, idle, or vicious. The 'points' of a good or of a bad citizen," he added, "are really far harder to discern than those of a puppy or a short-horn calf; many do not show themselves before the practical difficulties of life stimulate manhood to full exertion."[9]

Huxley attacked the idea that nature was a safe moral guide. It could not sanction moral behaviour because it was neither moral nor immoral, but amoral. Moral and immoral elements alike had evolved: the thief and murderer followed nature as much as the philanthropist. Cosmic evolutionism therefore, while it might be able to teach us how good and evil tendencies had come about, was unable to explain why what we call good is preferable to what we call evil.[10]

The moral progress of society depended, Huxley concluded, "not on imitating the cosmic process, still less in running away from it, but in combating it." That meant a course of conduct demanding self-restraint, cooperation, mutual aid, and an attitude that was directed "not so much to the survival of the fittest, as to the fitting of as many as possible to survive." And although Huxley believed that moral progress could be made, he warned that such progress would be slow. Because the animal element in man was ancient and strong and therefore hard to erase, the struggle against it would probably have to continue as long as the world lasted.[11]

Huxley's warnings were to the point, and his essay is still worth reading, but his conclusions do not follow from the premises. For how could man, in every respect a product of nature, be expected to overcome nature, or even want to do so? In the end Huxley could do no better than put his trust in human reason and the benevolent effects that a concerted human effort might have upon human nature. "The intelligence," he wrote, "which has converted the brother of the wolf into the faithful guardian of the flock ought to be able to do something towards curbing the instincts of savagery in civilized men."[12] He failed to mention, however, that the dog's evolution had been guided by an intelligence other (and higher) than its own. As a religious agnostic and a philosophical naturalist, Huxley could not assume that such transcendent guidance was available to humanity, and his hopes for moral improvement were therefore ill-founded. Indeed, the entire essay bears witness to the fact that, if belief in Darwinian evolutionism is maintained, no real substitute can be found for the naturalistic ethics which Huxley rightly rejected.

NOTES

[1] He mentioned this in a letter to W. Graham, written July 3, 1881. See *The Life and Letters of Charles Darwin, Including an Autobiographical Chapter*, ed. Francis Darwin, I, p. 285. See also *ibid.*, p. 282.

[2] Herbert Spencer, *Principles of Ethics* (New York: Appleton, 1898), I , p. xiv.

[3] Herbert Spencer, *Social Statics* (New York: Augustus M. Kelley, 1969; London: Chapman, 1851), p. 323.

[4] See Copleston, *A History of Philosophy*, VIII (Westminster, Maryland: Newman Press, 1966), ch. 5.

[5] On Darwin's attitude toward Spencer's theory, see John C. Greene, *Science, Ideology, and World View: Essays in the History of Evolutionary Ideas* (Berkeley: University of California Press, 1981), chs. 5, 6, and James R. Moore, *The Post-Darwinian Controversies* (Cambridge University Press, 1979), ch. 7.

[6] Greene, *Science, Ideology, and World View*, p. 158.

[7] Darwin, *The Descent of Man and Selection in Relation to Sex* (New York and London: Merrill and Baker, 1874), pp. 151f.

[8] *Ibid.*, pp. 152ff. See also pp. 706f.

[9] Thomas H. Huxley, *Evolution and Ethics and Other Essays* (New York: Appleton, 1929 [1896]), p. 23.

[10] *Ibid.*, p. 80.

[11] *Ibid.*, pp. 81-85.

[12] *Ibid.*, p. 85.

XIII. Positivism, Idealism, and the Study of History

We have seen that the heritage of Romanticism and the interest in history were important elements in the arrival of evolutionism, and therefore in the shaping of the nineteenth-century worldview in general. By mid-century the Romantic revolution had run its course, but the interest in history remained strong. It was not, of course, the only intellectual force in the nineteenth century. History shared the stage with other philosophical trends. Among them were, in addition to an all-pervasive evolutionism, the philosophies of positivism and idealism, both of which had connections with historiography. In this chapter we will look at the manner in which the three movements interacted. We will begin with descriptions of positivism and idealism, looking at them as independent philosophies and as influences on historical study, and then turn to the rise of historicism, another development in the field of history.

Positivism

Nineteenth-century positivism was inspired by the belief that the natural sciences were on the threshold of bringing about a truly rational age. The term positivism was invented by the Frenchman Auguste Comte (1798-1857), who believed that scientific knowledge was the only worthwhile or "positive" kind. Comte was the founder of sociology and the great advocate of a renovated culture, one wherein science and its methodology would take the place of religion and bring about the long-awaited utopia.

The great trust in science, which Comte shared with many of his contemporaries, was in large part a result of science's explanatory power, although its effect on technology would increasingly play a role as well. Little of that influence, however, was evident in the first half of the nineteenth century. The industrial revolution had begun without the benefit of science. The harnessing of steam power and its application to industry and transportation, for example, were the work of engineers and artisans, who relied on their own inventiveness rather than on scientific discoveries. It was not until the second half of the century that Francis Bacon's belief in the technological potential of science at last appeared to be justified. Largely (although not solely) as a result of scientific developments, that period witnessed a major technological revolution. Among the advances were the application of electricity, the development of electrical generators and of the internal combustion engine, the production of industrial chemicals, and the invention of telephone and telegraph. Innovations in the medical field included the manufacture of drugs and the application of the findings of microbiology in immunology.

No less impressive than the advances in technology and medicine were nineteenth-century developments in the pure sciences. Especially important among them were the theory of electromagnetism, the modern atomic theory (which was followed by the formulation of the "atomistic" cell theory for organic beings), the law of the conservation of energy, and Darwin's theory of evolution. The philosopher Alfred North Whitehead, who selected these four developments as the century's most important ones, writes that "the convergent effect of the new power for scientific advance, which resulted from these four ideas, transformed the middle period of the century into an orgy of scientific triumph.... Thus to the excitement derived from technological revolution, there was now added the excitement arising from the vistas disclosed by scientific theory. Both the material and the spiritual bases of social life were in process of transformation."[1]

The excitement was probably the greater because three of the generalizing theories, the law of the conservation of energy, the atomic theory, and Darwin's evolutionism, eliminated the need for a Creator and divine providence, and so allowed for an autonomous universe. The nineteenth century thus provided the scientific foundations for the fully secular worldview that the eighteenth had been looking for. To Comte the scientific advances suggested that similar explanatory laws could be developed for the advancement of the human and social sciences, and that in attempting to find these laws social scientists should follow the procedures that had been so successful in disciplines like physics and chemistry. The human sciences were to be subsumed under the natural sciences and both man and society explained in naturalistic terms.

The idea that man and society could be analyzed simply as natural objects was not all that strange in a period when materialistic philosophies had for some time already reduced humanity to nature. Life, thought, and behaviour were to be explained, according to these philosophies, in purely physical terms and were therefore subject to natural laws. Shortly after Comte completed his work, the naturalistic explanation of human life and action would be applied in biology and in such pan-evolutionist theories as Social Darwinism and evolutionary ethics. It would also be applied in history and in other areas of knowledge, and it would dominate sociology, Comte's own discipline. Comte believed that by following the naturalistic approach he would be able to do for man and society what Galileo and Newton and their colleagues had done for the natural sciences. By placing human thought and action on a positivist basis, sociology could ensure, among other things, that at some time in the future discord and war would cease and true harmony prevail among men.

For Comte this was not just a utopian dream. A believer in the idea of progress, he was convinced that the age of harmony was bound to arrive sooner or later. He showed its inevitability in his so-called law of the three phases. According to that law society and the individual pass through three phases or stages of progressive development. In the first stage, the religious one, people still believe in God or gods and in direct supernatural intervention in life and nature. Next comes the philosophical or metaphysical stage, when they become aware of the existence of natural laws, but still believe in a supernatural lawgiver. In the final stage, man realizes that there is no external lawgiver. Nature obeys its own unchanging laws, and all natural and human phenomena can be explained with reference to these laws. Once this is realized, progress is guaranteed. The positive phase had already been reached in the natural sciences. Comte spent great effort attempting to hasten its arrival in the sciences of man and society, teaching his contemporaries that intellectual inquiry must be restricted to the search for scientific, observable, "positive" facts, rather than for religious and metaphysical explanations. The only criteria to be used in judging propositions were empirical and logical ones.

Positivism and the study of history

Comte propagated his positivist philosophy in a six-volume work, which was published between 1830 and 1842. In that same period historians were in the process of turning history, which had long been an adjunct of theology, philosophy, and literature, into an autonomous discipline, one that would be on an equal footing with the natural sciences. This meant that a rigorous, "scientific" methodology had to be established. The attempt, which was begun in the eighteenth century, accelerated and was largely completed in the nineteenth. Hans Meyerhoff describes how it was done:

> As a result of the opening of diplomatic archives and in conjunction with the "auxiliary sciences" of biblical scholarship, mythology, philology, numismatics, and archaeology, history...began to develop logical tools and analytic techniques of its own. Critical methods were devised for sifting, testing, collating, and evaluating documentary sources; rigorous standards were employed for judging the impartiality, objectivity, and truthfulness of a historical work; and the new techniques were taught and applied in the academic seminars of the [Prussian] Historical School, to which students flocked from all over the world.[2]

Although the work had first of all been inspired by the methods of classical philology, the positivist movement with its stress on empiricism, logic, and a critical attitude also played a role. In its demand for exactitude and an objective approach, the influence of positivism on historiography was generally benign. There were also negative consequences, however, one of them being that history became an ancillary to mechanistic social sciences. History in this set-up provided data on human behaviour which the social sciences, especially sociology, would use for the construction of sociological laws. It meant that in history as in sociology free will and human responsibility became illusory. Although certainly not all nineteenth-century historians were positivists, the prevailing belief in the all-sufficiency of empiricism and the trust in method led many of them, also those who rejected positivism, into a position that was close to the positivist one.

Positivism also encouraged the development of the naturalistic branch of speculative history. Speculative history (or meta-history) refers to the attempt to find patterns and laws in history and so to determine the meaning of the historical process. The search may simply be for an explanation of the past, but in many cases the patterns that are discovered are also used to predict the future. We encounter this type of speculative history in Comte, who used his law of the three phases to explain both past and future, and also in a pan-evolutionist like Herbert Spencer.

The best-known naturalistic meta-historian of the nineteenth century, and indeed of all time, is Karl Marx, the father of "scientific socialism" or communism. A materialist and economic determinist, Marx called his socialism scientific because it was based on empirical laws which could be verified by way of historical study. One of these laws was that the means of production form the substructure of any society, and that all other aspects of social life – laws, religion, social and political institutions, and so on – are no more than the superstructure. The mere product of the economic set-up, they are replaced, or even abolished altogether, when there is a change in the means of production (for example, when feudalism is replaced by capitalism, or capitalism by Marx's brand of socialism). Another law established the inevitability of conflicts between the have-nots and the rich, conflicts that were destined to be won by the poor. Yet a third one stated that oppression is the result of the institute of private property, which in turn is protected by the state, so that, for a just society to be established, both private property and the state must be abolished. This would happen after the final war between the classes, when an impoverished industrial proletariat had overthrown its capitalist oppressors and the golden age of communism had begun. In short, history might appear to be no more than sound and fury, signifying nothing, but Marx showed it to have a pattern, a plan, and a purpose.

Idealism and the study of history: Kant

Positivism was strong in England and France but did not make much of an inroad in Germany. A notable exception is of course Karl Marx, but, as will become apparent, Marx was influenced as much by the German idealist Hegel as by the positivism of a man like Auguste Comte. Idealism (although not necessarily the Hegelian version) was the dominant philosophy in Germany, and idealism was the opposite of empiricism and positivism. Empiricists, following Locke, taught that there are no innate ideas and that knowledge therefore derives not from the mind but from the data of sense experience. Idealism, on the other hand, stressed the central function of the mind in the process of cognition. In its more radical forms, it denied the reality of the external world apart from the thinking self. Only the idea existed as an independent reality, which meant that the world as we know it was created by human thought.

Idealism was inspired by the philosophy of Immanuel Kant. Although Kant was far less radical than some of his followers, the idea that nature's order is the creation of the human mind was central to his epistemology. As we saw in chapter 10, Kant admitted that scientific knowledge cannot be had apart from the data of sense experience, but he disagreed with the empiricist position that the mind contains nothing but that which the senses bring to it. Rather, the mind is central in Kant's system and in fact orders and structures the physical world. It possesses a set of *a priori* categories by means of which it establishes the so-called natural laws (such as the law of causation), which it then imposes on nature. In the last analysis, therefore, in Kant also it is thought that creates the world.

In nineteenth-century Germany there was much interest in the study of the past, and Kant's German followers generally dealt with or even concentrated on the philosophy of history. Although this absorbing concern was not shared by Kant, he did write a number of essays on history topics. His interest was not primarily historical but philosophical. Like many Enlightenment thinkers who turned to history (and also like the nineteenth-century positivists we just met), he looked at the past as a speculative historian, attempting to determine the meaning and outcome of the historical process. That goal he pursued most systematically in an essay entitled, "Idea for a Universal History from a Cosmopolitan Point of View," which was published in 1784.[3]

This essay shows that Kant, like other thinkers of the period, saw history as the record of human progress toward rationality and freedom. Mankind, he believed, had begun as part of an amoral and deterministic Nature but was moving toward a truly moral and rational existence. Kant said that he could point to empirical evidence in support of this view, but he relied primarily on *a priori* arguments. He started from the premiss that Nature does nothing in vain and therefore ensures that all the capacities it has instilled in its creatures will be fully realized. The natural capacities of man (and the ones that distinguish him from all other living beings) are rationality and the potential to act as a moral agent. In order for these capacities to develop fully, Kant said, a civil society is needed, one that has the power to administer rational laws and so to eliminate the lawlessness humanity inherited from its savage past. What is required is not only the establishment of the civilized state, but also of an association of states, a cosmopolis; for only by worldwide cooperation can war and other international conflicts be avoided and mankind live a fully rational and moral life.

Nature's goal or "secret plan" is to bring about this pleasant situation. But the process it follows is not a pleasant one, at least not for the individual. Nature does not really care for the individual. Its concern is for the species, which alone is immortal and therefore capable of reaching humanity's final goal. To ensure the ultimate happiness of the species, individuals throughout history have to toil for the realization of that goal, and the means by which Nature forces them to do so is a combination of reason and what Kant calls mankind's "unsocial sociability." By this he means that, while man cannot live without society, his character flaws – such as his inherent competitiveness, heartlessness, and love of self rather than of the neighbour – make him at the same time utterly unsocial. The suffering this unsociability causes, not just to others but also to himself, will serve to convince him of the need to work for the establishment of a truly lawful society. In short, present evil brings about future redemption. And this is not mankind's doing; it is the work of Nature which, Kant says, knows better than man what is good for the race.

Although Kant introduced some novel aspects, the idea of history's progress through suffering was not new. A secularization of the Christian message, the idea had been used already in the early eighteenth century. Kant's predecessor in this regard was the Italian philosopher Giambattista Vico (1668-1744) whose philosophical work *The New Science* inspired not only speculative philosophers but also academic historians.[4] We will meet him again when discussing the historicism of the German Historical School. In his speculative work Vico anticipated Kant in teaching that in progressing from savagery to civilization humanity is guided by a power of which it is not aware and which it obeys without realizing its existence. Although Vico called that power divine providence, he usually treated it not as a supernatural power but as an immanent force. Human history in his system developed in accordance with laws that operated in what can only be called a mechanical fashion. It is true that Vico objected to the mechanistic philosophy of his day, and also that he distinguished between the methodologies to be followed in the natural and in the human sciences. Nevertheless, there are striking similarities between his view of history and the mechanistic model of the physical universe. The same thing is noticeable in Kant and in nineteenth-century speculative philosophers like Hegel and Marx.

Hegel's philosophy of history

Georg Wilhelm Friedrich Hegel (1770-1831) was a philosophical idealist and as such a successor of Kant, whose philosophy he used as a starting point for his own. Like that of Kant, Hegel's thought ranged over many areas. Among them was the field of religion, an aspect to which we will give attention in the next chapter. At this point we will concentrate on his philosophy of history, although, as will become apparent, it is not always possible to separate that part from the rest of his work.

An important element in Hegel's philosophy is his dialectic. Following the German idealist philosopher Johann Fichte (who died in 1814), Hegel used a method according to which opposites resolve themselves into a synthesis. The three steps of his dialectic are well known, if not through the work of Hegel himself, then through that of Marx, who borrowed Hegel's method. The first step in the dialectic is the thesis, which, when its inadequacies become apparent, gives rise to its opposite, the antithesis. The antithesis, in turn, is followed by a synthesis, which contains the two previous stages within itself, reconciling them and bringing them together at a higher level. To give an example from Marxism: medieval feudalism was the thesis, modern capitalism the antithesis, and communism would constitute the synthesis. It would retain the best of feudalism and capitalism while avoiding the evils of the two systems. An example from Hegel's work is the progress of freedom as exemplified in the history of Greece, Rome, and the modern West. The Greek concern with democracy and individual freedom constituted the thesis; the aristocratic Roman state with its stress on law served as the antithesis, and the modern Germanic state, which contained the positive aspects of both the Greek and the Roman systems while again avoiding their negative characteristics, formed the synthesis.

For Hegel as for Kant, history was the process toward the triumph of reason and freedom. Specifically, the historical record bore witness to the self-realization of the Spirit. Hegel called the Spirit also Reason, *Logos*, and the Absolute, and often referred to it as God. His Spirit, however, like all deities created by philosophers, was different from the God of the Bible. It was impersonal, non-transcendent, and, like man and nature, in a stage of constant development. It progressively realized itself through nature and human history by a process of dialectical unfolding. The unfolding of the Spirit through nature did not mean, Hegel said, that the world was divine. He objected to a pantheistic explanation of his system. Nor did it mean that the universe was illusory. As the objective manifestation of the Spirit it was truly real. The Spirit, Hegel taught, was the invisible universe, and the universe the visible Spirit.

In Hegel's philosophy, then, spirit was the ultimate reality, and because the nature of spirit is freedom, the historical process would culminate in the triumph of freedom. This ideal would be reached with the establishment of a united political community wherein the citizens were their own lawgivers; for Hegel agreed with Rousseau that true freedom is possible only in a state wherein the individual obeys laws he himself has set. To reach this stage is history's goal. Hegel's book *The Philosophy of History* shows that in moving toward this goal the Spirit (which in this context he called the World Spirit) makes use of what Hegel calls world-historical peoples: nations that at their appointed time play a decisive role in the history of the world. It also makes use of world-historical individuals, such as Alexander the Great, Julius Caesar, and Napoleon, people who are, in a sense, the World Spirit incarnate. Although these nations and individuals believe that they are pursuing their own goals, they are in fact no more than instruments of the World Spirit. The Spirit uses human achievements, but also human passions and the ensuing conflicts and wars and every other kind of evil that history witnesses, in order to bring about the perfection toward which it is striving. Hegel speaks in this connection of "the cunning of Reason," a mechanism that is similar to Kant's "secret plan of history."

Hegel, Kant, and Marx

Hegel has other traits in common with his predecessor, and also with his successor, Karl Marx. For one thing he builds, like Kant and Marx, on the idea of progress. This is implied in the dialectic, which proceeds in a continuous and progressive fashion. Each synthesis becomes a new thesis, giving rise to a repetition of the dialectical process until at last the highest synthesis is reached wherein the remaining contradictions are resolved. In Kant and Hegel this happy situation will arrive with the establishment of a rational political system that ensures full human freedom; in Marx with the triumph of communism.

Another similarity is that for these thinkers the golden age will come, as Vico already taught, by means of conflict and suffering. In essence their philosophies are secularized versions of the old theodicies, that is, they are means of justifying the ways of God (or Nature, or Reason, or History) with man. (Hegel, in fact, concludes his *Philosophy of History* by calling his system "the true *Theodicaea*, the justification of God in History."[5]) In all cases, human suffering may seem to be an evil but actually it is a blessing, since it is necessary for future freedom and happiness. As the poet Alexander Pope had said in the previous century, all partial evil is universal good. And as Darwin would express it a few decades after Hegel's death, the war of nature, famine, and death serve a higher purpose, namely the evolution of "forms most beautiful and most wonderful." The individual is sacrificed for the species, and the known present for an unknown future.

And finally, these systems have in common their deterministic view of man and history. Much as the speculative historians exalt human freedom, they in fact make the individual the tool of forces over which he has no control, which he does not even understand and therefore cannot resist. Reason or providence or the logic of history, or whatever the controlling force is called, uses the works of individuals, nations, and socio-economic classes – their good deeds as well as their crimes – for the fulfilment of a destiny of which it alone is aware. Mortals have no will of their own and are therefore not responsible for what they do. In that respect the meta-historians, also those of the idealist stripe, objectified the human being just as much as did all-out positivists like Comte.

Historicism

Historicism, which developed out of Romanticism, strongly opposed the approach of the meta-historians. Historicists were nominalists and made a point of stressing the difference between history proper, that is, history as the record of actions that are essentially unpredictable, and speculative history with its assumption of historical regularities. History for them was concerned not with the predetermined, the permanent, and the universal, but with human freedom, change, and the particular. There were no repetitions or cycles; each age was unique. The study of history therefore could not yield laws.

Historicists objected not only to the work of the speculative historians, they also opposed the use that Enlightenment *philosophes* had made of history. Enlightenment thinkers like Gibbon, Voltaire, and Condorcet and their peers had believed that the past was worth studying not first of all for its own sake, but because it provided examples that demonstrated the truth of Enlightenment philosophy. Believing that the eighteenth century was the crown of history's development so far, they judged previous epochs according to whether or not they had anticipated the Enlightenment achievement.

Romantics had rejected that view, and so did their historicist followers. They demanded an empathetic approach to the study of history and insisted that past societies and cultures be judged not with reference to the present, but on their own terms. Already in the late eighteenth century the Romantic philosopher Johann Gottfried Herder had taught the equality of all periods. In the nineteenth century Leopold von Ranke, the leading German historicist, expressed the same sentiment when he said that each epoch is "immediate to God."

The belief in the equality of all periods did not mean that historicism ignored the differences between past and present, nor did it mean that it denied progress. Although it did not evolve out of scientific evolutionism, it arose in the same period and was influenced by the same progressive view of history. But the conviction that much progress had already been made was no reason for historicists to adopt a condescending attitude toward earlier ages. Instead of judging past cultures, they wanted simply to describe them, and to do so with empathy. It was the only way truly to understand the past.

It was also the only way to understand the present. For an important element in historicism is the conviction that the roots of things present are in the past. Historicists believed that institutions, philosophies, religions, legal systems and so on are to be explained by studying their historical development, and that their validity can be established in no other manner than with reference to their supposed genesis. The modern tendency to explain and evaluate phenomena by their origin is part of the historicist inheritance.

Historical relativism

Historical research and writing flourished under historicism. But while great advances were made in the practical field, all was not well in the realm of theory. Academic historians experienced ongoing difficulties in their search for an underlying philosophy, one capable of answering questions about the goals history should pursue, about the methodology appropriate for historical study, and about the nature and legitimacy of history as an intellectual discipline.

One difficulty they encountered was the threat of an all-out historical relativism, a problem that was especially serious because it played havoc with what historians believed to be the social function of history. Historicism, and indeed the nineteenth century in general, saw history as a source of values, one that in a secular age could take the place of religion. This implied the need for historians to distinguish between good and evil, true and false, the moral and the immoral. But it was also of the essence of historicism to judge past epochs on their own terms, rather than according to nineteenth-century norms or – least of all – transcendent ones. In a historicist age there were no universal and unchanging standards. This view encouraged the relativizing of moral values. As Geoffrey Barraclough writes, under the rule of historicism

> ...Everything is related, judged and evaluated in relation – and far too often solely in relation – to time, place, context and environment; there are no absolutes; there is no transcendent sanction for man's action; morality itself is atomized, particularized, pulverized, until in the end it is held to be "impossible to think one man essentially more wicked than another." The historian is taught to discover, not whether Charles I – or Hitler – was right or wrong, but "how his action was historically conditioned...."[6]

Another problem concerned methodology. Like the practitioners of sociology and other social sciences, historians wanted a method that was truly scientific, and more than one historian, as we noted, heeded the positivist advice and attempted to follow the approach of the natural sciences. By the end of the century it became increasingly evident, however, that this methodology was not really applicable to human studies. It was not simply that positivism denied the unrepeatability of historical events. Equally important was the growing awareness that the type of objective approach which the scientific method demanded was not possible in history. There was an unavoidable subjective component in historical research and theorizing, which meant that historical interpretation would always be tentative.

There were several reasons for the increased awareness of the uncertainties in historical knowing. An important element was that in the final decades of the nineteenth century much attention was given to the implications of perspectivism, that is, the idea that our view of things is limited by our personal and cultural frames of reference, and that therefore our perception of reality is necessarily partial. The fact that historians looked at the world through the glasses provided by their individual and cultural idiosyncrasies and biases implied that a truly objective understanding of people from different periods and cultures was impossible. It also implied that history would constantly be rewritten, because different individuals and epochs would look at the past from different perspectives and therefore come with different conclusions.

The same period also witnessed a sustained attack on human rationality, and therefore on the traditional assumption that, as essentially rational beings, past individuals could indeed be understood. The turn to the irrational was influenced by the theories of men like Marx, Nietzsche, and Freud, who revealed the role of impersonal forces in history and of hidden, unconscious drives in human thought and behaviour. These theories showed that the objects of historical research were not only the product of a culture different from that of the investigators themselves, they were also individuals whose actions defied rational analysis. Indeed, perspectivism and the preponderance of the irrational in man constituted a dual obstacle to true knowledge of the past, since they affected both the historian and the peoples and societies he studied.[7]

The new historicism

The crisis that these developments caused inspired different responses. There were those who stuck to the positivist belief that only the natural sciences yield valid knowledge. Some of these historians continued to treat history as a natural science, while others, realizing the futility of that attempt and convinced that historical knowledge was by its very nature uncertain, resigned themselves to that fact. The school of historical relativism, which was especially strong in the United States, counted among its members the well-known American historians Charles Beard and Carl Becker.[8]

A different response came from a number of European philosophers. Prominent among them was the German idealist Wilhelm Dilthey, who lived from 1833 to 1911 and became the founder of the so-called "new historicism." Rejecting the belief in the universal applicability of the scientific method, Dilthey distinguished between *Geisteswissenschaften* (the humanities and the social sciences) and *Naturwissenschaften* (the natural sciences). The implication was that a natural science like physics and a human science like history were both truly scientific disciplines (in the sense that they were equally capable of yielding valid knowledge), but that they constituted different kinds of science. An important dissimilarity was that the subjective element was both unavoidable and necessary in historical studies, whereas the method used in the natural sciences aimed at eliminating that element. This difference was among the reasons why history, as historicists had always argued, required a different method from the one used in the natural sciences.

Dilthey's ideas as to the specifics of the historical method had much in common with those of Vico and of the earlier historicists. Like them, he stressed the need for an objective, scientific approach to history while insisting that that approach be enriched by an attempt to understand from the inside the feelings and thought processes of the individuals who had made history. He also followed Vico in believing that each period and culture had its own mentality, which distinguished it from all other cultures. This idea had been inherited by the Romantics and the early historicists, who had worked it out in their concepts of *Zeitgeist* and *Volksgeist* (respectively the spirit of the time and the spirit of a particular "folk " or culture). The concept of *Volksgeist* in particular has led some people to "spiritualize" their culture and encouraged a rabidly nationalistic interpretation of history. Yet as historicists pointed out, it can be used in a positive sense as well, namely as a means to arrive at a more comprehensive view of past epochs. To understand a historical society, they said, the historian should analyze its culture, and a first step in doing so was to come to know the *Zeit-* and the *Volksgeist* which informed the various manifestations of the culture in question and so gave them a certain "family likeness." An understanding of a period's legal traditions or its art or literature, for example, would therefore facilitate the understanding of the period as a whole.

Dilthey and his peers, in short, refuted the positivist notion that scientific detachment was either possible or desirable in history while at the same time insisting that historical knowledge could be reliable. They showed that the subjective element was not only a liability but also an asset. It was only as a thinking, feeling, and imagining human being that the historian could understand fellow human beings. Of course, the presence of the subjective element meant that historical interpretation would always be influenced by the times wherein the historian lived and by his own personality and beliefs. Historical interpretation would therefore never be uniform and history would continually be rewritten, even though many past histories would retain their value. But the lack of uniformity in historical interpretation, historicists argued, was unavoidable and not necessarily a drawback. The different points of view that different historians brought to their task ensured a more comprehensive view of the past and so enriched historical understanding.

Furthermore, although there was a danger of all-out subjectivism in historical studies, that type of problem, they pointed out, was not insurmountable. The historical method with its stress on the need for objectivity served as a safeguard against one-sidedness. As was the case in the natural sciences, so it was (at least in principle) in the human ones. Historians were accountable for the use they made of their sources, and scrutiny by their peers would constitute a safeguard against arbitrariness. The very awareness of his personal involvement, moreover, would warn the conscientious historian to guard against bias and so serve the cause of objectivity.

Although they did much to place the discipline of history on a sound and solid basis, Dilthey and his peers failed to eliminate the fundamental flaw of historicism, namely its encouragement of moral relativism and of the related belief that all truth is historically determined. A relativistic attitude would, at least in part as a result of the historicist tradition, characterize the late-modern and postmodern worldview as a whole. But to admit historicism's role in this development is not to deny the movement's positive contributions. Under its guidance history was freed from its subservience to other fields of knowledge and enabled to develop into an independent discipline. In distinguishing between natural and human sciences, moreover, historicism challenged the positivist belief that there is no truth beyond that which can be seen and measured and logically demonstrated. More than that, it served to strengthen a growing conviction that there is a subjective component not only in human studies, but in all disciplines, including the natural sciences. In doing so it contributed to the wave of skepticism that characterized late- and postmodern times, but it also influenced the search for epistemologies which avoided the one-sidedness of a positivistic Cartesianism. We will describe these developments in later chapters.

NOTES

[1.] Whitehead, *Science and the Modern World*, pp. 92-6.

[2] Hans Meyerhoff, ed., *The Philosophy of History in Our Time* (Garden City, New York: Doubleday, Anchor Books, 1959), pp. 12f.

[3.] Immanuel Kant, *On History*, ed. Lewis White Beck, trans. Lewis White Beck, Robert E. Anchor, Emil L. Fackenheim (Indianapolis: Bobbs-Merrill, Library of Liberal Arts, 1963), pp. 11-26. A helpful analysis is given in the editor's introduction to the volume.

[4.] Vico published the first edition of his *Scienza Nuova* in 1725. A much revised edition appeared in 1730, and again in 1744, the year of Vico's death. For an analysis of Vico's ideas on history, see Isaiah Berlin, *Vico and Herder: Two Studies in the History of Ideas* (New York: Viking Press, 1976); Peter Burke, *Vico* (Oxford: Oxford University Press, 1985); Amos Funkenstein, *Theology and the Scientific Imagination,* ch. 4; Leon Pompa, *Vico: A Study of the 'New Science'* (London: Cambridge University Press, 1975).

[5] Georg Wilhelm Friedrich Hegel, *The Philosophy of History,* trans. J. Sibree, with an introduction by C. J. Friedrich (New York: Dover Publications, 1956), p. 457. For an analysis of Hegel's philosophy of history, see William H. Dray, *Philosophy of History* (Englewood Cliffs, N.J.: Prentice-Hall, 1964), ch. 6; W. H. Walsh, *Philosophy of History: An Introduction* (New York: Harper and Row, Harper Torchbooks, 1967), ch. 7. Helpful overviews of Hegel's philosophy as a whole can be found in Charles Taylor, *Hegel* (Cambridge: Cambridge University Press, 1978 [1975]), and John Edward Toews, *Hegelianism: The Path Toward Dialectical Humanism, 1805-1841* (Cambridge: Cambridge University Press, 1985 [1980]).

[6] Geoffrey Barraclough, "The Historian in a Changing World," in Meyerhoff, *The Philosophy of History in Our Time,* p. 30.

[7] On these developments, and also on the "new historicism" in the next section, see the Editors' Introductions to Hans Meyerhoff, ed., *The Philosophy of History in Our Time,* pp. 1-25, and Fritz Stern, ed., *The Varieties of History: From Voltaire to the Present* (Cleveland: World, Meridian Books, 1964 [1956]), pp. 11-32, as well as Trygve R. Tholfsen, *Historical Thinking: An Introduction* (New York: Harper and Row, 1967), ch. 5, 6, 8.

[8] Tholfsen, *Historical Thinking,* pp. 220-24.

XIV. The Higher Criticism

In the early-modern period cultural leadership in Western Europe had come from Italy, France, and England. Germany, disunited and suffering from the aftermath of the disastrous Thirty Years' War (1618-48), had lagged far behind its neighbours to the south and west. This situation changed in the course of the eighteenth century. Germany then moved to the centre of the cultural scene, a position it would retain throughout the next century. In this period it would catch the world's attention with its great works in music and literature, with its achievements in the fields of philosophy, political theory, and historiography, and also with its work in biblical studies, the topic of the present chapter. Especially important in this area was the development of the so-called higher criticism. Although this form of biblical criticism was practised throughout the West, it was nineteenth-century Germany that assumed the leadership in the field. Its scholars recruited disciples from both Europe and North America, and some of its universities became international centres of biblical studies.

Modern biblical criticism was not a development that belonged to the nineteenth century alone. Seventeenth- and eighteenth-century thinkers had already questioned the historicity and reliability of Scripture. Among them was the German deist Hermann Samuel Reimarus (1694-1768), whose work was published shortly after his death.[1] As a deist, Reimarus did not intend to eliminate religion, but he did want to make it fully "rational." It had to include faith in a Creator, in morality, and in the existence of a future life, but not in any of the supernatural events the

Bible recounts. Jesus, for example, was for Reimarus simply a Jewish political and religious reformer. Accounts of miracles and other supernatural events had been invented by his followers, which meant that the interpretation provided in the New Testament was fraudulent.

Most of the newer critics rejected that conclusion. They were heirs of eighteenth-century rationalism, but also of a variety of nineteenth-century theories such as positivism, evolutionism, idealism, and a Romantic historicism. Positivism taught them to approach the work of biblical interpretation in a "scientific" spirit, which meant that the same methods were to be applied to the Bible as to any other historical document. This implied, as in the case of Reimarus, the exclusion of the supernatural elements. These, however, were no longer rejected as fraud. Instructed by evolutionism, idealism, and historicism, the new critics saw past religions as essential for the development of humanity's religious consciousness. Because religion was ever evolving, all its phases had been necessary. In that sense, every religion, even the most primitive one, was "immediate to God." The fact that the truths of the past could not be the truths of the present therefore did not mean that past beliefs were to be labelled as deceptions. They had been necessary for their own times and should be respected as such.

When dealing with the supernatural elements in the Bible, most nineteenth-century critics interpreted these as the product of myth. By that term they referred to stories which they believed primitive societies unconsciously created in an attempt to give historic form to their religious or national experiences – and which in fact usually contained a historical element. The myth concept, which had been developed by Vico, had earlier been used to explain Old Testament accounts, but in the nineteenth century it was increasingly applied to the New Testament as well. In the many books this century produced on the "historical Jesus," for example, the miracles and other supernatural events in the gospel accounts were often interpreted as creative legends by means of which the early church supported its belief in Jesus as the promised Messiah. Although these interpretations were not based on historical truth, they were important in that they helped modern theologians to understand the Bible. Meanwhile, to make the Bible relevant for the present, it simply had to be demythologized, so that whatever lasting truth it might possess could be revealed.

Although the higher criticism was destructive of the Christian faith, this was not what the majority of the critics intended. There no doubt were some who embarked on the work because of a rabid anticlericalism or a hatred of Christianity. The motive that inspired most of the nineteenth-century critics, however, was similar to the one that had inspired Reimarus and other deists: they wanted to rescue the Christian religion from oblivion by re-interpreting it in such a way that it would be suitable to their own rational and scientific age. That work, however, which took most of the nineteenth century and continued into the twentieth, left behind it a religiosity that was still called Christian but that had all but lost its connection with biblical revelation. In many cases the approach also led to an outright rejection of Christianity, even of Christianity in its watered-down form, and to the adoption of a full-fledged atheism. In what follows, we will look at both developments.

Schleiermacher's religion of feeling

Two men who had a strong impact on the nineteenth-century critical movement, and indeed on modern theology as a whole, were the theologian Friedrich Daniel Ernst Schleiermacher (1768-1834) and the philosopher Hegel, Schleiermacher's contemporary (1770-1831).

As a child, Schleiermacher had been educated in the Pietist tradition, but later he came under the influence of Rousseau and of German Romanticism. Although frequently heterodox, German Romantics were greatly interested in religion. Because he had studied theology and served as a clergyman, Schleiermacher was asked by his Romantic friends to explain his religious views. He responded with his book *On Religion: Speeches to Its Cultured Despisers*, which he published in 1799. In this work, his first major religious writing, he did not attempt to give a rational defence of religion but, in Romantic fashion, tried to explain what he believed to be its essence and ultimate meaning.

That essence was not morality, as Locke and Kant believed, nor was it assent to biblical truths, as taught by orthodox Lutheranism and orthodox Pietism. It was, rather, an "intuition of the universe," a "sensibility and taste for the infinite," or, as he expressed it in a later writing, a "feeling of utter dependence." Essentially, it was a craving for union with the "absolute." Schleiermacher described the absolute in impersonal terms, usually referring to it as "the universe," "the infinite," or "the highest." Sometimes, it is true, he called it "the deity," but this was not meant to convey the idea that religion required faith in a personal God. Belief in a personal deity, he stated, did not constitute the "hinge" or "chief article" of religion.[2] Although later he tried to come across as somewhat more orthodox, he continued to deny that the assumption of theism was of primary religious importance. The goal of religion was not to know a personal God but to strive toward union with the cosmos.

Schleiermacher believed that religious faith was a universal phenomenon, that all religions were valid, and that therefore religious plurality should prevail. Diversity was necessary and unavoidable because no religion could possess religious truth in all its fullness. He did state that Christianity was exceptional in that it had been "raised to a higher power" than other religions. This was so because it recognized "that everything finite requires higher mediation in order to be connected with the divine."[3] But the fact that Christianity possessed this insight did not mean that it should want to rule the world and refuse to welcome other religious forms. Nothing was more unchristian, Schleiermacher said, than to seek religious uniformity.[4] Nor did Christianity's superior status mean that it possessed final truth, or that the Christian Scriptures were infallible. Much of the Bible was to be understood not in a literal and historical, but in a symbolic sense. In this way Schleiermacher tried to make his peace with rationalistic attacks on Christianity while satisfying the contemporary craving for spirituality.

Hegel and the Romantics

The Romantics of Schleiermacher's day were heirs to Kant's philosophy, and one of their most pressing concerns was to reconcile Kantian principles with those of Romanticism proper. Among these principles were Kant's dualisms – especially his sharp separation between man and nature – and his belief in human freedom and autonomy. For Kant these two ideas were inseparably connected. It was in order to save humanity from becoming part of nature and so losing its freedom that he insisted on the absolute distinction between the two.[5]

Kant's Romantic followers adopted his principle of man's radical autonomy and indeed made it central to their ideology, but they rejected Kant's dualisms. Romantics were holists. Believing that physical nature and man were of the same substance, they longed for communion, even for a mystical union, with the universe. This mystical craving was expressed in Romantic poetry and in the visual arts and was also clearly evident in Schleiermacher's theology. The problem in this craving for union with nature was that it could – and indeed often did – lead to some version of pantheism. Pantheism, however, implied man's immersion in nature and therefore his loss of freedom. The two most cherished beliefs of Romanticism, in short, were irreconcilable.

It was this problem that Hegel came to solve. Like Schleiermacher,

Hegel belonged to the generation of early German Romantics, but unlike Schleiermacher he chose, quite early in his career, a rationalist approach to philosophy. He believed that it was only by acknowledging the absolute rule of reason in life and thought that Romanticism's central problem could be resolved.

In attempting to bring about the required synthesis, Hegel made use of his idea of the cosmic Spirit, which, as we saw in the previous chapter, was central to his philosophy. His Spirit had similarities with the world soul of pantheism in that it, too, expressed itself in nature. But although it evolved out of nature, Hegel's Spirit was also prior to and separate from it, and a similar status was guaranteed to the human being. Since it came to self-consciousness in man, the Spirit united man with the universe, but it at the same time established man's independence from the world of nature. The essence of Spirit was freedom, and mankind shared in that freedom.

By means of this construction Hegel managed to reconcile the irreconcilables of Romanticism – at least for the time being. Ultimately it would become clear that man and the infinite could not co-exist as equal partners; that man either had to give up his claim to autonomy or, if he refused to do so, transfer the Spirit's powers to himself. In course of time the second alternative would for many become the more logical one. But although destined to fail in its central goal, Hegel's synthesis would exert a strong influence on nineteenth-century religious thought and therefore demands our attention.

Hegel on religion

Hegel's belief in human autonomy determined his reinterpretation of the Christian faith. That reinterpretation was as radical as any of those produced by the nineteenth-century critical movement. This is not to suggest that Hegel had nothing good to say of Christianity. In fact, he esteemed it highly. Anxious to protect it, he objected to the tendency of Schleiermacher and other Romantics to move the centre of gravity from God to the worshipping individual, and he also rejected their belief that God was essentially unknowable. The intimate relationship between God (as cosmic Spirit) and man guaranteed that the human being could know God. Hegel also went further in protecting the historicity of the biblical record than many other nineteenth-century critics. For him, even more than for Schleiermacher, Christianity was the absolute religion.[6]

The fact that it was absolute did not mean, however, that it was true for all times. Like everything else in Hegel's system, religious truth underwent a process of development, and each epoch possessed the form that was appropriate to it. In that sense every religion in history, even the most primitive kind, had been absolute. Christianity was superior to earlier ones because in Hegel's system development meant progress and Christianity happened to be the culmination of a long evolutionary history. But its advantages over previous religions would not save Christianity from sharing the fate of these religions. Like them it would, once it had served its purpose, be absorbed by the Spirit, which meant that in fact it would be discarded. For it was not in religion, but in Hegel's dialectic philosophy that the cosmic Spirit would reach the end of its development and become Absolute Spirit.

Christianity, meanwhile, had a role to play in that development. A major reason why Hegel wanted to protect the historicity of much of the Bible was that he could use biblical doctrine to illustrate the "deeper truths" of his own philosophy. A well-known example is the use he made of the central doctrine of Christianity, the Incarnation. Hegel liked this doctrine because he thought it showed how God as the thesis united himself with man as the antithesis in the person of Christ as the synthesis, thereby underlining Hegel's own doctrine of the union between the infinite and the finite. But while not denying the historicity of the Incarnation, Hegel did not believe that Christ was the ultimate mediator between God and man. For him the meaning of Christ's incarnation was to show that in the end all men would become one with the divine. But an even better illustration of that was given, he believed, at Pentecost, when the Spirit descended on the believing community. Because at that time the church – that is, an ever-growing number of individuals – replaced Christ as the locus of the divine presence, Pentecost was a more adequate symbol of the divinization of all mankind than the Incarnation had been.[7]

It is important to keep in mind that for Hegel the divinization of humanity did not imply its immersion in the divine. It remained his goal all along to safeguard human autonomy, and human autonomy meant for him, as it did for Kant and the Romantics, that man was not to be subjected to external laws, not even to laws that were imposed by a supernatural authority. To be autonomous was to live by one's own reason and to be one's own lawgiver. Hegel therefore had to make sure that the union between God and men was established on a basis of equality. He believed that his concept of the cosmic Spirit allowed him to do so. That Spirit was, on the one hand, prior to and in that sense superior to man. It was also in control of the historical process and able to use nations and individuals in a manner over which they themselves had no control. On the other hand, however, the Spirit depended on man for its very existence: it was human beings who served as "the vehicles, and the indispensable vehicles, of his spiritual existence, as consciousness, rationality, will."[8] Therefore man was not simply a creature, he was also a creator, one whose authority could hardly be less than that of the Spirit.

It was at this point that Hegel ran into the problem which after his death would result in the collapse of his synthesis. The problem was that while his theory guaranteed the independence of man, this was achieved at the cost of the Spirit's power and status. Hegel's theory could and indeed would be interpreted to mean that the existence of the supernatural was no longer a necessary hypothesis. If the Spirit was dependent on man, it was possible to conclude to human superiority over the Spirit and to proceed from there to the transfer of its authority to man.

Those of Hegel's disciples who drew this conclusion destroyed the master's philosophy and eliminated whatever he had left intact of a supernatural faith. They replaced theism with atheism, transformed theology as knowledge of God into anthropology or knowledge of man, and so substituted the nineteenth-century "religion of humanity" for the supernatural religion of Christianity. Although Hegel would have been aghast at this secularization of his work, the seeds of the development were present in his own philosophy. By creating a God whose reason was dependent on human reason and who became conscious of himself only through the developing consciousness of mankind, he began the transformation of theology into anthropology. For this reason he can indeed be called the originator of the nineteenth- and twentieth-century "death of God" theologies.[9]

Strauss and the Young Hegelians

The attack on Hegel's synthesis began almost immediately after his death in 1831. It was led by some of his younger followers. One of the first to join it was David Friedrich Strauss (1808-74), who became internationally famous because of his *Life of Jesus,* the first volume of which he published in 1835, while still in his twenties. In it he tried to reconstruct the life of Jesus in purely natural terms, an attempt that would be made by various other nineteenth-century critics.

The publication of Strauss's work brought into the open a growing division among Hegel's followers. One group, the so-called right wing, consisted mainly of older disciples, men who wanted to keep Hegel's religious inheritance intact. Hegel had called Christianity the absolute religion and insisted that his philosophy did not supersede the Christian faith but rather, by revealing its inner truth, fulfilled it. Even when admitting the existence of discrepancies between Hegel's philosophy and the biblical record, many older Hegelians believed that, compared to the positive support Hegel gave to Christianity, these discrepancies were of minor significance and should be ignored.

The left wing, on the other hand – a group that became known as the school of the Young Hegelians – concluded that the discrepancies invalidated Hegel's synthesis. It was this group which completed the process toward the replacement of faith in the supernatural with a religion of humanity. This was done by replacing Hegel's doctrine of the reconciliation between God and man by one of the ultimate unity of mankind, a situation wherein, in the poet Schiller's words, all men became brethren.

Although the outcome was largely the same, the left-wing Hegelians did not all follow the same route. Some wanted to retain at least a residue of Hegel's theological thought. His philosophy had intended to safeguard Christianity, and its abandonment might lead to a collapse into a fully secularized, materialistic culture, a possibility that these disciples wanted to avoid. But while they followed Hegel in attempting to reconcile philosophy and religion, they departed from him in their radical denial of the historicity of the biblical record, an attitude that would lead sooner or later to the elimination of whatever transcendent elements were left in Hegel's theology. Strauss was among the Young Hegelians who followed this approach. Other members of the group, however, rejected the Hegelian synthesis outright, and with it the ideal of a Christian culture. This group included Karl Marx and Friedrich Engels, who in 1848 would proclaim the religion of communism, and the "death of God" theologian Ludwig Feuerbach. In what follows we will give attention to the work of Strauss and Feuerbach.[10]

As a student, Strauss had turned from Schleiermacher to Hegel, whose rationalism he thought provided a more secure basis for religious certainty than did Romantic subjectivism. His trust in Hegelianism sustained him when confronted with the need to go against Hegel's precepts in the matter of biblical criticism. As a critic, Strauss was influenced by Schleiermacher, but although he admired Schleiermacher's critical approach, he did not believe that it went far enough. Fearful of removing the entire basis of the Christian faith, Schleiermacher had hesitated to apply the historical-critical method to such central doctrines as the Incarnation. Strauss, however, was convinced that not even the most radical criticism could endanger religion. While revelation was not infallible, speculative philosophy was; and speculative philosophy, as Hegel had shown, confirmed the inner meaning of Christianity. It could therefore be trusted to eliminate whatever doubts a critical approach might create for the believer. "Philosophy would give back what historical criticism had taken away."[11]

Attempting to describe the "historical Jesus" as distinct from "the Christ of faith," Strauss made use of the myth concept to eliminate the historicity of miracles and other supernatural elements in the gospels. While not denying the historicity of Jesus himself, he taught that Jesus had to be seen as a man among other men. Like Hegel, Strauss believed that the essential message of Christianity was the unity of man with the "absolute," and that the doctrine of the Incarnation symbolized this unity. That was, for Strauss as for Hegel, the present-day relevance of the gospel. Meanwhile Strauss began the process of replacing Hegel's Absolute Spirit with "the spirit of humanity."

Strauss would influence Protestant theology in Germany and abroad, but his re-interpretation of the Bible was too revolutionary for his own day and he was dismissed from his university post. On a number of occasions he attempted to restore his professional fortunes by detracting some of his most radical conclusions, but in the end he clung to them. Toward the end of his life, convinced that speculative philosophy could not safeguard a religious culture and worldview after all, he rejected Hegel and turned to Darwinism instead.

Feuerbach and the religion of man

Ludwig Feuerbach (1804-72) explained his views on religion in a variety of works. Best known among them is his *Essence of Christianity*, which he published in 1841. Unlike Strauss, Feuerbach did not even attempt to reconcile philosophy and religion, and he welcomed the arrival of a non-Christian culture. Rejecting all belief in the transcendent, Feuerbach taught that religion had arisen as a result of mankind's feelings of alienation and that the deities people worshiped were projections of human fears, ambitions, and desires.

Feuerbach would become one of the prophets of the atheistic materialism that was gaining ground in the 1830s and '40s, the period that, after Hegel's death, witnessed the decline of philosophic idealism and the triumph of positivism. His work would be highly acclaimed, not only by men like Karl Marx and Friedrich Engels and their communist followers, but also by many other doubters and atheists, both in Germany and abroad. The novelist George Eliot (Marian Evans), for example, liked it so well that she translated it into English. Her translation, which was first published in 1854, is still in use.

Feuerbach's explanation of the idea of God as wish-fulfilment would grab the attention of many of his contemporaries and would be popularized further by Marx, Nietzsche, and Freud. Like Feuerbach, these men assumed that their "explanation" of the origin of mankind's belief in God amounted to a disproof of God's existence. As has been pointed out before, the idea that the validity of a thing or a belief can be determined by tracing its presumed origin is typical of the historicist mindset. The example of Feuerbach shows how easily this idea can give rise to the so-called genetic fallacy. Feuerbach's conclusion is fallacious because, while it is indeed true that something does not have to exist because we desire it, it is illogical to conclude that it *cannot* exist because we desire it. Faith in God, for example, can also be explained by the fact that, in Augustine's words, God has made us for himself, so that our hearts find no rest until they find it in him.

Feuerbach did not despise religion. He agreed with Strauss and other critics as to its historical value, believing that it had played a necessary role in humanity's earlier stages. But these times of ignorance were now past. The day had come to declare religion for what it was, an illusion, and to replace the worship of God with what in fact it had always been: the worship of man. With the term "man" Feuerbach referred not first of all to the individual, but to humanity as a whole. Like the other Young Hegelians he shared Hegel's (and Rousseau's and Kant's) desire for an ideal community, one wherein competitiveness would be replaced with co-operation and humanitarianism. Such a community constituted the true deity. "Man with man," Feuerbach exclaimed, " – the unity of I and Thou – is God."[12]

The belief that God was dead and that the worship of God was to be replaced with the worship of mankind was not confined to Hegelians like Feuerbach and Marx. It was shared by the positivist Auguste Comte, Feuerbach's contemporary, who spent much energy trying to organize his own "religion of humanity." What is striking is the supreme confidence with which these men greeted what they believed to be the demise of Christianity. For Feuerbach and Comte and their followers the loss of belief in God and in divine providence was not accompanied by a sense of dread, but by a feeling of liberation. In that respect they were, as a commentator observed, true children of their age: people who, unlike their twentieth-century successors, "did not know death and misunderstood evil."[13]

Feuerbach was a true child of his age not only in his optimistic humanism, but also in his analysis of the essential nature of the Christian religion. In a review of Feuerbach's *Essence of Christianity* and other works, the theologian Karl Barth calls Feuerbach's conclusions "extraordinarily, almost nauseatingly, trivial," but he adds that the same adjective applies to the theology of the period as a whole.[14] Feuerbach, he shows, did little more than draw the consequences of a theology that had already become an anthropology. His work illustrates what is bound to happen when theologies reign that are not concerned with God but concentrate on meeting mankind's subjective desires, such as its craving for security, spirituality, and participation in a larger whole. In that sense Feuerbach's work continues to be relevant.

Old Testament criticism

Not all biblical-critical schools that flourished in the nineteenth century were Hegelian in origin. Some critics followed Kant or Schleiermacher or other influential thinkers, and still others were led to biblical criticism primarily by the prevailing historicist and positivist trends, or else by anti-religious or anticlerical sentiments. Nor did biblical criticism end with the nineteenth century. Although various modifications were introduced over time, the approach itself continues. It is not our intention to describe the various schools, either those of the past or of the present, but something must yet be said about the one that revolutionized Old Testament studies by explaining the religion of Israel in evolutionary terms. The leader of that school was Julius Wellhausen (1844-1918).[15]

Wellhausen sought to confirm the theory, proposed by earlier historical and literary critics, that the Pentateuch (the five books of Moses) consists of records derived from four major sources or codes. Building on the work of predecessors regarding the relative chronology of these sources, he chose the so-called Priestly code as the most recent of the four. His conclusions were in conformity with evolutionary philosophy, according to which ideas, institutions, and beliefs are subject to a law of progressive development, so that the earliest stages are necessarily the most primitive ones. Wellhausen taught that Israel's religion had begun with a polytheistic stage and had culminated, via the period of the Prophets, in the elaborate and ritualistic religion of the Law, which was fully monotheistic.

These conclusions made necessary a re-dating of Old Testament history, a task to which Wellhausen devoted himself as well. In his theory the history of Israel began not with the patriarchs. The Bible portrayed these as monotheists, but since such a belief was too advanced for the time in which the patriarchs were supposed to have lived, the stories must be the product of later legend. For Wellhausen Israel's history began with the Exodus, when Moses had welded a number of nomadic Hebrew tribes together, providing them with a religion and a country. That religion was not monotheistic; other gods existed. The early stage was followed by that of the Prophets, who attacked the pagan elements in Israelite religion, introduced the idea of a transcendent and universal God, and stressed the ethical implications of the faith. The third and final period was the period of the Law with its centralized, formalized worship and elaborate ceremonial. The Levitical law therefore dated not from the Exodus but from a time much later in Israel's history. Wellhausen placed its origins in the period following the exile.

In liberal circles some of Wellhausen's ideas are still accepted, but much of his work has been shown to be in need of revision. His school has been criticized for concentrating so single-mindedly on the possible sources and prehistory of the biblical text that the text itself was ignored. Since his time more attention has been given to the final document, and where Wellhausen and his colleagues saw little more than a patchwork of fragments derived from a variety of disparate sources, newer critics have found that the Old Testament narratives, the Old Testament as a whole, and also the Old and New Testament combined, possess a unity that the earlier critics, who followed the historical-critical method to the letter, failed to see.

Other developments have shown additional weaknesses in the work of Wellhausen and his school. Archaeological investigations in the Middle East, for example, have provided evidence that advanced cultures flourished there in the time of the patriarchs. Newer research has also made clear that ideas like the covenant, holiness, and atonement were not introduced by the prophets, as Wellhausen's school believed, but were present in Israel's religion from the very beginning, and that the same was true of belief in monotheism and in high ethical principles such as those expressed in the Decalogue. The idea that everything develops necessarily from simple to more complex has been shown to be incorrect by workers in fields as far apart as language studies, palaeontology, and the history of religions. Scholarly work on newly discovered manuscripts and other sources, meanwhile, has shed new light on cultures in biblical times and shown a variety of customs that are similar to those described in the Old Testament. It has also established the essential accuracy of the manuscripts upon which earlier Bible versions were based. Modern scholarship, in brief, serves not only to attack the Bible's trustworthiness, but also to bolster its claims to authenticity.[16]

Relativizing the criticism

The nineteenth century was a complex one, filled with contradictions and contrasts. This was true of secular and religious developments. As to the latter: in religion there was progress as well as regress, and by concentrating on the march of secularization, this chapter has given a one-sided picture of the period. For the Christian religion was far from disappearing. As had been the case during the eighteenth-century Enlightenment, so it was in the nineteenth century. In reaction to the liberalism that dominated mainline churches and seminaries, orthodox biblical scholarship sharpened its critical tools, and religious revivals and reforms took place throughout the Christian world. Missionary efforts expanded greatly, making the nineteenth century the greatest missionary epoch in history. Missionary societies and Bible societies mushroomed, Christian schools and colleges were established in many countries, and much attention was given by Christians to such social issues as hospital and prison reform, the alleviation of poverty, and the abolition first of the slave trade and then of slavery itself.

But although Christianity survived and even greatly expanded, secularism continued its progress and, more than ever before, came to dominate the culture of what had once been a Christian Europe. It is with that process that the present chapter has dealt. It placed the process within the context of the nineteenth-century belief in speculative philosophy and positivistic science, and also in that of the shift from a belief in the fixity of truth to one in evolutionism and ever-changing norms. The single-minded belief in becoming and progressive change constituted a major turning point in western history and may well be the most destructive heritage of the nineteenth century. It certainly was destructive of religious faith. Culminating in the historical-critical approach to biblical studies with its creed that religion is the product of time and place and that the origins of the Christian faith are shrouded in legend, the turn to a developmental worldview probably made more victims than did Darwinism as a mere scientific theory. The Frenchman Joseph Ernest Renan, himself a biblical critic and author of a "Life of

Jesus," wrote in his memoirs that he lost his faith as a result of historical criticism, and we are told that George Eliot, who translated both Strauss and Feuerbach into English, paid little attention to the possibly negative implications of Darwinism for her religious faith, having already been "nurtured in the hardier school of German Biblical criticism."[17] And Renan and Eliot were not the only ones to be so nurtured. The higher biblical criticism has slain its thousands.

It is therefore good to realize the irony of the atheistic response. It was based on a philosophy that, in view of the age's general climate of opinion, should have been recognized as impermanent. For the belief in idealism, evolutionism, historicism, and scientific objectivity was itself culturally conditioned, as was the historical-critical method which was based on it. That the nineteenth century failed to realize this shows how difficult it is to discern the biases and preconceptions of one's own time. Often it is only later generations that can, with the benefit of hindsight, notice the blind spots of people living in earlier periods.

The fact remains that the approach of the nineteenth-century critical thinkers was insufficiently critical. They failed to notice that the method they followed in their biblical criticism signified not a move from a subjective understanding of the Scriptures to a scientific-objective one, but a move from one belief system to another. For none of the speculative, scientific, and historicist principles they applied can be demonstrated as objectively valid. They are matters of belief and should therefore be considered, according to the philosophy of the critical thinkers themselves, mere prejudices.

The need to be aware of the worldviews and prevailing biases of both past and present is one of the lessons to be learned from the nineteenth-century history of ideas. A second lesson is that absolute objectivity is an impossible goal, in historical research as in any other investigation – including that of the natural sciences. Knowledge necessarily has a subjective, personal dimension. With few exceptions the nineteenth century, and indeed the modern period as a whole, failed to take this fact into account. It fell to postmodern thinkers to make us aware of its truth, and to begin developing a theory of knowledge in accordance with it.

NOTES

[1] The original title of Reimarus' treatise was *Apology for or Defence of the Rational Worshippers of God*. Reimarus himself left it unpublished, but in the 1770s the German philosopher Gotthold Ephraim Lessing, saying that he had

discovered the manuscript at Wolfenbüttel, published parts of it, anonymously, under the title *Wolfenbüttel Fragments*.

2. Friedrich Schleiermacher, *On Religion: Speeches to Its Cultured Despisers*, trans. and ed. Richard Crouter (Cambridge: Cambridge University Press, 1990 [1988]), p. 135. A good account of the origin and general content of the volume, and also of later revisions, can be found in the editor's Introduction to this work.

3. Schleiermacher, *On Religion*, pp. 214, 218.

4. *Ibid.*, p. 222.

5. See on this topic chapter 10 above. For a fuller description of the problem the Romantics struggled with, and for the manner in which Hegel attempted to solve it, see Taylor, *Hegel*, ch. 1, 2.

6 For Hegel's religious theory see Taylor's volume, as well as Toews, *Hegelianism*, and Copleston, *A History of Philosophy*, VII (Westminster, Maryland: Newman Press, 1963), chs. 9-11.

7 Taylor, *Hegel*, pp. 208-11, 491-2, 495.

8. *Ibid.*, p. 45.

9. *Ibid.*, p. 495.

10. The split between right- and left-wing Hegelians and the work of Strauss and Feuerbach are well described in Toews, *Hegelianism*. On these topics, and on the historical-critical movement as it affected New Testament studies in general, see also C. Stephen Evans, *The Historical Christ and the Jesus of Faith: The Incarnational Narrative as History* (Oxford: Clarendon Press, 1996); Fred H. Klooster, *Quests for the Historical Jesus* (Grand Rapids: Baker, 1977); Eta Linnemann, *Historical Criticism of the Bible: Methodology or Ideology? Reflections of a Bultmannian turned Evangelical*, trans. Robert W. Yarbrough (Grand Rapids: Baker, 1990); Eta Linnemann, *Is there a Synoptic Problem? Rethinking the Literary Dependence of the First Three Gospels*, trans. Robert W. Yarbrough (Grand Rapids: Baker, 1992); James M. Robinson, *A New Quest of the Historical Jesus* (London: SCM Press, 1971 [1959]); Albert Schweitzer, *The Quest of the Historical Jesus: A Critical Study of Its Progress from Reimarus to Wrede*, trans. W. Montgomery (New York: Macmillan, 1950). Of special interest are the works of Eta Linnemann who, as the title of one of her books shows, was a disciple of the radical twentieth-century critic Rudolf Bultmann before turning to the biblical faith, and who is therefore able to critique the movement from the inside.

[11.] Toews, *Hegelianism*, 257f, 263.

[12.] Quoted by Karl Barth in an introductory essay to Ludwig Feuerbach, *The Essence of Christianity*, trans. George Eliot (New York: Harper and Brothers, Harper Torchbooks, The Cloister Library, 1957), p. xiii.

[13] *Ibid.*, p. xxviii.

[14.] *Ibid.*, p. xix.

[15] On Wellhausen, and on Old Testament criticism in general, see Ronald E. Clements, *A Century of Old Testament Study* (Guildford and London: Lutterworth Press, 1976); Herbert F. Hahn, *The Old Testament in Modern Research* (Philadelphia: Fortress Press, 1970 [1954]); John H. Hayes, *An Introduction to Old Testament Study* (Nashville: Abingdon, 1980 [1979]); John Rogerson, *Old Testament Criticism in the Nineteenth Century: England and Germany* (London: Society for Promoting Christian Knowledge, 1985 [1984]).

[16] For the manner in which modern scholarship has bolstered the Old Testament's claim to authenticity, see especially Hahn, *The Old Testament in Modern Research*.

[17.] Franklin L. Baumer, *Modern European Thought: Continuity and Change in Ideas 1600-1950* (New York: Macmillan, 1977), p. 315; Gertrude Himmelfarb, *Darwin and the Darwinian Revolution*, p. 450.

XV. The Fin de siècle

Central to modernism was the belief that the proper use of human reason would guarantee progress. That belief arose in the Enlightenment and culminated with the rise of nineteenth-century positivism. The era of positivism's triumph was short-lived, however. Its dominant position came under attack during the century's closing decades, a period that has become known as the *fin de siècle*. In its opposition to positivism, the *fin de siècle* was reminiscent of the earlier Romantic movement, which had also challenged aspects of the modernist creed, and it foreshadowed the rejection of modernism that would characterize the late twentieth century.

If the postmodern rejection of modernity can be explained by the all too apparent failure of the modern promise of progress, such is not the case with the *fin de siècle*. Europe was doing well during the second half of the nineteenth century. Science advanced rapidly, and its technological applications stimulated economic expansion. Politically there was progress as well. Liberalism was spreading throughout western Europe, and much of the unrest among the working classes that had plagued the century's earlier decades had abated, thanks to the growing prosperity and to increasingly progressive social legislation. Europe's global position, moreover, seemed secure. The closing decades of the century witnessed a renewal of the race for colonies, as a result of which European dominion of other continents was greatly extended. The West was in control of the rest of the world, and in the opinion of many westerners this situation was both inevitable and permanent. It was the white man's manifest destiny.

All this is not to suggest that the political horizon was cloudless. A cause of considerable worry was the rising economic and military strength of Germany. In 1871 the Prussian Chancellor Otto von Bismarck had managed to bring about the unification of Germany by defeating Austria and France, two of the continent's greatest powers. Germany became a superpower which posed a danger not only to its continental neighbours, but also to the military and economic might of England. In the race for colonies it used military threats to back up its demands. The situation contributed to the armament race and the system of entangling alliances that would contribute to the outbreak of World War I.

German aggressiveness, and the threat of armed conflict which the new imbalance of power entailed, added to the feeling of unease that characterized the *fin de siècle*. It is not surprising that France, a country that had been traumatized by the defeat of 1871 and forced to sign a humiliating peace treaty, was among the first to experience the *fin de siècle* mood of dejection. Yet the German threat and the prospect of war do not provide a sufficient explanation of the phenomenon. The malaise was also felt in victorious Germany. Indeed, a central figure in turn-of-the-century thinking was a German, Friedrich Nietzsche, and other German nationals played a prominent role as well. Among them was the historian of cultural decline Oswald Spengler.

Spengler, who held to a cyclical view of history, stated that the collapse of western civilization was inevitable and simply a matter of time. Although he wrote much of his *Decline of the West* during the First World War, he was not inspired by the fear of a German defeat in that war. Like most of his fellow Germans he believed that his country would be victorious. Nor was his pessimism inspired by the outbreak of war *per se*. Spengler believed in the benevolent effect of warfare. So did many of his contemporaries, both at home and abroad, although not necessarily for the same reasons. Spengler thought that an armed conflict might delay (although it could not prevent) Europe's slide into decadence and nihilism, whereas much of the rest of the pro-war crowd was inspired by the more optimistic creed of Social Darwinism. Believing that war would weed out the unfit among the nations and enlarge the opportunities of the fit, and confident that their own country was among the latter, they welcomed war for nationalistic reasons.

A spiritual void

If Europe enjoyed unprecedented wealth and global power, if technology had not yet as clearly shown its destructive potential as it would in the next century, and if even a possible European war was not universally felt to be a negative thing, how is one to account for the *fin de siècle* feeling of malaise?

There is, as we will see, a variety of explanations, but the underlying reason was that Europeans were beginning to realize the consequences of the atheism their society had embraced. Christianity had been at the core of European civilization, but in the course of modern history the moulders of public opinion increasingly turned away from the Christian faith. The process of secularization began well before the nineteenth century. An early milestone was the acceptance of the Cartesian epistemology, which, insisting upon the autonomy of human reason, declared that certainty of knowledge depended on the jettisoning of tradition and authority, including divine authority. The most radical consequence of the secularizing process, atheism, was kept at bay, however. It is true that the early-modern period had its atheists, as did earlier centuries. But the atheists remained a minority, in part because they could provide no real alternative to the Christian explanation of the world. This was among the reasons why the ideas of a man like David Hume, for example, did not spread as widely in his days as they might have otherwise. That situation changed with the triumph of a materialistic evolutionism. In providing a solution to the problem of origins that had stymied earlier agnostics and atheists, Darwin made atheism possible.

The spread of atheism had a dual effect. Some experienced it as liberating. Karl Marx can serve as an example, and so can thinkers like Auguste Comte and Ludwig Feuerbach. For these men the defeat of faith in the supernatural allowed mankind finally to come into its own; and an autonomous humanity, they believed, would be capable of producing the earthly utopia that Christianity had failed to bring about. But not everyone shared this feeling of optimism. It was also realized, and increasingly so as the century progressed, that the acceptance of atheism meant the orphaning of humanity. The denial of the biblical faith signified a break with all that had gone before, for western civilization had been shaped by the teachings of the Bible. It implied the rejection of practically every traditional belief system and moral code and their replacement with something new and untried.

Nietzsche and "the death of God"

The philosopher Friedrich Nietzsche (1844-1900) was among those who tried to make their contemporaries aware of the implications of life in a godless universe – that is, in a world which believes that there is no God and that there never has been one. A man who was strongly influenced by his times, Nietzsche also played an important role in shaping them, and those who want to understand the *fin de siècle* and its postmodern sequel cannot afford to ignore him and his work.

The son of a Lutheran minister, Nietzsche in his student days turned away from the faith of his fathers to become the most influential spokesman of the new atheism and the main prophet of its world-shaking consequences. He described those consequences most memorably in a parable contained in his book *The Gay Science*. Although well known, the passage is worth quoting because it so well expresses the magnitude of the changes that would follow western society's rejection of faith in God. The parable tells of a madman who went into the market place in broad daylight with a lantern, crying out that he was looking for God. When the onlookers, unbelievers all, made fun of him and of his search, asking him where God had gone, and if perhaps he had lost his way, or embarked upon a voyage, or gone into hiding, the madman replied:

> "Whither is God?... I will tell you. *We have killed him* – you and I. All of us are his murderers. But how did we do this? How could we drink up the sea? Who gave us the sponge to wipe away the entire horizon? What were we doing when we unchained this earth from its sun? Whither is it moving now? Whither are we moving? Away from all suns? Are we not plunging continually? Backward, sideward, forward, in all directions? Is there still any up and down? Are we not straying as through an infinite nothing? Do we not feel the breath of empty space? Has it not become colder? Is not night continually closing in on us? Do we not need to light lanterns in the morning?... God is dead. God remains dead. And we have killed him.
>
> "How shall we comfort ourselves, the murderers of all murderers? ... Is not the greatness of this deed too great for us? Must we ourselves not become gods simply to appear worthy of it? There has never been a greater deed; and whoever is born after us – for the sake of this deed he will belong to a higher history than all history hitherto."

Here the madman fell silent and looked again at his listeners;

and they, too, were silent and stared at him in astonishment. At last he threw his lantern on the ground, and it broke into pieces and went out. "I have come too early," he said then; "my time is not yet. This tremendous event is still on its way, still wandering; it has not yet reached the ears of men. Lightning and thunder require time, the light of the stars requires time; deeds, though done, still require time to be seen and heard. This deed is still more distant from them than the most distant stars - *and yet they have done it themselves.*"[1]

Nietzsche's response to atheism was not one of despair. Although aware of the traumatic changes that were bound to follow the rejection of religion, he also welcomed the new age, for he passionately hated Christianity. Furthermore, as the parable of the madman shows, he agreed with men like Comte and Feuerbach that the end of the age of supernaturalism would enable man (or at least some men) to take the place of God. He did not share, however, the naive optimism of the earlier nineteenth-century atheists. They had left the impression that in a godless world, life would go on more or less as before, except that it would be better than ever before. Nietzsche realized that the absence of belief in God would change the world unrecognizably, and not necessarily for the better. With the loss of faith in the Christian gospel, mankind would no longer be ruled by the Christian commandment of compassion and justice, but by the dictates of naked power. The human being was a product of amoral nature and, freed from the moral restraints the Christian religion had imposed, would behave accordingly.

The new morality

Nietzsche influenced the twentieth century at least as much as he did his own age, and we will return to him when dealing with the topic of postmodernism. At that time we will pay special attention to his ideas on language. Here some of his other teachings will be mentioned, such as his views on morality, his proclamation of the superman and the will to power, his rejection of truth, and his view of history.

One of the reasons Nietzsche gave for his hatred of Christianity was the morality it taught, which he believed was a slave or herd morality, one that benefited the masses while limiting the power of the noble and strong. That type of morality accounted for much of the decadence of western society. He disagreed with Karl Marx on the origin of Christian values. For Marx, religion was the superstructure of an oppressive, class-based society, enabling the oppressor to keep the workers under control with the promise of eternal rewards and the threat of eternal punishment. In Marxism, the Christian religion was the proverbial pie in the sky, the opiate of the people, and the Christian moral law was imposed by the powerful. Nietzsche, however, explained it as the invention of the weak and the product of resentment and fear. Unable to protect themselves by force, the masses, with the help of the priests, had sought to curb their masters' power by universalizing such ideals as kindness, humility, compassion, and pity. Having found these ideals in the Christian religion, they conspired to impose that religion on their society. This Christian herd morality had affected all of western culture and explained such uniquely western systems as socialism and democracy, both of which Nietzsche found contemptible.[2]

The morality of the new age would have to be altogether different from that of the Christian tradition. Indeed, Nietzsche said, there would have to be a "transvaluation of all values," an *Umwertung aller Werte*. He did not make clear, however, how the new values would differ from the old ones. On the whole, he appears to have been unable to depart too drastically from traditional morality. Yet the terminology he used suggested that the new values would be the opposite of the Christian ones; that the post-Christian age would glorify, among other things, murder, treachery, tyranny, oppression of the weak, egotism, and violence and war. This was indeed the conclusion some of his followers would draw, such as the German National Socialists, who adopted him as their prophet.

Nietzsche himself did not advocate a Nazi type of morality, at least not consistently so. At times he does come across as a racist and a believer in the positive effects of violence and war, but at other times he strongly rejects these ideas. He more and more wrote in an aphoristic manner, and he often contradicted himself. As a result people can draw from his writings just about any message they wish. Commentators have portrayed him as a gentle humanist and as an advocate of violence, as a veiled liberal and as a proto-Nazi, as an anarchist and as an authoritarian, as an idealistic reformer and as a nihilist. Few if any of these portrayals are a hundred percent correct, but for all of them there is textual evidence. As to his influence on Nazism, Nietzsche was, as one author puts it, liked by the Nazis for what he condemned: democracy, pacifism, individualism, Christianity, humanitarianism, and for what he praised: authority, racial purity, the warrior spirit, "the stern life and the great health,"[3] but he also wrote much that the Nazis could not use.

Whatever his intentions, there is little doubt that with his nihilism and elitism, his concept of the will to power and his admiration of such beings as the Teutonic "blond beast,"[4] Nietzsche reflected disturbing cultural forces. He did so also with his concept of the superman. Nietzsche rejected Darwin's theory of evolution. Since it promised the improvement of humanity as a whole, it was too reminiscent of Christianity. For Nietzsche there was no automatic and universal improvement. Development toward a superior status would have to be consciously willed, and the common herd, decadent as it had become, did not qualify. Only a limited number of people would rise to the occasion, and it was these people, the supermen, who would rule in the new dispensation. Nietzsche foresaw a society of leaders and followers; of masters with their own master morality (for the superman would be "beyond good and evil" and establish his own laws), and of a common herd that existed to serve the masters. In this manner, Christian decadence would be overcome and life would triumph.

Nietzsche on truth and progress

Nietzsche scorned not only the religion and moral traditions of western civilization, he rejected that civilization as a whole. This implied, among other things, the denial of the traditional view of knowledge. From its Greek beginnings onward, the West had believed in the possibility of finding universal truths. Influenced by the skeptical currents of his age, Nietzsche denied that such truths could be found, or even that people were interested in them. The world and all it contained, including mankind, were energized not by the will to truth but by the will to power; hence mankind's goal in searching for knowledge was not to understand the world, but to master it. All the so-called eternal verities – such as universally valid laws of logic, universal moral truths, the uniformity and orderliness of the cosmos, the immutable laws of nature – were fictions. As often as not they were necessary ones: people needed to believe in certain fictions to be able to function, but the idea that the so-called truths by which humanity lived were absolute and universal was a myth. The search for truth was therefore to be abandoned. "The falseness of a judgment," he stated in a well-known passage, "is for us not necessarily an objection to a judgment.... The question is to what extent it is life-promoting, life-preserving, species-preserving, perhaps even species-cultivating."[5]

Another tradition Nietzsche rejected was the western view of history. Unlike pagan civilizations which tended to hold either to regressive or to cyclical views of the historical process, the West had adopted a progressive one. The belief that history has a goal and is therefore meaningful was derived from Christianity; and the Enlightenment view of progress, as well as the teleological philosophies of men like Hegel and Marx, were reminiscent of that Christian view. So, in an important sense, was Darwinian evolutionism. Rejecting progress and a goal-directed philosophy of history, Nietzsche had to find an alternative. In the end he adopted the idea of eternal recurrence, which was a version of the cyclical view of paganism.

Although he had thought about it earlier, Nietzsche announced the idea in his book *Thus Spoke Zarathustra*, which was completed in 1885, in the last decade of his career as a writer.[6] (Early in 1889 he would collapse into the insanity that lasted until his death eleven years later.) The principle of eternal recurrence implied the endless return of everything that had ever happened: every event and thought and action, every pain and victory and defeat would infinitely be repeated. The principle could not but give rise to despair, and Nietsche's decision to affirm it was made with reluctance and fear. He did affirm it in the end because it implied for him the giving of his assent to life as he had lived it; the "yea-saying" to all the choices and decisions he had made and to all the experiences he had undergone. An additional reason was no doubt that it bestowed immortality on the earth-bound being he had created.

Nietzsche added to the principle of eternal recurrence the idea of man's ability to redeem the past by saying of all that had happened: "Thus I willed it."[7] This doctrine has given rise to various interpretations, as has the idea of eternal recurrence. One possible explanation is that it provided mankind with a means of controlling its fate. By affirming the past, one avoided harbouring vain regrets about what had happened, which made it easier to reach the goal of overcoming oneself and evolving toward superman status. A person could accept the past (and himself), in Nietzsche's view, because there were no objective values: the individual was responsible to himself alone. Ultimately it was Nietzsche's delusion of divinity which inspired the doctrines of eternal recurrence and of the redemption of the past.[8] His entire project depended on the possibility of man's taking the place of God, and since divinity implied the ability to control not just the present and the future, but also the past, ways had to be found to endow mankind with at least a semblance of such divine power.

The extent to which Nietzsche's doctrine of eternal recurrence was adopted by his followers is difficult to determine. It is clear, however, that the belief in some version or other of the cyclical view of history was in the air. The formulation of the second law of thermodynamics, which was widely interpreted to mean that at some time in the distant future the universe would freeze up, could allow for a cyclical view of cosmic history – assuming that each freeze-up was followed by a new beginning. The turn of the century was primarily concerned, however, with cyclical explanations not of cosmic history but of the history of civilizations. The idea that the two thousand years of Christianity were coming to a close and that a new and far less gentle era was approaching, was expressed, for example, in W. B. Yeats's well-known poem "The Second Coming," which was published shortly after the First World War and spoke of the collapse of society into anarchy and violence. Yeats's statement, "Things fall apart; the centre cannot hold," reminds one of the conclusion of Nietzsche's madman that the end of faith means the unchaining of the earth from its sun.

Yeats's vision of the replacement of Christian innocence by antichristian evil was also reminiscent of Oswald Spengler's theory. Spengler's *Decline of the West,* which appeared in 1918, constitutes the period's best-known cyclical interpretation of history. It explained the fate of civilizations in organic terms. Just as living organisms went through the process of birth, growth, decline, and death, all of it in accordance with unchanging natural laws, so it was with civilizations. Their ultimate demise was inevitable. And European civilization, in the view of Spengler (who admitted that he had been greatly influenced by Nietzsche), was well past its prime, its disintegration being only a matter of time.

The attack on positivism

Although the mood of cultural pessimism to which Nietzsche, Spengler, Yeats, and various others bore witness was widespread, its sway during the *fin de siècle* was not total. The belief in the altogether benevolent potential of science and technology was not dead, and neither was the belief in progress. A more general decline in these beliefs had to await the disasters of the twentieth century, beginning with the devastations of the First World War. Similarly, more than one *fin de siècle* thinker clung to the creed of positivism. Although in the late nineteenth century it came under attack, the belief proved tenacious, and positivism would return, in a modified form, in the period between the two world wars.

But during the *fin de siècle* it was no longer the dominant philosophy, as it had been during the four decades before the 1890s. The feelings of uncertainty, as expressed by men like Nietzsche and Spengler, played a role in its diminishing appeal. The period also witnessed a rebellion against the reductionist view of man that the positivist philosophy encouraged. Since Marx and Darwin that view had been widely accepted, and Freud's naturalism would strengthen the trend. But in spite of the prestige of these men, there was a growing unease with a philosophical tendency that made man part of nature and explained human behaviour with reference to mechanistic laws.

The role of positivism was also affected by changing conceptions of the nature of science. There was an increasing awareness that subjective factors play a role in the choice of theories and in the decision as to what constitutes a fact. Nietzsche already challenged the positivist claim that "there are only *facts*" by declaring that there are no facts at all, only interpretations.[9] Scientific developments would underline the message. The new physics of the early twentieth century played a major part in eroding the belief that full scientific objectivity is possible, and in the course of the twentieth century evidence that observation and scientific theorizing are influenced by such factors as the scientists' prior knowledge, their experience, their expectations, their language, and the paradigm to which they adhere, accumulated rapidly. Meanwhile findings in the field of mathematics were undermining the belief in the existence of universally valid truth. We will turn to these developments in a later chapter.

Science and the demotion of man

Science affected the *fin de siècle* mood in other ways. Far more clearly than their predecessors, thinkers in this period realized that advances in scientific knowledge, although they gave evidence of the amazing power of human reason, did not necessarily redound to mankind's feeling of self-worth. The negative implications of scientific knowledge were twofold. Firstly, it appeared that science, while contributing to the emancipation of man, at the same time diminished his status both spiritually and in relation to the cosmos. And secondly, it was becoming clear that the further the fund of scientific knowledge expanded, the less certain man was that he possessed any true knowledge. We will look at both these apparent paradoxes.

Among those who expressed the first of these insights – the one concerning humanity's diminishing status – was Nietzsche, who wrote:

Has not man's determination to belittle himself developed apace precisely since Copernicus? Alas, his belief that he was unique and irreplaceable in the hierarchy of beings had been shattered for good; he had become an animal, quite literal and without reservations; he who, according to his earlier belief, had been almost God.... Ever since Copernicus man has been rolling down an incline, faster and faster, away from the center.... All science (and by no means astronomy alone, concerning whose humiliating and discrediting effect Kant has left us a remarkable confession – "It destroys my importance") all science, natural as well as *unnatural* (by which I mean the self-scrutiny of the "knower") is now determined to talk man out of his former respect for himself, as though that respect had been nothing but a bizarre presumption.[10]

In a well-known passage in his *Introductory Lectures*, Sigmund Freud dealt with the same topic. Like Nietzsche, he traced the beginning of the development to Copernicus, stating that the first blow to man's self-love and megalomania (to borrow Freud's terminology) had come with the Copernican removal of humanity and its habitat from the centre of the universe. Another theory with similar effects, he said, was Darwin's evolutionism, which demoted man from a being made in God's image to one made in the image of an animal. And yet a third one was Freud's own contribution to the science of man, namely his theory of the unconscious. According to that theory the ego, whose position had been vaunted so highly by western philosophers from the Greeks onward, was little more than the plaything of irrational drives and instincts.[11] The last two of these theories suggested that the critical intelligence of man, while greatly increasing his understanding of and power over nature, at the same time threatened to make him part – and an insignificant part at that – of the nature he sought to control.

Other scientific theories would, in the nineteenth and twentieth centuries, underline the message. Developments in astronomy confirmed the conclusions drawn by earlier scientists about the unimaginable extent of cosmic space and, by implication, of the relative insignificance of man's position in the universe. Occupying no more than a speck in an unbelievably large cosmos, man's habitat, as the seventeenth-century poet John Donne had already said, was lost in space. And what was true of the earth was true of the solar system as a whole. The earth's sun was only one of billions of suns in its galaxy, the Milky Way, and the Milky Way itself was one of perhaps a billion other galaxies dispersed through space. Distances were becoming truly astronomical. Whereas it takes only eight minutes for light to travel the 93 million miles that separate the sun from the earth, the time required for light to travel from one end of the Milky Way to the other was estimated at 100,000 years, and distances among galaxies were expressed in millions of light years. Christians would admit that the greatly expanded space attests to God's power and majesty, but they would also, with the rest of society, share in Pascal's sense of alienation when contemplating "the eternal silence of those infinite spaces."

Science diminished humanity's status not only in a spatial but also in a temporal sense. Theories were developed suggesting that the universe was billions of years old, that the age of the earth also was far greater than had previously been believed, and that the human species was no more than a late (and chance) development in an evolutionary process that had spanned eons. And while it was true that evolutionary theory allowed for man's further development, it also showed that that development was in danger, since extinction threatened humanity as much as it threatened other species. Untold numbers of them had already disappeared, and there was no guarantee that humanity would not meet the same fate. Indeed, no species was any longer believed to have an unlimited life span. This was the conclusion drawn from the second law of thermodynamics, to which we already referred. Formulated in the 1850s, it stated that in a thermally isolated system the amount of entropy cannot be decreased. Assuming that this law applied to the universe as a whole, the implication was that ultimately the universe would run down and that life would be extinguished.

Reductionism

Yet another factor in the demotion of man is scientific reductionism, that is, the practice of analyzing and explaining complex systems in terms of the properties of their parts. As a methodology, reductionism has often played a positive role in science. It proved its worth first in physics and then, with the introduction of Dalton's theory that ordinary matter is composed of corpuscles or atoms, also in chemistry. Its successful application in these two areas encouraged its use in biology and subsequently in the human sciences. That even in the human sphere the approach could be fruitful became evident with the discovery of the role played by biochemical factors in certain mental illnesses and in advances made in such fields as genetics and brain research.[12]

Although in many areas methodological reductionism has been and continues to be fruitful, there are, as we will notice in later chapters, limitations to its use. Furthermore, it often provides the basis for a far less benign version of reductionism, namely the ontological (or metaphysical) one. According to the latter, complex systems are not only analyzable in terms of their parts but are in fact nothing but organizations of these parts. It means that chemistry can be fully reduced to physics, biology to chemistry, and human thought and behaviour to biology and biochemistry. It therefore implies that matter – ultimately the atom – is all that exists. This type of reductionism has become pervasive in modern times. It has influenced fields of knowledge as far apart as ethics (think of the reduction of ethics to evolutionary biology), religion, linguistics, psychology, sociology, and political theory. An example from the last-mentioned field is the social contract theory, according to which the individual is logically prior to the community,[13] just as the atom is logically prior to complex natural entities. Indeed, atomism as a metaphysics is behind much of the individualism of the modern period and behind much of the modern worldview as a whole. There is truth in Ludwig Wittgenstein's observation that it is not propositions and statements, but pictures and metaphors (in this case the metaphor of reality as consisting of disconnected, miscroscopic material entities) that determine our philosophical convictions.[14]

As to its effect on humanity's feeling of self-worth, by reducing life and thought and behaviour to the laws of physics and chemistry, ontological reductionism denies, among other things, the idea of a mind-body duality. Consciousness and thought are held to be simply secretions from the brain, just as bile is a secretion from the liver. Often this materialistic view of man is combined with a mechanistic one, which means that like the universe in general, the human being also is seen as a complex machine. Ontological reductionism makes free will and human responsibility illusory. The individual is determined by his biology and becomes the helpless victim of experts in human engineering.

Ontological reductionism, in short, plays an important part in reducing mankind's "former respect for himself," and with the prevailing trust in Darwinism, Freudianism, behaviourism, and other materialistic and mechanistic explanations of human thought and behaviour, it will continue to do so. But as the theories discussed in the previous section make clear, it is not possible to explain the decline of man's sense of self-worth as a result of ontological reductionism alone. The lament of the ancient Teacher that those who increase knowledge increase sorrow seems to apply across the board; at least, that was the conclusion increasingly drawn during and since the *fin de siècle*. The shock produced by the realization of science's negative implications was not the only reason for the denial of progress around the turn of the century, but it was an important contributing factor.

Science and skepticism

The second negative effect of scientific advances was that they showed the limitations of human reason. Since the beginning of the scientific revolution a battle had been waged against the skeptical implications of the sciences and of the scientific epistemology, and by the end of the nineteenth century it was becoming clearer than ever that the battle was a losing one.

The problem of skepticism had scientific and philosophical causes. As to the former, technical advances, such as the invention of the telescope and the microscope, showed already in the early phases of the scientific revolution that the world which science revealed was different from what people had assumed it to be. Scientific theories had a similar effect. The Copernican-Newtonian system, for example, presented a universe that was the opposite of what the senses suggested and common sense dictated, and further advances served only to underline the message. By the early twentieth century science had reached the point that it could explain nature only by means of abstract mathematical formulas, metaphors, and analogies. The idea that one could know the world as it was "in itself" was discarded.

The skepticism this caused was reinforced by philosophical conundrums. We have dealt with these in previous chapters and can restrict ourselves to a brief recapitulation. At the centre of the philosophical problem was the difficulty of explaining how the human mind can have knowledge of external nature. Christian thinkers had answered that question with reference to the fact that God had created man and given him the ability to understand the outside world. In the course of the early-modern period, however, this faith eroded, and with that erosion the relationship between subject and object, the knower and the known, became problematic. We have seen how philosophers from Descartes onwards struggled with the problem but failed to provide a satisfactory answer. Eventually the problem was inherited by Immanuel Kant. Believing in the universal validity of Newtonian physics and Euclidean geometry and convinced that truly objective knowledge could be had, Kant attempted to solve the problem of skepticism by proposing a shift in the centre of gravity from the object, nature, to the subject, the human mind. Where formerly it had been thought that the mind had to follow the testimony of the external world in order to understand it, it was now believed that the mind in fact structured the world.

Kant's subject-centred epistemology appeared convincing because he spoke not of any individual human mind, but of the mind as a universal, or, to use a modern term, of human consciousness-as-such. That was still possible in his days. The Enlightenment believed that human nature was uniform. The fact that all men, regardless of time, class, or culture, partook of that nature meant that they could all reach the same conclusions. The danger of a philosophical and moral subjective relativism was thus avoided. The danger of skepticism also was reduced, for the belief in the rationality and goodness of mankind continued to be strong in Kant's days, so that the mind could safely be entrusted with the responsibilities that were now placed on it. A rational being and the possessor of an unerring sense of the moral imperative, man had the ability to distinguish between truth and error and good and evil.

The Kantian theory of knowledge remained influential, but Kant's solution of the problem of skepticism lasted only as long as the scientific basis on which he built remained unshaken and as long as the humanistic belief he relied on remained intact. As it happened, the scientific base would collapse in the course of the twentieth century,[15] and the humanistic belief began to crumble as early as the nineteenth. The ultimately most serious blow against that belief was delivered by Darwin, who, by declaring man to be the chance product of an non-rational and amoral nature, fatally undermined the trust in mankind's rationality and natural goodness. Around the same time Marxism assailed the belief in the uniformity and rationality of human nature by proclaiming that man's convictions are determined by the socio-economic conditions within which they arise, and by stating that what man may think is his search for truth is in fact inspired by his desire for economic gain. And Nietzsche in his turn strengthened the tendency toward relativism and skepticism by teaching that we all look at the world from our own limited perspective, and that our so-called search for truth is in effect a search for power.

In short, the basis for the postmodern disbelief in the possibility of reaching objective, universally valid truth was laid in the nineteenth century. We will see in the next chapter how the early twentieth century built on that basis.

NOTES

1. Friedrich Nietzsche, *The Gay Science,* trans. and ed. Walter Kaufmann (New York: Random House, Vintage Books, 1974), par. 125.

2. For Nietzsche's views on master and slave morality, see part V (especially par. 195-203) and part IX (especially par. 260) of his *Beyond Good and Evil,* trans. and ed. Walter Kaufmann (New York: Random House, Vintage Books, 1966), as well as the "First Essay" of his *The Genealogy of Morals* in *The Birth of Tragedy and The Genealogy of Morals,* trans. Francis Golffing (Garden City, New York: Doubleday, Anchor Books, 1956).

3. Crane Brinton, *Nietzsche* (Cambridge, Mass.: Harvard University Press, 1948 [1941]), p. 216.

4. See the section "The 'Improvers' of Mankind," 2, in Nietzsche's *The Twilight of the Idols: Or, How to Philosophise with the Hammer,* trans. Anthony M. Ludovici (New York: Russell and Russell, 1964).

5. Nietzsche, *Beyond Good and Evil,* Part I, 4.

6. He mentioned it, but without using the term itself, in section 341 of *The Gay Science,* the first edition of which appeared in 1882. See also Part III, "Of the Vision and the Riddle," 2, and "The Convalescent," 2, and Part IV, "The Intoxicated Song," 9-11, in his *Thus Spoke Zarathustra,* trans. R. J. Hollingdale (Harmondsworth: Penguin Books, 1964 [1961]).

7. Nietzsche, *Zarathustra,* Part II, "Of Redemption"; Part III, "Of Old and New Law-Tables," 3.

8. On Niezsche's delusions of divinity, see below, pp. 263f.

9. Nietzsche, *The Will to Power,* trans. Walter Kaufmann and R. J. Hollingdale, ed. Walter Kaufmann (New York: Random House, Vintage Books, 1968), p. 267, aphorism. 481.

10. Nietzsche, *The Genealogy of Morals,* XXV.

11. Sigmund Freud, *Introductory Lectures on Psychoanalysis,* trans. and ed. James Strachey (New York: Norton, A Liveright Book, 1977), Lecture XVIII.

12. On the benefits of methodological reductionism, and on the issue of scientific reductionism in general, see Nancey Murphy, *Anglo-American Postmodernity: Philosophical Perspectives on Science, Religion, and Ethics* (Boulder, Colorado: Westview Press, 1997), pp. 12-35.

13. *Ibid.,* pp. 14-18.

14. *Ibid.,* p. 87.

15. This happened with the development of non-Euclidean mathematics and the rise of the new physics, which destroyed Kant's argument regarding the universal validity of Euclidean geometry and Newtonian physics. On these developments see chapter 17 below.

XVI. The Turn to the Irrational

The real break between the nineteenth and twentieth century happened not in 1900 but in 1914, the year of the outbreak of the Great War. During the first decade and a half of the new century, Europe's political, social, and economic affairs continued to run largely in nineteenth-century grooves. While signs of an approaching disintegration of the old order were certainly not absent, many Europeans continued to believe in social and economic progress.

The belief in the continuation of the West's dominant global position was not challenged either in these years, at least not substantially. There was an increasingly strong tendency to question Europe's cultural superiority, and predictions of a reversal of its fortunes multiplied, but few of these had yet come to pass. The most striking exception was the defeat of Russia (in the Russo-Japanese War of 1905) by a non-European and a non-white nation. But this could be explained by the fact that Russia was itself partly an Asian power, so that the humiliation it suffered did not have to reflect on the prospects of the rest of Europe.

If the period inherited the late nineteenth-century belief in stability and progress, it also shared in the sense of uncertainty of the preceding epoch, and it followed it in its turn toward relativism and the irrational. It is these developments, especially as they accelerated after the outbreak of the war, that will have our attention in the present chapter. We will begin with the rise of psychoanalysis and with the work of its founder and most famous practitioner, Sigmund Freud, who straddled the two periods. He was born in the middle of the nineteenth century but published most of his work in the twentieth, some of it before 1914. The section will be followed by brief accounts of the work of Freud's erstwhile disciple, Carl Gustav Jung, and of the rise and implications of the sociology of knowledge. In the next chapter we will show how developments in mathematics and the natural sciences contributed to the mood of uncertainty.

The rise of psychoanalysis

Sigmund Freud (1856-1939) spent practically his entire life in Vienna, the capital of the multi-ethnic and slowly disintegrating Habsburg empire, which would suffer dismemberment after the First World War. For centuries a cultural leader, Vienna in the early twentieth century was the European centre of avant-garde art, *fin de siècle* thinking, and Nietzsche-inspired neo-paganism.[1] It was also a hotbed of anti-Semitism and helped nurture the ideas of both Adolf Hitler, who spent part of his youth in the Austrian capital, and Theodor Herzl, the father of Zionism and of the idea of a Jewish homeland. Freud, himself a Jew, moved to England when in 1938 Hitler revisited Austria and annexed it to his German Reich. He died in the country of his exile, a few weeks after the outbreak of the Second World War.

Freud ranks with Karl Marx as the creator of one of the West's great post-Christian mythologies. The two men had other traits in common. Both were German-speaking Jews who embraced atheism. Heirs of the Enlightenment and of positivism, both were also rationalists and firm believers in the competence of the scientific method to locate and define human problems. Furthermore, both presented their theories as scientific ones and saw them accepted as such, although in fact they were based more on speculation than on empirical evidence.

But if there were close similarities between the two men, the dissimilarities were also profound. A comparison of the two mythologies shows the radical differences between the worldviews of their creators, as well as the vast distance Europe had travelled, in the space of a few decades, from the belief in progress and rationality to a pessimistic irrationalism. Marx, who was Freud's older contemporary (he died in 1883 when Freud was 27), was a staunch believer in progress. And although his concept of ideology would throw doubt on the independent power of human reason (a point to which we return later in this chapter), Marx did not explicitly deny mankind's essential rationality. Freud did precisely that. While never doubting that he himself was a rational agent, he made it his life's work to show the preponderance of the irrational in the rest of the human family. He also rejected belief in progress, not only in progress of the Marxist type, but even in that of the far more limited Nietzschean one. In Freud's system there was no promise of the rise of supermen capable of revitalizing a decadent culture. While Marx was still a utopian, Freud had few if any illusions left.[2]

In spite of his pessimism, Freud's ideas were widely accepted. It is no exaggeration to say that he influenced the contemporary view of man more profoundly than any other late-modern thinker. His influence and popularity are to be explained in part by the promised therapeutic value of his psychoanalysis. In the late nineteenth and the early twentieth century neurotic symptoms began to multiply, especially among members of the upper and middle classes, and Freud believed that he was able to explain and cure these disorders. Another reason was that Freudianism was indeed a mythology, containing a view of human existence that was believed to be capable of replacing the Christian one, which was now increasingly being rejected.

It is this aspect of Freudianism, more than its therapeutic potential, that explains both its influence in Freud's own days and its survival value. Today not many psychoanalysts would want to call themselves pure Freudians. There is overwhelming evidence that Freud cheated and effected few if any lasting cures. His mechanistic approach and his reductionism also have come under attack, especially his insistence that the majority of neuroses are to be explained by sexual experiences or fantasies, many of them dating from early childhood. It is now recognized, moreover, that mental disorders do not have to be a result of repressed guilt feelings or traumas. As often as not the causes are physical, requiring drug treatment rather than months or even years of expensive psychoanalytic therapy. But while his reputation as a psychotherapist has eroded, Freud's explanation of the origins of man's misery remains a strong cultural force, and his view of human nature continues to be influential.

Guilt and the unconscious

Central to Freud's psychoanalytical system was his explanation of human guilt, the problem that he believed was behind the mental and emotional disorders he dealt with. For him guilt was not a result of man's transgressing divine commandments or the commandments of natural law. Its origins were to be found in the complexities of man's evolutionary development and in the restraints imposed upon him by society. Discarding the concepts of sin and human responsibility, Freud attempted to remove the problem of guilt by simply tracing what he considered to be its biological and social origins.

Freud explained the feeling of guilt with reference to the workings of the unconscious. He did not invent the idea of the unconscious, which had been talked and written about for some centuries. It was Freud, however, who made a point of examining the concept's psychological implications and who showed its relevance for a theory of human nature. By making it the basis of both his psychoanalysis and his anthropology, he also popularized the concept.

The unconscious for Freud was the seat of instinctual drives, such as the death wish, the drive for power, and the drive for sexual satisfaction. The sex drive was the dominant one, and was, Freud taught, already strong in infancy. Sill uninhibited, the child made no attempt to refrain from satisfying its instinctual desires. When in growing up it learned that the subject of sexuality was surrounded by taboos, however, it began to repress these desires, together with any memories of sexual fantasies, which it now experienced as shameful.

The repression of instinctual drives did not have to cause debilitating problems. Mentally healthy persons learned to live (although often only precariously) with the conflicting dictates of social morality and of the unconscious. In the neurotic person, however, the repressed desires and memories would sooner or later trigger symptoms of emotional maladjustment and sometimes even of physical illness. The fact that this could happen was evidence of the strength of the unconscious, which Freud believed to be much more basic to human nature than man's rational faculty. Humanity had descended from a long line of animal precursors, and human reason was therefore a late acquisition. The instinctual drives, which originated in mankind's pre-human past and resided in the unconscious, were far older and therefore a far more integral part of the human psyche.

Human nature, then, continued to be close to animal nature. The acquisition of reason had made a difference and could be considered progress, but in Freud's view that progress was had at the price of human happiness. It had led to the establishment of a civil society which, in order to function properly, demanded the repression of man's animal instincts and so became a major cause of emotional disorders. Freud devoted his book *Civilization and its Discontents*, published in 1930, to this topic, but he mentioned it in other writings as well (for example, in his *Future of an Illusion* of 1927). Since a return to a "state of nature" was out of the question, the struggle between the demands of the instincts and those of society could be expected to continue indefinitely.

Id, ego, and superego

To explain the nature of that struggle, Freud introduced his well-known division of the human psyche into three parts, that of the id, the ego, and the superego. The id was the repository of the instinctual drives, among which the libido or sex drive was the most powerful. The direct successor of man's primordial animal nature, the id was ruled by what Freud called the pleasure principle, and its concern was with the satisfaction of the individual's instinctual desires and needs. The ego was the actual human person, the "self," which was endowed with consciousness and intelligence and for that reason was weaker than the id. It was in charge of a variety of defence mechanisms to help it cope with the pressures exerted by the id. The superego, finally, grew out of the awareness of parental and societal restraints upon instinctual demands and filled the role of the individual's conscience. Its task was to supervise the ego and make sure that the id and the libido were kept under control. Because this meant an ongoing inner struggle, the inevitable result of its efforts was the creation of new traumas.

To help people suffering from neuroses it was necessary, Freud said, to bring the underlying causes of the neurotic symptoms to the surface. Healing was a matter of understanding, of making the patient realize that his problems were not caused by personal failures. The analyst listened to the patient's accounts of his past, analyzed his dreams, and used a variety of other means to probe his thoughts and memories, in the hope of finding the cause of the guilt feelings. If these feelings could be explained as the result of natural processes over which the patient himself had no control, a cure could be achieved. To understand, in Freud's theory, was to be cured.

Freud's mythology

Several of Freud's ideas originated in the nineteenth century. Among those who had broached ideas similar to Freud's were Arthur Schopenhauer – a German philosopher whose nihilistic pessimism had strongly influenced Nietzsche and other *fin de siècle* thinkers – and Nietzsche himself. Freud denied that he had made use of their insights, insisting that he had read their works only late in life, but he was probably guilty here of special pleading. Students of Freud's life have shown that turn-of-the-century Viennese thinkers paid a great deal of attention to Schopenhauer and Nietzsche, and as a university student

Freud himself belonged to a reading society which one author describes as "a radical, pan-German organization in which the views of Schopenhauer, Wagner, and Nietzsche were avidly discussed."[3] Members of the reading society even corresponded with Nietzsche. Having belonged to this group for five years, Freud must have been aware of the work of Schopenhauer and Nietzsche, which makes it hard to believe that the similarities between their ideas and his own were coincidental.

The most direct influence on Freud was Charles Darwin, whose book on human evolution (*The Descent of Man*) had appeared in 1871, and whose theory was finding wide acceptance by the time Freud began to develop his system. Darwin's theory of human evolution established a new anthropology, one that described man not as a being made in the image of God, but as closely akin to the animal and the product of a mindless evolutionary process. This anthropology made necessary a new psychology, one that "was not based upon the philosophy of mind, or upon perception, or upon conditioned reflexes, or upon man's spiritual qualities, but one which was rooted in his kinship with animals. The time was ripe for a psychology based upon 'instinct'; that is, upon the basic biological forces or 'drives' motivating the behaviour of both man and animals...."[4]

It was this need that Freud intended to fill. But as mentioned earlier, he was not satisfied with simply developing a new psychology; he also wanted a new cosmology that could serve as framework for his psychology and anthropology. Freud was militantly atheistic and a sworn enemy of both the Jewish and the Christian religion. Having rejected the biblical account of the origin of human guilt, he searched for an explanation that was equally coherent. He believed he had found it by adapting a number of classical legends.

One of these was the story of the Greek King Oedipus, who had killed his father and married his mother. This legend became the basis of the so-called Oedipus complex. Freud, who had a strong "mother fixation," recalled that as a child he had been in competition with his father for the love of his mother and (as was his custom) he universalized this personal experience. As he wrote in October 1897 to a friend: "I have found, in my own case too, [the phenomenon of] being in love with my mother and jealous of my father, and I now consider it a universal event in early childhood...."[5] Since infant girls were plagued by similar incestuous fantasies, a basis had been found for the universal sense of guilt. The Oedipus complex would become a central concept in Freud's psychology and anthropology.

Freud later supplemented the idea of the Oedipus complex with that of the so-called primal crime, the story of the killing and eating of the abusive and incestuous primeval father by his sons. He told this story in the last chapter of his book *Totem and Taboo* (1912-13), using it, like the Oedipus complex, as evidence for his contention that the desire for incest and parricide is a universal human trait which accounts for the phenomenon of guilt.

It accounted also for the institution of society with its customs and laws. The sons had both hated and loved their father and were devoured by remorse for their deeds of parricide and cannibalism, a feeling of guilt that was passed on from the primal horde to the rest of humanity. They realized, moreover, that for the family to survive, it must outlaw the acts that had cost the father his life (his aggressiveness and his monopolizing of the women of the tribe), as well as their own heinous deed. This led them to institute laws which forbade parricide and incest and put restraints on the sexual and aggressive drives in general. So they made organized society possible.

This was not yet the extent of the explanatory power assigned to the Oedipus complex and the primal crime. They also explained cultural achievements like art, which in Freud's system resulted from the "sublimation" of instinctual energy and drives, that is, their redirection into socially acceptable channels. Not in the last place, they accounted for the rise of religion. According to Freud, all religions were inspired by the attempt to deal with the primal guilt; all of them were to be seen as "reactions aiming at the same great event with which culture began and which ever since has not let mankind come to rest" (*Totem and Taboo*, IV, 5).

This was not Freud's only account of the origin of religion. He also explained it with reference to the need for a father figure, someone who would exorcise for man the terrors of nature, reconcile him to the cruelty of fate, and compensate him for the suffering and privations which civilized life imposed on him (*Future of an Illusion*, III). But he kept returning to the Oedipus complex and the primal crime, no doubt because their explanatory power was so much greater, accounting, as they did, for every aspect of human life and culture. His use of these concepts provides an example of the type of reductionism we can meet in Freud. His own peculiar childhood experiences served as proof of one of his central premises, namely that civilization and all it stands for can be explained with reference to incestuous desire and a primordial murder.

An appraisal

One reads Freud with mixed feelings. On the one hand, one cannot help being impressed by his lively imagination and his virtuosity as a system-builder. He deserves credit, moreover, for his often keen insight into human nature and his courage in exposing the dark side of the human psyche. But on the other hand it is difficult not to lose patience with his special pleading, his doctrinaire reductionism, and his almost superstitious trust in the validity of his self-invented theories, no matter how absurd.

Of Freud's reductionism, to start with that topic, we have already given various examples. Freud made a point of digging up dirt and of reducing everything, even the best that civilization has produced, to the lowest possible motive. By doing so he completed the devaluation of traditional norms and values that Nietzsche had begun. The results were similar, although (again like Nietzsche) Freud left it to his followers to draw most of the ethical implications of his theory. The expedient of reducing tensions by relaxing the rules that traditionally held society and the family together was implied in his system. It meant, as his followers properly deduced, that the way to mental health could no longer be sought in the traditional counsels of self-discipline and restraint, but only in a policy of permissiveness. The beast in man must be given its due.

Freud's tendency of reducing the highest to the lowest extended, as we saw, to his explanation of religion. Here as elsewhere one is struck not only by his reductionism, but also by his gullibility. He kept insisting, always in strident tones, that the religious explanation of life was too far-fetched to merit even a moment's consideration. Yet he substituted an explanation that he himself admitted sounded fantastic, and that has stretched the patience of even some of his most loyal supporters. They may be willing to accept the idea of the Oedipus complex as an explanatory metaphor but are embarrassed by Freud's insistence that it, and the concept of the primal crime, refer to actual historical events. Their embarrassment is the greater because Freud based these ideas on data provided by anthropologists whose theories have by now been fully discredited.

For Freud, the historicity of the stories had to stand. It provided proof that his psychoanalytical theories had universal validity and therefore held the key to neurotic symptoms and their cure in all civilized societies. He refused to admit, however, that his theories were based on the stories. Always careful to defend his reputation as a scientist, he insisted that his work was truly empirical. In his anthropological works he repeatedly stated that the events the stories related, bizarre and unbelievable as they might seem, were to be accepted as true because they were in agreement with his findings as a clinical psychologist. Critics have mentioned the extent to which he was able to deceive himself and allow his premisses to dictate his conclusions. "Time and again," in the words of one commentator, "Freud saw in his patients what psychoanalytical theory led him to look for and then to interpret the way he did; and when the theory changed, so did the clinical findings."[6]

One difficult question Freud faced was how events that had taken place at the beginning of human history could still affect humanity. He answered it with reference to the theory of the Chevalier de Lamarck, the French evolutionist who had taught that acquired characteristics can be inherited. That theory was already under attack in Freud's days, but like other psychoanalysts, Freud refused to relinquish it.[7] His entire system depended on the assumption that dispositions such as the primal herd's inclination toward parricide and incest could be and in fact were inherited by the most distant generations, and that man recapitulates, either in infancy or later in life, the psychic history of the race. But if Lamarckianism is indeed to be rejected as untenable – and there are few evolutionists today who would deny this – then much of Freudianism must be rejected as well.

And finally, there is Freud's failure to apply his beliefs about human nature to himself and his own theories. A critical and highly intelligent man, he should have admitted that he would have to qualify his theory with the admission that his insights, too, were determined by instinctual drives, and therefore suspect. But to admit this would have meant that he had to remain silent, a sacrifice that Freud, as Nietzsche before him, refused to make. Yet it remains true that, as one commentator put it, the "renaturalization" of man is self-devouring, a sawing off of the branch on which the renaturalizer sits.[8] The fact that Freud and his followers have denied the fact does not negate the truth that their logic destroys their argument.

Jung and the collective unconscious

Freud attracted students who would become influential in their own right. The Swiss Carl Gustav Jung (1875-1961) was the most famous of the early disciples. For a number of years he was close to Freud, who at one time called him his adopted son and heir, but he later broke with the master. Among the causes of the estrangement was Jung's questioning of Freud's single-minded insistence upon the sex drive as the predominant cause of neuroses. He also rejected Freud's dismissal of religion. Although Jung himself had abandoned the Christian faith, he believed that man had spiritual needs that must be satisfied. He was especially interested in eastern and primitive religions and in various manifestations of the occult.

Jung departed from Freud also in his description of the mind. Like Freud, he distinguished three levels in the human psyche, which he called the conscious, the personal unconscious, and the collective unconscious. The conscious and the personal unconscious were similar to the Freudian ego and id, except that Jung rejected Freud's stress on the dominance of the sex drive. The personal unconscious, moreover, was not only the seat of instinctual appetites, but also of other elements that influenced man's thought and behaviour, such as his spiritual needs.

Like Freud, Jung was a Lamarckian. It was this theory that enabled him to arrive at the idea of the collective unconscious. Formed in the evolutionary process, the collective unconscious served, among other things, to join the individual's experiences to those of the entire human race, all the way down to its pre-human past. It formed the repository of archetypes or primordial images, such as the image of God, rebirth, hero, mother-goddess, and numberless others. The existence and accessibility of these images explained why individuals, no matter how far apart in time and space, tended to perceive reality in ways that were not altogether dissimilar. The concept of the archetypes can therefore be seen as an elaboration of Kant's idea of the universal categories of the mind, although it is rather more mystical and fanciful. The idea also shows that for Jung the past played a more positive role than it did for Freud. For Freud it was the source of all present problems; in Jung's view it supplied wisdom that man could draw on to meet present needs.[9]

The idea of the collective unconscious and the archetypes would become influential not only in Jungian psychology but also in a multitude of other areas, such as anthropology, literary criticism, and the study of comparative religion and primitive cultures. Jung's tendency toward Gnosticism, mysticism, and the irrational, and his interest in the occult, are among the reasons for his appeal among members of New Age religions. It probably also helps explain his anti-Semitism and his admiration of National Socialism with its pagan spirituality – factors that may have constituted additional reasons for his break with Freud.[10]

The sociology of knowledge

The Enlightenment had viewed man as a rational and autonomous agent, whose ideas were not necessarily influenced by subjective elements such as personal beliefs or the beliefs of the society in which they arose. With his celebration of the irrational, Jung, as Nietzsche and Freud before him, contributed to the demolition of the Enlightenment view of man. His concern with the collective unconscious and the archetypes shows, however, that he had not fully abandoned the belief in universals and in the unchanging nature of reality. Therefore the danger of relativism, while certainly not absent, was kept at bay in Jung's psychology. More openly relativistic were the implications of developments in a number of other human sciences which in the early twentieth century culminated in the rise of the sociology of knowledge.

The sociology of knowledge stresses the social foundations of human knowing and the changing character of truth over time. It was influenced by developments in such disciplines as history (especially since the rise of historicism), cultural anthropology, and sociology proper. In a previous chapter we already noted the relativistic implications of historicism with its refusal to evaluate preceding cultures. Sociologists and anthropologists drew conclusions similar to those of the historians. Noticing the role played by environment and history in the genesis of belief and value systems, they concluded that it was impossible to distinguish among these systems with reference to universal, overarching standards. What was good for one society might be bad for another. The criterion to be used in judging belief systems was not whether they were true or false, but whether they worked for their society.

The sociology of knowledge was also influenced by the Marxist concept of ideology. Marx was not a relativist by choice, but in his fight against those who failed to see things the way he did, he had recourse to the idea that a person's situation in the world can influence his view of things. Marx did not think that this error threatened proletarians and their advocates. They, he was convinced, were free from ideological confusion and saw reality in its true light. He employed the concept only against his bourgeois opponents. But of course, the weapon could boomerang and be used against Marxism itself. Once this happened, and the conviction spread that all thought is subject to ideological distortions, the parts needed for the construction of the sociology of knowledge were in place.[11]

The discipline arose in the 1920s. It was the brainchild of the German philosopher Max Scheler, who held a moderately relativistic view of human knowing. For him society determined the presence of certain ideas but not necessarily their entire content. His successor, the sociologist Karl Mannheim, removed that restriction. More radical and also more influential than Scheler, Mannheim taught that all ideas, with the sole exception of those of mathematics and of some of the natural sciences, were social constructs. And because societies changed over time, so did concepts of truth. None of them were eternal; all had arisen at a particular point in time, and presumably all would be discarded when the social and cultural substructures changed.

The problem with this theory was that, on its own premises, it could claim to be no more than a temporary phenomenon. All-out relativism suffers from the same defect as Nietzsche's and Freud's irrationalism: it is self-referentially incoherent. If there is no truth, then relativism cannot be true either. Mannheim realized this and made a point of denying that his approach was relativistic in any arbitrary sense. He called his theory not a relativistic but a relationist one, and relationism, he said, does not signify that there are no criteria of rightness and wrongness. But he added that relationism does insist "... that it lies in the nature of certain assertions that they cannot be formulated absolutely, but only in terms of the perspective of a given situation." The idea that truth can be discovered in a form that is "independent of an historically and socially determined set of meanings" had to be given up as "a vain hope."[12] Clearly, Mannheim was not able to avoid the shoals of a doctrinaire relativism.

To say that the sociology of knowledge runs the danger of logical incoherence is not to deny that the individual's social and cultural backgrounds influence his view of the world. They do. But the admission of this truth does not have to lead to an all-out relativism. That it frequently does so in the tradition of the sociology of knowledge is evidence of the tendency to move from one extreme to its opposite, a tendency that is characteristic of much of modernism and was in large part inspired by its belief in scientific infallibility. That belief led to the conclusion that either exhaustive truth can be reached, or, if that turns out to be impossible, no truth can be had at all. But the fact that our cultural and social rootedness is undeniable does not prove that therefore we are determined by our society. Experience shows that we have access to criteria of truth and falsity and of right and wrong beyond those which our society acknowledges – which means that we are personally responsible for our beliefs and actions.

The basic problem with the sociologists of knowledge was not that they went too far in their criticism of Enlightenment certainties, but that they did not go far enough. The Enlightenment tradition of human reason was all-inclusive: it taught not only that the human mind was an infallible source of universal truths, but also that it was the only such source. Revelation, established authorities, tradition, collective and individual experience and plain common sense yielded only subjective opinions. To demolish, as the sociology of knowledge did, the first of these beliefs while leaving the second intact, was a sure route to the doctrinaire relativism that characterizes the work of so many late-modern thinkers, from historicists and anthropologists to the sociologists of knowledge themselves.

As the work of Nietzsche, Freud, Jung and their followers shows, it was also a sure route to the enthronement of the irrational. The late nineteenth and early twentieth centuries made clear that the denial of a transcendent source of truth, and the refusal to accept as knowledge whatever cannot pass the grid established by a scientific rationalism, mean the death of man as a rational being.

NOTES

[1] A good source on Viennese culture at the turn of the century is Carl E. Schorske, *Fin-de-siècle Vienna: Politics and Culture* (New York: Random House, Vintage Books, 1981 [1961]).

[2] It is true that in the last chapter of his *Future of an Illusion* (chapter 10) he states that at some distant point in time reason (and science) will become stronger than unreason, but this was said primarily to show the superiority of scientific atheism over religion. The proclamation of some kind of progress is not typical of his work.

[3] Frank J. Sulloway, *Freud, Biologist of the Mind: Beyond the Psychoanalytic Legend* (New York: Basic Books, 1979), p. 468. For various myths created by Freud and his followers to bolster his claims to originality see chapter 13 of the same book.

[4] Anthony Storr, *Freud* (Oxford: Oxford University Press, 1990 [1989]), p. 121. On Darwin's influence on Freud, see also Sulloway, *Freud, Biologist of the Mind*, ch. 7 and *passim*.

[5] Quoted in Storr, *Freud*, p. 23. On Freud's peculiar relationships with his parents, see further Clarence J. Karier, *Scientists of the Mind: Intellectual Founders of Modern Psychology* (Urbana: University of Illinois Press, 1986), pp. 194-200.

6. Sulloway, *Freud, Biologist of the Mind,* p. 498.

7 *Ibid.,* pp. 439f.

8. Ernest Gellner, *The Psychoanalytic Movement, Or the Coming of Unreason* (London: Paladin Books, 1985), p. 217.

9. Philip Rieff, *Freud: The Mind of the Moralist* (Chicago: University of Chicago Press, 1979 [1959], p. 200n.

10. On Jung's Gnosticism and anti-Semitism, see Karier, *Scientists of the Mind,* ch. 8.

11. For the origins of the sociology of knowledge, see Karl Mannheim, *Ideology and Utopia: An Introduction to the Sociology of Knowledge,* trans. Louis Wirth and Edward Shils (New York: Harcourt, Brace and World, A Harvest Book, 1936); and Peter L. Berger and Thomas Luckmann, *The Social Construction of Reality: A Treatise in the Sociology of Knowledge* (Garden City, New York: Doubleday, Anchor Books, 1967), pp. 1-18.

12. Mannheim, *Ideology and Utopia,* pp. 283, 80.

XVII. The New Mathematics and Physics

While psychologists and other social scientists were questioning the power of human reason, natural scientists went about their business as usual. That business flourished. The nineteenth century had been a time of great scientific advances. In the first half of the twentieth century these advances, in so far as they applied to the physical sciences, culminated in what came to be called the new physics.

The breakthroughs were so spectacular that people have referred to them as constituting a second scientific revolution, comparable in importance to the one effected two centuries earlier by Newton and his colleagues. And it was not only the theories that were trailblazing. Their applications were equally revolutionary. By making possible the use of nuclear power and by inaugurating the age of electronics and the computer, the new physics greatly extended the West's technological know-how, thereby fundamentally changing its culture.

The second scientific revolution confirmed in a striking manner the modern trust in the ability of science to harness the powers of nature for human use. It was, however, far less successful than the first one had been in *explaining* nature and its workings. Although Copernicus' astronomy had been opposed to experience, classical physics in general had provided a picture of nature that appeared utterly rational and self-evidently true. As Alexander Pope described it in the well-known couplet: "Nature and nature's laws lay hid in night; God said, 'Let Newton be!' and all was light." The cosmos was a machine, intelligible and altogether predictable in its operations. The new physics challenged that view. In that sense it was in tune with the age of uncertainty in which it arose, just as Newtonianism was in tune with the growing trust in reason of its era. Stupendous as its achievements were, the new physics confirmed Nietzsche's and Freud's observations about the negative implications of scientific advances for humanity's self-esteem.

The blow delivered by the new physics was the more painful because developments with similar implications were taking place in the related field of mathematics, the discipline that had long been recognized as the key to the understanding of nature. The beginnings of these developments can be traced back to the nineteenth century, and we will therefore turn to them first.[1]

The prestige of mathematics

For more than two thousand years mathematics had been considered the queen of the sciences. It was held in awe because of both its inner logic and its ability to advance human knowledge in general. The contribution of mathematics to the progress of knowledge was twofold. In the first place, it provided a method of deductive or axiomatic reasoning which promised to lead to more certain conclusions than the inductive kind. Inductive reasoning begins with the collection of empirical evidence, which serves as the basis for a generalization or law. The inductive approach, although much used, is not foolproof. No matter how much evidence is gathered, the possibility that counter-evidence will turn up, tomorrow or next year or perhaps in the next century, can never be discounted. Induction gives rise to probabilities, not to necessary truths.

One could reach such necessary truths, the modern age believed, by applying the deductive method. Here one began with axioms or self-evident truths, from which, by careful reasoning, further truths were derived. If the premises were true, and if the proper logical approach was followed, then the conclusion had to be true as well. This was the case in Euclidean mathematics. It was also the case in syllogistic reasoning, another example of the deductive approach. If it is indubitably true that all men are mortal and that Socrates is a man, then it necessarily follows that Socrates is mortal.

Although earlier civilizations like Egypt and Babylonia had used mathematics, the Greeks were the first to make it into an organized system with its own methodology. It was from them that Christian Europe inherited its view of both the nature of mathematics and the type of reasoning based on it. The outstanding modern advocate of the mathematical approach to reasoning was the seventeenth-century philosopher René Descartes. A mathematician himself, Descartes developed a theory of knowledge that was based on the mathematical method. He started with first principles or self-evident truths (his "clear and distinct ideas"), and, moving step by step and following a strictly logical method, arrived at what he believed were necessary, universally valid conclusions. As we have seen in chapter 7, the approach even enabled him to reach certainty about the independence of the mind and the existence of God. The method he followed, Descartes believed, was essentially a mechanical one, so that everyone could learn to use it, "however mediocre his mind."[2]

A main reason for the enduring appeal of the Cartesian approach was its vindication in the scientific revolution. Modern science benefited not only from the mathematical method, however, but also from mathematics as such. Here we come to the second contribution of mathematics to human knowledge, which is that it provided, as the Pre-Socratic Pythagoreans had already taught, the key with which to unlock the secrets of nature. This quality contributed to the feeling of awe which mathematics inspired in modern times. The scientist Albert Einstein once said that the most incomprehensible thing about the world is that it is comprehensible. And it is mathematics – the fact that the laws of nature can be expressed in mathematical terms – which ensures this comprehensibility.

Mathematics in a secular age

Why does nature have this mathematical structure? And how is it possible that human beings can discover the mathematical laws governing nature? Christians have traditionally answered these questions with reference to divine creation. It was God who endowed the universe he had made with mathematical properties. Having assigned to man the task of guarding and developing nature, he gave him a mind capable of understanding nature's mathematical structures and of responding to its mathematical language. This meant that both man and nature, although in different ways, reflected the laws the Creator had instituted. Early-modern scientists still believed in this God-given harmony. It explains Kepler's conviction that in their work scientists were thinking God's thoughts after him.

This faith lasted well into the seventeenth century. That same period, however, witnessed a decline in the belief in God as sovereign Creator. We noted in earlier chapters that scientific advances contributed to that decline, although early scientists by no means intended such an outcome. But the success of science led people to place their trust in scientific progress. Mathematics, the scientists' tool, was similarly revered. Its very effectiveness in describing the structure and operations of the universe – and therefore in revealing what Kepler called God's thoughts – gave rise to the idea that the authority of mathematics must at least be equivalent to that of the Bible. The concern with God's general revelation tended to push his special revelation into the background. From there it was but a step to seeing mathematics not as God's creature, but as an autonomous power, which determined both the nature and the operations of the universe. That step was indeed taken. It implied that God himself was bound by the laws of nature and logic; that he could not have made a world different from the existing one.[3]

The history of early-modern thought shows that once this stage was reached, belief in God was no longer considered necessary. Mathematics became an idol. God could the more easily be dispensed with because the mathematical method of reasoning shared in the status of mathematics itself as a tool to find truth and certainty. First considered equivalent to divine revelation as a means of reaching truth, the Cartesian method soon displaced revelation. Before long it would be used as the means to judge it.

The decline of the biblical faith caused philosophical problems. One of them was the question how, in the absence of a rational Creator, it was to be explained that nature had a rational structure. That question, being a purely theoretical one, could perhaps be ignored. More disturbing was the problem of the harmony between man and nature. Why was it that man could understand the structures of the universe? Or, more urgently: if God was not the sovereign Creator of both man and nature and the ultimate guarantor of truth, how could one be certain that reliable truth about these structures could indeed be reached? Descartes, Locke, and Hume were among the philosophers struggling with that question. None of them found a satisfactory answer, and by the eighteenth century, if not earlier, skepticism about the validity of human reasoning was beginning to replace certainty.

Kant, Hume's younger contemporary, tried to solve the problem of skepticism by discarding the idea of a harmony or correspondence between mind and nature. Rather than assuming that man had to discover the order of nature, he taught that the human mind creates that order and imposes it on the universe. Nature was no longer to be understood on its own terms but on those of the human mind. But Kant could not prove that all minds had similar structures, so that every person, regardless of time and place, was capable of perceiving and interpreting nature in the same way. In the end his theory would therefore contribute to the rise of subjective relativism, according to which every individual creates his or her own reality.

A different solution was proposed by evolutionists, who taught that man can understand nature because he evolved from it and continues to be part of it. This theory suffers from even more serious defects than the Kantian one. Still under the influence of classicism and Christianity, Kant believed in an overarching reason, but evolutionists teach that the universe and all it contains are the product of randomness. The problem with the evolutionary type of argument is the difficulty of explaining how a random process can produce rational structures and give rise, moreover, to minds that understand these structures.[4]

The collapse of certainty

The lack of a satisfactory explanation of the harmony between nature and the human mind did little to diminish the prestige of mathematics. The scientific advances throughout the modern period showed its great worth as a scientific tool. They also bolstered the Cartesian belief in the ability of mathematics and its method to solve whatever problems still plagued humanity. So long as this belief remained unimpaired, the skepticism and relativism that were creeping up in other fields of knowledge could be kept at bay. It was the very trust in mathematical universality and infallibility, however, that came under attack in the nineteenth century and would collapse in the early twentieth. Its collapse struck a fatal blow at what remained of the western belief in universal truths.

The problem began in the field of geometry. The authority in that discipline was the Hellenist Euclid, who had lived in Alexandria around 300 B.C. The heir to two or three centuries of Greek mathematical studies, Euclid had collected the work of his predecessors, systematized it, and so transmitted it to posterity. It was Euclidean geometry, more than anything else, that instilled in Europeans the belief in both the infallibility of the axiomatic method and the ability of mathematics to reveal absolute truths about the physical world. Euclidean axioms, postulates, and theorems were in accordance with the facts of nature and had universal validity; at least mathematicians had for more than two millennia been certain that this was so.

In the course of the nineteenth century, however, work on one of

Euclid's postulates resulted in the formation of different geometric systems. It appeared that Euclidean geometry applied to plane surfaces and was therefore the proper tool for the type of measurements that scientists had normally been concerned with, but that it did not work for areas where curvature had to be taken into account. For these situations alternative geometries were needed. These geometries yielded triangles the sum of whose angles was either less or more than 180 degrees, depending on whether the curvature was negative or positive.

The problem was not that such alternative systems did not work, for they did. They were internally consistent and appeared to be no less effective in their own domain than Euclid's in his. Einstein's general theory of relativity of 1915, for example, was based on a non-Euclidean geometry, and the empirical validation of his theory four years later proved that the geometry he had used indeed described the physical world.[5] What was disturbing about the new geometries was that a system with universal validity no longer existed. If different geometrical systems were equally true, then truth ceased to be an absolute, universal concept in mathematics and therefore, according to many – for such was the prestige of mathematics – also in all other fields of knowledge.

The slide toward relativism accelerated when problems arose in other areas of mathematics as well. Different algebraic systems had to be constructed, each of them designed for a specific set of phenomena. As in geometry, experience decided which system was applicable in a certain situation.

Another unsettling development was that logic, on which mathematical reasoning is based, was also becoming problematic. The difficulties came in the form of logical paradoxes or antinomies. Some of these had been known of old: the so-called liar's paradox, according to which a statement is true and false at the same time, is a good example. A well-known version is that of the Cretan poet who says that all Cretans are liars. Since he himself is a Cretan, the verdict applies to him as well. But if he is a liar, then his statement is a lie, and the Cretans are not liars, which means that he is not a liar either, ... and so on, ad infinitum. In former ages the belief in the universal validity of mathematics and logic had been strong enough to take this type of paradox in stride. The situation changed when mathematicians, chastened by the rise of non-Euclidean geometries, attempted to enhance mathematical certainty by placing all mathematical systems, including algebra and arithmetic, on a strictly logical basis. The paradoxes that kept turning up threatened to play havoc with these attempts.

An even more serious blow came when in 1931 the mathematician Kurt Gödel revealed the vanity of ongoing attempts to make mathematics into a system that could be shown to be both complete and consistent. The dream that, given time, a unified system could be established for mathematics, one that was logically consistent and included every branch of the discipline, had to be given up. Mathematics was forever incapable of producing a coherent and complete system of thought.

Post-Euclidean relativism

Although theories were developed to eliminate the logical paradoxes, they were insufficiently convincing to remove the doubt that had been cast on the universal validity not only of mathematics, but also of the logic on which mathematics was based. Aristotle's logic had established certain "laws of thought," such as the law of non-contradiction (according to which a proposition cannot be both true and false) and that of the excluded middle (according to which a proposition must be either true or false), which had ever since been considered to be self-evidently true. The logical paradoxes seemed to suggest, however, that at least in some cases these laws do not apply; that there are things which can be both A and not-A. Gödel's incompleteness theorem, which showed that some propositions are neither provable nor disprovable, seemed to have similar implications.[6] In short, developments in both mathematics and logic – the two disciplines that had been considered the great sources of indubitable truths – now strengthened the tendency toward relativism.

People were quick to notice this. The relativistic reasoning followed by those who took their cue from mathematical developments led to conclusions similar to those reached by historicism and the sociology of knowledge. The fact that the new geometric and algebraic systems were internally consistent and effective in their own domain was used as a starting point. If in mathematics one could begin from different principles and nevertheless reach valid results, then, these people argued, it must be so in other fields as well. This meant that religions and legal systems and moral codes could no longer be judged according to universally-valid norms. It also meant that no culture or religion or moral system could be considered intrinsically superior or inferior to any other. As long as the systems worked for those who used them, they were to be considered valid.

The reactions to non-Euclideanism and the relativism to which it gave rise were varied. In the period following the First World War when rebellion against authority and tradition was in the air, many welcomed the developments as a justification for the abandonment of traditional morality and social restraints. Non-Euclideanism also seemed to vindicate a tendency (which was especially strong in America) to follow a pragmatist and empiricist approach in law and the social sciences, rather than one based on deduction from established norms. What counted was what society demanded at any given time.

And so, as Edward A. Purcell has shown,[7] legal theorists and social scientists were in the front ranks of those who applauded the new mathematics. It offered what they considered solid proof that the way to plan a just society was to follow an empirical approach. Non-Euclideanism could be used to justify the adoption of political, social, and legal theories and practices that were altogether different from the traditional ones. Most of the scholars in question were reform-minded and anxious for an overhaul of what was increasingly seen as a very imperfect status quo. Mathematical developments encouraged experimentation with a variety of new forms.

These ideas did not remain unchallenged. Opponents warned – increasingly so in the turbulent 1930s – of the anti-democratic implications of an all-out political, ethical, and legal empiricism. Mankind, they pointed out, was not intrinsically moral, and the absence of a higher law to which not only common people but rulers and judges also were subject, would lead to despotism and the rule of force. Hitler's experiment with "non-Euclidean" political, ethical, and legal systems proved their point. The refusal to rejoice in the triumph of a relativistic empiricism was inspired not only, however, by the fear that it might prove to be a two-edged sword. Many also mourned the loss of certainty because it implied the collapse of any remaining hope that human reason could aspire to absolute knowledge.

That fear was the stronger because the relativistic and skeptical mindset affected increasingly large areas. The victims included social, political, and legal thought, ethics and religion, traditional logic, and even science. As to logic, people began to argue that Aristotle's "laws of thought," for example, were social constructs and were adhered to because of their social utility, not because they expressed necessary truths. The way was therefore open to the formulation of "non-Euclidean" logical systems. The possibility of reaching truth in the natural sciences was similarly denied, and scientific theories too were declared to be social constructs. They were accepted not because they were true, but because they were in agreement with the belief systems that prevailed in the society in which they arose, and ultimately, of course, because they "worked."

Thomas Kuhn and the notion of paradigms

Those who held that scientific theories are social constructs were able to back up their claims with reference to theories of the sociology of knowledge. They could also refer to the work of a number of twentieth-century philosophers of science, who, while rejecting all-out relativism, did question the traditional view of science as an altogether objective enterprise. Among these philosophers was Thomas Kuhn, whose pioneering work on the history of science appeared in 1962.[8]

Rejecting modern scientist philosophies, Kuhn taught that scientists work within a certain conceptual model or framework, which shapes the way they look at the scientific problems they deal with. Aristotelian, Newtonian, and Darwinian science could serve as examples of such frameworks, but Kuhn included less comprehensive ones as well. He called these frameworks paradigms.[9] The influence of a scientist's paradigm could be sufficiently strong, he said, to prevent him or her from seeing evidence in the same way as someone adhering to a competing paradigm. The paradigmatic glasses one wore determined not just what one was looking for, but often also what one actually saw.

The scientists' concern in normal science, Kuhn said, was not first of all to prove a theory true or false, but to work out the implications of their paradigm. They used it as a basis for the gathering of further evidence and the solving of remaining problems. Loyalty to or belief in the paradigm meant that anomalies would long be ignored or explained away. And when the accumulation of contradictions at last led to a paradigm shift, scientists who accepted the new paradigm did not do so because it could be proven to be more "true" than the previous one. Non-objective factors played a role, such as "idiosyncrasies of autobiography and personality," considerations of beauty, the desire for simplicity, and the conviction that the new theory had greater explanatory power. Often, Kuhn said, it was a simple matter of faith that the new paradigm would produce better results than the previous one. He even spoke in this connection of a scientist's "conversion."

Kuhn's theory served as a corrective to the modernist tradition, which saw the scientific method as fully objective. It undoubtedly had relativistic implications.[10] If the scientist's own belief systems, those of his scientific community, and even those of society at large influence the way he sees the world, then absolutely objective knowledge remains a dream. But intellectual modesty in any event demands the admission that man cannot see the world with the eyes of God. That admission does not have to lead to a stance of extreme relativism, nor did it do so in Kuhn's case. There is much in science that is not affected by one's presuppositions and can be shown to be objectively true.

Furthermore, even in those areas where presuppositions do intrude, the world does not let the scientist get away with fantasy. There are reality checks. And while it is true that we cannot take hold of absolute knowledge, history, experience, and logic show that we can reach reliable conclusions. With its amazing track record, science itself testifies to this. Following the typical western all-or-nothing approach, however, relativists (among them some of Kuhn's more radical followers) ignored this testimony and used the work of Kuhn as evidence that scientific truth is altogether subjective.

The new physics

Developments in the physical sciences strengthened the general trend toward relativism. The new physics played a role similar to that of non-Euclidean geometry in that it did not invalidate the old system but rather supplemented it. Yet it strongly affected people's conception of the physical world.[11]

Newtonian or classical physics was in tune with people's normal experiences. It left the impression, for example, that time and space were absolute (in the sense that they were the same for observers everywhere and at all times), and conceived of matter and energy as distinct entities. For classical physics nature was a unified system, and natural laws were universally valid. The world operated in a machine-like fashion and was fully determinate, which meant that strict causality ruled. One could predict things with certainty. Newtonianism also held that there was a clear distinction between the human mind and external nature. Separate from the world of objects, the mind could study that world as an outsider or spectator, in an objective manner. All these assumptions seemed to be confirmed by common sense.

The view of the universe as a mechanism governed by fixed laws worked well for most of the modern period, and many of the Newtonian laws are still accepted as valid. Around the turn of the century, however, scientists discovered that the Newtonian system is incapable of accounting for phenomena at the remote edges of nature – that is, in the macrocosm of interstellar space and in the microcosm of the atomic and subatomic world. In 1905, for example, Albert Einstein published his special theory of relativity. This theory disproved the idea, expressed in

Newton's *Principia* (although, admittedly, not applied in classical mechanics), that space is absolute, showing that the location and movement of bodies in space can only be described in terms of their relationship to each other. There are no boundaries or directions in space, which means that there is no absolute frame of reference. One can give an accurate measurement of the location of a body in space only by stating the position of the person who does the measuring.

If there is no absolute spatial frame of reference, neither is there, Einstein showed, an absolute chronological or temporal one. Time is subjective. We can make it objective by using clocks and calendars, but since these are based on the earth's rotation on its axis and its orbit around the sun, these measuring devices are not applicable to other areas in the universe. The relativity of time means that we cannot apply our sense of "now" to the cosmos as a whole, a conclusion Einstein expressed in his concept of the "relativity of simultaneity." Like space, time is relative to the observer's "system" or frame of reference.

Einstein's special theory of relativity had other implications. It changed scientists' conception of the relationship between mass and energy by establishing that mass, too, is relative. It varies with its motion: the greater the velocity of an object, the greater its mass. Since motion can be seen as a form of energy, Einstein concluded that the increased mass of a moving body results from its increased energy, and that mass and energy are equivalent. He expressed this equivalence in an equation which showed that energy equals mass multiplied by the square of the velocity of light – the famous equation $E=mc^2$, which contributed to the rise of nuclear physics and, in the realm of technology, to the development of nuclear medicine, nuclear electrical power generation, and nuclear weaponry.

If Einstein's theory had far-reaching implications as to the relationship between mass and energy, so did the related work of Einstein's contemporary, the German physicist Max Planck.

In 1900 Planck noted that the energy radiated by a cooling body is emitted not in a continuous stream but discontinuously, in small bundles, which he called quanta. This suggested that radiation is to be regarded not only as a wave, but also as a particle. Later it was found that the electron, which had been assumed to be a particle, could in turn be looked at as a wave. These discoveries, which introduced quantum physics, showed that nature cannot really be pictured at the micro level. It is possible to observe and measure effects, but the reality underlying them is beyond our imagination: no metaphor can be found to illustrate the wave-particle duality and other phenomena at the sub-atomic level.

Quantum physics differed from classical physics in other ways. For one thing, it destroyed the belief, fostered by the mechanistic philosophy, that science can fully understand the processes of nature, that these processes are strictly determinate, and that science can therefore predict with certainty. It became apparent, for example, that an electron's position and its velocity cannot both be accurately measured at the same time. The act of measuring its velocity affects the electron's position and *vice versa*. It is only possible to measure the average velocity or position of a large number of electrons; precise knowledge of both properties (velocity and position) of a single electron cannot be had. These insights found expression in Heisenberg's uncertainty principle of 1927, which expresses the degree of uncertainty in a mathematical formula. The principle confirmed the conclusion that at the subatomic level we are dealing not with laws of certainty but of probability. The findings also refuted the modern dualist philosophy of an airtight division between the observer and the observed. The observer affects the object of study: in the act of observation the world is changed.

Quantum physics showed, we noted, that particles can be observed to behave like waves and waves like particles, depending on the instruments used in the observation. The two aspects cannot be observed at the same time and are in that sense mutually exclusive. Yet since neither can explain the nature of an electron fully, both must be accepted. The wave-particle duality led the Danish physicist Niels Bohr, shortly after the publication of Heisenberg's principle of uncertainty, to formulate the so-called complementarity principle. Bohr's principle speaks of the different information obtained under different sets of experimental conditions as not contradictory, but as complementary to each other.

As Gerald Holton points out,[12] the idea of complementarity is already evident in Heisenberg's principle, which tells us that both position and velocity cannot be accurately measured at the same time. Complementarity is restricted there, however, because position and velocity *are* capable of being observed and measured (with at least a limited degree of certainty) in the same experiment and are therefore not mutually exclusive. Such mutual exclusivity does apply to the wave-particle aspects. They cannot be exhibited simultaneously and must therefore be accepted as fully "complementary" features of the same object.

The complementarity principle, as Bohr realized, had philosophical and epistemological implications in that in at least one area it replaced the "either-or" logic of Aristotelianism (and of modernism) by a logic of complementarity, of "both-and." In that sense developments in physics reinforced the conclusions drawn from the development of non-Euclidean mathematics.

Religion and the new physics

The cultural reactions to the new physics were similar to those following the appearance of non-Euclidean mathematics. Some people welcomed the relativism that they believed was implied in the scientific theories, while others deplored it. A novel element, however, was the attempt to give religious significance to the discoveries. This was done not only by New Age pundits, who thought they had found in quantum physics a confirmation of their mystical and pantheistic beliefs, but also by Christians.

Some Christians, noticing the seemingly paradoxical nature of the world that quantum physics revealed, concluded that this reflected negatively on the rationality of the Creator and therefore rejected the new theories out of hand. Many others, however, saw the new physics as an ally of the faith. For two centuries or more unbelievers had used Newtonian science to attack Christianity. They had argued that since the universe is a machine, operating mechanically and according to unchangeable laws, there is no room for grace, divine providence, or human freedom and responsibility. By challenging the determinism and materialism of the old system, quantum physics removed these obstacles to Christian faith and was therefore welcomed.

There were Christians who went further and declared that the new physics gave direct support to Christian doctrine. "Christian theologians, often confusing the language of relativity with its scientific content," historian Erwin Hiebert writes, "used Einstein's theories to support doctrines ranging from immortality to the existence of the Holy Spirit."[13] Quantum physics was used in a similar fashion. It was marshalled, for example, to bolster the belief in human freedom. This was done by people who reasoned that freedom could simply be defined as the absence of ascertainable causes. Heisenberg's principle of indeterminacy, according to which no cause-and-effect relationship can be observed for certain phenomena at the subatomic level, they interpreted to mean that human acts also can be without causes and therefore free.

In short, people again made use of science for cultural purposes. They repeated the approach that had often been followed under the old physics, when the tendency had also been to explain complex systems in terms of their most basic constituents and to reason by analogy from science to the rest of life and thought. They failed to realize that indeterminacy at the microphysical level, where we appear to be confronted with randomness or chance, is altogether different from responsible action by a reflective, free, and moral agent.[14] To reason, Ian Barbour writes, that "if atoms are determined, so are people; if atoms are indeterminate, so are people" is to compare entirely different concepts.[15] Similarly, attempting to prove the existence of the supernatural with reference to scientific theories involves the danger of reducing God, in physicist Sir Arthur Eddington's words, "to a system of differential equations."[16]

Although there were even physicists who indulged in this type of reductionistic reasoning, many in the scientific community rejected the approach. When asked about the religious implications of relativity, Einstein vehemently denied that as a purely scientific theory relativity had anything to do with religion. Nor had science anything to say about human freedom. According to Einstein, "The present fashion of applying the axioms of physical science to human life is not only entirely a mistake but has also something reprehensible in it."[17] Various other physicists agreed in denying a direct connection between religion and science. And the absence of such a connection, as one of them said, is all for the good, for science is fallible and tentative and scientific theories are bound to be replaced sooner or later. And therefore, "to hitch a religious philosophy to a contemporary science is a sure route to its obsolescence."[18]

Most physicists agreed, however, that while their findings did not support religion, they did not contradict it either; and it is indeed possible to marshal arguments showing that the new physics is more religion-friendly than the Newtonian system was. For one thing, as we already noted, it removed the obstacles that a materialistic and deterministic mechanism, in the view of many, placed on the way of religious faith. Furthermore, quantum physics, although it allows for methodological reductionism, is less hospitable to such an approach than classical physics was. Whereas under classical physics it was often assumed that systems can be fully explained with reference to the laws governing their component parts, in quantum physics it can be seen that wholes are more than the sum of their parts and exhibit properties that are not found in these parts.[19] Abstraction and reductionism are making room for holism.[20]

Arguments against reductionism as the only viable approach in science can also be derived from the complementarity principle which

Niels Bohr formulated in connection with the wave-particle duality. As Bohr himself suggested, this principle can be given a wider application. Specifically, it can be used to remind us of the fact that phenomena can be studied at more than one level. Human life, for example, can indeed be described in terms of material factors, but it certainly cannot be exhaustively explained in this fashion. And neither can religion exhaustively be explained in terms of psychology, psychology in terms of biology, or biology in terms of physics and chemistry. Life can be analyzed at the highest and lowest level and at any level in-between. Various historians and philosophers, Christians as well as non-Christians, have in fact battled ontological reductionism on these terms.[21]

And lastly, quantum physicists have made it clear that their methods do not provide a literal picture of the universe but only sets of mathematical formulas or, as Eddington expressed it, a "shadow world of symbols."[22] Newtonianism held that its physics gave an exact replica of the world and so could give rise to the idea that science can be used to proclaim on the truth of all things, including the existence or non-existence of God. Although most modern scientists are realists in that they believe their theories to refer to an external world rather than being mere mental constructs,[23] quantum physics has destroyed the belief that science can get hold of all reality, let alone that it can pronounce on the Infinite. Deeper scientific insight has led to greater intellectual modesty. It is now admitted that the way of science is not the way to all truth.

And that counsel of modesty is one of the more important philosophical lessons to be learned from the developments in physics. A second counsel, related to the first and no less important, is to avoid the error of making a fallible scientific theory into a philosophy of life and an essential support of, or obstacle to, religious faith.

NOTES

[1.] Morris Kline, *Mathematics: The Loss of Certainty* (New York: Oxford University Press, 1980) provides a good account of developments in mathematics. Also helpful is Stephen F. Barker, *Philosophy of Mathematics* (Englewood Cliffs, N.J.: Prentice Hall, 1964). For a Christian approach to the topic, see the lucid account by Pearcey and Thaxton, *The Soul of Science*, Part Three; as well as James Nickel, *Mathematics: Is God Silent?* (Vallecito, California: Ross House Books, 1990).

2. Quoted in Grene, *The Knower and the Known*, 1966), p. 66.

3. On this process, see Pearcey and Thaxton, *The Soul of Science*, ch. 6. The process started already with Kepler and Galileo, for whom mathematical truths were eternal, existing independently of God, a conclusion that the voluntarist Descartes opposed. Osler, *Divine Will and the Mechanical Philosophy*, pp. 126f.; Funkenstein, *Theology and the Scientific Imagination*, pp. 117f.

4. This particular problem remains unresolved in George Lakoff and Mark Johnson's study *Philosophy in the Flesh: The Embodied Mind and its Challenge to Western Thought* (New York: Basic Books, 1999). For this study's explanation of reason and the mind, as well as language, as products of evolution, see pp. 4, 17, 476, 509.

5. A prediction of Einstein's general theory was that the rays of light from a star would be deflected by a specified amount by the sun's gravitational field. The prediction was confirmed by English scientists when during the solar eclipse of 1919 they were able to take photographs of stars in the sun's immediate neighbourhood. It was this well-publicized empirical validation that popularized both non-Euclidean mathematics and Einstein's relativity theory.

6. Kline, *Mathematics*, p. 264.

7. Edward A. Purcell, Jr., *The Crisis of Democratic Theory: Scientific Naturalism and the Problem of Value* (Lexington: University Press of Kentucky, 1973), chs. 4, 5, and *passim*. My description of the nature of post-Euclidean relativism and of the reactions it inspired is based on Purcell's study.

8. Thomas S. Kuhn, *The Structure of Scientific Revolutions* (Chicago: University of Chicago Press, 1962, with a revised edition in 1973). (References in the text are to the latter edition.) See also the same author's *The Essential Tension*, especially chs. 6, 7, 9, 11, 12, and 13, and his contributions to Imre Lakatos and Alan Musgrave, eds., *Criticism and the Growth of Knowledge* (Cambridge: Cambridge University Press, 1970). For an appraisal of Kuhn's theory and its implications by a Christian author see Del Ratzsch, *Philosophy of Science: The Natural Sciences in Christian Perspective* (Downers Grove, Ill.: InterVarsity, 1986), ch. 3.

9. Kuhn defined paradigms as (*inter alia*) "universally recognized scientific achievements that for a time provide model problems and solutions to a community of practitioners," *Structure*, 1973, p. viii. See also *ibid.*, Postscript 2; and Kuhn, *The Essential Tension*, ch. 12 and *passim*.

[10.] For a critique of the relativistic implications of Kuhn's theory see the contributions by Imre Lakatos, Karl R. Popper, Stephen Toulmin and others in Lakatos and Musgrave, eds., *Criticism and the Growth of Knowledge.*

[11.] On the new physics (Einstein's relativity theories and quantum physics), see Ian G. Barbour, *Issues in Science and Religion* (New York: Harper and Row, Harper Torchbooks, 1971 [1966]), ch. 10; *idem, Religion and Science: Historical and Contemporary Issues* (New York: HarperCollins, HarperSanFrancisco, 1997), ch. 7; Lincoln Barnett, *The Universe and Dr. Einstein* (New York: Bantam Books, 1968 [William Morrow, 1948]); Barbara Lovett Cline, *Men Who Made A New Physics: Physicists and the Quantum Theory* (New York: New American Library, Signet Science Library Books, 1965); Albert Einstein, *Out of My Later Years: The Scientist, Philosopher and Man Portrayed Through His Own Words* (New York: Wing Books, Random House, 1996 [1956]); Philipp Frank, *Einstein: His Life and Times,* trans. George Rosen, ed. Shuichi Kusaka (New York: Knopf, 1947); Peter Gibbins, *Particles and Paradoxes: The Limits of Quantum Logic* (Cambridge: Cambridge University Press, 1987); Gerald Holton, *Thematic Origins of Scientific Thought: Kepler to Einstein,* rev. ed. (Cambridge and London: Harvard University Press, 1988 [1973]); Gerald Holton and Yehuda Elkana, eds., *Albert Einstein: Historical and Cultural Perspectives. The Centennial Symposium in Jerusalem* (Princeton: Princeton University Press, 1982); Ken Wilber, ed., *Quantum Questions: Mystical Writings of the World's Great Physicists* (Boston: New Science Library, 1985 [1984]). For excellent Christian accounts, see Pearcey and Thaxton, *Soul of Science,* chs. 8, 9, and Erwin N. Hiebert, "Modern Physics and Christian Faith," in *God and Nature,* eds. Lindberg and Numbers, pp. 424-47.

[12.] Holton, *Thematic Origins,* pp. 102, 139f., n4.

[13.] Hiebert, "Modern Physics and Christian Faith," p. 432. For additional examples of and comments on the practice of assigning religious and philosophical significance to the new scientific theories, see *ibid.,* esp. pp. 430-34; Barbour, *Issues,* ch. 10 and *passim; idem, Religion and Science,* pp. 184-91; Pearcey and Thaxton, *Soul of Science,* ch. 9; Wilber, *Quantum Questions,* ch. 1.

[14.] Barbour, *Issues,* pp. 307-9.

[15.] *Ibid.,* p. 313.

[16.] Wilber, *Quantum Questions,* p. 8.

[17.] *Ibid.,* p. 5

[18.] *Ibid.*, pp. ixf.

[19.] Barbour, *Issues*, pp. 294-97. See also Murphy, *Anglo-American Postmodernity*, pp. 18-35.

[20.] The term holism, which is derived from the Greek word *holos* (meaning "whole") can be defined in a number of ways. Firstly it refers, as in this chapter, to the belief that complex wholes are often more than the sum of their parts. Secondly, it applies to a philosophy like that of Thomas Kuhn, which holds that the system in its entirety – the paradigm, in Kuhn's case – strongly influences observation and theorizing. Thirdly, it is used for the medical practice of not just dealing with the symptoms of a disease but of considering also the patient's mental and social background and conditions. Similarly in education, holism stresses the development of the student as a whole, rather than simply concentrating on the mind. And lastly, it refers to the postmodern tendency of rejecting Cartesian dualisms and other dichotomies in favour of a more integrative approach and, often, even of a monistic philosophy. For examples of the last-mentioned application, see ch. 19 below.

[21] See, for example, Barbour, *Issues*, ch. 11 and *passim*; *idem, Religion and Science*, pp. 173-5, 182-4; C. A. Coulson, *Science and Christian Belief* (London: Fontana Books, 1964 [Oxford University Press, 1955]), especially ch. 3; Donald M. MacKay, *The Clockwork Image: A Christian Perspective on Science* (Downers Grove, Ill.: InterVarsity, 1977 [1974]); Wilber, *Quantum Questions*, pp. 11-29; Murphy, *Anglo-American Postmodernity*. See also Michael Polanyi's conception of a hierarchy of analyzable levels in *The Tacit Dimension* (Garden City, New York: Doubleday, 1966), ch. 2. A well-known anti-reductionist philosophy written from a Christian perspective is the one by the Reformed philosopher Herman Dooyeweerd, one of the originators of the Cosmonomic or Cosmic Law Philosophy (also called the Amsterdam Philosophy). In a later chapter we will give attention to the work of Polanyi and Dooyeweerd.

[22.] Wilber, *Quantum Questions*, p. 8.

[23.] Barbour, *Issues*, pp. 168-74.

XVIII. Logical Positivism and Existentialism

When the twentieth century came around, philosophy had lost much of its ancient prestige to science, which provided a means for the acquisition of more practical knowledge. Science did not, however, have much to say about the meaning of life, the destiny of man, or the manner in which he should live on this earth. Because that type of question was still being asked, philosophy continued to be practised.

In the twentieth century as before, people were able to choose among a variety of systems. Idealist philosophies like those of Kant and Hegel still found practitioners, at least at the universities. Among Roman Catholics the philosophy of Thomas Aquinas was experiencing a revival. People of a more secular bent could turn to Marxism, the phenomenology of Edmund Husserl, or the pragmatism of Americans such as William James and John Dewey. And for those who wanted a philosophy based on developmentalism, there were among the newer versions the creative evolutionism of the Frenchman Henri Bergson and the process philosophy of the Anglo-American Alfred North Whitehead.

Some of these systems (the majority of which date from the late nineteenth or early twentieth century) have had our attention earlier; the remainder can be mentioned only in passing. In this chapter we will focus on two other philosophies, namely logical positivism and existentialism. Both illustrate some important aspects of the twentieth-century climate of opinion, including its postmodern phase.

Logical positivism

Although they flourished at the same time, logical positivism and existentialism did not have a great deal in common. Apart from criticizing naturalistic philosophies, existentialism paid little heed to the world of science and technology, concentrating instead on questions about the meaning of life and the problem of human freedom. Logical positivism dismissed that type of question as meaningless. Despising metaphysics and all kinds of speculative philosophy, it reflected the scientific aspect of the twentieth-century world of thought. Also, while existentialism could and indeed did serve as a means of social criticism, its focus was on the individual, whereas logical positivism was sufficiently utopian to aim at cultural transformation.

Logical positivism (or logical empiricism, as it was also called) is no longer around as a formal philosophy, but its spirit is still with us. It was influenced by British empiricists such as Locke and Hume and, more immediately, by the writings of British mathematician and philosopher Bertrand Russell (1872-1970) and some of his colleagues. The movement did not originate in England, however, but in Vienna, among scholars like R. Carnap, O. Neurath, and Moritz Schlick. Vienna was also the home of Ludwig Wittgenstein, who had been a student of Russell and would strongly influence the positivist school. By mid-century the movement had spread to various other countries, becoming especially popular in England and the United States.[1]

Organized in the 1920s by the so-called Vienna Circle, logical positivism constituted a revolution in the history of philosophy. In former ages philosophy had concerned itself with several branches of knowledge, including metaphysics and physics, politics, ethics, and epistemology or theory of knowledge. Logical positivism, however, restricted itself to a single discipline, namely the logical analysis of language.

The decision to impose this restriction was influenced by the fact that most of philosophy's traditional concerns had been taken over by independent disciplines, a development that seemed to threaten its very *raison d'être*. If in a pragmatic age philosophy was to retain any relevance, it would have to find ways and means to support those disciplines that promoted worthwhile knowledge, namely the natural and social sciences. Since the one thing all the sciences had in common was language, the decision to concentrate on the study and analysis of language and its meaning was a logical one. For centuries the queen of the sciences, philosophy would now become their handmaiden.

There were other reasons for the choice. Among them was the fact that by this time the study of the nature and function of language was assuming an important place in many areas of thought. In that sense logical positivism functioned as a mainstream philosophy. Its practitioners were also motivated, especially in the movement's earlier phase, by socio-political considerations. The Vienna Circle itself was active in the 1920s and 1930s, a period when a variety of ideologies – nationalist, fascist, racist, and Marxist ones – were in the air. Members of the Circle believed that people submitted to these ideologies because of careless thinking and a faulty use of language. Fearful of the power which, especially in Germany and Austria, was given to abstractions such as state and culture, *Volk* and race and blood, they turned to the English nominalist tradition for a method to purify language.

And so logical positivists assumed what they believed to be an essential cultural task. If they could persuade people to examine their beliefs in a scientific, positivistic manner, they might yet ensure the survival of a democratic society. Their aim was to rid language of all that could not be scientifically verified, which implied the need to remove all abstractions. That there are also abstractions or universals that express truths without which life becomes meaningless, was ignored.

Its nature and limitations

Logical positivists liked to quote the maxim with which Wittgenstein concluded his *Tractatus Logico-Philosophicus*: "Whereof one cannot speak, thereof one must be silent." As Wittgenstein scholars have argued, they misinterpreted that famous saying.[2] Wittgenstein himself, who tended toward mysticism, meant by it that about all that really matters we must remain silent, whereas the logical positivists interpreted it to mean that what we can speak about is all that really matters. They agreed with that sentiment. It meant that they could remake society by restricting language to what they themselves considered to be the only worthwhile type of propositions, namely scientifically verifiable ones. All the rest could be declared meaningless and so banished from human discourse. They also adopted Wittgenstein's proposition, "The limits of my language mean the limits of my world." It served as another affirmation of their belief that language can indeed serve as a tool to create a better world.

In that world the realm of the sayable (and therefore of the knowable) was to be severely restricted. Specifically – and in agreement with the empiricist and positivist traditions on which they built – logical positivists declared that sense experience and logic are the means by which to judge the validity of any statement. They incorporated this view in their notorious verification principle, which limited meaningful propositions to two categories: factual ones, which were verifiable by the senses, and formal ones, like those of logic and mathematics, which were self-evidently true (such as the statement that a triangle has three sides or that if A and B are both equal to C, then they are also equal to each other).

These two categories, then, were the only ones logical positivism recognized. If a statement expressed anything that could not be empirically tested or shown to be self-evidently true, it was by definition meaningless. As the skeptic David Hume had famously put it in the eighteenth century, works dealing with such matters should be thrown into the fire. The verification principle denied the validity not only of ideological abstractions, but also of religious and moral statements. To say, for example, "God exists," was a nonsense statement, since it was unverifiable. (The same verdict applied to its opposite: the statement that God does not exist.) In the field of ethics, the statement, "You are now stealing money," was a valid proposition, for it could be verified. But to say, "Stealing money is wrong," was again to speak nonsense, since the judgment expressed only the speaker's personal feelings. Someone else might disagree, and neither of them could prove his point.[3]

And what applied to religious and moral judgments applied to aesthetic and metaphysical ones. Indeed, statements about practically everything that conveys meaning to people were declared meaningless. If one did not want to talk nonsense, one had to stop speaking of these matters. And so the wisdom of the ages was summarily dismissed.[4] For while it is true that logical positivism did not say that religious, ethical, and metaphysical statements are false, by declaring them meaningless it assigned them to the realm of the irrationally subjective. What all this amounted to was that a movement which officially rejected metaphysical questions as meaningless introduced a metaphysics of its own, one that based the hope for social salvation on a system of language which allowed the label of truth only to what can be seen and touched and logically demonstrated.

Logical positivism arose in response to the desperate cultural and political crises of the 1920s and 1930s. It would come under attack in the more relaxed and more skeptical atmosphere of the period following the Second World War. The attack focused on the verification principle. Among its fatal weaknesses, critics pointed out, was that the principle could not itself be verified, since it was neither logically self-evident nor based on sense experience. Its own criteria therefore declared it to be nonsensical. The word "meaningful" also was problematic, since it is not at all synonymous with "empirically verifiable." Another objection to the movement was the implied assumption that the scientific method itself is altogether objective. By the middle of the century it was becoming increasingly clear that this is not the case; that the personal element intrudes in the choice of hypotheses, the acceptance and rejection of theories, and even in something as basic as perception.

It should be noted, however, that only the positivist trust in the scientific method was abandoned. The belief in the ability of language to change the world, which had already been promoted by Nietzsche, survived and became one of the creeds of postmodernism.

Existentialism

Like logical positivism, existentialism has had its day, but its influence is still strongly felt. Indeed, without a knowledge of this philosophy it will be difficult to understand either modern art and literature or much of modern theology, psychology, ethics, and educational theory and practice, for the existentialist movement has had an effect in all these fields.

It is not easy to define existentialism, for there are many differences among those to whom the label has been applied. The term itself, which was popularized by the French existentialist Jean-Paul Sartre (1905-80), was questioned by a number of his colleagues who went on record saying that they were not existentialists in Sartre's sense of the term. In spite of their protests, the label stuck. Historians therefore have no choice but to work with it and try to come with a definition that covers the more important themes and tendencies found in the works of existentialists. Because of the differences among these thinkers, it is difficult to give a list of themes to which no exceptions can be found. All that can be done is to provide a partial definition by describing some of the more obvious similarities among leading existentialist thinkers.

The definition that is here proposed has four parts. Firstly, existentialism stands for the affirmation of the individual as someone who possesses freedom and must therefore assume responsibility for the choices he makes in life. Sartre said that existence comes before essence and explained this to mean that man does not have a ready-made nature, but creates himself by the way he lives. "Man is nothing else but what he makes of himself."[5] That, he said, is the first principle of existentialism.

The fact that the individual is responsible for his own acts implies the rejection of the mass-man, the one who follows the crowd, or public opinion, or a gang-leader or dictator. To be told what to do by someone else makes life a lot easier, but it is a way of life that existentialism rejects. The individual must stand on his own two feet and make his own choices, agonizing as that may be. Man, as Sartre put it, is *condemned* to be free. Although the roots of existentialism go further back, the philosophy caught on during the Second World War in occupied France. The call to affirm one's freedom and assume responsibility for one's actions was as urgent at that time as it had ever been.

Although other existentialists would not subscribe to every aspect of Sartre's creed, they did join him in affirming human responsibility and the need of personal commitment. They also agreed with him as to the heaviness of the burden human freedom imposes. This applied with special force to the atheists among them, because for them man was entirely on his own, deprived of all external norms and guidelines. Traditionally, those who rejected religion as the source of moral values had turned to reason for guidance, or else to nature or society, but none of these sources remained. The power of reason had been shown to have serious limitations; nature, since Darwin, was amoral and indifferent; and a society plagued by divisions and ruled by pragmatism and relativism was also unable to provide objective norms. The individual could therefore never be certain that the choices he made were indeed the right ones; yet he remained fully responsible for them.

The concern with the individual leads to the second trait that existentialists have in common, namely their rebellion against a philosophical tradition, as old as Plato, that concentrates on such abstractions as essences or universals while ignoring the individual person in his concrete, flesh-and-blood existence. The Dane Søren Kierkegaard (1813-55), the first modern existentialist philosopher, saw this essentialist tradition personified in the German philosopher Hegel, whose work dominated the Danish philosophical scene in Kierkegaard's days. Hegel's philosophy seemed to Kierkegaard "to reduce the individual human person to a mere moment in the life or self-unfolding of the Absolute."[6] As existentialists increasingly recognized, scientific naturalism posed a similar threat in that it made the individual "a transitory resultant of physical processes,"[7] a mere object in a mechanistic and fully materialistic universe. Here also the individual as a responsible human being was declared illusory.

Existentialists rebelled not only against essentialism and scientific naturalism but also against the tyranny of reason as such, a tyranny that, like the essentialist tradition, western civilization had inherited from the Greeks. This brings us to the third part of our definition. Existentialists were not irrationalists, but they did reject the dominant creed of the all-sufficiency of human reason. Most of them would have agreed with the Frenchman Blaise Pascal, a seventeenth-century forerunner of modern existentialism, who wrote that reason's last step is to recognize that there is an infinity of things that lie beyond it.[8]

Fourthly and finally, existentialists distinguished between objective and subjective knowledge and truth and, while not necessarily rejecting the former (although it is true that some of them at times tended to do so), they stressed the latter. It has to be pointed out here that subjectivity is not to be confused with subjectivism with its connotations of relativism and arbitrariness. The term refers, rather, to a search for truth wherein man is involved not with his intellect only, but with his entire being, and wherein he does not look first of all for theoretical knowledge, but for a truth that he can embrace and act upon in his life.

Here, too, the approach was a revolutionary one, for the western tradition had long stressed the superiority of objective over subjective knowledge. This is not to say that the existentialist brand of knowledge and truth was new in the history of human thought. As William Barrett has reminded us in a study comparing Hebraic and Greek attitudes to knowledge,[9] the approach to truth involving the whole man, intellect as well as emotions and will, is biblical. Nor was it ever totally forgotten in the Christian West; but it was submerged both by the Greek tradition, which prized theoretical over personal knowledge, and by modernism.

Kierkegaard

Existentialist philosophy can be divided into two branches, a theist and an atheist one. The former included men like Søren Kierkegaard, Karl Jaspers, Gabriel Marcel, Nicolai Berdyaev, and the Jewish scholar Martin Buber. Prominent within the latter group were Friedrich Nietzsche, his compatriot Martin Heidegger, and the French thinkers Jean-Paul Sartre, Simone de Beauvoir, and Albert Camus. In this chapter we will restrict our attention to Kierkegaard and Sartre as representatives of the two branches.

Neither Christian nor secular existentialism would catch people's attention and become a movement until the troubled twentieth century. Kierkegaard, who died in 1855, was therefore well ahead of his time. His concern, however, was similar to that of his twentieth-century successors. It was to assume responsibility for his own existence and life and destiny, which in his case were defined in uncompromisingly religious terms. Kierkegaard's two-fold goal was to find out what it meant to be a Christian and how a person could become one. The rash of books he wrote in rapid succession between 1843 and his death twelve years later were intended to awaken his contemporaries to the urgency of these questions.

Among the best-known of these books is *Fear and Trembling* (1843), in which Kierkegaard presents his view of the levels of human existence. He distinguishes three such levels: the aesthetic, the ethical, and the religious. The first level is the one of irresponsibility and sensual pleasure, where a person behaves as he feels like behaving without regard for norms. In the end it leads to despair, and this motivates people to move on to the ethical level. Kierkegaard calls the ethical level the universal, because unlike the previous one it provides objective norms to which everyone is subject. Adherence to the universal is necessary for an orderly communal life, and Kierkegaard says that in this sense the universal is higher than the individual. Sin at this level is asserting one's individuality before the universal.

There are times, however, when we must leave the universal behind, either because our conscience or peculiar situation forces us to do so or because religious conviction makes it imperative. With religious conviction faith comes in, and faith is the function of what Kierkegaard calls the religious centre of our existence. Acting at the religious level may mean that we go against the ethical one. Because we are placing ourselves outside the pale, we enter the religious level with "fear and trembling"; yet to obey the divine command, no matter what the cost, is the only way to live authentically as a Christian. Kierkegaard's great example was Abraham, the father of believers and the "knight of faith," who was ordered to sacrifice his son, an act that at the universal level would be called murder. Although unable to explain the demand, Abraham nevertheless obeyed, because God, even more than Isaac, was the centre of his existence. He obeyed for God's sake, and so also for his own, for in trusting God he became God's confidant and friend.[10]

Here, then, is the answer to the first question Kierkegaard raised. The Lutheran state church to which he belonged had settled into a comfortable coexistence with the world. All that was required to be called a Christian was church membership, acceptance of certain doctrines, and living an outwardly decent life. Reacting against this easy-believism, Kierkegaard stressed the responsibility of the individual who stands alone before God, who trusts him and obeys the divine command, regardless of the cost. He at the same time denied that man deserves anything in God's sight by obeying the moral law. Salvation is a gift, which can be appropriated only by turning from the self and the world to God. That is, it can be appropriated only by a total conversion, which will be evident in a changed life. Being a Christian, Kierkegaard never tired of saying, is *living* the faith, and religion is *being* religious.

But again, the moral life is not a guarantee of eternal life; salvation is God's gift. In his rejection of Pelagianism and legalism Kierkegaard clearly shows his Lutheran heritage.[11] God takes the initiative, and man replies because he despairs of saving himself. Moralism and legalism, as Luther (and Augustine, and Paul) well knew, are not helps but hindrances to faith, because by promoting self-reliance they deny the need for grace. The function of the moral law is not to enable us to earn salvation but rather, as Paul teaches, to make us aware of our utter inability to save ourselves and so to show us that we need Christ.

How to become a Christian

If *being* a Christian means total reliance on God and total obedience – that is, if it means a willingness to live on the religious level, as Abraham did – how then does one *become* such a Christian? What must we do to turn from unbelief to a saving faith? Much of modern Christianity had answered this question by stating that it is possible to climb up to God by one's moral efforts and/or by one's reasoning powers. Having shown the impossibility of the first of these counsels, Kierkegaard turned to and demolished the second one.[12]

The question about the relationship between faith and reason, or revelation and philosophy, is as old as Christianity. Kierkegaard's concern was first of all with ongoing attempts to harmonize Christianity and philosophy, attempts that most recently had been made by Hegel and his followers. Kierkegaard attacked the presumption that human reason is capable of apprehending the holy and infinite God. He reminded the Hegelian philosophers and theologians of his day that God is altogether different from man, and that man can know God and his saving truth only because, and in so far as, it has pleased God to reveal himself.

Kierkegaard also turned against the practice of attempting to prove the existence of God by rational arguments. We have seen how especially in the modern period, when Christianity increasingly came under attack by the new sciences (or by the philosophies based on them), apologists turned to rational and empirical proofs to shore up the faith. These proofs were declared inadequate by Hume and Kant, and Kierkegaard agreed with their verdict. He rejected the proofs not only because they are ambiguous, but also because Christian truth in all its depth cannot be demonstrated. Philosophy can perhaps show that there must be a supreme being, but it cannot conceive of a God who so loved a lost humanity that in his Son he came down to rescue it. Faith, for Kierkegaard, is not a matter of rational evidence; it is the affirmation of a truth that can only be appropriated by personal commitment.

Kierkegaard was not satisfied with rejecting logical reasoning as a way to faith; he treated empirical evidence in much the same manner. Although the confession of God's historical revelation of himself in Christ was central to his faith, he all but denied the importance of historical evidence as given in the Bible. There were two reasons for this attitude. For one thing, such evidence, he believed, could yield only probability, not certainty, and faith must rest on certainty. Yet he also made a point of stressing the element of risk and uncertainty in faith and objected to reliance on historical evidence because it would tempt people to base their trust on objective proofs rather than strive for inner conviction. By relying on objective certainty, one did away with faith itself. As one commentator remarks, the approach was therefore rejected for two apparently contradictory reasons: for failing to give certainty and for presuming to give it.[13]

Kierkegaard's rejection of the objective element in faith can be explained in terms of his mission, which was to convince people that faith cannot be based on empirical evidence or the pronouncements of philosophers, but requires conversion and rests on a personal relationship. Yet it is on this point that the strongest criticism must be directed against his philosophy. The danger of the approach is that it can, and in fact did, lead to a diminished concern for the historical reliability of the Bible. Kierkegaard was an enemy of theological liberalism; yet his refusal to value historical evidence could not but diminish the importance of the written Word. That the single-minded stress on subjectivity encourages that approach is shown in the history of the twentieth-century school of dialectical theology which Kierkegaard inspired, and which concluded by openly adopting the historical-critical method in biblical studies.

There is more to be said about Kierkegaard's subjective approach. We will attempt a further evaluation of his work, and that of existentialism in general, at the end of this chapter. First we turn briefly to Sartre, the representative of the atheistic brand of existentialism.

Sartre

Sartre differed from most other existentialists in that he was still a follower of Descartes, and therefore a dualist. This meant that for him truth was a matter of the intellect only, and that a chasm existed between mind and nature. Descartes had tried to bridge the gap by positing the existence of God, but for Sartre there was no God. Therefore the universe was alien, irrational, and absurd; and human consciousness found itself in opposition to a nature which was fully determined and which constituted a threat to human freedom.[14]

Man's freedom, for Sartre, was unlimited, and therefore human responsibility was total. Although he admitted the influence of heredity and environment on the human personality, he did not allow that influence to be used as an excuse for the individual's failures. Freudian and all other kinds of determinism he dismissed as escapist. Man had to judge himself not by what he could or could not have done, but by the choices he in fact had made. Sartre talked in this connection of bad faith. Acting in bad faith was what Heidegger called living the inauthentic life. It meant the refusal to accept responsibility for the choices one makes by looking for excuses, or by following authority or public opinion or the crowd.

It was by assuming this total responsibility for his actions that man created himself. It was the same total responsibility which made life under existentialism such a hazardous affair. Because man was only a chance development rather than a being created by God, there was no divinely determined human essence or universal, and therefore no blueprint that one could follow in shaping one's life. Nor were there any objective values. The Christian Kierkegaard had been able to posit the ethical level as a universal, but for Sartre there was no such level. The individual had to find his own norms. He had to choose, moreover, in such a way that, as Kant had taught, he would want his choice to be universally valid; yet, unlike Kant, he could never know whether that choice was the right one. This predicament, which to a greater or lesser degree we meet in other existentialists, goes a long way in explaining the themes of guilt, absurdity, dread, and despair, which keep turning up in existentialist writings.

Existentialism: an evaluation

As a system of thought and a guide for action, existentialism had defects. As more than one author has said, it is far more valuable as a corrective than as a philosophy. Particularly valuable has been its protest against the intellectual, social, and political forces that threaten the individual's freedom. These include, on the intellectual side, philosophies such as Marxism, Freudianism, and behaviourism, all of which are deterministic and regard man as little more than a thing to be manipulated. On the political and social levels, they include totalitarian dictatorships and democratic public opinion, which destroy freedom by their regimentation and demand for conformity. The existentialists' defiance of such intellectual, social, and political forces has been a positive and bracing thing in twentieth-century history.

There is something heroic, even titanic, in the best of existentialism. It is that very element which explains why this philosophy, although it greatly influenced the culture wherein it arose, never attracted a great many practitioners. It demands too much self-denial and – especially in its atheistic branch – it offers too few rewards. The stoical nature of existentialism is especially striking in Sartre's version. David E. Roberts speaks of a "sado-masochistic character structure" underlying Sartre's ontology and complains that this philosopher is asking us "to undergo the painful process of outwitting our own egotism, will-to-power, moralistic shibboleths, and idolatrous illusions for the sake of a freedom which has no point other than itself."[15]

Atheistic existentialism has few positive answers to the questions that Immanuel Kant asked of philosophy, namely: What can I know? What ought I to do? What may I hope? The knowledge that can be attained is limited; there is very little left for humanity to hope for; and moral guidance is lacking altogether. And life in a godless world is risky. In the words of the Russian novelist Dostoevsky: if there were no God, everything would be permitted. Sartre agreed that this was so.[16] Although he and his atheist colleagues would have liked to decide upon criteria that could avoid complete arbitrariness in moral matters, they could not find any. The "death of God" and the fact of the individual's absolute freedom made it impossible.

Moral uncertainty is not a characteristic of atheistic existentialism only. Kierkegaard's stance also gives rise to questions. He speaks of the man of faith who temporarily leaves the moral law behind him in order to obey God, but he does not make it clear how the individual can know God's will. Does one go by intimations and "religious experiences"? But it is this type of approach that can lead to the Münsters and Jonestowns of history. There is of course the work of the Holy Spirit in the life of the believer, but Christian theology has always warned against a subjectivist usage of that doctrine and taught that the Spirit does not work apart from the written Word. In that Word ethical criteria can indeed be found. But the authority of the Bible was, as we noted, undermined by Kierkegaard's philosophy.

There are other weaknesses in existentialism. The stress on the individual's struggle for authenticity is so pronounced that it threatens to shut him off from society and community. This danger has been recognized by twentieth-century existentialist thinkers such as Martin Buber and Gabriel Marcel, who have given attention to the individual's responsibility toward others. Sartre tried to do the same – but without really succeeding – by turning to socialism and communism. And this problem also was not restricted to atheistic existentialism. Kierkegaard, while rightly stressing the individual's personal responsibility before God, was in danger of losing sight of the church as the community of believers. Indeed, the church appears to have had but limited value for him. The emphasis throughout was on the lone individual and his needs and responsibilities. This excessive individualism accounts not only for Kierkegaard's attitude toward the church; it is also among the reasons for his ignoring of the covenantal aspect in the Christian religion and his questioning of the appropriateness of infant baptism.[17]

The danger of subjectivism

Yet another danger in existentialism is its tendency to exalt subjective over objective truth to such an extent that the validity of the latter is all but denied. We have mentioned this weakness in connection with Kierkegaard, and in what follows we will again concentrate on him, but it must be kept in mind that an excessive stress on the subjective is encountered among other existentialists as well.[18]

We must begin by stating once again that Kierkegaard's rejection of religious rationalism was to the point. The attempt to harmonize faith and reason led too easily to a type of religion that saw religious truth as a matter of logic rather than of inner conviction, and that replaced the God of the Bible by a deity created in man's image. A religion based on reason also ignored the role that the will plays in faith. Kierkegaard acknowledged the importance of that role when he exclaimed that belief is difficult because it is so difficult to obey.[19] The intellect could not resolve that moral problem. Salvation had to come from beyond man, and when it was offered it had to be humbly believed and embraced. Faith started where thought stopped; which meant that it started regardless of any objective evidence. That was what made it faith, as distinguished from objective knowledge. And because faith was a matter of the will, it had to become evident in discipleship. Kierkegaard's "leap of faith" was not simply a leap of thought, but also of personal commitment.[20]

Kierkegaard was very much aware of the limitations of reason not only in its relationship to the will, but also in its own field, that of the understanding. Human thought, he knew, is finite. It is also historically and culturally conditioned. And reason can never decide on such questions as the existence or the non-existence of God, which means that atheists too are in error when basing their belief on rational arguments.

In short, Kierkegaard's battle against a reason that transgressed its limits was good and necessary. Yet in rejecting the important role of reason and of the objective element in faith, his reaction was excessive. It was also dangerous and encouraged, among other things, the type of subjectivism in faith and morals that became all too common in the twentieth century. Kierkegaard himself was not a subjectivist. Although there are ambiguities in his ethical stand, he upheld the universal validity of the moral law. Nor was he an anti-intellectualist: his attack was directed not against the intellect as such, but against an arrogant and idolatrous intellectualism. The fact remains, however, that the demand for inwardness and subjective certainty was so strongly emphasized that the role of reason and the importance of the objective element in faith were all but denied.

This deficiency is especially striking in Kierkegaard's attitude toward historical evidence. His argument, as we have seen, was that such evidence was either too uncertain, or that reliance on it negated the need for faith. He ignored the fact that, although historical evidence can indeed not prove the mysteries of the faith, it is nevertheless basic to the Christian religion and has been given as an aid to faith. To reject it for the sake of inwardness is arrogant and cannot but lead to the rejection of the historical faith.

How are we to explain this excessive concern with the subjectivity of truth? The answer would seem to be that existentialists were still too strongly influenced by the modern belief that knowledge can be accepted as true only if it passes scientific criteria. Rightly condemning that belief as deadly, Kierkegaard and other existentialists went to the opposite extreme of all but denying the objective element in truth. They remained stuck, in other words, in the dichotomy between objectivity and subjectivity which had been around throughout the modern period and became a virtually unassailable creed in the positivistic nineteenth century. It was not until the next century that a theory of knowledge would be developed which, rather than positing an opposition between the subjective and the objective, united them. If existentialists had been able to apply that view of knowledge they might have overcome the subjectivist tendency in their thinking. Still caught in the modernist dichotomy, they appear to have felt that they could do little more than replace an exclusive trust in objective evidence with an equally excessive reliance on subjectivity and inwardness.

The deficiencies in existentialism are many. To list them cannot, however, be the end of the story. Existentialism deserves credit for having begun the revolt against a positivistic scientism, for having affirmed the truth of human freedom and human responsibility, and for having rediscovered the ancient truth that knowledge is not a matter of the intellect only, but also of the will and the emotions. In addition to all this, Christian existentialism deserves credit for attempting to awaken Christendom to the dangers of an externalized religiosity. On these counts the message of Kierkegaard and of those who followed him continues to be valid.

NOTES

[1.] On the history of logical positivism see its major publicist, Alfred Jules Ayer, *Language, Truth and Logic* (New York: Dover Publications, 1952 [1936]), and *idem,* ed., *Logical Positivism* (Glencoe, Ill.: The Free Press, 1959). For what follows see also David Crystal, *Linguistics, Language and Religion* (London: Burnes and Oates, Hawthorn Books, 1965), ch. 12; Leszek Kolakowski, *The Alienation of Reason: A History of Positivist Thought,* trans. Norbert Guterman (Garden City, New York: Doubleday, Anchor Books, 1969), ch. 8 and Conclusion; and Robert C. Solomon, *Continental Philosophy since 1750: The Rise and Fall of the Self* (Oxford: Oxford University Press, 1988), ch. 10. The cultural background of the Vienna Circle, and the role that Ludwig Wittgenstein played in the movement, is well described in Allan Janik and Stephen Toulmin, *Wittgenstein's Vienna* (New York: Simon and Schuster, 1973).

[2.] See, for example, Janik and Toulmin, *Wittgenstein's Vienna,* p. 191 and *passim.*

[3.] Ayer, *Language, Truth and Logic,* pp. 114-16, 107f.

[4.] Crystal, *Linguistics, Language and Religion,* p, 162.

[5.] Jean-Paul Sartre, *Existentialism,* trans. Bernard Frechtman (New York: Philosophical Library, 1947), p. 18.

[6.] Frederick Copleston, *Contemporary Philosophy: Studies of Logical Positivism and Existentialism* (Westminster, Maryland: Newman Press, 1956), p. 105.

[7.] Henry Sturt, quoted by Copleston, *Contemporary Philosophy*, p. 107.

[8.] *Pascal's Pensées*, ed. and trans. H. F. Stewart (New York: Modern Library, 1967), p. 49.

[9.] Barrett, *Irrational Man*, ch. 4.

[10.] Søren Kierkegaard, *Fear and Trembling*, in *Fear and Trembling; Repetition*, ed. and trans. Howard V. Hong and Edna H. Hong (Princeton: Princeton University Press, 1983), pp. 59, 77.

[11.] David E. Roberts, *Existentialism and Religious Belief*, ed. Roger Hazelton (New York: Oxford University Press, Galaxy Books, 1963 [1957]), p. 70.

[12.] On this topic see especially Kierkegaard's *Philosophical Fragments*, trans. and ed. David F. Swenson, ed. Niels Thulstrup, trans. Howard V. Hong (Princeton: Princeton University Press, 1969 [1936]), and his *Concluding Unscientific Postscript*, trans. David F. Swenson and Walter Lowrie (Princeton: Princeton University Press, 1964 [1941]).

[13.] C. Stephen Evans, *Subjectivity and Religious Belief: An Historical, Critical Study* (Washington, D. C.: University Press of America, 1982 [1978]), p. 83.

[14.] A brief description of Sartre's philosophy can be found in his *Existentialism*. His major philosophical work is *L'être et le néant*, 1943 (English title: *Being and Nothingness*). Sartre made use also of the essay, the novel, the drama, and the short story to spread his existentialist ideas. His *La nausée* (*Nausea*), published in 1938, is among the best known of his philosophical novels.

[15.] Roberts, *Existentialism and Religious Belief*, pp. 223f.

[16.] Sartre, *Existentialism*, p. 27.

[17.] Kierkegaard, *Postscript*, Book Two, Part Two, Ch. IV, Section I, par. 1-3.

[18.] For discussions of Kierkegaard's subjectivism see Roberts, chs. 2, 3; Evans, chs. 3, 6, 7.

[19.] Walter Lowrie, *A Short Life of Kierkegaard* (Princeton: Princeton University Press, 1942), p. 86.

[20.] Roberts, *Existentialism and Religious Belief*, p. 94.

XIX. Postmodernism:
Theories of Language and Literature

In the course of the twentieth century many of the traditions of modernism, and indeed of western civilization as a whole, have come under attack. The attacks have been so sustained, and the accompanying changes in worldview so profound, that people are speaking of a paradigm shift, a massive cultural transformation not unlike the one that separated the modern period from the Middle Ages. Although the origin of the troubles can be traced to the late-nineteenth century and beyond, the changes did not reach a critical mass until the second half of the twentieth century. It was after the Second World War, somewhere in the 1960s or 1970s, commentators believe, that the modern age began to make room for what has come to be called the postmodern one.

To describe the causes and nature of this shift in any detail would be beyond the scope of this book. We will limit ourselves to the central element in the cultural revolution of our times, namely the changing attitude toward truth, a change that is directly related to the epistemological problems modernism left in its wake. In the present chapter our focus is on one kind of response to these problems, namely the postmodern turn to language and the attempt to replace theory of knowledge with theories of interpretation. In subsequent chapters we will concentrate on an alternative (and more promising) approach, where the goal is not to discard the idea of theory of knowledge as such, but to develop an epistemology capable of replacing the defunct modern one.

The Romantic legacy

We have described the modern view of knowledge in earlier chapters. For two centuries or more it was believed that objective, universally valid truth could be had if humanity followed the lead of an emancipated human reason. By relying on his reason, man could free himself from all that had previously encumbered and imprisoned him. It would deliver him from the cruelties of nature, from the tyranny of religious and political authority, and even from the irrational side of his own nature.

The idea of progress through reason took a firm hold in the eighteenth century and remained strong throughout the nineteenth. But it was never without detractors, and in the second half of the eighteenth century, with the rise of Romanticism, doubts about the all-sufficiency of reason multiplied. The Romantics questioned the rationalistic basis of the Enlightenment project, believing that far too little attention was given to feelings and the imagination. Reason, they argued, was not the only faculty with creative powers; the imagination also possessed them. Rousseau's switch from Descartes' "I think, therefore I am" to his own "I feel, therefore I am," served Romantics as a programme and rallying cry.

This so-called "turn to the aesthetic" – that is, to art and language and interpretation – did not imply a rejection of the idea of progress. Under Romanticism reliance on the imagination was believed to be as good a basis for progress as reliance on reason had been. Nor was it seen as endangering the search for truth. For the Romantics as for their Enlightenment predecessors, the self was "a bastion of virtue and epistemic certainty,"[1] and therefore altogether capable of leading humanity into the promised land.

The Romantic period went the way of all cultural periods, but Romanticism as a philosophy survived and became, like Enlightenment rationalism, an ingredient in the western worldview. It influenced Friedrich Nietzsche, the nineteenth-century thinker who openly and persistently attacked modernity, including its Romantic phase. Among the Romantic ideas Nietzsche objected to was the belief in the self and its ability to reach universally valid truth. For Nietzsche universally valid truth did not exist, and neither did the self: it was nothing but a bundle of desires. Nietzsche also rejected the Romantics' idea of progress. But he followed Romanticism in its turn to the aesthetic, stressing especially the centrality of language in human affairs. In this respect, as in a variety of others, he indicated the direction postmodernism would take. His influence upon postmodernism has been so great that the movement cannot really be explained without reference to his ideas. In this chapter such references will often be made.

Language in the Bible

In emphasizing the importance of language, Nietzsche was well within the tradition of his culture, even though he made use of that tradition in order to pervert it. But to stress the importance of language as such was neither perverse nor revolutionary. Christianity had always believed in the centrality of the word, and this belief had become ingrained in western thought.

It was based on Scripture, and before we turn to the postmodern view of language, it will be good to call to mind the biblical one. The Bible has much to say on language, for God is the God of the Word, who, when creating man in his image, extended to him the gift of language, so that he might hear the divine Word and respond to it. That Word, we learn, has world-creating power. The first chapter of the Old Testament relates how by a speech act God made the heavens and the earth, and in the New Testament we read that it was through the *Logos*, the Word of God, that all things were made (John 1:3). The same Word, taking upon himself human flesh and blood, brought about redemption for those who hear the gospel and believe it.

As various commentators have pointed out, the biblical emphasis on the word, and therefore on hearing and obeying and personal commitment as the way to knowledge and truth, is different from the Greek tradition, which has also strongly influenced our culture. Although it is true that the Greeks never ignored the aural element in knowing, they tended to stress the visual. This is evident in their language. Our word "idea," for example, is derived from the Greek verb *eidein* (to see), and the word "theory" (Greek *theoria*) from *theatai*, which means to view, to look at or gaze, to behold, having the element of spectacle. For the Greeks not voice and word and listening, but seeing and beholding were primarily associated with knowing. We express the same preoccupation with the visual when we use the expression "I see" when we mean, "I understand." Various other metaphors, such as "insight," "mind's eye," and "worldview," point to the same tradition, as does the colloquial expression "seeing is believing."

The element of the visual is certainly not absent from biblical language about knowing. Nevertheless, the Bible stresses hearing and listening. That this is not simply a matter of theoretical interest should be clear. God did not reveal himself to the eyes of man, and he forbade the making of any images of him. Man could know God only by listening to him. If he did that, enlightenment would follow: "Your Word is a lamp to my feet and a light for my path" (Psalm 119:105). But it is indeed the *Word* that brings light: hearing precedes seeing. Faith comes from what is heard (Romans 10:17; RSV). The "immediate seeing of the heart of things," as Abraham Kuyper called it, will be "the characteristic of our knowledge in another sphere of reality."[2]

The importance of the element of listening was largely forgotten in the modern era, and this has had consequences for human understanding. Walter Ong tells us that the shift from a preoccupation with the word to a preoccupation with space took place in the eighteenth century. This shift, he says, made the human being a spectator and manipulator in the universe, rather than a participant, and it contributed to the deist conception of God as not the One who speaks, but as the Great Architect. It explains why the eighteenth-century philosopher Kant spoke of intellectual knowledge in terms of "phenomena," that is, of appearances, rather than of things as they are in themselves. If understanding is to be reached by sight alone, Ong says, then we are by that very fact condemned to dealing with surfaces only, for sight reveals nothing but surfaces. The real thing, the noumenon, can then never be known.[3]

The exclusive concern with the visual has important religious consequences. Modern history shows that a culture which stresses seeing to such an extent that it ignores listening, loses the Word, and therefore also the awareness of God's presence. It has been said, and rightly so, that "it is the *invisible* which poses a series of almost insurmountable problems for much contemporary philosophy."[4] In a sight and image-oriented culture like ours, it poses problems in theology and religion as well. A first step in attempting to solve them is to recognize once again the importance of listening as a way to knowledge.

Human beings received the gift of language not only so that they could know God in his self-revelation and respond to him. The gift was also to be employed in the task they were given to develop creation. We read in Genesis 2 that Adam began executing the creation mandate by naming the animals God had brought to him. This episode shows that all cognition – knowledge of the divine, but also of scientific and cultural matters – requires language. "To discover what a thing is 'called'," Richard Weaver writes, "... is the essential step in knowing, and to say that all education is learning to name rightly, as Adam named the animals, would assert an underlying truth. The sentence passed upon Babel confounded the *learning* of its builders."[5]

It also disrupted their community. For yet another function of language is to bind people together – horizontally, as members of a community existing at a particular point in time, and vertically, as members of a community that spans the ages. By allowing us to transcend the limitations imposed by our temporality, language gives us access to that which endures. And therefore, to quote Weaver once again, "one of the most important revelations about a period comes in its theory of language, for that informs us whether language is viewed as a bridge to the noumenal or as a body of fictions convenient for grappling with transitory phenomena."[6]

Social uses of language

Postmodernism, generally speaking, does not believe in a noumenal or supersensory world. Most postmodernists are nominalists, for whom language is indeed little more than a body of fictions. It is arbitrary and slippery, and therefore quite incapable of fulfilling the intellectual and social and religious functions that have traditionally been laid upon it. But while denying the reliability of language, these postmodern thinkers are far from doubting its importance. They do not believe that it can lead to truth, but, like the logical positivists before them, they are convinced that it can serve as a means to achieve power.

There are various reasons why radical postmodernists believe that language cannot lead to truth, but the underlying one is the conviction that truth does not exist, or, if it does exist, that it is forever inaccessible to us. This thoroughgoing skepticism is among postmodernism's defining characteristics. It is also one of the features that distinguishes it from modernism. For although modernism was from its beginnings plagued by skepticism, it believed in the possibility of reaching objective truth – at least in those disciplines that were amenable to scientific analysis. Postmodernism says that not even science leads to truth. Like everything else, it is engaged in for the sake of power and control.

The developments leading to this all-out skepticism have been described in previous chapters and need not be related here. It is apparent that in postmodernism we have both a consummation of modernism and a reaction against it. The consummation is evident in postmodernism's secularism and belief in human autonomy. The reaction is a result of disillusionment with modernism, a disillusionment that was present already in the Romantic movement and was again keenly felt in the period of the *fin de siècle*. In the twentieth century the sense of betrayal was reinforced by a multitude of factors, such as the political and military disasters the period experienced, and the dangers posed by environmental degradation and the unrestricted growth of technology.

Radical postmodernism, then, rejects whatever belief in truth modernism still possessed. Here the pride of modern humanism led to its nemesis. Descartes taught that by doubting away all received truths, unaided human reason could reach ultimate truth, even truth about God. Reason was a better guide to truth than revelation. On that doctrine Descartes' successors built their utopian belief in human perfectibility and unlimited progress. Now that the failure of the great modern project has become apparent, reason is rejected.

But the road to faith remains closed as well. Rather than taking the route back to God as the Author of truth, postmodernism continues modernism's rejection of God. The result of the denial of both reason and faith is intellectual and moral nihilism and led Nietzsche to proclaim the will to power as the force that energizes man and the world. It is also the force that energizes mankind's use of language and the pursuit of science. Neither of them, for Nietzsche as for his followers, leads to truth; both are simply instruments of power.

This being so, the question must be asked why postmodernists choose language as their primary power tool rather than science, in spite of the latter's proven track record. Part of the answer is that language has greater flexibility than science and therefore, in postmodernist thinking, also greater potential. For science must follow a strict logical method and pay attention to "irreducible facts." It faces reality checks at every turn. Language is not so limited. Here the imagination can roam freely and create whatever reality it fancies. The post-Freudian world is a therapeutic world, and language has far greater therapeutic potential than science.

For many postmodernists, however, the reach of language goes beyond the power of making people feel good. Properly employed, it has virtually unlimited potential. It is capable – and here we come to another reason why radical postmodernists choose language over science – of both destroying worlds and cultures and creating new ones. This belief they derived from Christianity, that is, from the biblical teachings about the power of the divine Word. They learned it also from history, for have not many world-transforming events – from the establishment and expansion of the Christian church to the modern secularization of society and the widespread belief in atheism – been brought about by the use of language? By wielding the power of the word, prophets and apostles and reformers, as well as philosophers and poets, have been transformers of culture.

Modernism devoted itself to the transformation of culture by secularizing it, and radical postmodernists want to complete that process, using language as their tool. Language must serve (as under logical positivism) to bring about a world that is fully secular and wherein all the old values and all the traditional ways of thinking have been replaced. There must be, in Nietszsche's words, a "transvaluation of all values." If we want to understand this desire to destroy and create, it helps to turn back to Nietzsche, who initiated the dream.

Nietzsche's mission

The world Nietzsche wanted to destroy was the one he inhabited. As has been noted in chapter 15, he was driven by a life-long hatred of western civilization and of the Christian religion. The two were related. Christianity had been at the core of western culture and accounted for many of the features that Nietzsche found particularly objectionable in it. It had provided an avenue, for example, for the Greek philosophical tradition to enter Western Europe. Although on occasion Nietzsche had good things to say of Greek philosophy, on the whole he disliked its rationalism, and also its metaphysical tendencies. To restore the health of a civilization that he believed was sick to the point of death, man had to turn back to the earth, whose creature he was, and the Greek philosophers with their search for the Absolute discouraged that.

As a supernatural religion Christianity itself was guilty of turning man away from his earthly concerns. Furthermore, by preaching compassion and equality, it promoted a morality that exalted the weak and mediocre, which Nietzsche believed was a major reason for the decline of western civilization. In order to flourish, a culture needed the presence of a privileged class of creative supermen who were free to establish their own morality. Because it was his ambition to overthrow a decadent Christian culture and replace it with a vital and vibrant neo-pagan one, Nietzsche had to discredit the Christian faith. In short, there was a variety of cultural reasons for his hatred of and preoccupation with Christianity.

There were personal ones as well. Nietzsche liked to compare himself to Christ. He saw him as his sworn enemy whom he liked to ridicule and scorn, but also as his rival, and at times even as his great example, who had been charged with the kind of world-historical task that Nietzsche had taken upon himself. Nietzsche seems to have believed, for example, that in order to bring forth a new epoch he, too, had to sacrifice himself.

He signed some of his last letters, written in 1889, just before his collapse into the insanity that would end with his death more than a decade later, as "The Crucified One." The last book he wrote (an embarrassingly boastful autobiography) he named *Ecce Homo* – thereby calling to mind the words Pilate had used when presenting Christ to the Jews on the morning of the crucifixion.

There are other indications of his delusions of divine grandeur. Nietzsche stated that not the birth of Jesus should henceforth be seen as the dividing point in history (B.C. and A.D.), but that "his [Nietszsche's] unmasking of the nihilism of Christian morality should be the point by which time is measured from now on."[7] He also thought that by writing what he considered to be his most important book, *Thus Spoke Zarathustra,* he had given his fellow-men "the greatest gift that [had] ever been bestowed upon them." Later he added that in the future university chairs might be "founded and endowed for the interpretation of *Zarathustra*."[8] Obviously, it was comparable in importance to the Bible and would serve, together with other Nietzschean writings, as the revelation that was to bring about the new world.

But before that world could be established, the old one had to be destroyed, and that project occupied Nietzsche for much of his life. Since the old world also was the creation of the word, its dismantling required him to repudiate the very language and traditions that he relied on to complete his project of rebuilding. It was here that Nietzsche met his reality check. Language, also human language, has the power to build, but only if it is used and accepted as a trustworthy tool. By denying its trustworthiness, as Nietzsche was forced to do, he could destroy but not rebuild. He was aware of his inability to create a new language, a new logic, and new values apart from and in opposition to the traditional ones. The incoherences and contradictions in his philosophy, which he vainly attempted to resolve, could not but destroy him in the end.

If Nietzsche was destined to fail as a builder, he executed his program of destruction with brilliance, and he had successors eager to continue the work he had begun. These people can count on the help of modern linguistics, philosophy of language, and theories of literary criticism, for the study of language has become a major concern in the twentieth century, and much of it supports the Nietzschean position on both the arbitrariness of language and its centrality. The idea is gaining ground that just as at one time religion was replaced by science as the centre of human knowledge, so science is now to be replaced by literature and become, in the words of American philosopher Richard Rorty, no more than a literary genre.[9] Theories of language and interpretation will take the place of theory of knowledge. The implication of such a turn to the linguistic is that the search for objective truth is to be abandoned in favour of a subjective approach to knowledge, one that is fuelled by pragmatic considerations rather than by the desire for truth.

Language as prison and power tool

Following Nietzsche, his postmodern disciples teach that each language has its own peculiarities and creates its own truths. These truths are therefore relative. An example they often use is that the grammar of the Indo-European linguistic family forces us to think in terms of dualisms or binary oppositions. Among them are the oppositions divine-human, Creator-creation, subject-object, good-evil, male-female, body-mind, absolute-relative, and various others. Because we cannot but think in terms of oppositions, postmodern critics say, we believe that they reflect reality, but that is not necessarily so. There are other grammars that stress unity, rather than opposition, and the people using these grammars have for that very reason a different view of reality. They believe in the essential oneness of God and nature, God and man, good and evil, male and female, subject and object, and so on. Examples of such monistic views can be found in eastern pantheism and in other pagan religions. Since the western dualistic and the non-western monistic concepts of reality cannot both be true, and since there is no transcendental *logos* or meta-language by which we can judge local languages, it follows that we have to look at truth as relative.

The idea of perspectivism as taught by Nietzsche (and as implied in historicism and the sociology of knowledge) has similar implications. Perspectivism refers to the fact that we are unable to see things objectively and in their totality; that we look at them from our own limited perspective or frame of reference. My perspective is different from that of people living in a different culture or historical period. According to some of Nietzsche's more radical followers, it is even different from that of my neighbour, especially if that neighbour is of another racial or ethnic or social background, or if he or she is of the other sex, or of a different "sexual orientation." This again means that there is not one overarching truth, but an infinitude of personal and often contradictory ones.

Because our language and its grammar both determine and limit our understanding of the world, we are, according to postmodernist teachings, imprisoned in our language, in the sense that we cannot think beyond it. This explains why Nietzsche said he feared that "we are not getting rid of God because we still believe in grammar"[10] for much of our linguistic usage, including several of the binary oppositions in western languages, presupposes the existence of a transcendent God. It also explains Ludwig Wittgenstein's maxim, which we quoted in the previous chapter, that the limits of one's language mean the limits of one's world.

How did Nietzsche, and how do his postmodernist followers, propose we break out of the prison created by language? Or, more importantly, how are they going to use their insights into the arbitrariness of language in order both to destroy and to build? They have a number of strategies in place. One of them is to show the relationship between a society's grammar, vocabulary, and dominant metaphors on the one hand, and its view of reality on the other. People have to be made aware that a language can do no more than establish what is true for the society it serves; that there is no universal, overarching truth. Once they realize this, they will learn not to take their language and the traditions of their culture too seriously.

Another strategy is to look at the *origin* of grammatical structures, vocabulary, and moral codes, in order to find out why they arose and who benefited by them. For language is a social construct. Nietzsche said that its construction was the work of the so-called ontotheologists, the people who originally established western cvilization on the basis of Greek philosophy and biblical theology. Many of his modern-day followers, especially the political activists among them, have replaced these ontotheologists with the capitalist, misogynous, heterosexual, and ethnocentric western male. But no matter how the culprit is described, the strategy to be followed is the same. It is to discredit traditional concepts and structures by showing that they are the product of the dominant few, invented to serve them as tools to establish and maintain their control.

Much use is also being made of the idea of the mask as promoted by Marx, Nietzsche, and Freud. These men taught that there is a hidden agenda behind all we say and do, even if we ourselves are unaware of it. For Marxists that agenda is inspired by greed and the struggle for socio-economic control; for Nietzsche by the universal will to power; and for Freud by the desire to satisfy our instincts (especially the sexual one). We are inherently hypocritical, and selfishness rules all our deeds, words, and thoughts. Our religious beliefs and philosophical systems, our art, literature, and moral codes, our promotion of freedom and equality, even our acts of piety and pity and charity – all of these can be reduced to the striving for economic gain, the will to power, and/or the desire for sexual satisfaction. And again, once this becomes generally known, people will become sufficiently critical of their culture to reject it.

Considerable progress has been made in the work of demolition. The building of a new society by means of language proceeds far less rapidly, however. That work is pretty well restricted to attempts at changing language in such a way that the power of the dominant group is weakened in favour of the so-called marginalized. It is the task of what has become known as the political correctness movement, which executes it by rejecting discriminatory terms, promoting "inclusive language," and employing traditional language to "transvaluate" traditional norms.

Deconstruction

In attacking western culture Nietzsche's heirs do not make use of language only. They try to accomplish their goal also by other means, for example, by restricting access to the western cultural heritage. One of the strategies they follow here is to reduce the time which schools and universities traditionally devoted to western history and the western literary canon and to fill the gap with courses on non-western cultures and their writings.

Another means of reaching the common goal is to re-interpret western writings, with the aim of exposing their "hidden meanings" and so making them ineffective. This is not the least deadly of the weapons radical postmodernists like to employ. The texts of a civilization are, after all, the main instruments by which the dominant group grounded and maintains its power. If they can be shown to be the products of hypocrisy and lust for power, the foundations of society will be certain to crumble.

To interpret a text, one can choose among a number of literary theories. One can try, for example, to contextualize the message by giving much attention to author, historical background, and original recipients. This approach, which is known as that of *authorial intent*, has advantages and disadvantages. Contextualization can help to clarify the message, but it is also possible to place so heavy a stress on context that the text itself receives insufficient attention. Believing that we know all there is to know about the author's ideas, we may be tempted to read our own preconceptions into the text and so misread it. We may even be altogether mistaken about the author's true intent. It was to avoid this type of danger that early in the twentieth century the so-called "new criticism" arose. This school, which adopted the theory of *textual intent*, ignores author and background in favour of the text itself, trying to get its message by studying its structure and its use of imagery, irony, paradox, metaphor, and so on. And finally, there is the so-called *reader's response* or *reception theory*, which concentrates neither on author nor textual structure, but on what the text says to the present reader. All three theories have positive aspects, and all three have been and are being followed, sometimes separately, often also in combination.

Following the example of the French philosopher Jacques Derrida, postmodernists have added yet another theory to the list, namely post-structuralism or deconstructionism. It is similar to reception theory in that it gives priority not to the apparent intention of the author or the apparent message of the text, but to the response of the reader. But it also differs from conventional reception theory. The important thing is no longer the reader's interaction with a text which has an inherent meaning; the reader now analyzes the text in order to find its "hidden" meaning and show that it does not say what it purports to say. This does not necessarily mean what opponents of deconstructionism sometimes assert, namely that arbitrariness rules. Derrida himself has always denied that his theory is essentially relativistic and nihilistic. It is true, however, that at least among some of his followers there is a tendency to manipulate the text in such a way that it pretty well says what they want it to say. According to the pragmatist Richard Rorty, for example, the strong textualist asks essentially the same question about a text that "the engineer or the physicist asks himself about a puzzling physical object: how shall I describe this in order to get it to do what I want?"[11] But putting it in this way may be giving too much power to the individual reader, for radical postmodernism also teaches that the reader himself, like the speaker, is imprisoned in a web of language and cannot wield it as an instrument fully under his own control.

Nevertheless, deconstructionism is a power tool. Derrida's theory allows radical postmodernists to complete Nietzsche's project of freeing their culture from the shackles imposed by language, history, and tradition. It provides them with a means of destroying the ontotheological foundations of western civilization. More and more it is also being used in the culture wars of our own time, where the battle is waged on behalf of what are called the marginalized, such as women, racial and ethnic and religious minorities, and homosexuals. The concepts of mask and hidden agenda play a central role in these efforts, since they can be employed to discredit the ideas embodied in the written texts of our culture – in religious writings, in works on ethics, in philosophical, historical, and legal texts, and in literature proper – and so make room for new values. This postmodernist hermeneutics has properly been labelled a "hermeneutics of suspicion."

Although the intention of much of deconstructionism is to right past wrongs, the results are, as often as not, the establishment of new imbalances and injustices. Nor is this surprising. If Marx, Nietzsche, and Freud are indeed correct, then the values to be created can have no other foundation than desire and the will to power, which means that the justice of whoever happens to be the most powerful – in this case the critic – prevails. For the truly radical critics such arbitrariness is no problem. They deny that there is truth or anything else beyond language, and conclude that therefore they have the freedom to use language (and written texts) as is most convenient to them. Truth is not discovered but made. Nietzsche was among the first to teach this, and to conclude from it that literal truth is unimportant. He therefore felt justified to play fast and loose with both biblical data and historical information – a point which even some of his admirers have admitted.[12]

The question that Nietzsche and his followers failed to address is who is to control the new power-brokers. For it is obvious that many of the critics are as much on a power trip as the ontotheologists and other builders of western culture have ever been. In a sense, of course, comparing the two groups is comparing incommensurables. The founders of western society knew themselves to be bound by a truth that remained valid regardless of man's wishes, and their conclusions could be verified (and falsified) according to universally accepted standards. Radical deconstructionism does not know of such standards, which means that its interpretations can be arbitrary and that critics can keep deconstructing texts (including each other's writings) ad infinitum. Like Nietzsche, the philosophers and literary theorists he inspires are better at destroying than at building. For the more radical among them, building – that is, the creation of a new society once the old one has been dismantled – is no longer even a goal. Endless deconstruction is.[13]

An evaluation

The postmodernist theories on language and literature are having a strong impact on our culture. Nor is that surprising, for, destructive as they frequently are, they contain more than a grain of truth. It cannot be denied that words are arbitrary, that to a large extent language is the product of the society it serves, and that our personal and cultural perspectives, together with the language we use, influence our perception of reality. It is also true that language is employed to oppress and to commit violence, that people wear masks and pursue hidden agendas, and that many of the texts of our culture serve to maintain structures benefiting dominant groups. A dislike of the critics' hidden agenda should not blind us to these truths. In fact, much of what these critics remind us of – such as our abuse of language, the evils of the tongue we perpetrate, and the "deceitfulness and desperate corruption" of the human heart (Jeremiah 17:9; RSV) – we already knew from the Bible.

But if the facts are incontrovertible, the relativistic and nihilistic conclusions that are being drawn from them are not. Among the reasons why they are nevertheless widely accepted – not just by radicals but also by people who have no political or ideological axe to grind – is what Karl Popper has called the habit of "exaggerating a difficulty into an impossibility,"[14] a habit that is fed by our society's tendency toward an all-or-nothing approach. Unable to relativize relativism, many people assume that if infallible truth cannot be found, no truth can be had at all, and that the relative validity of an oral statement, a written text, or a cultural tradition cannot be established by any means. The possibility that they may be tested with reference, for example, to their social consequences is often not even considered.

The same type of argument applies to other problems postmodernists have raised in connection with language. The admission that language is largely a social construct, for example, and that it strongly influences our view of the world, does not have to lead to the conclusion that it imprisons us. We can transcend the limitations that language and culture impose by looking at and learning from the belief systems of cultures separate from ours in space and time. The Roman philosopher Cicero already taught that historical knowledge can help us to escape the tyranny of the present. And a modern-day philosopher has suggested that Wittgenstein's maxim, "the limits of my language mean the limits of my world," could be reversed and made to say, "the limits of my world mean the limits of my language"[15] – a world (and therefore a language) that could be greatly extended if religion and metaphysics were again accepted as sources of truth. But these roads to freedom postmodern critics cut off by deconstructing the texts that provide access to religion, metaphysics, historical knowledge, and the literary canon.

The suggestion that the social aspect of language is necessarily a drawback must be challenged as well. Although we are not the products of society, we are social beings whose ability to communicate is essential for survival. We cannot divorce either ourselves or our language from our community and its history. Nietzsche's desire for divine autonomy notwithstanding, it remains true that "we are aware of the world through a 'we' before we are through an 'I'."[16] Sociologist of knowledge Karl Mannheim and his followers are right in saying that knowing is not an individual but a social act, even if they are wrong to conclude that this makes truth relative. But it is incontrovertible that we either function as members of a community – one that extends in time and space – or we do not function at all. To close off the road to the past, and to destroy belief in the dependability of the communal language of past and present, is therefore to place individual and community in jeopardy, as is indeed happening in our days.

In short, the intellectual and moral nihilism in which a radical postmodernism threatens to engulf our culture is not an inescapable fate. Logic, reason, and experience are on the side of those who reject the absolutism of today's intellectual trends. So is the Christian faith, based on divine revelation. Ultimately, it is the rejection of revelation that forms the basis of the postmodern view on language – for this rejection implies the denial of what the new hermeneutics calls a transcendental *logos*, that is, of an overarching and transcendent truth.

Excursus: the binary oppositions

To show that revelation indeed sheds light on the questions which postmodernism raises, we will conclude this chapter by looking briefly at the matter of the binary oppositions.

The postmodern age is holistic and anxious to get rid of all dualisms. Part of the reason is that Descartes and his followers widened certain dichotomies to such an extent that the divides became virtually unbridgeable. It is increasingly realized that the sharp dualisms which Cartesianism poses between subject and object and between man and nature have contributed to the environmental problems plaguing western society. Placing the human mind over against a nature that was seen as no more than a machine led to attempts not to understand and develop nature as something organic, but to control and manipulate it as if it were a lifeless thing. Nor was it only the West that suffered the effects of this approach. As a result of western imperialism the entire world became a victim of the European will to power.

But if a reaction against the Cartesian tradition was overdue, the alternative proposed under postmodernism is hardly an improvement. In the rebellion against the Cartesian heritage, the western propensity for falling off the opposite side of the horse is again evident. People today are not just searching for more holistic and integrative approaches, but often reject the western tradition altogether, turning for solace and light to cultures that have traditionally been anti-dualistic. This is among the reasons for the current appeal of pantheism and other monistic systems. It means that not only truly divisive dichotomies are rejected, but also those that society has always experienced as positive and indeed necessary for a well-ordered life.

The tendency toward monism was evident in the philosophy of the German existentialist Martin Heidegger (1889-1976), who was, after Nietzsche, the most influential prophet of postmodernism. Rejecting the Cartesian tradition, Heidegger taught that man is not a consciousness separate from the world, standing over against it and capable of analyzing it in a detached manner. Rather, he must be seen as *Dasein,* or being-in-the-world; as someone who is at home in the world, cares for it, and is bound up in it; who is not only in but also of the world. By so obliterating the dualisms between man and nature and subject and object, Heidegger became, in his own estimation, a world-transforming figure; a philosopher who brought about a truly new age of thought. That honour had evaded Nietzsche, whose work, because of its stress on the will to power, Heidegger qualified as not the replacement but the consummation (as well as the inversion) of the millennia-old Greek and European philosophical tradition.

Heidegger's philosophy has much appeal for a world suffering from the ravages of modernism. But before we rush to embrace it, it is well to realize that with its exaltation of nature and its "renaturalization" of the human being, it is also a contributor to the paganization of the world. For paganism thrives on monism. Christianity, on the other hand, while rejecting dualisms of the Cartesian kind, does not deny the validity of dichotomies *per se.* It knows that the Bible itself teaches us to maintain certain oppositions, distinguishing as it does between God and man, Creator and creature, good and evil, man and nature, male and female. It is because western civilization was nurtured by Christianity (and not because of a conspiracy by dominant cliques) that our language is characterized by these dichotomies.

A study of history also makes clear that dichotomies are not necessarily a means of oppression but that often they serve to protect human liberty. This can be shown with reference to the rise of political freedoms in Western Europe and the establishment of royal absolutism in the East. In the Eastern Roman Empire and in its Byzantine successor, the emperor controlled the church. That tradition was inherited by Russia when in 1453 Constantinople fell to the Turks and Moscow replaced it as the capital of Eastern Orthodoxy. Although it is not the only cause of subsequent developments, Byzantium's political monism strongly encouraged the development of czarist despotism in Russia, and later the acceptance of communist totalitarianism. In Western Europe, meanwhile, a tradition of political freedom developed, thanks in large part to drawn-out conflicts for supremacy between church and state. These medieval conflicts prevented both the temporal power and the church from dominating the political scene. The dichotomous mindset that was then established continues to dominate constitutional democracies. They refuse to give extensive powers to the government and insist upon the separation of church and state, of executive and legislature and judiciary, of the public and the private realms. In totalitarian states no such dichotomies exist. Church and religion, legislature and judiciary, education and science, public and private life, all are subject to the omnipotent state.

Liberal political theory, which has flourished in the West for centuries, has always insisted upon a system of checks and balances. As American political scientist Glenn Tinder has shown in a recent article,[17] medieval theorists were not the first to demand this approach to politics. They were preceded by the church father Augustine. In promoting dichotomies in politics and other areas of life, Augustine was motivated, Tinder says, by the imperative to love God and therefore to eschew idols. For ultimately the denial of the divinely instituted oppositions leads to idolatry. That is why monism thrives under paganism; and if it triumphs in the Christian world, it does so in times of apostasy and secularization. In such times the danger of totalitarian rule, with the absolute state or a charismatic leader serving as substitute divinity, is a real one. It is not all that surprising that the monist Heidegger at one time openly promoted Hitler's cause.

The destructive effects of the collapse of all dichotomies are not restricted to the field of politics. The consequences of disturbing the proper balance between faith and reason, subjectivity and objectivity, free will and determinism, freedom and necessity, rights and responsibilities, are no less destructive. In our days the tendency to reject complexities and to absolutize one element is strong; and because idols cannot save, there often are sudden switches from one extreme to another. The modern idolatry of reason has collapsed into postmodern irrationalism, that of freedom into moral and social anarchy or, in the end, into a state-directed totalitarianism, that of scientific objectivism into all-out subjectivism, that of an excessive trust in human competence into the very denial of selfhood. And the list could go on.

As Augustine knew, the biblical dichotomies were instituted because of sin, to limit its effects, so that human life could continue in an imperfect and broken world. Their maintenance depends on the acknowledgement of human guilt before God, and on faith in the promise that that guilt is removed in Christ. For it is in Christ that all things, including these dichotomies, hold together. In him they are also resolved. For in establishing dichotomies, the Bible does not portray them as unbridgeable dualisms, as elements that stand in hostile opposition to each other. The Bible stresses relationships and ultimate reconciliation. "There is," Paul writes, "neither Jew nor Greek, slave nor free, male nor female, for you are all one in Jesus Christ" (Galatians 3:28). It is divine grace that makes possible both the maintenance of the divinely-instituted dichotomies and their ultimate resolution.

In a broken world the maintenance of the biblical dichotomies is essential for the survival of freedom and civilization. And this, Tinder believes, "is why Augustine, as the first great God-centered philosopher in the West, played so essential a part in the recovery of the West from the catastrophe of the fall of the Roman Empire. It is also why the modern world, in its inability to preserve the breadth, complexity, and balance of Augustine's universe, has come so near to experiencing the collapse of Western civilization."

NOTES

[1] Roger Lundin, *The Culture of Interpretation: Christian Faith and the Postmodern World* (Grand Rapids: Eerdmans, 1993), p. 237.

[2] Abraham Kuyper, *Principles of Sacred Theology*, trans. J. Hendrik De Vries (Grand Rapids: Eerdmans, 1965 [1898]), p. 62.

[3] Walter J. Ong, *The Presence of the Word: Some Prolegomena for Cultural and Religious History* (Minneapolis: University of Minnesota Press, 1986 [1967]), pp. 73f.

[4] Don Ihde, *Listening and Voice: A Phenomonology of Sound* (Athens, Ohio: Ohio University Press, 1976), p. 14.

[5.] Richard M. Weaver, *Ideas Have Consequences*, p. 149 (italics added). On the topic of the biblical approach to language see also Moisés Silva, *God, Language, and Scripture: Reading the Bible in the Light of General Linguistics* (Grand Rapids: Zondervan, 1990), especially ch. 2, and the references given there.

[6.] Weaver, *Ideas Have Consequences*, p. 150.

[7.] Brian D. Ingraffia, *Postmodern Theory and Biblical Theology* (Cambridge: Cambridge University Press, 1995), p. 22; see also *ibid.*, p. 90. For Nietzsche's last letters see *Nietzsche – Briefwechsel: Kritische Gesamtausgabe*, III, 5 (Berlin/New York: Walter de Gruyter, 1984), pp. 572-9.

[8.] Nietzsche, *Ecce Homo*, trans. Anthony M. Ludovici (New York: Russell and Russell, 1964), "Preface," par. 4; "Why I write such excellent books," par. 1.

[9.] Richard Rorty, *Consequences of Pragmatism* (Minneapolis: University of Minnesota Press, 1982), p. 141.

[10.] Nietzsche, *Twilight of the Idols*, "'Reason' in Philosophy," 5.

[11.] Rorty, *Consequences of Pragmatism*, p. 153.

[12.] As shown, for example, by Ingraffia, *Postmodern Theory*, pp. 62f.

[13.] For helpful Christian analyses of postmodern literary theory, see several of the essays in Clarence Walhout and Leland Ryken, eds., *Contemporary Literary Theory: A Christian Appraisal* (Grand Rapids: Eerdmans, 1991).

[14] Quoted by E. D. Hirsch, Jr., *The Aims of Interpretation* (Chicago: University of Chicago Press, 1976), p. 148. Popper used the expression in connection with perspectivism and Kuhn's philosophy of science.

[15.] Copleston, *Contemporary Philosophy*, p. 76.

[16.] Charles Taylor, quoted in Janet Martin Soskice, *Metaphor and Religious Language* (Oxford: Clarendon Press, 1987 [1985]), p. 179, n. 18. For the fact that all our knowledge, including the knowledge of religion, has a "social face" and that we constantly rely on the knowledge and experience of "authoritative others," see Soskice's fine essay "Knowledge and Experience in Science and Religion: Can We be Realists?" in Robert John Russell *et. al.*, eds., *Physics, Philosophy, and Theology: A Common Quest for Understanding* (Vatican City State: Vatican Observatory, 1988), pp. 173-84. See also the comments on the same topic by Michael Polanyi as summarized below, ch. 22.

[17.] Glenn Tinder, "Augustine's World and Ours," *First Things,* No. 78 (December 1997), pp. 35-42.

XX. A Christian Critique of Modernism

In the opening chapter of this book we mentioned the impact that theories of knowledge have on our lives. Even if we are not aware of the prevailing one, and perhaps do not even know that theories of knowledge exist, the answers they give to such questions as, "How do we know?" "What can we know?" and "How certain is our knowledge?" strongly influence our life and thought.

The prevailing theory of knowledge is therefore comparable to a period's worldview. The similarity extends to the temporary nature of these theories, which change in tandem with profound cultural changes. That this is also happening in the transition from modernism to postmodernism became evident in the previous chapter. There we noted that the concept of epistemology itself is under attack, and that the attempt is being made to replace theory of knowledge with theories of language and interpretation.

Although that attempt has widespread appeal, it is by no means the solution sought by all present-day thinkers. There are also those who, in a less radical fashion, propose to replace the prevailing theory of knowledge with one that avoids that theory's weaknesses while retaining its strengths. They refuse, that is, to make a clean break with the western epistemological tradition as such.

These alternative approaches are the subject of the concluding chapters of this book, beginning with the present one. The present chapter describes a Christian critique of the modern epistemology, namely that by the Dutch theologian Abraham Kuyper, who already in the late nineteenth century drew attention to the problems inherent in the scientist view of knowledge. Although he developed neither a systematic philosophy of science nor a new theory of knowledge, his work is important to us in that he revealed some of the unacknowledged presuppositions that govern the modern approach to knowledge. In doing so he returned to the epistemological tradition of Augustine, while at the same time anticipating many of the arguments that would be used by postmodern critics of the modern epistemology.

Before turning to Kuyper's work, we will briefly review the origins and nature of the prevailing theory of knowledge, in order to show how it could assume its controlling influence.

The objective ideal

The task of theories of knowledge is to help people cope with skepticism and uncertainty. They tend to come about when worldviews fragment and much of what long seemed self-evidently true is called into question. Such a period of crisis arose in the later Middle Ages, lasted well into the seventeenth century, and repeated itself in the centuries following. As we have seen in earlier chapters, the problems the seventeenth century experienced were not narrowly epistemological but extended to practically all of life. There were at that time deep religious divisions within and among European countries; the new capitalism had given rise to serious economic crises; England and other nations suffered political upheavals and sectarian unrest; and voyages of overseas exploration were making Europeans aware that there were religions and advanced cultures beside their own, thereby encouraging an attitude of relativism. The new astronomy, meanwhile, placed in question whatever traditional verities had survived the religious, socio-political, and economic turmoil.

In this situation people clamoured for certainty, for a foundation on which they could rebuild their lives, and the epistemology that was now being developed promised to provide such a foundation. The approach Descartes followed was different from the traditional one. Like the English empiricist Sir Francis Bacon, he was convinced that many of the problems Europe faced were caused, or at least aggravated, by the medieval practice of relying on tradition and authority, rather than on the thinkers' own insights. The solution he proposed was the well-known method of universal doubt of received wisdoms, followed by a rational, axiomatic approach to knowledge. To attain full objectivity, every effort had to be made to exclude the personal element. As in mathematics, the discipline on which it was modelled, the method would lead to conclusions that were logically necessary and therefore indubitably true. In this way human fallibility would be overcome.

In his battle with skepticism Descartes was first of all concerned with the defence of the scientific pursuit, but he believed that his epistemology could also resolve the theological, political, and social problems that Europe faced. Contemporary thinkers tended to agree, empiricists as well as rationalists. For although there were differences between the two schools, with Cartesian rationalists emphasizing mathematical exactitude and deductive logic, and Baconian and Lockean empiricists stressing observation, both schools held that objective knowledge in science and elsewhere can be assured if, and only if, scientists and others follow the so-called scientific method of detachment and doubt.

Because of its apparent success in the natural sciences the new method was indeed applied in the so-called human sciences, and so helped lay the basis for the Enlightenment expectation of human and social perfectibility. According to the modern creed, every difficulty, including those caused by religious disagreements, would yield to the new, scientific way of problem-solving. Trust was placed in method, and the ideal of scientific objectivity came to permeate the modern worldview. Only knowledge that could be scientifically tested was considered true knowledge; all the rest was held to be merely subjective opinion.

Although this scientist belief was most clearly evident in late-modern positivism, its origins are to be found in the philosophies of the seventeenth and eighteenth centuries. And in spite of occasional rebellions against it, it survived into the twentieth century. Indeed, much of it survives even under postmodernism.

Protestantism and modern science

The reason for the theory's long life and widespread appeal was not only its promise of intellectual certainty but also its scientific efficiency. This helps to explain why, in spite of its absolutist claims, it met with little sustained criticism even among Christians. It is true that Protestant as well as Roman Catholic theologians attacked the rationalist philosophy of Descartes. But the Cartesian approach did not in the long run fail to influence orthodox Christianity, and the empiricist version of the theory was popular from the beginning, especially among Protestants. It worked well in the scientific domain, and on the whole it was felt that the Christian faith had little to fear from science. During much of the modern period Protestantism had been in favour of the scientific enterprise. On occasion disagreements did arise, but Christians were usually able to reconcile apparent oppositions between the pronouncements of science and the contents of revelation. Furthermore, although the very success of science was hastening the spread of skepticism and agnosticism, the Newtonian understanding of nature could also be used against the enemies of Christianity.

And it was so used, also after Hume's attack on the foundations of natural theology. In fact, for a century or so following his death, Hume's approach was not considered as persuasive as it would be later, after the triumph of Darwinism. Well-argued eighteenth- and nineteenth-century works on natural theology seemed to have refuted his skeptical conclusions. In the absence of a substitute cosmology (such as eventually Darwin would provide), there was hardly an alternative to the belief that the world was the product of intelligent design. Especially influential in convincing their age of the harmony between faith and science were two English apologists, the Anglican Bishop Joseph Butler (1692-1752), author of the famous *Analogy of Religion* of 1736, and his co-religionist William Paley (1743-1805), whose *Evidences of Christianity* and *Natural Theology* appeared in 1796 and 1802 respectively. Both authors were widely read and remained popular well into the nineteenth century.

The widespread belief in intelligent design – that is, in a rational and presumably benevolent Creator – implied for most modern thinkers the rationality of human beings and the uniformity of human nature. This meant that for all people at all times perception and reasoning led to essentially the same conclusions. Culture, historical situation, personal idiosyncracies and personal and communal belief systems had little or no effect on the manner in which people viewed and interpreted reality. This conviction, which was still at the basis of Immanuel Kant's theory of knowledge and moral philosophy, would come under attack in late-modern times. Darwin, Marx, Nietzsche, Freud, the historicists and the sociologists of knowledge, all would do their share in demolishing it. During the eighteenth century and during much of the nineteenth, however, the belief remained strong, also among Christians. It was another reason why few of them considered it necessary to scrutinize the principles on which the prevailing epistemology was based.

Such scrutiny was not absent altogether. The American theologian and philosopher Jonathan Edwards (1703-58), a Calvinist, did question the assumption that there is no connection between faith and understanding. True knowledge of God, of man himself, and of nature, he taught, depends on the mind's being enlightened by God's grace. But

Edwards' voice was a solitary one, even in his own community. In conformity with the general perception of the age, most American Evangelicals held that theories of knowledge were religiously neutral, that the scientific method truly guaranteed the elimination of subjective elements, and that the conclusions reached by those who followed the proper method must therefore be objectively true. The fact that, as natural theologians showed, the scientific understanding of reality was in essential agreement with that of Christian theology, reinforced the belief in the objectivity of the scientific method. Science and revelation, it was widely held, could not truly and permanently clash. Science served Christians as a trustworthy ally.[1]

After Darwin

That belief was demolished in the final decades of the nineteenth century, when both Darwinism and the historical-critical method of biblical studies established themselves at the universities. The two-pronged attack on the trustworthiness of revelation, which was as sudden as it was unexpected, confronted Christians with the urgent need to rethink their trust in the objective ideal. The responses were far from unanimous. Some people tried to reach a compromise between scientific evolutionism and biblical Christianity by opting for a theistic version of evolutionism. Others responded to the challenge by either renouncing the Christian faith altogether, or by following the direction indicated by men like Kant and Schleiermacher. That is, they stressed the subjective element in faith and made man's moral sense or his religious experience, rather than divine revelation, the basis of religious certainty. This allowed them to disregard the attacks on the historicity of the Bible. In the twentieth century the neo-orthodox school of Karl Barth, although starting from different premises, made its peace with the higher criticism in a similar manner.

Yet another response was to cling to the faith in biblical Christianity, reject the findings of the evolutionists and the higher biblical critics as false, but at the same time maintain that the scientific method, if properly applied, led to fully objective truth. Those who chose this approach believed that the way to salvage orthodox Christianity was by the traditional means of proving the truth of Scripture and of the Christian worldview in a scientific, evidentialist manner. This tendency was strong especially in America, where the relationship between the Evangelical religion and Baconian science had always been close. It helps explain, as historians of the American Evangelical movement have suggested, why so many Evangelicals responded to the challenge of the higher biblical criticism and Darwinism by embracing such movements as dispensationalism (with its attempts to prove the truth of the Bible with reference to the fulfillment of biblical prophecy), and scientific creationism.

We encounter here what has been called the "anti-modernist modernism" of much of American Evangelicalism. It is anti-modernist in its objection to attacks on the faith, but it is modernist in attempting to battle the enemy with its own scientist weapons. Jonathan Edwards' teaching on the role of presuppositions in the scientific enterprise continued to be ignored among his American co-religionists. It was the Dutch theologian Abraham Kuyper who returned to it, more than a century after Edwards' death.

Kuyper's critique of scientism

Abraham Kuyper (1837-1920) received his theological education at the university of Leiden. Taught in one of the modernist traditions, he turned as a young pastor to orthodox Calvinism. Later, in 1886, he would lead a secession from the liberal state church and contribute to the establishment of a separate church community (the strictly Calvinistic Reformed Churches). Convinced that the struggle on behalf of the Reformed faith had to be waged in all areas of life, Kuyper had six years earlier established a Reformed university (the Free University of Amsterdam), where he himself taught. He also assumed the leadership of a Christian political party (the Anti-Revolutionary one), represented that party in Parliament, and from 1901 to 1905 served his country as Prime Minister. Meanwhile he maintained contact with the home base by constant journalistic labours. In 1898 he travelled to the United States to deliver the Stone Lectures at Princeton Seminary. Later published under the title *Lectures on Calvinism*, they served to make his Calvinistic principles known to English-speaking readers.

As his *Lectures* and other writings make clear, Kuyper spoke of Calvinism not only as a theological system, but also as an all-embracing worldview, one that is informed by the Scriptures and acknowledges the cosmic rule of Christ. It was his desire to bring the principles of that worldview to bear on the nation's life and so make possible a wide-ranging cultural renewal. That goal inspired all his work, including his pronouncements on the nature and limitations of science, the topic we are concerned with.

Like most of his co-religionists, Kuyper was a scientific realist, which means that he believed in the objective existence of the external world. He also believed that we are able to reach a true understanding of the operations of that world. Kuyper adhered to the ancient and still widely held *logos* doctrine, according to which we can understand nature because we were created in God's image, as rational beings, who are enabled to "think God's thoughts after him."[2] But he also realized that our faith commitments – specifically our response to divine revelation – play a decisive role in the way in which we understand and explain nature. As a result there is a division, an antithesis, between the work of believing and unbelieving scientists. Kuyper said that when scientists were simply engaged in weighing and measuring, the division was not evident. In those preliminary activities they generally reached the same results. But such uniformity became far more difficult when the scientists theorized about the results of their observations. Then, in many cases, religious presuppositions came in, and it was the conflicts between these ultimate belief systems that led to mutually antagonistic explanations.[3]

The stress was on the antagonism between these explanations. Subjectivity itself, Kuyper believed, was part of man's creaturely make-up. Even if sin had never entered the world, different people would still reach different conclusions in their theorizing, but these would then not reflect opposing convictions about ultimate reality. The existence of such non-antagonistic differences was all for the good. It stimulated further research and so contributed to scientific progress.[4] The danger lay not in human subjectivity. It lay in the refusal to *admit* the subjective element and, specifically, the role which religious commitments play in human thought. Kuyper's fight was not so much against unbelieving science as against the prevailing belief in scientific objectivity and infallibility. It was that dogma that constituted the great stumbling block for Christians.

Against skepticism

It also contributed to the culture of doubt in general. "All Scepticism," Kuyper states at one point, "originates from the impression that our certainty depends upon the result of our scientific research."[5] Kuyper was concerned about the problem of skepticism. It is true, he did not believe that a Pyrrhonist attitude was inevitable. In fact he was able, as we will see, to list elements in human life and thought that have historically prevented a lapse into all-out skepticism and that presumably would be able to do so in the future. Yet he admitted that the temptation to skepticism was there, and a major reason was that the differences among scientific theories were too evident for the belief in scientific objectivity to be maintained. Scientists and other thinkers should therefore admit the subjective element in their work. Unbelieving scientists should do so by acknowledging their naturalistic starting point; Christians by confessing that in their work they are guided by faith in divine revelation.

There were other reasons why full scientific objectivity was difficult to attain. Kuyper listed several, all of them a result of human finitude and fallenness.[6] The list included [deliberate] falsehoods, unintentional mistakes in observation, in memory, and in the processes of thought, self-delusion and self-deception, a wrong use of the imagination, and the influence of other minds – an influence to which we are subject through nurture, through formal education, and also through our use of language. As to the language element, Kuyper reminds us that "all kinds of untruths" have entered our everyday speech, and that the words, names, proverbs, and common sayings we unconsciously use, "mould our self-consciousness."[7] Still other factors preventing full objectivity are bodily and psychological weaknesses, the influence exerted by one's political and social environment, and the temptation to pursue one's own selfish interests. And finally, there is what Kuyper calls the "darkening of our consciousness," by which he means our frequent lack of sympathy toward the object of our investigation, which causes us to stand not alongside but over against it. Anticipating a typically postmodern conviction, he concludes that "this *estrangement* from the object of our knowledge is the greatest obstacle in the way to our knowledge of it."[8]

In view of all these impediments to the attainment of objective knowledge, the temptation to lapse into radical skepticism was real. But, Kuyper argued, "the process of history" was against such an outcome. "However often Scepticism has lifted up its head," he wrote, "it has never been able to maintain a standing for itself, and with unbroken courage and indefatigable power of will thinking humanity has ever started out anew upon the search after truth."[9] What accounted for mankind's ability to escape the ever-present snare of Pyrrhonism? Kuyper said that the explanation was to be found in the power of three subjective elements, namely human wisdom, common sense, and, above all, faith.

Wisdom he defined as immediate insight, that is, an insight that is acquired apart from science and discursive thought.[10] It refers to a knowledge of things that expresses itself not theoretically, but intuitively and practically, giving to those who possess it an insight that is in harmony with reality as it is daily experienced. Such wisdom, he pointed out, does not depend on education: an illiterate person can possess it, while highly educated people may fall far short of it. Its presence constitutes a safeguard against conclusions that may seem logically necessary (and are therefore considered inevitable by those who allow themselves to be guided by logical reasoning alone), but that are in fact opposed to human experience.

Wisdom is more discerning than common sense, the second element Kuyper mentions; yet possession of the latter also implies a soundness of intuition and of mind and an openness to the nature of experienced reality. Therefore, whereas the subjective element in discursive thought encourages skepticism, common sense and wisdom counteract that trend. They do so by providing a sense of certainty that is "constantly confirmed in the fiery test of practical application in daily life"[11] and so help their possessors to maintain the conviction that they are able to determine what is real. This practical wisdom can never take the place of discursive thought and empiricism, "but it has the general *universal* tendency to exclude follies from the processes of discursive thought, and in empirical investigation to promote the accuracy of our tact."[12] By doing so it serves as a bastion against all-out skepticism.

Faith

And finally, there is the role of faith, which, Kuyper says, counteracts skepticism even more effectively than wisdom does. When speaking of the role of faith in this connection, he wants it to be taken in a formal sense only, apart from any religious content. This means that it does not refer to saving faith in Christ, or even to faith in the existence of God, but only to a faculty or function of the human mind. Kuyper calls it the "formal function of the life of our soul which is fundamental to every fact in our human consciousness."[13] Faith in this sense is present in human beings generally, a point that Kuyper emphasizes. Although it is a subjective element in knowing, its universality ensures that it is not "of an individual-subjective character," but can be called "subjective in a general and communal sense."[14]

Like wisdom and common sense, this faith operates immediately, without the help of demonstrative proof. It places a check upon the human consciousness "which is first unstable, uncertain, and tossed about," and so provides stability and certainty.[15] Indeed, Kuyper says, in the end faith is the only true source of certainty in human thought, including scientific thought. This is so, first of all, because it gives us the starting point of our knowledge, namely the certainty of the existence of our own ego. It also provides the bridge from ego to non-ego, or from subject to object, and so assures us that we can believe what our senses tell us. For the skeptics are correct in saying that the reliability of our perceptions and observations cannot be demonstrated. It can only be believed, and in fact it is believed. If it were not, science, and life itself, would be impossible.[16]

Faith plays an essential role not only in observation, but also in demonstration, and in human reasoning in general. In reasoning we rely on axioms or first principles – or, as Descartes called them, clear and distinct ideas – as starting points. Such fundamental principles (for example, that I myself and other minds exist, that there is a real world out there, and that A is not not-A) are, again, not the result of demonstration and are not even capable of logical proof. They are simply propositions which we, together with other people, accept as self-evidently true, believing where we cannot prove. The power of faith serves as the "mysterious bond" that binds our ego to the axioms. By doing so, it makes human reasoning possible.[17]

Faith is equally indispensable, Kuyper continues, in the business of formulating scientific laws, and of accepting them as valid once they have been properly verified. Faith is needed here because definitive proof of the laws' universal validity can never be reached. Such proof is impossible for the simple reason that our demonstration cannot go further than our observation, and our observation is strictly limited. Even if it were possible for us to take account of every relevant aspect as it exists today (which in itself is highly unlikely), we would still have no way of ascertaining that the law in question applied also in the past, or that it will continue to apply in the future. Science is possible only if we believe in notions such as the uniformity and stability of nature.

And if the validity of specific empirical laws cannot be demonstrated, neither can it be proven that natural laws *as such* exist. Logic teaches, and correctly so, that no conclusion from the particular to the general is demonstratively valid; yet we constantly draw such conclusions. We do that not because we can prove that the general exists in the particular, but, again, because we believe this to be so.[18]

As this summary of his view on the role of faith makes clear, Kuyper goes well beyond the arguments of Locke and of a skeptic like Hume. He agrees with them that most of our so-called certainties are based on faith rather than demonstrative proof, but he rejects the conclusion that as a source of truth and certainty faith is inferior to demonstration and observation. Such a conclusion, he says, is altogether erroneous, and the antithesis between faith and science is a false one. It is wrong to say that science establishes truths that are equally binding on all people, but that faith belongs to the realm of suppositions and uncertainties. Faith in this formal sense is at the foundation of all knowledge, including the demonstrative kind.[19] And because it is part of the human consciousness, and therefore universal, it is able, Kuyper concludes, to build a solid dam against Pyrrhonic skepticism.

Antithesis and common grace

In the foregoing Kuyper has been speaking of faith as a function of the human mind in general, and therefore as something religiously neutral. It is a faculty that gives the same type of certainties to all people, regardless of their beliefs about ultimate truths. But the fact that at this level it is devoid of specifically religious content does not, of course, imply that faith remains religiously neutral throughout. In fact, as we have seen, Kuyper asserts the existence of a religious antithesis, one that is evident in all of human life and thought, and therefore also in the realm of the sciences, and he maintains that this antithesis is the result of ultimate faith commitments. The division lies between those who accept divine revelation as given in the Scriptures and those who reject it and believe in a closed universe.

Faith in this religious sense also gives certainty, to the non-Christian as much as to the Christian. This implies for Kuyper that reconciliations between religiously antagonistic scientific systems are well-nigh impossible. The proper thing for scientists to do, therefore, is to admit their religious presuppositions. Doing so does not place the science of Christians on a lower level than that occupied by the science of unbelievers, for both kinds are based on religious faith. Kuyper believes, as we saw, that the differences between believing and unbelieving scientists are not perceptible at the level of weighing and measuring and numbering. Near the ground, the tree of science is united, but at a certain height the stem separates and so, ultimately, do the branches. That opposing conclusions reached at these levels are a result of different belief systems becomes clear, he says, in such theories as evolutionism. The "fundamental opposition" which Darwin's theory has aroused among "men of repute" makes clear that it has no compulsory character.[20] In other words, it was not evidence which decided that issue, but religious presuppositions.

In this type of situation, Kuyper believes, the dividing wall between the sciences of believers and unbelievers is virtually unscalable. Although at the beginning levels the two groups can still benefit each other – they can use each other's findings, scrutinize each other's observations and logical reasoning, and ask each other to justify their conclusions – such cooperation is no longer possible when faith commitments begin to play their part. Once that happens, "every effort to understand each other will be futile in those points of the investigation in which this difference comes into play; and it will be impossible to settle the difference of insight. No polemics between these two kinds of science, on details which do not concern the statement of an objectively observable fact, or...a logical fault in argumentation, can ever serve any purpose."[21]

This belief in the power of religious presuppositions, it may be added, is also among the reasons why Kuyper believes that apologetics and natural theology have little effect in bringing unbelievers to faith and can even be counter-productive. Unless the discussion begins with an analysis of the underlying belief systems, he insists, the two parties will talk past each other. More than that: unless the Holy Spirit works faith in his or her heart, a person cannot discern divine truths. "Without the sense of God in the heart," Kuyper writes, echoing Calvin's teachings, "no one shall ever attain unto a knowledge of God...."[22] All efforts to prove the truth of Christianity by so-called evidences are therefore bound to fail. Saving faith in God is worked by grace, not by logical argument or empirical proof.

In Kuyper's system, then, an antithesis existed between belief and unbelief. It was found in the realm of religion as in that of culture and science and scholarship in general. But he met with a difficulty here. While insisting that whatever was not "of faith" was false, Kuyper was also very much aware of the good things that unbelieving thought in general, and unbelieving science in particular, had brought about. He was, moreover, anxious to avoid an Anabaptist type of escapism from the world. Convinced that there is "not a square inch in the whole domain of human life of which Christ, who is Sovereign of all, does not say 'Mine!'," he wished to remind Christians of their duty to proclaim Christ's Kingdom in scholarship, politics, and every other field of culture. Rather than shunning the world, Christians had to be culturally engaged. This implied (for example in the field of politics and in various areas of scholarship) that cooperation with unbelievers was unavoidable.

The difficulty Kuyper faced here was to reconcile the belief in total depravity with the apparent ability of unregenerate man to produce works that are of value to church and Kingdom. In attempting to solve this problem he had recourse to the concept of common grace. A gift of God, this grace was common or general in the sense that it was provided to both the elect and the non-elect. Kuyper made it very clear that, unlike particular grace, it did not lead to regeneration; nor did it remove the ultimate consequences of the fall into sin. In that sense the religious antithesis remained in force. Common grace, in fact, stressed the seriousness of sin by proclaiming, against the opinion of humanists of all stripes, that whatever is good in life is not man's doing but God's gracious and undeserved gift. Meanwhile, although fundamentally different from particular grace, common grace did serve the former. By making it possible for history to continue after humanity's fall into sin, and by checking the disastrous consequences of sin, it allowed for the survival and expansion of the church, and so served the consummation of God's Kingdom.[23] It did so for example by making it possible for unbelievers – scientists and others – to produce work of real value.

An evaluation

The concept of common grace as Kuyper developed it has not escaped criticism. One objection that has been raised against it is that it can have a secularizing effect. If much of the work of unbelieving culture and scholarship is a product of God's grace – even if it is only *common* grace – then it would seem to follow that the Christian can make use of that culture and scholarship to their fullest extent. This was not the conclusion Kuyper intended. He wanted to maintain the antithesis. It is true, however, that he lived at a time when belief in progress was still strong, and this fact may have contributed to his own tendency toward cultural optimism, a tendency that is evident in his concept of common grace. Another objection to Kuyper's teaching on common grace is, of course, that he failed to reconcile the doctrine with his conviction that mutual understanding between believing and unbelieving science is, at the level of theories and worldviews, severely restricted. Indeed, the concept is difficult to harmonize with his presuppositionalism not only in science but also in apologetics.

Kuyper's insistence on the division between believing and unbelieving science leaves us with other questions. He rightly stresses the importance of faith commitments in scientific theorizing, but he does not explain how Christian scientists are to work with the antithesis he has shown to exist. Specifically, he fails to answer the admittedly difficult question how we are to judge a scientific theory or explanation on religious grounds. Darwinism provides a clear-cut example of a theory based on anti-Christian premises, but in that sense it is exceptional. It is much harder to evaluate the religious principles that are at the basis of, let us say, Newtonianism, or quantum physics, or relativity theory. Few

Christian scientists will believe that they have to reject such theories on religious grounds, but neither will they be able to prove that the theories were inspired by or based on faith in revelation.

In this connection one also wonders if Kuyper should not have made it clear that, while one's religious commitment indeed plays a role in one's scientific reasoning, believers are not necessarily more successful in their scientific work than are unbelievers. It is true that faith in divine creation and providence has inspired fruitful scientific theorizing, but we also know of important theories that are not only the work of unbelievers but in fact owe their existence to their creators' unbelief. Apparently, as Kuyper's follower, the Dutch philosopher Herman Dooyeweerd, concludes, "God uses the apostate powers in culture to further unfold the potentials which he laid in the creation."[24]

One could argue, furthermore, that Kuyper could have placed greater stress than in fact he does on the tentativeness of scientific models and theories. By doing so he could have shown that their ultimate religious significance is not as great as people often assume. The strong belief in the scientist ideal – a belief that Kuyper rightly rejected as both unfounded and disastrous – was possible precisely because of the prevailing habit of assuming the permanence of scientific theories and so absolutizing them. Nor does it hurt to be reminded in this connection of the fact that the data available to scientists can often accommodate more than one theory, sometimes even conflicting ones, which nevertheless account for many of the same phenomena. And that, it should be added, is not necessarily a drawback. As is more and more realized in our days, rather than limiting our understanding of a phenomenon, a proliferation of theories can in fact enlarge it.[25]

On a different level, one could object to Kuyper's indiscriminate use of the word "faith." At one point he defines it as a function of the human mind in general, quite apart from any religious content. In that context he speaks of it as the means by which we are sure of all those things, also in the natural world, "of which [we] have a *firm conviction*, but which conviction is not the outcome of observation or demonstration."[26] At other times, however, he uses it as referring to a personal belief in God and in the saving work of Christ. This is confusing. But it may be that we are confronted here with the limitations of our language. Although in the former case the word "faith" could perhaps be replaced by the word "trust," that word would not quite convey the idea Kuyper had in mind. Nor would it convey what a later philosopher, Michael Polanyi, meant when he referred to "faith" as the conviction we have of a reality that is still hidden or only dimly perceived, but on which we nevertheless build with strong personal commitment and "universal intent."[27] Perhaps the term "presupposition" is a more adequate alternative. When defined as "a personal commitment that is held at the most basic level of one's network of beliefs,"[28] the term comes close to the meaning of Kuyper and Polanyi when they speak of faith in a non-religious sense.

To ask these various questions, however, is not to deny the positive aspects in Kuyper's pronouncements on the prevailing theory of knowledge. His contributions are many. In an age when not only the general public, but even many believers subscribed to the belief in scientific infallibility, Kuyper reminded people of the subjective element in science, of the fact that scientists are prone to err in their reasoning, and of the consequent fallibility of the scientific method. By doing so he provided a means of escape from the scientist stranglehold on religious faith.

And this is by no means the full extent of his work. He also reasserted the antithesis, which at least in the field of science Christians had too often ignored, and showed that it runs through all of life and all of scholarship. He made manifest the arrogance of a scientism that declares, without a shred of proof, that science is the only source of knowledge and certainty, so that everybody, including the believer, has to bow to its dictates even in matters of religion. He showed the extent to which the misplaced belief in scientific infallibility has contributed to the radical skepticism and relativism of late-modern times, and he made clear the incoherence of the culture of doubt. Not in the last place, he showed faith (in both meanings of the term) to be the ground of knowledge and humanity's greatest safeguard against debilitating doubt. As we noted in the introduction and as we will show in the following chapters, many of these insights would be confirmed by secular critics of the cult of scientism.

NOTES

[1.] For the continuing belief of American Evangelicalism in scientific objectivity, see Mark A. Noll, *The Scandal of the Evangelical Mind* (Grand Rapids/Leicester: Eerdmans/Inter-Varsity Press, 1994), and the references given in that work.

[2.] Albert Wolters, "Dutch Neo-Calvinism: Worldview, Philosophy and Rationality," in *Rationality in the Calvinian Tradition,* eds. Hendrik Hart *et al.* (Lanham: University Press of America, 1983), pp. 124-6. For Kuyper's explanation of man's ability to understand the cosmos, see also his *Principles of Sacred Theology*, pp. 77f., 83, 175, and his *Lectures on Calvinism: The Stone Foundation Lectures* (Grand Rapids: Eerdmans, 1970 [1931]), pp. 113f.

[3] Kuyper, *Principles of Sacred Theology*, pp. 91, 104, 168. In the Second Division of this work (pp. 56-227), Kuyper deals in considerable detail with epistemology and the nature of scientific inquiry, and most of my references are to this work. A helpful analysis of Kuyper's philosophy of science can be found in George Marsden, "The Collapse of American Evangelical Academia," in *Faith and Rationality: Reason and Belief in God*, eds. Plantinga and Wolterstorff, pp. 219-64, and in Ratzsch, "Abraham Kuyper's Philosophy of Science," in *Facets of Faith and Science*, II, ed. van der Meer, pp. 1-32.

[4] Kuyper, *Principles*, pp. 106, 169f., 178.

[5] *Ibid.*, p. 125.

[6] *Ibid.*, pp. 106-14.

[7] *Ibid.*, p. 108.

[8] *Ibid.*, p. 111.

[9] *Ibid.*, p. 119.

[10] For Kuyper's discussion of wisdom and common sense, see *ibid.*, pp. 119-25.

[11] *Ibid.*, p. 123.

[12] *Ibid.*, p. 124.

[13] *Ibid.*, p. 125. For Kuyper's discussion of the role of faith, see *ibid.*, pp. 125-46, as well as his *Lectures*, pp. 131f.

[14] *Principles*, p. 126.

[15] *Ibid.*, p. 127.

[16] *Ibid.*, pp. 129-36.

[17] *Ibid.*, p. 136.

[18.] *Ibid.*, pp. 137-39.

[19.] *Ibid.*, pp. 125, 140, 143; *Lectures*, p. 131.

[20.] *Principles*, p. 91.

[21.] *Ibid.*, p. 160.

[22.] *Ibid.*, p. 112.

[23.] A brief exposition of the concept of common grace is given in Kuyper's *Lectures*, pp. 121-6. For an exhaustive treatment, see his three-volume *De gemeene gratie* (Kampen: Kok, n.d.). For the analysis, explanation, and evaluation of the concept I have made use of Jochem Douma, *Algemene Genade: Uiteenzetting, vergelijking en beoordeling van de opvattingen van A. Kuyper, K. Schilder en Joh. Calvijn over 'algemene genade'* (Goes: Oosterbaan & Le Cointre, 1966). (The study, which is written in Dutch, closes with a brief but helpful English summary.)

[24.] Herman Dooyeweerd, *Roots of Western Culture*, p. 108.

[25.] Nancey Murphy (*Anglo-American Postmodernity*, ch. 4) illustrates this point with reference to two major models in the mental health sciences (the medical and the psychosocial one), showing that although apparently conflicting, these models are in fact complementary: each provides relevant information that is not available through the other.

[26.] Kuyper, *Principles*, p. 131.

[27] See below, p. 303.

[28] For this definition see Greg L. Bahnsen, *Van Til's Apologetic: Readings and Analysis* (Phillipsburg, New Jersey: Presbyterian and Reformed Publishing Company, 1998), p. 2, n4. Bahnsen's fuller definition runs as follows: "A 'presupposition' is an elementary assumption in one's reasoning or in the process by which opinions are formed. ... [It] is not just any assumption in an argument, but a personal commitment that is held at the most basic level of one's network of beliefs. Presuppositions form a wide-ranging, foundational *perspective* (or starting point) in terms of which everything else is interpreted and evaluated. As such, presuppositions have the greatest authority in one's thinking, being treated as one's least negotiable beliefs and being granted the highest immunity to revision." (I thank the Rev. Wes Bredenhof, a former student, for this reference.)

XXI. Postmodernism:
New Ways of Knowing (1)

Well-known among postmodern critics of modernism is the Anglo-Hungarian scientist and philosopher Michael Polanyi (1891-1976). It is on his work that we will focus in this chapter and the next one. The reason for choosing him is not that he was the only twentieth-century critic to attempt a replacement of the modern theory of knowledge. As will become apparent in these concluding chapters, several other thinkers have been involved in the attempt. Polanyi did, however, make some of the more important contributions to the formulation of a new epistemology. His work is of interest, moreover, because of the clear implications it has not only for scientific thinking but also for other fields of knowledge, including theology and politics.

In what follows we will give attention to a number of these implications. We will begin with the connections Polanyi draws between the modern view of knowledge and the political and moral disasters of the twentieth century, then outline his suggestions for a replacement epistemology, and conclude, in the next chapter, with some of the religious and theological implications of that epistemology.

The cult of scientism

In his critique of the prevailing theory of knowledge Polanyi pays a great deal of attention to two elements in that theory, namely the ideal of scientific detachment and that of systematic doubt. The preface to

Personal Knowledge, his major work, calls the ideal of scientific detachment a false one. Polanyi believes that in the exact sciences it may well be harmless, because scientists in these disciplines ignore it, but states that it has a destructive effect in other areas of thought and "falsifies our whole outlook far beyond the domain of science."[1]

This is so because the ideal of scientific detachment implies reliance on a method that is both impersonal and foolproof. A major reason why that approach has had destructive consequences is the type of society in which the ideal arose. It happened to be a society that placed as much stress on humanitarian reform as on scientific certainty. Indeed, the devotion to social improvement was one of modernism's most striking characteristics. The humanitarian impulse was inherited from Christianity, but under modernism it became secularized. It also grew more intense and culminated in the modern belief in unlimited progress and in human and social perfectibility. Polanyi explains this utopianism with reference to the prevailing belief that the mere application of the scientific method would fully and permanently solve all human problems. It is that belief, he says, that produced the dynamite which caused the near-destruction of western civilization in the twentieth century and still threatens our culture.

The coupling of moral perfectionism with the belief in a fully objective, infallible method is a major theme in his work. He became aware of its destructiveness as a result of his own experiences. Born in 1891 in Budapest, Polanyi witnessed in his lifetime, as a commentator writes, "both the unity and the dissolution of European culture.... He recalls the greatness of European centers of thought and compares what they were with what they are today. In thinking of this contrast and the magnitude and the madness of the killing of more than fifty million persons since 1914, he seeks an answer to the question of how the most morally motivated and the most liberally inquiring period in history could culminate in such destruction."[2]

His answer is, firstly, that the coupling of moral perfectionism with trust in an impersonal method created a belief in the automatic attainment of social perfection. He points out that that belief would necessarily be disappointed and so lead to coercion. In this scientist approach, it should be noted, the profound difference between the secularized humanitarian impulse and the Christian one becomes evident. Aware of the reality of sin, Christianity knows of the need to live with imperfection. The heavenly city will come, but not as a result of human effort or the outcome of a historical process. Not man is its architect, but God. The Christian tradition is based, moreover, on the command to love one's neighbour as oneself, and therefore enjoins costly commitment, even self-sacrifice. But under modernism trust in science has replaced faith in God, and science, according to the popular view, does not require personal commitment. It follows a method that works in an automatic manner.[3]

Secondly, the coupling took place in a time when the spiritual foundations of moral truths were being undermined. Universal doubt was at the basis of both the Cartesian epistemology and the so-called scientific method and soon pervaded all of society. The culture of doubt resulted first in the rejection of traditional moral values and then in the discrediting of all expressions of morality. As a consequence of the intellectual inheritance of thinkers like Marx and Nietzsche, such expressions were now seen as instruments of hypocrisy and oppression wielded by the dominant group. As a result, moral passions were distrusted to such an extent that they expressed themselves in an attitude of anti-moralism. The Marquis de Sade, who gave us the word sadism, has been called the first anti-moralist of this kind, and Nietzsche, Polanyi says, may have been the first theorist.[4] It was this anti-moralism, coupled with the trust in method, that fuelled much of the twentieth-century drive for the transformation of society.

Thirdly, the coupling led to a sense of self-righteousness, a refusal to acknowledge the possibility of error, and an intolerance to opposing beliefs. All this became evident already in the French Revolution, the first time the Enlightenment recipe for social perfection was put to the test. Promising liberty, equality, and universal brotherhood, the revolution derailed into a reign of domestic terror and two decades or more of war. Another example, one to which Polanyi refers often, is the rise of communism, which resulted in the death of untold millions. More clearly so than the French revolutionaries, Marx presented his system as a truly scientific one, insisting that the predicted outcome was inevitable. In accordance with unchangeable laws of logic and history, the class struggle would lead to the overthrow of capitalism and the establishment of the socialist utopia.

The fact that communism found adherents throughout the world, including the democratic West, testifies to the strength of the scientist belief. That it could survive even the revelations of the system's violence and inhumanity under Lenin and Stalin is to be explained by the fact that it was based on the coupling of belief in method with the humanitarian impulse. "Alleged scientific assertions, which are accepted as such because they satisfy moral passions," Polanyi writes, "will excite these passions further, and thus lend increased convincing power to the scientific affirmations in question – and so on, indefinitely."[5] The coupling is also effective in its own defence. Objections to its scientific component can be refuted by the exalted moral goal that is being served, while any moral objections can be dismissed with reference to its scientific nature. "Each of the two components ... takes it in turn to draw attention away from the other when it is under attack."[6]

The cult of scientism today

Times have changed since Polanyi wrote. In most of the western world totalitarianism as we experienced it in the twentieth century has had its day, at least for now. It has left behind a revulsion with utopian systems of all descriptions, including the Marxist one. Our age calls itself not only postmodern but also post-ideological. On this issue the boundary line between modernism and postmodernism appears to be clearly drawn.

The present-day view of the relationship between humanitarianism and the scientist attitude, however, is rather more difficult to determine. On the one hand, the postmodern age tends to count the trust in science and its method among the ideologies that are to be rejected. It opposes the modern quest for certainty and meaning and proclaims the relativity of all truth and the absence of all ultimate meaning. Yet the moral impulse persists, witness the concern for what are called the marginalized; and the belief in the perfectibility of society is as strong as it was under modernism, and also as radical. In that sense the trust in method would seem to have survived.

Indeed, even when rejecting communism because of its violence, moulders of public opinion continued to promote the detached, skeptical approach to problem-solving as the cure-all for society's ills. And the fact that the promised utopia continues to evade us explains, Polanyi concludes, the reformers' increasing radicalism. It also explains our culture's self-doubt and cynicism. Having been indoctrinated with the perfectionist ideal, more and more people – and especially the younger generation – interpret their culture's failure to live up to that ideal as hypocrisy and turn their back on society.

It is time, Polanyi says, that as a society we learn to curb our inordinate moral demands. Unjust privileges can be reduced only gradually; those who try to eliminate them overnight bring about greater injustices than they remove.[7] This is not to suggest that efforts at moral improvement are to be abandoned. It means, rather, that we must work for the improvement of our society while knowing that the ideals we pursue cannot possibly be achieved.[8] Our pledge has to be a personal one. Far too long we have lived in what Polanyi calls a fool's paradise, trusting that we were free from personal responsibility because we followed an objective method. It is this denial of personal accountability which explains why the scientist belief could be applied to systems, such as Marxism and National Socialism, which relieve the individual of moral responsibility.[9]

Morality in an age of skepticism

But again, although lamenting its excesses, Polanyi does not reject the reformist effort as such. Modern humanitarianism, he says, has resulted in unprecedented political and social reforms and produced "a society that was with all its evils, more free and more humane than any that had existed before."[10] Moral passions have led to great social improvements.

But the contradictions inherent in a morality that was based on philosophical and religious skepticism could not be contained, and in the course of modern history this became increasingly evident. The evil effects were most clearly noticeable in regions where secularization proceeded most rapidly. The fact that religion remained strong in eighteenth-century England was among the reasons, Polanyi believes, why that country, together with its American colonies, was saved from the political radicalism which would wreak havoc in revolutionary France, even though much of the new philosophy originated in the former country.

For it was the Englishman John Locke who, more than anyone else, inspired the Enlightenment thinkers and their revolutionary followers. Anxious for religious peace, Locke put forward the argument of uncertainty, arguing that "since it is impossible to demonstrate which religion is true, we should admit them all." The implication of such an argument is, Polanyi says, that a belief which is not demonstrably true is not to be made obligatory. Applied to moral principles, this means that unless such principles can be demonstrated, we should not only refrain from imposing them on society but even tolerate their total denial. And they indeed cannot be demonstrated: one cannot *prove* the obligation to uphold truth, justice, and mercy. It follows that a system of lies and cruelty and lawlessness is to be accepted as a logical alternative to traditional moral principles.[11] While England and America avoided drawing this conclusion, a secularized France did not. It was in France (and in the twentieth-century totalitarian systems) that the destructive potential of philosophic and moral skepticism became apparent: if you allow traditional ideals like freedom, truth, loyalty, goodness, and mercy to be placed in doubt, Polanyi says, you have no weapons to prevent their opposites from taking hold.

A survey of that process reads like a history of ideas of modern and late-modern times. Most modern thinkers still believed in personal responsibility and in moral standards that were universal and unchanging. That belief was given a philosophical basis by Kant and survived into the nineteenth century. In the course of that century, however, it would increasingly come under attack. The teachings of Hegel and of historicism gave rise to the belief that moral standards, rather than being universal and unchanging, are dependent on time and place. Marxism followed by stating that ideas of truth and goodness are by-products of class interests, which implies the denial of a common moral code among different classes. Marxism also stated that traditional morality is used as a cover-up for the exploitation of the economically weak. Their destruction by revolutionary violence thus becomes a moral act.

The erosion of the ancient moral code and its foundations continued during and after the *fin de siècle*. Nietzsche, much like Marx, taught that moral actions mask the desire for power. Proclaiming the need for a transvaluation of values, he implied that the pursuit of evil is less hypocritical and more "natural" than obedience to traditional moral precepts. Freud, in turn, made man's instinctual nature the determining force in life. Although admitting that much of traditional morality cannot be dispensed with, he qualified that admission by teaching that moral restraint is the cause of humanity's neuroses, and therefore at best a necessary evil. Good and evil, moral restraint and self-indulgence were now, Polanyi says, defined in terms of emotional sickness and health.[12] By implication the individual's personal responsibility was denied.

It was these late-modern perversions of morality that explain why moral forces were turned into violent and nihilistic channels. Destroying belief in the reality of justice and reason, the prevailing skepticism "stamped these ideas as mere super-structures; as out-of-date ideologies of a bourgeois age; as mere screens for selfish interests hiding behind them; and indeed, as sources of confusion and weakness to anyone who would trust in them." And so a generation grew up with strong moral passions, yet despising reason, justice, and morality. Following Marx, Nietzsche, and Freud, they believed "in the forces which were left for them to believe in – in Power, Economic Interest, Subconscious Desire....

Here they found a modern, acid-proof embodiment for their moral aspirations. Compassion was turned into merciless hatred and the desire for brotherhood into deadly class-war. Patriotism was turned into Fascist beastliness; the more evil, the more patriotic were the people who had gone Fascist."[13]

That outcome, Polanyi believes, was inevitable. If, as Marxism teaches, traditional morality is nothing but the superstructure of bourgeois society, then Marxists and their fellow-travellers can only reject it. In doing so they will be able to enlist support not only from moral nihilists, but also from men and women who are fired by a strong moral impulse but have been taught that that impulse can be satisfied only by destroying bourgeois hypocrisy. The fact that Marxist objectivism relieves the individual of all responsibility for his actions (since whatever happens in life and politics is a matter of scientific inevitability) is an added attraction. And the same kind of moral inversion happened under National Socialism. Hitler's program inspired people not in spite of but because of its very wickedness: his followers accepted acts of cruelty as a moral obligation.[14]

Personal knowledge

If the modern epistemology of detachment and doubt has indeed promoted the disasters of nihilism and totalitarianism of late-modern times, the questions as to the validity of that epistemology and the possibility of its replacement become urgent. Polanyi deals with these questions throughout his works. In what follows we will look at some of the arguments he uses to refute the traditional theory of knowledge and to support the alternative he proposes. That alternative he refers to as the concept of *personal knowledge*.

Among the elements he attacks in the traditional theory is its belief in automatism and detachment. As we already noted, Polanyi says that natural scientists do not really approach their work in a spirit of detachment, even if they think they do. Science would be impossible if they purged their minds of all subjective elements and simply applied a mechanical method. The scientist is fully part of the project he is working on. Although there are differences between science on the one hand and art and the humanities on the other, the distinction is not nearly as sharp as modern thinkers have assumed. Just as a work of art depends not only on the artist's skill, but also on his personality, imagination, creativity, and other tacit elements, so it is with science. All knowledge, whether in science or art or religion, is personal, which means that the human being is involved in it with all its faculties – and also with all its limitations.

Science is therefore not based, as the empiricist Francis Bacon and his followers would have us believe, on value-free observation and experimentation. These activities are guided by hypotheses, which are human creations, and are often not the result of empirical fact-finding but of thought experiments and hunches and creative insights. This fact explains, we may add, the striking correspondence between scientific theories and general worldviews – for scientists are, after all, members of their community. The heliocentric model of the universe and Darwinian evolutionism – to restrict ourselves to these two examples – came about only when society was ready to accept the type of cosmology that depended on these scientific theories.

The scientist's personal involvement also accounts for Thomas Kuhn's observation that scientific theories are frequently rejected or accepted not because of empirical evidence but in spite of it. As often as not it is a matter not of sight, but of personal preference and even, Kuhn says, of faith. This applies, for example, to Neo-Darwinism. As Polanyi writes, that theory "is firmly accredited and highly regarded by science, though there is little direct evidence for it, because it beautifully fits into a mechanistic system of the universe and bears on a subject – the origin of man – which is of the utmost intrinsic interest."[15] In short, science is not a simple matter of collecting facts and expecting them to dictate conclusions. The subjective element is indispensable and affects the scientific process from beginning to end. In that sense the gap between non-scientific and scientific knowledge is not nearly as wide as modernists supposed.

Skepticism and the quest for certainty

Polanyi attacks not only the detachment and automatism of the modern theory, but also its skepticism.[16] The idea of universal doubt as prerequisite for the acquisition of objective knowledge he considers, as has become apparent, to be among the most harmful aspects of the Cartesian epistemology.

It is also one of the most unrealistic. For one thing, most of our knowledge, he shows, is tacit, which means that often we are not even conscious of it and that we know far more than we can tell, and therefore also far more than we can doubt away. Moreover, to say that scientists have to ignore all they have ever learned is to suggest that each one of them has to reinvent the wheel, which is obviously nonsensical. The work of science, like other human projects, builds on the experiences, insights, and accomplishments of previous generations. Much knowledge is transmitted rather than discovered, which means that the pursuit of knowledge is impossible if one assumes, as modern epistemology says we must, that authority and tradition and inherited wisdom are necessarily suspect.

Knowledge depends, Polanyi says, on the willingness to accept information in the absence of definitive logical or empirical evidence. While admitting that there is a place for doubt in science (as in other branches of human knowledge), Polanyi balances that admission by stressing, as Kuyper did, the central role of faith, a term that must again be defined in a largely non-religious sense. In Polanyi's case the object of faith is first of all the rationality of nature, a rationality to which man, who is himself endowed with reason, is able to respond.[17] Science makes use of the senses (Polanyi is committed to an empirical approach), but it also transcends them.

Faith plays additional roles. It is needed for the reception of transmitted knowledge, and it serves as remedy against the infinite regress to which our constant questioning would otherwise lead. In the search for knowledge, after all the necessary questions have been asked, we must fall back on faith. Polanyi more than once quotes the church father Augustine, who said that unless we believe we will not understand. No thinking, he keeps telling us, can be done outside a fiduciary framework. This was tacitly taken for granted before the rise of critical philosophy, and before moderns like Locke declared knowledge of faith to be inferior to scientific knowledge. "We must now," Polanyi says, "recognize belief once more as the source of all knowledge."[18]

And finally, Polanyi attacks the modern obsession with *certainty* of knowledge. Like the other critics of the modern epistemology, he rejects Cartesian foundationalism. His concept of personal knowledge implies the risk of failure, for human beings are fallible. Errors are possible no matter what method is followed. This does not imply a collapse into skepticism, nor does it mean the enthronement of the subjective. It was never Polanyi's intention to replace the objective ideal with a subjective one, and he makes it clear that such a conclusion does not follow. For one thing, he points out, scientists believe that truth is real and will be recognized by all who sincerely seek it.[19] Furthermore, they pursue their researches with what Polanyi calls *universal intent* – which means that they are committed to achieving results they believe have universal validity, even while admitting that they may be mistaken. Still other safeguards against a subjectivist arbitrariness are the role the scientific community plays in the screening of theories and the fact that these theories can be validated by whether or not they lead to further knowledge. Nevertheless, the possibility of error is always present. The modern belief that perfection can be achieved – in knowledge as in the organization of society – ignores man's finitude.

In this connection Polanyi also attacks the notion that there is an infallible method of testing and verifying scientific theories. Contrary evidence, he shows, does not necessarily lead to the rejection of a theory, and corroborating evidence has in the end been shown to be invalid.[20] As Thomas Kuhn also taught, scientists do not necessarily rely on criteria of reproducibility of experiments; subjective factors play a role in the acceptance and rejection of evidence. It is, Polanyi says, the scientist's belief about "the general nature of things" – a holistic concept – that influences his reaction to the available evidence.[21] Using Kuhnian terms, we could say that the prevailing paradigm performs that function. But again, this does not imply subjectivism or skepticism, for the belief about the general nature of things is held with universal intent. Personal knowledge as Polanyi defines it avoids the pitfalls of both modern objectivism and postmodern skepticism. The theory has, as we will see in the next chapter, other positive implications.

NOTES

[1.] Michael Polanyi, *Personal Knowledge: Towards a Post-Critical Philosophy* (Chicago: University of Chicago Press, 1962 [1958]), p. vii. On his philosophy see this work, as well as his *Science, Faith and Society* (Chicago: University of Chicago Press, 1964 [1946]); *The Tacit Dimension* (Garden City, New York: Doubleday, 1966); *The Study of Man* (Chicago: University of Chicago Press, Phoenix Books, 1967 [1959]); *The Logic of Liberty: Reflections and Rejoinders* (Chicago: University of Chicago Press, 1980 [1951]); *Knowing and Being: Essays by Michael Polanyi,* ed. Marjorie Grene (Chicago: University of Chicago Press, 1969); and (with Harry Prosch), *Meaning* (Chicago: University of Chicago Press, 1975). A helpful summary of Polanyi's work is Richard Gelwick, *The Way of Discovery: An Introduction to the Thought of Michael Polanyi* (Oxford: Oxford University Press, 1977).

[2.] Gelwick, *The Way of Discovery,* pp. 4f.

[3.] For Polanyi's formulation of the Christian answer to the problem of perfectionism, see his *Meaning,* p. 215.

4. Polanyi, *The Tacit Dimension*, pp. 58f.

5. Polanyi, *Personal Knowledge*, p. 230.

6 *Ibid.*

7. *Ibid.*, p. 245.

8. *Ibid.*

9. *Ibid.*, pp. 268, 323.

10 Quoted by Gelwick, *The Way of Discovery*, p. 21; see also Polanyi, *Personal Knowledge*, pp. 222f.

11. Polanyi, *The Logic of Liberty*, p. 97.

12. Polanyi, *Knowing and Being*, p. 43.

13. Polanyi, *The Logic of Liberty*, p. 5.

14. Polanyi, *Personal Knowledge*, p. 232.

15. *Ibid.*, p. 136.

16. *Ibid.*, especially chapter 9, "The Critique of Doubt."

17. Polanyi, *Science, Faith and Society*, p. 73; *Personal Knowledge*, pp. 5, 6, 15, 64, and *passim*.

18. *Ibid.*, p. 266. Polanyi is not the only contemporary thinker to stress the cognitive function of faith (in the sense of a general mental function). We meet the same idea in other late-modern and postmodern thinkers. Well-known among them are, besides Thomas Kuhn, Ludwig Wittgenstein and Albert Einstein.

19. Polanyi, *Science, Faith and Society*, p. 73.

20. Polanyi, *Personal Knowledge*, pp. 12f.; *Science, Faith and Society*, Appendix 3.

21. *Ibid.*, pp. 10f.

XXII. Postmodernism:
New Ways of Knowing (2)

Against reductionism

We noted in the previous chapter that Polanyi upholds the need for objectivity while rejecting the scientist trust in the possibility of absolute certainty. Belief in "complete objectivity as usually attributed to the exact sciences," he writes, "is a delusion and is in fact a false ideal."[1]

It is, as we have seen, also a dehumanizing one. To give one more example of its negative consequences: the emphasis on objective certainty contributes to the habit of reducing complex things to their component parts. That has led, among other things, to the reduction of life and of the human mind to physics and chemistry. These material elements are considered the most real because, unlike complex living and thinking beings, they lend themselves to an objective, naturalistic analysis. And so we have come, in the words of Polanyi scholar Richard Gelwick, "to an absurd position, where many are concerned about the preservation of life, while we have at large an understanding that equates living persons with complex biochemical machines. Before we can expect from science and government the kind of respect for and understanding of life that are necessary, we have to have in operation a mode of knowing that can acknowledge the distinctive character of living things."[2]

With his refutation of objectivism, his view of the thinker as a feeling and purposive being, his stress on the tacit element in knowledge, and his holistic approach in general, Polanyi has contributed to this alternate way of knowing. He has done it also with his concept of a universe that is stratified and hierarchically ordered, a concept which allows him to refute the idea that the laws governing lower levels account for the operations of higher ones. In *The Tacit Dimension* he illustrates the idea of hierarchy with reference to the art of speaking, showing that one cannot derive a vocabulary from phonetics, or a grammar from a vocabulary, or a good style from a correct use of grammar, or the content of a piece of prose from a good style. In short, "it is impossible to represent the organizing principles of a higher level by the laws governing its isolated particulars."[3]

And what applies to the art of speaking applies to the levels found in living beings, from the vegetative one at the bottom of the hierarchy to those of consciousness, intellect, and moral sense at the top. Since all these successive levels are situated above the inanimate, they all rely for their operations on the laws of physics and chemistry. But it does not follow that therefore, as modern scientism takes for granted, all manifestations of life can be fully explained by these laws. That assumption is nonsense, Polanyi says. "The most striking feature of our own existence is our sentience. The laws of physics and chemistry include no conception of sentience, and any system wholly determined by these laws must be insentient."[4]

Polanyi concludes that the study of life must therefore "ultimately reveal some principles additional to those manifested by inanimate matter... ."[5] He does not say that these principles are to be found beyond nature. He rejects mechanistic Darwinism, but believes in a type of evolutionism that he says has similarities with the theory of the French thinker Henri Bergson, who posited a creative agency or *élan vital* in nature.[6] And indeed, for Polanyi also the creative agency is an immanent one. He explains life and sentience as the outcome of a process of emergence, a concept that allows for causation from the higher to the lower: rather than arising from the lowest levels, life and sentience emerge through the interaction of higher levels with lower ones. The direction of causation is reversed and in that sense reductionism is defeated, but life and sentience are still the products of nature; there is no acknowledgment of a transcendent, ultimate cause. Nor is there, as a result, a safeguarding of the independence of the mind, which appears to be simply a product of nature.[7] We will see in the next section that a concept of hierarchy has been developed which avoids such a naturalistic conclusion. But to reject Polanyi's explanation is not to deny the value of the idea of hierarchy as such, which shows on scientific and common-sense grounds the error of metaphysical reductionism.

Other attacks on scientism

Polanyi was not alone in warning against scientific objectivism and the reductionism to which this has led. Among those who fought the scientist attitude were the fifth-century church father Augustine and the seventeenth-century philosopher Blaise Pascal. Among Christians who have kept the tradition alive in the late nineteenth and twentieth centuries are, in addition to Abraham Kuyper, Kuyper's colleague Herman Bavinck, and the Reformed philosopher Herman Dooyeweerd.[8] Other religious thinkers who have challenged the all-sufficiency of the scientific approach are the Jewish existentialist philosopher Martin Buber and his Roman Catholic colleague Gabriel Marcel. The work of Dooyeweerd and of the two existentialists is of special import for the topic we are now dealing with, as will appear from the following brief (and necessarily oversimplified) summaries of their philosophies.

Inspired by Kuyper, and in cooperation with the philosopher Dirk Vollenhoven, Dooyeweerd (1894-1977) developed the so-called Cosmic Law Philosophy, which affirms the Augustinian maxim that unless we believe, we will not understand. Knowing God (the God of the Bible) is a necessary condition for understanding, which means that there can be no opposition between faith and knowledge. The prevailing reductionism Dooyeweerd calls idolatry, because it gives creative powers to whatever aspect of reality is selected as the causal one, whether this be number, matter (physics and chemistry), life, sensation, logic, or (under postmodernism) language.

Dooyeweerd distinguishes some fifteen aspects of reality, which like Polanyi he arranges in a hierarchical order. He moves from the numerical, spatial, kinematic, and physical aspects up to the biotic, sensory, logical, historical, linguistic ones, and so on, to the fiduciary or faith aspect, which he places at the summit. Dooyeweerd teaches that all these aspects are equally dependent on God, and that none has priority over the other. Of course there is preconditionality: the physical aspect, for example, precedes the biotic, the biotic the sensory, the sensory the ability to think. But the one is not a sufficient *cause* of the next one, and therefore none can be reduced to another; all are dependent on God alone. Dooyeweerd thereby leaves no room for a naturalistic view of emergence, and so avoids the risk of openly or surreptitiously providing nature with autonomous powers.

The existentialist thinkers Martin Buber and Gabriel Marcel concern themselves with the kind of knowledge that depends on trust in and commitment to a person. Distinguishing between theoretical and interpersonal knowing, they reject the modern belief that only the former ensures reliable knowledge. Martin Buber (1878-1965), whose work *I and Thou* appeared in 1923, speaks of an *I-It* and an *I-Thou* relationship. The first applies when we treat something or someone as an *it*, an object that we can control, manipulate, and classify. In the second case we approach the other as a *thou*, a person who addresses us and to whom we respond. Here we do not objectify the other, attempting to control him; instead we open up to him and commit ourselves to him. Such interpersonal knowledge is non-scientific but is not therefore less certain. Indeed, it is the only way truly to come to know a fellow human being. It is also the only way to know God. Biblical scholarship and theology floundered when they attempted to treat revelation in a purely analytical fashion instead of listening to it as to the living word of a God who is himself a Person and who addresses human beings as persons.

In his collection of essays entitled *Creative Fidelity,* first published in 1940, Buber's younger contemporary Gabriel Marcel applies the insights of interpersonal knowing to the problem of religious skepticism. Marcel (1889-1973) says that if we want to know our neighbour we must approach him as a person, in self-giving fidelity. Only in that way can the path of love be opened and knowledge of the other replace mere "opinion." Similarly, to know God we must respond to him as a *Thou* – as the One who commits himself to us in love and fidelity, and who awaits our response. For religious faith applies not simply to a set of propositions we hold to be true, but – more intimately and more profoundly – to the Person of whom these propositions speak.[9]

Marcel's work implies that one cannot really be a biblical interpreter if one is not a believer. The same conclusion was explicitly drawn, nearly two decades later, by Michael Polanyi, when he wrote, "Only a Christian who stands in the service of his faith can understand Christian theology and only he can enter into the religious meaning of the Bible."[10] While such a stance implies circular reasoning, the circularity is not vicious. As Polanyi has often reminded us, all our ultimate commitments are circular. We begin with belief in a reality that may still be hidden or is only dimly perceived, and in our quest for further knowledge we build on that belief with strong personal commitment – and also with universal intent. In that respect the situation of the radical biblical critic is no different from that of the Christian. He also has his starting point in belief, namely in the conviction that the universe is a closed one, and that the only truth claims deserving consideration are the ones that can be logically or empirically verified.

Criticisms of Polanyi's theory

The similarities between the work of Polanyi, Buber, and Marcel are not coincidental but testify to a shift in paradigms or world-views. That such a shift is underway is also clear from the fact that many other thinkers, religious and non-religious ones, are turning from the old scientism to a more personal and a more holistic approach to knowledge. They include the philosophers Ludwig Wittgenstein, Martin Heidegger, and Alisdair MacIntyre, the hermeneuticist Hans-Georg Gadamer, the philosophers of science Thomas Kuhn, Imre Lakatos, and Stephen Toulmin, and various others. Among them are philosophers, theologians, natural scientists, linguists, psychologists, sociologists, and historians, all of whom are, in one way or another, reacting against the tyranny of scientist objectivism.[11]

Not all these people were influenced by Polanyi. The work of some of them, in fact, preceded his. Nor will all these thinkers agree with Polanyi's theory as a whole. Aspects of his work have been criticized by thinkers who nevertheless share his anti-positivist views and agree with many elements in his theory of personal knowledge. The objection has been raised, for example, that in attempting to prove the personal element in science, Polanyi tends to downplay the distinction between scientific knowledge and other ways of knowing rather too much. One of Polanyi's critics, the Belgian philosopher Chaim Perelman, has dealt with this issue in some detail. He argues that in each epoch the scientific community agrees (at least provisionally) on certain sets of propositions, but that such a body of accepted truths does not exist in philosophy, law, art, morality, or religion, at least not if one crosses the boundary from one culture to another. Similarly, there is progress in science, so that past science is out of date, whereas new conceptions in art, literature, philosophy, or religion do not disqualify older ones in those disciplines. This is so, he says, because there are techniques of prediction, proof, and verification in the sciences for which there are no equivalents in other disciplines. While rejecting with Polanyi the modern theory of science with its stress on doubt, detachment, and objective certainty, Perelman nevertheless wants to emphasize – and rightly so, in my opinion – the special place of science in our culture.[12]

Polanyi has also been criticized for explaining the acceptance and rejection of theories not with reference to objective standards, but on psychological and sociological grounds. Among those who have made that charge is Polanyi's compatriot, the Anglo-Hungarian scholar Imre Lakatos (1922-74), who accuses Polanyi of an overly subjective approach to scientific truth and blames him for failing to provide proper criteria by which to evaluate competing theories.[13] Although Lakatos does little to substantiate his charge that Polanyi tends to "water down the ideal of proven truth" to "truth by [changing] consensus,"[14] he is correct in stating that the Polanyian approach lacks a specific set of fully objective criteria for the appraisal of scientific theories. Lakatos himself has attempted to provide such criteria with his methodology of what he calls research programmes. That methodology serves as an alternative to Polanyi's theory and should therefore have our attention.[15]

Lakatos agrees with Polanyi, Kuhn and other contemporary philosophers that scientists don't necessarily reject a theory because of contrary evidence. Scientific theories, he states, are tenacious and are not abandoned simply because observation or experiments appear to contradict them. He explains this tenacity with reference to the nature of research programmess, which he defines as descriptive units of scientific achievements (such as Newtonian science, Einstein's relativity theory, quantum mechanics, Marxism, Freudianism, and so on). In brief, they are similar to Kuhn's paradigms. These research programmes, Lakatos says, consist of a central theory or set of theories that serves as the hard core, a protective belt of auxiliary hypotheses, and a problem-solving machinery. All research programmes, including such well-established ones as those of Newton and Einstein, have unsolved problems. These problems do not, however, refute the hard core but lead only to adjustments in the protective belt of auxiliary hypotheses.

If all theories have unresolved problems and anomalies, and if both verification and falsification are well-nigh impossible, how does one distinguish between what Lakatos calls "degenerating" research programmes and "progressive" ones? Whereas Polanyi and Kuhn held that subjective elements play an important role in choosing between competing theories, Lakatos believes that the process is, or at least can be, a wholly rational one. Progressive programmes, he says, are distinguishable from degenerating ones by the fact that they "predict novel facts, facts which had been either undreamt of, or have indeed been contradicted by previous or rival programmes." Lakatos proves the point with examples from Newtonian and Einsteinian theories. In degenerative programs, on the other hand – and here Marxism serves him as an example – "theories are fabricated only in order to accommodate known facts" and to explain away unsuccessful predictions.[16] The choice between rival programmes, in short, can be made on purely objective grounds.

In his anxiety to exorcize the spectre of scientific subjectivism and irrationality Lakatos undoubtedly underestimates the subjective element in the acceptance and rejection of theories. There is abundant evidence in the history of science that subjective factors – such as the desire for simplicity, estimations of a theory's explanatory power, social needs and expectations, and also a scientist's religious and metaphysical beliefs and his idea of the "general nature of things" – play an important part in the evaluation of theories. Well-known examples are the early acceptance of Copernicanism and of Darwinian evolutionism, as well as Einstein's and other scientists' belief in his general theory of relativity before strong empirical justification had been forthcoming and also in spite of what seemed to be contradictory experimental evidence.[17] Lakatos is correct, however, in pointing out that objective touchstones are available for the appraisal of a theory – if not immediately, then once it has reached a certain maturity. Although Polanyi did not deny the existence of such touchstones nor downplay the importance of empirical testing, the lack of a clearly-delineated set of objective criteria in his system can give rise to confusion about the nature of scientific truth. In that sense Lakatos' theory serves indeed as a corrective.

On a different level, questions could be raised about Polanyi's explanation of political developments. It can be argued, for example, that while one cannot but agree with the connections he draws between Cartesian skepticism and the rise of totalitarianism and nihilism, it is doubtful that the cult of objectivism fully explains these phenomena. There were other developments that contributed to the rise of religious, philosophical, and moral skepticism. We have in earlier chapters alluded to such factors as the West's growing acquaintance with previously unknown cultures, the new scientific model of the universe, and a number of scientific theories of a more limited scope. Also influential were the break-up of religious unity and, later, the development of technology, which increased popular doubt about the value of knowledge that did not contribute to technological progress.

These criticisms and corrections, though valid, do not detract from Polanyi's central thesis regarding the culturally destructive influence of the objectivist epistemology. Nor do they cast doubt on the significance and promise of the theory of knowledge he proposes as an alternative. So far we have concentrated on the socio-political and cultural implications of that theory, but Polanyi's view of personal knowledge has a bearing on religious knowing as well. We will conclude this chapter with a look at some of these religious implications.

Personal knowledge and religion

Attempts by scholars to determine Polanyi's religious convictions have been largely unsuccessful. The reason is the lack of consistency in his statements on religion. As one theologian complains, "At times he speaks as if he were a Christian believer and forecasts a religious revival that will furnish a true cultural solution to modern skepticism. At other times he appears completely agnostic and more so, it seems, as he gets older. And at still other times he seems to advocate a merely secular Christianity."[18]

This is indeed the impression Polanyi's statements leave with the reader. He appears to have been sympathetic to Christianity and anxious to uphold its rationality but does not indicate a strong personal commitment. He gives the impression of entering the domain of theology with some trepidation, and while expressing agreement with "many passages" in the writings of the liberal existentialist theologian Paul Tillich, he does not ally himself fully with him or with any other theologian.[19] His concern with religion and theology will probably have to be explained largely (although perhaps not exclusively) by the bearing they have on his conclusions in the field of epistemology. Since it is these conclusions that interest us, we will focus on them, rather than speculating further on his religious convictions.

The reader will already have noted several of the implications Polanyi's theory has for religious knowledge. Christians will appreciate his attacks on skepticism and universal doubt, his defence of authority and tradition, and his insistence on the importance of the transmission of knowledge in the search for further knowledge. They will also agree with his acknowledgement of the need of commitment in the search for truth, a commitment that follows from belief in an independently existing reality which will reveal itself to those who passionately seek it. In the field of religion, the idea of responsible commitment reminds one of the Lord's parable about the man who gave up everything in order to find the pearl of great value (Matthew 13:46); and also of the biblical warning that those who come to God "must believe that he exists and that he rewards those who earnestly seek him" (Hebrews 11:6). Polanyi's concept of circularity is a biblical one. Belief is the precondition of knowledge. And in religion as in science, it affirms an *objective* reality – one that is not the product of our minds, but exists apart from us and regardless of our wishes and dreams.

Also applicable to the field of religion are Polanyi's statements on the stability of scientific knowledge. Under modernism it was generally assumed that scientific knowledge was superior to religious knowledge because of the scientists' techniques of verification and falsification, which made their conclusions objectively certain. But Polanyi has shown (as have Kuhn, Lakatos, and other contemporary philosophers of science) that contrary evidence does not necessarily lead to revisions of scientific theories. Nor is the reproducibility of experiments necessarily a proof of their correctness. Both contrary and corroborating evidence can later turn out to have been erroneous. For Polanyi, as we saw, it is the scientists' belief in "the general nature of things" that determines the use they make of such evidence. If that belief supports the theory in question, it will be able to withstand a great deal of evidence that would appear to negate it. The stability of the neo-Darwinian theory of evolution, which is upheld in spite of the scarcity of supporting evidence, served Polanyi as an example.[20] The same kind of procedure, he implies, is followed in the case of religion. "A fiduciary philosophy," he states, "does not eliminate doubt, but (like Christianity) says that we should hold on to what we truly believe, ... trusting the unfathomable intimations that call upon us to do so."[21]

Still other elements in Polanyi's epistemology that have a bearing on religion are his accounts of the acquisition of skills and of the human need to live and work together in community. As to the former, Polanyi shows that many of the skills the scientist possesses are unspecifiable and can therefore be taught only by example; and learning by example, he reminds us, implies submission to authority. It is by watching and imitating the master that the apprentice learns the rules of his trade, including those of which the master himself is not consciously aware. Such hidden rules can be learned only by someone "who surrenders himself to that extent uncritically to the imitation of another."[22] In his essay on Polanyi's relevance for biblical hermeneutics, Christian commentator Royce Gordon Gruenler applies this insight to religious knowledge, stating that what Jesus teaches his followers cannot simply be learned by precept, but demands "the practice of the art of discipleship."[23] It is only by trusting Jesus as our master, by imitating his faith, and by following him, that we can know the truth. And it is only by attending to his art – "the unspecifiable art of servanthood on behalf of the sinner, the poor, the sick, the oppressed, the widow, and the orphan and of his willingness to die for the lost"[24] – that our life as believers bears fruit.

The necessity of instruction implies the importance of what Polanyi calls "conviviality," that is, of membership in a society of people who share the same traditions and beliefs. Such a community provides not only for the transmission of knowledge and skills, it also protects the commonly held values and supports their cultivation.[25] As social beings who cannot survive in isolation, individuals need that protection and support. Translating this insight again into religious terms, it means that the life of faith requires membership and active involvement in the church as community of believers.

It also means, Gruenler writes, that advanced theological training must be entrusted not to the secular university but to the church. "The fellowship that underlies genuine biblical interpretation ... must include at its center the worshiping body of believers who are faithful to the patterns of tradition." And the interpreter needs to realize "that the secular university does not provide an objective perspective on the biblical data, although it claims to be neutrally objectivist. That has been the mistake of post-Enlightenment criticism, and it has culminated in the present crisis in biblical studies. It is Polanyi's point," Gruenler adds, "that no opinions, no matter how scientific and objective they are claimed to be, are outside a believing community. The secular university is no exception."[26]

The problem of "cultural conditioning"

But what about the objection that we hold our convictions simply because of our culture and upbringing in a specific community, and that therefore they are altogether relative? This objection is often raised. Rousseau already opposed the transmission of knowledge, insisting that children should be allowed to find the truth for themselves. Other moderns, including Nietzsche, have similarly complained that nurture and education fill our minds with social and cultural prejudices and so deprive us of our intellectual autonomy. Many of today's educators agree with the opinion that children should be taught as little as possible and be told, instead, to find truth – including religious truth – on their own.

Polanyi's answer to these objections goes directly against the grain of a relativistic and individualistic culture. Rejecting the ideas of Rousseau, Nietzsche, and their followers as nonsensical, he reminds us that we are links in a succession of generations and heirs to the insights of our predecessors, which must be transmitted to us if we are to accomplish anything at all. An acquaintance with our culture and its traditions is indispensable for our social and intellectual development. Should we be left with empty, untutored minds, he says, we would be no more than imbeciles.[27]

This serves as yet another reminder that membership in a community is essential in the search for knowledge. We cannot start our explorations as disembodied, non-historical, non-contextual beings. The only starting point we have is the one given us in the community, civilization, and historical epoch in which we find ourselves. That is where we take up our task, realizing that we are unavoidably part of our culture and our upbringing. As Polanyi writes in another connection, "Tacit assent and intellectual passions, the sharing of an idiom and of a cultural heritage, affiliation to a like-minded community: such are the impulses which shape our vision of the nature of things on which we rely for our mastery of things. No intelligence, however critical or original, can operate outside such a fiduciary framework."[28] And what applies to secular knowledge, we may add, applies to the knowledge of faith. Here, too, a tutoring in the truth of the Scriptures and in the traditions of the church, and membership in the communion of believers, are essential means given us to come to faith and to have it preserved and strengthened.

By stressing the need for the transmission of knowledge Polanyi does not mean that we undergo traditional truths in a passive manner. Although they come to us from the past, we ourselves seek them out and interpret them and we do so within the context of our present needs and problems.[29] That is, we personally work with these truths and so make them our own. The undeniable fact – indeed the indispensability – of our cultural rootedness does not deprive us of our personal responsibility. No matter what culturalists and historicists may teach, individuals, Polanyi says, have "some measure of direct access to the standards of truth and rightness."[30] This means that they are capable of making responsible choices and of testing their cultural heritage.

The fact remains that the criteria by which we test the rationality of our culture and the validity of its assumptions are dependent on that same culture, so that a truly objective view of things is denied us. Toward the end of his discussion on commitment Polanyi returns to the question how, under these circumstances, we can arrive at responsible judgments, that is, judgments we hold with universal intent. He replies that from the point of view of the traditional theory of knowledge our cultural rootedness "would reduce all our convictions to the mere products of a particular location and interest" and therefore constitute a most serious drawback. Polanyi rejects that conclusion. "Believing as I do in the justification of deliberate intellectual commitments," he states, "I accept these accidents of personal existence as the concrete opportunities for exercising our personal responsibility. *This acceptance is the sense of my calling.*"[31]

That these "accidents of personal existence" confer opportunities could be illustrated with reference to the history of science. Many an important scientific theory had to await a particular time and culture before it could be conceived and accepted. But to state these advantages is not to deny that our being located in a particular culture also imposes limits, in that it prevents us from a truly objective view of reality. Polanyi acknowledges these limits and sees them as imposed by human finitude. We have no choice but to accept them, since it is impossible to hold ourselves responsible beyond them. To ask how we would think had we been raised outside any particular society is as meaningless as to ask how we would think if we had been born in no particular body, and therefore without particular sensory and nervous organs. "I believe, therefore," he concludes, "that as I am called upon to live and die in this body, struggling to satisfy its desires, recording my impressions by aid of such sense organs as it is equipped with, and acting through the puny machinery of my brain, my nerves and my muscles, so I am called upon also to acquire the instruments of intelligence from my early surroundings and to use these particular instruments to fulfil the universal obligations to which I am subject."[32]

Polanyi does not say – at least not in so many words – that it is God who called us, placed us in a particular culture, and assigned to us the task we are to fulfil within that culture. But whether or not that admission is implied in his message, Christian believers can and should take to heart his answer to the argument of "cultural conditioning." For at least since the Enlightenment that argument has been used to relativize religious truth, together with all other truths that cannot pass the grid of the sciences. Polanyi has reminded us that the argument's strength derives from our society's denial of human dependence and its mistaken belief in the so-called objective method of science as the infallible means to lead us into all truth. The difference between his epistemology and that of Cartesian modernism is profound. Polanyi presupposes human finitude and human dependence, whereas Descartes bases his theory on the belief that, given the proper method, man can look at reality with the eyes of God. Such pride, Polanyi's works show, cannot but be followed by its fall.

NOTES

[1.] Polanyi, *Personal Knowledge*, p. 18.

[2.] Gelwick, *The Way of Discovery*, p. 147.

[3.] Polanyi, *The Tacit Dimension*, pp. 35f. Polanyi's argument is more subtle than the brief summaries in this paragraph and the next one suggest (see the entire chapter he devotes to the subject, *op.cit.*, pp. 29-52).

[4.] *Ibid.*, pp. 36f.

[5.] *Ibid.*, p. 38.

[6.] *Ibid.*, p. 46.

[7.] On this point see Jeffrey Kane, *Beyond Empiricism: Michael Polanyi Reconsidered* (New York: Peter Lang, 1984), pp. 133-39, 214-16.

[8.] See Al Wolters, "Bavinck on Faith and Science," and Roy A. Clouser, "A Sketch of Dooyeweerd's Philosophy of Science," in *Facets of Faith and Science*, II, ed. van der Meer, pp. 33-55 and 81-97 respectively; as well as Roy A. Clouser, *The Myth of Religious Neutrality: An Essay on the Hidden Role of Religious Belief in Theories* (Notre Dame: University of Notre Dame Press, 1991).

[9.] Gabriel Marcel, *Creative Fidelity*, trans. Robert Rosthal (New York: Farrar, Straus, 1964), pp. 32f., 40, 129-36, 167-71, and *passim*. For a more detailed survey of the bearing of Marcel's philosophy on biblical hermeneutics than I have been able to give, see Royce Gordon Gruenler, *Meaning and Understanding: The Philosophical Framework for Biblical Interpretation* (Grand Rapids: Zondervan, 1991), pp. 111-26.

[10.] Polanyi, *Personal Knowledge*, p. 281.

[11] For several examples, see Gelwick, *The Way of Discovery*, ch. 5; Polanyi, *Science, Faith and Society*, pp. 12f.

[12.] Chaim Perelman, "Polanyi's Interpretation of Scientific Inquiry" in *Intellect and Hope: Essays in the Thought of Michael Polanyi*, eds. Thomas A. Langford and William H. Poteat (Durham, N.C.: Duke University Press, 1968), pp. 232-41.

[13] For Lakatos' criticisms of Polanyi (whom he quite consistently associates with Thomas Kuhn), see Imre Lakatos and Alan Musgrave, ed., *Criticism and the Growth of Knowledge*, pp. 92n2, 115, 163n2, 178.

[14.] *Ibid.*, p. 92.

[15.] A description of this methodology appears in Imre Lakatos, *The Methodology of Scientific Research Programmes,* ed. John Worrall and Gregory Currie (Cambridge: Cambridge University Press, 1978); see especially the Introduction and chapter 1. See also Imre Lakatos, *Mathematics, Science and Epistemology,* ed. John Worrall and Gregory Currie (Cambridge: Cambridge University Press, 1978) and, for commentaries on and critiques of Lakatos' system, R. S. Cohen, P. K. Feyerabend, and M. W. Wartosfky, eds., *Essays in Memory of Imre Lakatos* (Dordrecht-Holland/Boston-U.S.A.: D. Reidel Publishing Company, 1976).

[16.] Lakatos, *Methodology,* pp. 5f.

[17.] For the subjective elements in the acceptance of Copernicanism and Darwinism see, respectively, chapters 5 and 11 above. For the Einstein episode see Polanyi, *Personal Knowledge,* pp. 9-15.

[18.] T. Kennedy, quoted by Andy F. Sanders, *Michael Polanyi's Post-Critical Epistemology: A Reconstruction of Some Aspects of 'Tacit Knowing'* (Amsterdam: Rodopi, 1988), p. 242n.

[19.] Polanyi, *Personal Knowledge,* pp. 282, 283n1.

[20.] Above, p. 302.

[21.] Polanyi, *Personal Knowledge,* p. 318.

[22] *Ibid.*, p. 53.

[23.] Gruenler, *Meaning and Understanding,* p. 179.

[24.] *Ibid.*, p. 180.

[25.] Polanyi, *Personal Knowledge*, p. 203.

[26.] Gruenler, *Meaning and Understanding.,* pp.188f.

[27.] Polanyi, *Personal Knowledge,* p. 295.

[28.] *Ibid.*, p. 266.

[29.] *Ibid.*, p. 160.

[30.] Polanyi, *The Study of Man,* p. 89.

[31] Polanyi, *Personal Knowledge,* p. 322. (Italics in the original.)

[32.] *Ibid.*, p. 323.

XXIII. Epilogue

In the foregoing chapters we have traced the decline of the Christian faith in western society, together with that society's transition from belief in a well-nigh infallible human reason to the postmodern attitude of skepticism and irrationalism.

Our concern was with the role that ideas have played in these developments, especially ideas derived from religion, philosophy, and science. Because the central question has always been and continues to be the question of truth, we gave, in describing these ideas, a good deal of attention to theories of knowledge, focusing on the modern one. Looking at the origin and nature of the modern epistemology, we saw that it contributed to the success of western science, but also that it placed a stranglehold on religious faith and had a destructive effect on anthropology, ethics, politics, and social relationships as well. While the connection between rationalism and the secularization of society was noticeable throughout the modern period, rationalism's negative effects on the belief in truth in general would not become fully evident until the late twentieth century. The growing realization of the destructiveness and illusory nature of the rationalist belief system was a major cause of postmodernism's rejection of modernism and all it stood for.

The purpose of our inquiry was first of all to serve as a reminder that theories of knowledge exist, that they have social, political, and philosophical implications and that they are not neutral in a religious sense. Christians have always been aware of the need to test the prevailing worldview and so to evaluate the "spirits" of their age and culture, but they have frequently failed to pay attention to the answer that these worldviews give to questions about human knowing. All too often theories of knowledge were considered to be self-evidently true and religiously and ideologically neutral, so that in their case the mandate of testing the spirits did not apply. In this book we noted the consequences of this neglect especially in the case of the modern epistemology. Although there have been thinkers who showed the imperialism of that theory to be unfounded, their message was generally ignored, which meant that rationalism and scientism could continue their work.

A second aim was to warn against the skepticism and irrationalism which characterize the postmodern reaction to modern rationalism. That reaction, we saw, is in part a result of the western tendency to move from one extreme to its opposite, an attitude which expresses itself in the conviction that if we can't have fully objective knowledge, we deny the possibility of achieving any knowledge at all. Such a conclusion, widespread as its acceptance may be, goes flatly against human experience and is nonsensical. It is also dehumanizing, for men and women were created as rational beings with a hunger for knowledge and with both the mandate and the ability to pursue and find it. Not in the last place, it furthers the nihilistic aims of the Nietzschean school, which seeks the annihilation of the West's religious and intellectual heritages, both of which are built on the conviction that truth exists and can be found.

The solution to the problems left by modern scientism lies therefore not in denying the possibility of achieving true and reliable knowledge, a belief the West inherited from both Greece and Christianity. Our society's need is for a theory of knowledge that avoids the pitfalls of the modern one but retains its positive aspects. Contributions to such a theory have indeed been made. Important in this connection, we noted, is the work of the church father and philosopher Augustine and of the nineteenth-century theologian Abraham Kuyper, as well as that of twentieth-century thinkers like Herman Dooyeweerd, Martin Buber, Gabriel Marcel, Michael Polanyi, and several of their contemporaries.

Toward a new epistemology

The work of these thinkers deserves our attention. Whether their contributions, or any number of them, will coalesce into a theory of knowledge that one day will replace the modern one is too early to tell. It is undeniable, however, that a replacement theory capable of avoiding the pitfalls of both modern scientism and postmodern skepticism must incorporate several of the conclusions drawn by these people.

If such a theory should indeed come about, in what specific areas will it differ from its predecessor? And what will be some of its consequences?

For one thing, the new theory will leave no room for modernism's counsel of radical epistemic individualism. Descartes and his school envisioned the scholar as a solitary, autonomous thinker, who in the pursuit of knowledge cuts himself off from his community, its traditions, its belief systems, and its history. In the Cartesian scheme, in order to achieve indubitable knowledge the individual is expected consciously to ignore the ideas of his community and his predecessors and to rely exclusively on his own powers of logical thought. By following this advice and rejecting the aid of authority and tradition, he indeed, as Roger Lundin puts it, orphans himself.[1]

Descartes' critics have shown that the individualistic ideal is destructive of both society and true learning. It is socially destructive because it contributes to the atomization of society and, by declaring all authority and all tradition suspect, makes it impossible to reach a moral consensus. If the individual is the measure of all things, then a universal moral code is illusory. The demand for autonomy inhibits true learning because human beings are part of their history and build, if they are building at all, on the achievements of their predecessors. History and tradition, the critics in question have shown, are not obstacles to but sources of knowledge, and to ignore them by doubting them away is to impoverish oneself and one's society. It means that one fails to learn both from the positive insights of previous generations and from their mistakes and so is forced, in Santayana's well-known words, to repeat history.

And what applies to the historical community applies to community in general. Michael Polanyi, as we saw in the preceding chapter, shows the irrationality of expecting to find wisdom by ignoring the lessons of one's community and its history. The philosopher Alasdair MacIntyre brings the same message, reminding us of the Aristotelian teaching "that one cannot think for oneself if one thinks entirely by oneself, that it is only by participation in rational practice-based community that one becomes rational...."[2] And in stressing the importance of community and tradition Polanyi's and MacIntyre's are not solitary voices. The rejection of the individualistic ideal is common among postmodern thinkers.[3]

We may expect the new epistemology, then, to recognize history, tradition, and community as indispensable sources of knowledge. As proponents of the new view of knowledge have pointed out, paying heed to the wisdom of former generations and working as a member of a community does not have to mean, as the Cartesians feared it would, that one becomes the prisoner of his tradition and of the opinions of his fellow men. The teachings of radical culturalists and perspectivists notwithstanding, the individual has, as history and everyday experience make clear, "some measure of direct access to the standards of truth and rightness."[4]

This brings us to the matter of cultural conditioning to which, as we noted in the previous chapter, Polanyi has given a good deal of attention. Here again Alasdair MacIntyre's work complements that of Polanyi. Admitting that our reasoning is influenced by our community's history and traditions so that an impartial evaluation of our own and other traditions is difficult, MacIntyre nevertheless refuses to accept the widespread idea that we might as well, in relativistic fashion, assign equal value to all traditions. Establishing a methodology that has some similarity with that of Imre Lakatos, he shows that traditions can be "vindicated by the way in which they transcend the limitations of and provide remedies for the defects of their predecessors within the history of that same tradition."[5] The validity of the claims of rival traditions can be established in a similar manner.[6] In short, we are able to distinguish among standards and we can both evaluate and transcend traditional and cultural ones.

Another characteristic of the new theory of knowledge will be the rejection of the impersonality and detachment of the Cartesian approach and of the sharp dualism it established between the knower and the known. Like their Greek mentors, Cartesians saw the world as a theatre and the scientist as not an actor within but an observer of a nature that was altogether separate from the world of men. That view led to what Abraham Kuyper called the "estrangement from the object of our knowledge," an attitude which he saw as the greatest obstacle in our way of knowing that which we study.[7] It resulted in seeing the object of scientific study – nature, and also the human being – as a thing, something that could be used, exploited, and manipulated.

Rejecting such radical detachment and dualism, postmodern thinkers speak of personal knowledge and stress the need of engagement and relationality, of concern for the other, both in the world of humanity and in that of nature. The same need for personal engagement, we may add, is being recognized in the field of literary interpretation. With respect to biblical hermeneutics, for example, it has been said that to understand the biblical language is to enter sympathetically into the biblical world, and also that in order to enter that world it is important to take up its practices.[8] Understanding, like faith, demands personal commitment.

Yet another difference with its modern counterpart will be the new theory's relinquishment of the modern ideal of absolute certainty in human knowing. This means that it will reject classical or Cartesian foundationalism – the belief that knowledge claims can be fully justified with reference to underlying beliefs which are either self-evident or evident to the senses. Examples of such foundational beliefs are Descartes' first principles, the so-called "clear and distinct ideas." Constituting the basis of his deductive reasoning, these principles guaranteed that this reasoning (always assuming that a careful logical approach was followed) would reveal indubitable truth. Not all modern foundationalists followed the Cartesian approach to the letter, yet all of them, rationalists as well as empiricists, stuck to the belief that knowledge claims can be grounded in such a manner that they can be shown to be true beyond all doubt.

The foundationalist theory was plausible, as Nancey Murphy has suggested, because it was based on the metaphor of knowledge as a building.[9] Just as an actual building requires a solid, unshakable foundation, so it was with knowledge: at the basis of scientific and all other reasoning were to be truths that no skeptic could deconstruct. If no such foundation could be found, the one who proposed the knowledge claim was "on shaky grounds" and his claim had to be dismissed. The theory's original appeal, we saw in chapter 7 of this book, can in large part be explained with reference to the age wherein it arose. A time of Pyrrhonic skepticism and of great political, social, and economic instability, the seventeenth century felt a desperate need for epistemic certainty, and Cartesian foundationalism promised to fulfill that need. It did so, for many, even in the field of religion, witness the flourishing of natural theology, which sought to establish religious certainty by means of theistic arguments that were based on reason or observation or both.

Foundationalism collapsed when in the twentieth century it became increasingly evident that the subjective element intrudes in the act of observation, and that first principles such as those of Descartes are neither eternal nor universal but depend on time and place. The demise of Cartesian foundationalism has contributed to the mood of postmodern skepticism; to the belief that if we cannot have absolutely certain knowledge, we may as well abandon the search for truth. Not all of today's thinkers, however, confuse nonfoundationalism with the idea that knowledge claims are necessarily groundless, so that a collapse into all-out relativism is indeed the only logical response. Alvin Plantinga has shown the falsity of such a conclusion with reference to the Christian faith, which he shows is all but groundless.[10] Scientific certainties, he and others make clear, are not the only certainties. There are also moral and experiential ones; there is, as Martin Buber and Gabriel Marcel reminded us, the certainty of interpersonal knowledge; and there is the certainty of religious faith.

The bankruptcy of foundationalism does mean, however, that the Faustian ideal of indubitable and limitless knowledge – in science and in other fields – must be given up. Being a creature, man cannot know as God knows. We may expect the replacement theory to reflect that insight. We may also expect the new theory to replace foundationalism by holism, an approach wherein one does not distinguish between basic and non-basic beliefs but, in evaluating knowledge claims, gives attention to the degree of their consistency with the paradigm or belief system as a whole.

What difference will it make?

By acknowledging the limitations of human reason, the new epistemology should have consequences additional to those suggested in the previous section. It should, for example, act as a counter to today's debilitating intellectual skepticism, at least in so far as that resulted from the exorbitant claims made on behalf of science and its methodology. If Michael Polanyi is right, it should also contribute to the growing realization that perfection is not achievable here below, and so put an end to the disastrous efforts of the last few centuries to establish a heavenly city on earth by force and coercion. It may even lead to the conclusion that, in view of human fallibility and of man's proven inability to control the works of his hands, checks must be placed on the unrestrained development of technology.

Not in the last place, the new epistemology will demolish the claim that science can pronounce on the validity of religious faith. Showing the objective and foundationalist ideals to be illusory, it will remove the stumbling block which for centuries scientism and rationalism have placed on the way of faith. Because of the stress on the role of belief in human knowing and the implied acknowledgement of human dependence, the new approach to knowledge will, moreover, make room for the confession that God is the source of all knowledge and truth, and that in Christ all things hold together (Colossians 1:17). This means that it can serve as basis for a truly biblical view of knowledge.

If they want to understand their age and test its spirits, Christians are well advised to give heed to the work that is being done today in the field of epistemology.

NOTES
[1] Roger Lundin, "Interpreting Orphans: Hermeneutics in the Cartesian Tradition," in Roger Lundin, Clarence Walhout, Anthony C. Thiselton, *The Promise of Hermeneutics* (Grand Rapids/Carlisle U.K.: Eerdmans/Paternoster Press, 1999), pp. 1-64.

[2] Alasdair MacIntyre, *Whose Justice? Which Rationality?* (Notre Dame: University of Notre Dame Press, 1988), p. 396.

[3] For examples, see Nancey Murphy, *Theology in the Age of Scientific Reasoning* (Ithaca and London: Cornell University Press, 1996 [1990]), p. 201-04; as well as Nancey Murphy, Brad J. Kallenberg, and Mark Thiessen Nation, eds., *Virtues and Practices in the Christian Tradition: Christian Ethics after MacIntyre* (Harrisburg, Pennsylvania: Trinity Press International, 1997).

[4] Polanyi, *The Study of Man*, p. 89.

[5] MacIntyre, *Whose Justice?*, p. 7. The evaluation of tradition is a constant theme in this book. See on this topic also the same author's *After Virtue: A Study in Moral Theory*, 2nd ed. (Notre Dame, Indiana: University of Notre Dame Press, 1984), pp. 268, 270, and *passim*, and his *Three Rival Versions of Moral Enquiry: Encyclopaedia, Genealogy, and Tradition* (Notre Dame: University of Notre Dame Press, 1990), pp. 5, 145f.

[6] MacIntyre, *Whose Justice?*, pp. 401-3 and *passim*.

[7] Above, p. 284.

[8] Murphy, *Anglo-American Postmodernity*, pp. 148f. See also Polanyi's statement, quoted in the previous chapter, that "Only a Christian who stands in the service of his faith can understand Christian theology and only he can enter into the religious meaning of the Bible." (*Personal Knowledge*, p. 281.)

[9] Murphy, *Anglo-American Postmodernity*, pp. 9f.; see also pp. 26f.

[10] Alvin Plantinga, "Reason and Belief in God," in *Faith and Rationality*, eds. Plantinga and Wolterstorff, pp. 72-81.

Chronology

Dates from the ancient world and the Middle Ages are often only approximate, as are dates assigned to historical periods.

B. C.

8th century	Homer
7th century	Hesiod
600	Thales of Miletus
600	Beginnings of Pre-Socratic philosophy
525	Pythagoras
512-479	Persian Invasions
500	Heraclitus, Parmenides
500-400	Greek tragedians: Aeschylus, Sophocles, Euripides
500-428	Anaxagoras
484-424	Herodotus, the "father of history"
480-410	Protagoras
469-399	Socrates
460-370	Democritus
460-400	Thucydides, historian of the Pelopponesian Wars
450-400	The Sophist movement
431-404	Peloponnesian Wars (between Athens and Sparta)
428-347	Plato
384-322	Aristotle
360-270	Pyrrho of Elis, founder of Pyrrhonic school of skepticism
341-271	Epicurus, founder of school of Epicureanism

336-264   Zeno, founder of school of Stoicism
334-323   Conquests of Alexander the Great
323   Death of Alexander; beginning of Hellenistic Age
300   Euclid systematizes Greek geometry
270   Aristarchus of Samos proposes heliocentric theory
94-55   Lucretius, Epicurean, writer of *De Rerum Natura*
31   End of Roman Republic; establishment of Roman Empire
6-4   Birth of Christ

A. D.
50-52   Paul at Athens
100-165   Justin Martyr
150   Ptolemy's *Almagest*
160-220   Tertullian
200   Sextus Empiricus, historian of Pyrrhonism
1st-3rd cent. Compilation of Hermetic Corpus
3rd century Emergence of Neoplatonism
205-270   Plotinus, best-known representative of Neoplatonism
313   Edict of Milan: toleration of Christianity
330   Constantine the Great moves imperial capital from Rome
             to Constantinople
340-420   Jerome
354-430   Augustine
410   Visigoths sack Rome
426   Augustine's *City of God*
476   Fall of the Western Roman Empire
476   Beginning of the Middle Ages
480-524   Boethius
622   Beginning of Mohammedanism
711-718   Moorish conquest of Spain
800-1000   New waves of invasions: Muslim, Norsemen, Magyars
910   Beginning of Cluniac Reform
1000-1300   The High Middle Ages
1033-1109   Anselm
1079-1142   Abelard
1126-1198   Averroes
1135-1204   Maimonides
1150   Beginning of recovery of Aristotle's work
1175-1253   Robert Grosseteste
1200-1280   Albert the Great (Albertus Magnus)

1209	Establishment of Franciscan Order
1214-1292	Roger Bacon
1216	Establishment of Dominican Order
1225-1274	Thomas Aquainas
1264-1308	John Duns Scotus
1265-1321	Dante Alighieri
1277	Bishop Etienne Tempier's condemnation of Aristotelian theses
1285-1349	William of Ockham
14th century	Late-medieval science (North-Western Europe)
1300-1450	The Late Middle Ages (North-Western Europe)
1300-1530	Italian Renaissance
1309-1377	Babylonian Captivity of the Church
1323	Canonization of Thomas Aquinas
1329-1384	John Wycliffe
1337-1453	Hundred Years' War between England and France
1347-1351	Black Death comes to Europe for the first time
1372-1415	John Huss
1378-1417	Great Western Schism
1379-1471	Thomas a Kempis
1415	John Huss burned at the stake
1419-1489	John Wessel Gansfort
1450-1600	Northern Renaissance
1450	Invention of printing with movable type
1453	Constantinople falls to the Turks
1453	End of Eastern (Byzantine) Roman Empire
1455	Gutenberg Bible
1466-1536	Desiderius Erasmus
1483-1546	Martin Luther
1492	Christopher Columbus discovers America
1509-1564	John Calvin
1517	Luther posts his 95 theses; beginning of Protestant Reformation
1521	Luther excommunicated
1536	First edition of Calvin's *Institutes of the Christian Religion*
1543	Andreas Vesalius' book on human anatomy appears (*On the Structure of the Human Body*)
1543	Nicolaus Copernicus publishes *On the Revolutions of the Heavenly Spheres*
1561-1626	Francis Bacon

1572	Tycho Brahe discovers a supernova
1596-1650	René Descartes
1600	Giordano Bruno burned at the stake
1604	Christopher Marlowe's *The Tragicall History of Dr. Faustus*
1609	Johannes Kepler's first two laws of planetary motion (the third one follows in 1619)
1609	Galileo uses the telescope for the first time
1618-1648	Thirty Years' War
1620	Francis Bacon's *Novum Organum*
1623-1662	Blaise Pascal
1627-1691	Robert Boyle
1632-1704	John Locke
1637	Descartes' *Discourse on Method*
1638-1715	Louis XIV
1642-1648	England's civil war
1646-1716	Gottfried Wilhelm Leibniz
1651	Thomas Hobbes' *Leviathan*
1667-1745	Jonathan Swift
1668-1744	Giambattista Vico
1674	Anthony van Leeuwenhoek discovers microscopic organisms
1687	Sir Isaac Newton's *Principia*
1688	England's Glorious Revolution
1690	Locke's *Essay on Human Understanding* and *Two Treatises of Government*
1694-1778	Voltaire (François-Marie Arouet)
1695	Locke's *Reasonableness of Christianity*
1703-1758	Jonathan Edwards
1709-1784	Dr. Samuel Johnson
1711-1776	David Hume
1712-1778	Jean-Jacques Rousseau
1724-1804	Immanuel Kant
1734	Alexander Pope's *Essay on Man*
1744-1829	The Chevalier de Lamarck
1751	French *Encyclopédie* begins publication
1755	Lisbon Earthquake
1756-1763	Seven Years' War
1756	Voltaire's *Essay on the Manners and Customs of Nations*
1762	Rousseau's *Social Contract*

1762	Rousseau's *Emile, or On Education*
1770-1831	Georg Wilhelm Friedrich Hegel
1776	American Declaration of Independence
1776	Adam Smith's *On the Wealth of Nations*
1776-1788	Edward Gibbon's *Decline and Fall of the Roman Empire*
1778	Death of Voltaire and Rousseau
1779	Hume's *Dialogues Concerning Natural Religion*
1781-1788	Kant's *Critique of Pure Reason, Foundations for the Metaphysics of Morals, Critique of Practical Reason*
1788-1860	Arthur Schopenhauer
1789	Outbreak of the French Revolution
1790	Edmund Burke's *Reflections on the Revolution in France*
1793	Kant's *Religion Within the Limits of Reason Alone*
1795	The Marquis de Condorcet's *Outlines of an Historical View of the Progress of the Human Mind*
1798	Thomas R. Malthus' *Essay on the Principle of Population*
1799-1815	Napoleon I rules France
1799	Friedrich Daniel Ernst Schleiermacher's *On Religion: Speeches to Its Cultured Despisers*
1803	John Dalton proposes atomic theory of matter
1813-1855	Søren Kierkegaard
1818-1883	Karl Marx
1820-1903	Herbert Spencer
1830-1842	Auguste Comte's *Cours de Philosophie Positive*
1833	Charles Lyell's *Principles of Geology*
1835-1836	David Friedrich Strauss's *Life of Jesus*
1837-1920	Abraham Kuyper
1841	Ludwig Feuerbach's *Essence of Christianity*
1843	Kierkegaard's *Fear and Trembling*
1844-1900	Friedrich Nietzsche
1844-1918	Julius Wellhausen
1848	Karl Marx and Friedrich Engels publish the *Communist Manifesto*
1849-1851	Second Law of Thermodynamics
1854	Georg Bernard Riemann begins work on non-Euclidean geometry
1856-1939	Sigmund Freud
1859	Charles Darwin's *On the Origin of Species*
1871	Darwin's *Descent of Man*
1871	Unification of Germany

1875-1961	Carl Gustav Jung
1878-1965	Martin Buber
1880-1910	*Fin de siècle*
1886-1968	Karl Barth
1889-1976	Martin Heidegger
1889-1973	Gabriel Marcel
1891-1976	Michael Polanyi
1893-1947	Karl Mannheim
1894-1977	Herman Dooyeweerd
1894	Kuyper's *Encyclopaedie der Heilige Godgeleerdheid* (English translation, *Principles of Sacred Theology*, 1898)
1900	Freud's *The Interpretation of Dreams*
1900	Beginning of quantum theory (Max Planck)
1904-1905	Russo-Japanese War
1905	Albert Einstein's special theory of relativity
1905-1980	Jean-Paul Sartre
1914-1918	First World War
1915	Einstein's general theory of relativity; experimentally confirmed in 1919
1917	Outbreak of Russian Revolution
1918	Oswald Spengler's *Decline of the West*
1920	William Butler Yeats's "The Second Coming"
1921	Ludwig Wittgenstein's *Tractatus Logico-Philosophicus*
1923	Buber's *I and Thou*
1925	Alfred North Whitehead's *Science and the Modern World*
1927	Martin Heidegger's *Sein und Zeit*
1927	Werner Heisenberg's principle of uncertainty
1928	Niels Bohr's principle of complementarity
1929	Vienna Circle issues its manifesto
1931	Gödel's incompleteness theorem
1933	Adolf Hitler gains control of Germany
1938	Discovery of nuclear fission
1938	Sartre's *Nausea*
1939-1945	Second World War
1940	Marcell's *Creative Fidelity*
1943	Sartre's *Being and Nothingness*
1945	Dropping of atomic bomb on Hiroshima and Nagasaki
1946-1989	Cold War
1958	Michael Polanyi's *Personal Knowledge*
1962	Thomas S. Kuhn's *The Structure of Scientific Revolutions*

Bibliography

This list contains a selection of sources used.

Allen, Diogenes. *Christian Belief in a Postmodern World: The Full Wealth of Conviction*. Louisville, Kentucky: Westminster/John Knox Press, 1989.

Bahnsen, Greg L. *Van Til's Apologetic: Readings and Analysis*. Phillipsburg, New Jersey: Presbyterian and Reformed, 1998.

Barbour, Ian G. *Issues in Science and Religion*. New York: Harper and Row, Harper Torchbooks, 1971; 1966.

_____. *Religion and Science: Historical and Contemporary Issues*. New York: HarperCollins, HarperSanFrancisco, 1997.

Barnett, Lincoln. *The Universe and Dr. Einstein*. New York: Bantam Books, 1968; William Morrow, 1948.

Barrett, William. *Irrational Man: A Study in Existential Philosophy*. Garden City, New York: Doubleday, Anchor Books, 1962; 1958.

Baumer, Franklin L. *Modern European Thought: Continuity and Change in Ideas, 1600-1950*. New York: Macmillan, 1977.

_____. *Religion and the Rise of Scepticism*. New York: Harcourt, Brace, 1960.

Bavinck, H. *Christelijke Wereldbeschouwing*. 3rd ed. Kampen: Kok, 1929; 1904.

Berger, Peter L., *et al*. *The Homeless Mind: Modernization and Consciousness*. New York: Random House, 1973.

Berger, Peter L., and Thomas Luckmann. *The Social Construction of*

Reality: A Treatise in the Sociology of Knowledge. Garden City, New York: Doubleday, Anchor Books, 1967.

Berlin, Isaiah. *Vico and Herder: Two Studies in the History of Ideas.* New York: Viking Press, 1976.

Boas, Marie. *The Scientific Renaissance 1450-1630.* New York: Harper and Row, Harper Torchbooks, The Science Library, 1962.

Brinton, Crane. *Nietzsche.* Cambridge, Mass.: Harvard University Press, 1948; 1941.

Brooke, John Hedley. *Science and Religion: Some Historical Perspectives.* Cambridge: Cambridge University Press, 1991.

Brown, Colin. *Miracles and the Critical Mind.* Grand Rapids: Eerdmans, 1984.

_____. *That You May Believe: Miracles and Faith Then and Now.* Grand Rapids: Eerdmans, 1985.

Cline, Barbara Lovett. *Men Who Made a New Physics: Physicists and the Quantum Theory.* New York: New American Library, Signet Science Library Books, 1965.

Clouser, Roy A. *The Myth of Religious Neutrality: An Essay on the Hidden Role of Religious Belief in Theories.* Notre Dame: University of Notre Dame Press, 1991.

Cochrane, Charles Norris. *Christianity and Classical Culture: A Study of Thought and Action from Augustus to Augustine.* New York: Oxford University Press, A Galaxy Book, 1964; 1940.

Cohen, R. S., P. K. Feyerabend, and M. W. Wartofsky, eds. *Essays in Memory of Imre Lakatos.* Dordrecht-Holland/Boston-U.S.A.: D. Reidel Publishing Comp., 1976.

Copleston, F. C. *Contemporary Philosophy: Studies of Logical Positivism and Existentialism.* Westminster, Maryland: Newman Press, 1956.

_____. *A History of Medieval Philosophy.* New York: Harper and Row, Torchbook Library, 1972.

_____. *A History of Philosophy,* I. Garden City, New York: Doubleday, Image Books, 1962; Westminster, Maryland: Newman Press, 1946.

_____. *A History of Philosophy,* VI-VIII. Westminster, Maryland: Newman Press, 1960-1966.

Cornford, F. M. *Before and After Socrates.* Cambridge: Cambridge University Press, 1965; 1932.

Coulson, C. A. *Science and Christian Belief.* London: Fontana Books, 1964; Oxford: Oxford University Press, 1955.

Craig, William Lane. *Reasonable Faith: Christian Truth and Apologetics.* Wheaton, Ill.: Crossway, 1994; 1984.

Dobbs, B. J. T. *The Janus Face of Genius: The Role of Alchemy in Newton's Thought.* Cambridge: Cambridge University Press, 1991.

Dooyeweerd, Herman. *Roots of Western Culture: Pagan, Secular, and Christian Options.* Trans. John Kraay, eds. Mark Vander Vennen and Bernard Zylstra. Toronto: Wedge, 1979.

Douma, Jochem. *Algemene Genade: Uiteenzetting, vergelijking en beoordeling van de opvattingen van A. Kuyper, K. Schilder en Joh. Calvijn over 'algemene genade.'* Goes: Oosterbaan & Le Cointre, 1966.

Dray, William H. *Philosophy of History.* Englewood Cliffs, N. J.: Prentice-Hall, 1964.

Eagleton, Terry. *The Illusions of Postmodernism.* Oxford: Blackwell, 1997; 1996.

Evans, C. Stephen. *The Historical Christ and the Jesus of Faith: The Incarnational Narrative as History.* Oxford: Clarendon Press, 1996.

_____. *Subjectivity and Religious Belief: An Historical, Critical Study.* Washington, D. C.: University Press of America, 1982; 1978.

Frank, Philipp. *Einstein: His Life and Times.* Trans. George Rosen, ed. Shuichi Kusaka. New York: Knopf, 1947.

Geehan, E. R., ed. *Jerusalem and Athens: Critical Discussions on the Theology and Apologetics of Cornelius Van Til.* N.p.: Presbyterian and Reformed, 1971.

Gellner, Ernest. *The Psychoanalytic Movement, Or The Coming of Unreason.* London: Paladin Books, 1985.

Gelwick, Richard, *The Way of Discovery: An Introduction to the Thought of Michael Polanyi.* Oxford: Oxford University Press, 1977.

Gilson, Etienne. *Dante and Philosophy.* New York: Harper and Row, Harper Torchbooks, The Academic Library, 1963; Sheed and Ward, 1949.

_____. *Reason and Revelation in the Middle Ages.* New York: Scribner's, Scribner Library Books, 1938.

Gonzalez, Justo L. *A History of Christian Thought,* II. Nashville: Abingdon Press, 1983; 1971.

Grene, Marjorie. *The Knower and the Known.* London: Faber and Faber, 1966.

Gruenler, Royce Gordon. *Meaning and Understanding: The Philosophical Framework for Biblical Interpretation.* Grand Rapids: Zondervan, 1991.

Hahn, Herbert F. *The Old Testament in Modern Research.* Philadelphia: Fortress, 1970; 1954.

Hale, John. *The Civilization of Europe in the Renaissance.* New York: Macmillan, 1993.

Harbison, E. Harris. *The Christian Scholar in the Age of the Reformation.* New York: Scribner's, The Scribner Library, 1956.

Hart, Hendrik, *et al.,* eds. *Rationality in the Calvinian Tradition.* Lanham: University Press of America, 1983.

Hayes, John H. *An Introduction to Old Testament Study.* Nashville: Abingdon, 1980; 1979.

Hill, Christopher. *The World Turned Upside Down: Radical Ideas During the English Revolution.* Harmondsworth: Penguin Books, 1982; 1972.

Himmelfarb, Gertrude. *Darwin and the Darwinian Revolution.* New York: Norton, Norton Library, 1968; 1959.

Hirsch, Jr., E. D. *The Aims of Interpretation.* Chicago: University of Chicago Press, 1976.

Holmes, Arthur F. *Contours of a World View.* Grand Rapids: Eerdmans, 1983.

Holton, Gerald. *Thematic Origins of Scientific Thought: Kepler to Einstein.* Rev. ed. Cambridge and London: Harvard University Press, 1988; 1973.

Hooykaas, R. *Religion and the Rise of Modern Science.* Edinburgh: Scottish Academic Press, 1984; 1972.

Huizinga, J. *The Waning of the Middle Ages.* Trans. F. Hopman. Harmondsworth: Penguin Books, 1965; 1924.

Ihde, Don. *Listening and Voice: A Phenomenology of Sound.* Athens, Ohio: Ohio University Press, 1976.

Ingraffia, Brian D. *Postmodern Theory and Biblical Theology.* Cambridge: Cambridge University Press, 1995.

Janik, Allan, and Stephen Toulmin. *Wittgenstein's Vienna.* New York: Simon and Schuster, 1973.

Johnson, Phillip E. *Darwin on Trial.* Downers Grove, Ill.: InterVarsity, 1993; 1991.

Kaiser, Christopher. *Creation and the History of Science.* London/Grand Rapids: Marshall Pickering/Eerdmans, 1991.

_____. *Creational Theology and the History of Physical Science: The Creationist Tradition from Basil to Bohr.* Leiden/New York/Köln: Brill, 1997.

Karier, Clarence J. *Scientists of the Mind: Intellectual Founders of*

Modern Psychology. Urbana: University of Illinois Press, 1986.

Kline, Morris, *Mathematics: The Loss of Certainty.* New York: Oxford University Press, 1980.

Klooster, Fred H. *Quests for the Historical Jesus.* Grand Rapids: Baker, 1977.

Knowles, David. *The Evolution of Medieval Thought.* London: Longmans, Green, 1963; 1962.

Kolakowski, Leszek. *The Alienation of Reason: A History of Positivist Thought.* Trans. Norbert Guterman. Garden City, New York: Doubleday, Anchor Books, 1969.

Kuhn, Thomas. *The Essential Tension: Selected Studies in Scientific Tradition and Change.* Chicago: University of Chicago Press, 1977.

_____. *The Structure of Scientific Revolutions.* Chicago: University of Chicago Press, 1973; 1962.

Langford, Thomas A., and William H. Poteat, eds. *Intellect and Hope: Essays in the Thought of Michael Polanyi.* Durham, N.C.: Duke University Press, 1968.

Leff, Gordon. *The Dissolution of the Medieval Outlook: An Essay on Intellectual and Spiritual Change in the Fourteenth Century.* New York: New York University Press, 1976.

_____. *Medieval Thought: St. Augustine to Ockham.* Harmondsworth: Penguin Books, 1965; 1958.

Lewis, C. S. *Miracles.* New York: Macmillan, 1947.

Lindberg, David C. *The Beginnings of Western Science: The European Scientific Tradition in Philosophical, Religious, and Institutional Context, 600 B.C. to A.D. 1450.* Chicago and London: University of Chicago Press, 1992.

Lindberg, David C., and Ronald L. Numbers, eds. *God and Nature: Historical Essays on the Encounter between Christianity and Science.* Berkeley: University of California Press, 1986.

Linnemann, Eta. *Historical Criticism of the Bible: Methodology or Ideology? Reflections of a Bultmannian turned Evangelical.* Trans. Robert W. Yarbrough. Grand Rapids: Baker, 1990.

_____. *Is there a Synoptic Problem? Rethinking the Literary Dependence of the First Three Gospels.* Trans. Robert W. Yarbrough. Grand Rapids: Baker, 1992.

Lovejoy, Arthur O. *The Great Chain of Being: A Study of the History of an Idea.* New York: Harper and Row, Harper Torchbooks, The Academy Library, 1960; 1965; Cambridge, Mass.: Harvard University Press, 1936.

Lowrie, Walter. *A Short Life of Kierkegaard.* Princeton: Princeton University Press, 1942.

Lundin, Roger. *The Culture of Interpretation: Christian Faith and the Postmodern World.* Grand Rapids: Eerdmans, 1993.

MacIntyre, Alisdair. *After Virtue: A Study in Moral Theory.* 2nd ed. Notre Dame: University of Notre Dame Press, 1984.

_____. *Three Rival Versions of Moral Enquiry: Encyclopaedia, Genealogy, and Tradition.* Notre Dame: University of Notre Dame Press, 1990.

_____. *Whose Justice? Which Rationality?* Notre Dame: University of Notre Dame Press, 1988.

MacKay, Donald M. *The Clockwork Image: A Christian Perspective on Science.* Downers Grove, Ill.: InterVarsity, 1977; 1974.

Marcel, Gabriel. *Creative Fidelity.* Trans. Robert Rosthal. New York: Farrar, Strauss, 1964.

Mason, Stephen F. *A History of the Sciences.* New York: Macmillan, Collier Books, 1973; 1962.

Meyerhoff, Hans, ed. *The Philosophy of History in Our Time.* Garden City, New York: Doubleday, Anchor Books, 1959.

Murphy, Nancey. *Anglo-American Postmodernity: Philosophical Perspectives on Science, Religion, and Ethics.* Boulder, Colorado: Westview Press, 1997.

_____. *Theology in the Age of Scientific Reasoning.* Ithaca and London: Cornell University Press, Cornell Paperbacks, 1996; 1990.

Nickel, James. *Mathematics: Is God Silent?* Vallecito, Cal.: Ross House Books, 1990.

Noll, Mark A. *The Scandal of the Evangelical Mind.* Grand Rapids/Leicester: Eerdmans-Inter-Varsity Press, 1994.

Oberman, Heiko Augustinus. *The Harvest of Medieval Theology: Gabriel Biel and Late Medieval Nominalism.* Cambridge, Mass.: Harvard University Press, 1963.

Ong, Walter J. *The Presence of the Word: Some Prolegomena for Cultural and Religious History.* Minneapolis: University of Minnesota Press, 1986; 1967.

Osler, Margaret J. *Divine Will and the Mechanical Philosophy: Gassendi and Descartes on Contingency and Necessity in the Created World.* Cambridge: Cambridge University Press, 1994.

Ozment, Steven. *The Age of Reform 1250-1550: An Intellectual and Religious History of Late Medieval and Reformation Europe.* New Haven: Yale University Press, 1980.

Panofsky, Erwin. *Gothic Architecture and Scholasticism.* Cleveland: World, Meridian Books, 1968; 1951.

Pearcey, Nancy R., and Charles B. Thaxton. *The Soul of Science: Christian Faith and Natural Philosophy.* Wheaton, Ill.: Crossway, 1994.

Plantinga, Alvin, and Nicholas Wolterstorff, eds. *Faith and Rationality: Reason and Belief in God.* Notre Dame: University of Notre Dame Press, 1983.

Polanyi, Michael. *The Logic of Liberty: Reflections and Rejoinders.* Chicago: University of Chicago Press, 1980; 1951.

_____. *Personal Knowledge: Toward a Post-Critical Philosophy.* Chicago: University of Chicago Press, 1962; 1958.

_____. *Science, Faith and Society.* Chicago: University of Chicago Press, 1964; 1946.

Purcell, Jr., Edward A. *The Crisis of Democratic Theory: Scientific Naturalism and the Problem of Value.* Lexington: University Press of Kentucky, 1973.

Ratzsch, Del. *Philosophy of Science: The Natural Sciences in Christian Perspective.* Downers Grove, Ill.: InterVarsity, 1986.

Rieff, Philip. *Freud: The Mind of the Moralist.* Chicago: University of Chicago Press, 1979; 1959.

Roberts, David E. *Existentialism and Religious Belief.* Ed. Roger Hazelton. New York: Oxford University Press, Galaxy Books, 1963; 1957.

Robinson, James M. *A New Quest of the Historical Jesus.* London: SCM Press, 1971; 1959.

Russell, Robert John, *et al.*, eds. *Physics, Philosophy, and Theology: A Common Quest for Understanding.* Vatican City State: Vatican Observatory, 1988.

Sanders, Andy F. *Michael Polanyi's Post-Critical Epistemology: A Reconstruction of Some Aspects of "Tacit Knowing."* Amsterdam: Rodopi, 1988.

Schorske, Carl E. *Fin-de-siècle Vienna: Politics and Culture.* New York: Random House, Vintage Books, 1981; 1961.

Schweitzer, Albert. *The Quest of the Historical Jesus: A Critical Study of its Progress from Reimarus to Wrede.* Trans. W. Montgomery. New York: Macmillan, 1950.

Silva, Moisés. *God, Language, and Scripture: Reading the Bible in the Light of General Linguistics.* Grand Rapids: Zondervan, 1990.

Solomon, Robert C. *Continental Philosophy since 1750: The Rise and*

Fall of the Self. Oxford: Oxford University Press, 1988.

Soskice, Janet Martin. *Metaphor and Religious Language.* Oxford: Clarendon Press, 1987; 1985.

Storr, Anthony. *Freud.* Oxford: Oxford University Press, 1990; 1989.

Sulloway, Frank J. *Freud, Biologist of the Mind: Beyond the Psychoanalytic Legend.* New York: Basic Books, 1979.

Taylor, Charles. *Hegel.* Cambridge: Cambridge University Press, 1978; 1975.

Tholfsen, Trygve R. *Historical Thinking: An Introduction.* New York: Harper and Row, 1967.

Tinder, Glenn. "Augustine's World and Ours." *First Things,* No. 78, December 1997.

Toews, John Edward. *Hegelianism: The Path Toward Dialectical Humanism, 1805-41.* Cambridge: Cambridge University Press, 1985; 1980.

Toulmin, Stephen. *Cosmopolis: The Hidden Agenda of Modernity.* Chicago: University of Chicago Press, 1992; 1990.

_____. *The Return to Cosmology: Postmodern Science and the Theology of Nature.* Berkeley: University of California Press, 1982.

Tully, James. *An Approach to Political Philosophy: Locke in Contexts.* Cambridge: Cambridge University Press, 1993.

van der Meer, Jitse M., ed. *Facets of Faith and Science,* 4 vols. Lanham: The Pascal Centre for Advanced Studies in Faith and Science/University Press of America, 1996.

Walhout, Clarence, and Leland Ryken, eds. *Contemporary Literary Theory: A Christian Appraisal.* Grand Rapids: Eerdmans, 1991.

Walsh, W. H. *Philosophy of History: An Introduction.* New York: Harper and Row, Harper Tochbooks, 1967.

Weaver, Richard M. *Ideas Have Consequences.* Chicago: University of Chicago Press, 1948.

Webster, Charles. *From Paracelsus to Newton: Magic and the Making of Modern Science.* Cambridge: Cambridge University Press, 1984; 1982.

Westfall, Richard S. *Science and Religion in Seventeenth-Century England.* New Haven: Yale University Press, 1964; 1958.

Whitehead, Alfred North. *Science and the Modern World.* New York: New American Library, Mentor Books, 1964; 1948; Macmillan, 1925.

Willey, Basil. *The Eighteenth-Century Background.* Harmondsworth: Penguin Books, 1965; 1962; Chatto and Windus, 1940.

Wolterstorff, Nicholas. *Reason Within the Bounds of Religion.* Grand Rapids: Eerdmans, 1976.

Yates, Frances A. *Giordano Bruno and the Hermetic Tradition.* London: Routledge and Kegan Paul, 1964.

Index

Note: Numbers in boldface refer to definitions.

DISCARD